Sustainable Management of Water Resources

THE FONDAZIONE ENI ENRICO MATTEI (FEEM) SERIES ON ECONOMICS, THE ENVIRONMENT AND SUSTAINABLE DEVELOPMENT

Series Editor: Carlo Carraro, *University of Venice, Venice and Research Director, Fondazione Eni Enrico Mattei (FEEM), Milan, Italy*

Editorial Board

The Fondazione Eni Enrico Mattei (FEEM) was established in 1989 as a non-profit, non-partisan research institution. It carries out high-profile research in the fields of economic development, energy and the environment, thanks to an international network of researchers who contribute to disseminate knowledge through seminars, congresses and publications. The main objective of the Fondazione is to foster interactions among academic, industrial and public policy spheres in an effort to find solutions to environmental problems. Over the years it has thus become a major European institution for research on sustainable development and the privileged interlocutor of a number of leading national and international policy institutions.

The Fondazione Eni Enrico Mattei (FEEM) Series on Economics, the Environment and Sustainable Development publishes leading-edge research findings providing an authoritative and up-to-date source of information in all aspects of sustainable development. FEEM research outputs are the results of a sound and acknowledged co-operation between its internal staff and a worldwide network of outstanding researchers and practitioners. A Scientific Advisory Board of distinguished academics ensures the quality of the publications.

This series serves as an outlet for the main results of FEEM's research programmes in the areas of economics, energy and the environment.

Titles in the series include:

Trade and Environment
Theory and Policy in the Context of EU Enlargement and Economic Transition
Edited by John W. Maxwell and Rafael Reuveny

Green Accounting in Europe
A Comparative Study, Volume 2
Edited by Anil Markandya and Marialuisa Tamborra

Sustainable Management of Water Resources
An Integrated Approach
Edited by Carlo Giupponi, Anthony J. Jakeman, Derek Karssenberg and Matt Hare

Sustainable Management of Water Resources

An Integrated Approach

Edited by

Carlo Giupponi
Fondazione Eni Enrico Mattei and University of Milan, Italy

Anthony J. Jakeman
The Australian National University, Australia

Derek Karssenberg
Utrecht University, The Netherlands

Matt P. Hare
Seecon Deutschland GmbH, Germany

THE FONDAZIONE ENI ENRICO MATTEI (FEEM) SERIES ON
ECONOMICS, THE ENVIRONMENT AND SUSTAINABLE
DEVELOPMENT

Edward Elgar
Cheltenham, UK • Northampton, MA, USA

Published by
Edward Elgar Publishing Limited
Glensanda House
Montpellier Parade
Cheltenham
Glos GL50 1UA
UK

Edward Elgar Publishing, Inc.
136 West Street
Suite 202
Northampton
Massachusetts 01060
USA

A catalogue record for this book
is available from the British Library

ISBN-13: 978 1 84542 745 0
ISBN-10: 1 84542 745 9

Printed and bound in Great Britain by MPG Books Ltd, Bodmin, Cornwall

Contents

List of Contributors

Robert M. Argent, University of Melbourne, Australia

Olivier Barreteau, Public Agricultural and Environmental Research Institute (Cemagref), Irrigation Research Unit, France

M. Bruce Beck, University of Georgia, USA

John Bromley, Centre of Ecology and Hydrology, Wallingford, UK

Valerie Cogan, Fondazione Eni Enrico Mattei, Italy

Anita Fassio, Fondazione Eni Enrico Mattei, Italy

Jacobo Feás Vàzquez, Universidad de Santiago de Compostela, Spain

Pier Francesco Ghetti, University of Venice, Italy

Carlo Giupponi, University of Milan and Fondazione Eni Enrico Mattei, Italy

Matt P. Hare, Seecon Deutschland GmbH, Germany

Anthony J. Jakeman, The Australian National University, Australia

Ron Janssen, Free University of Amsterdam, The Netherlands

Derek Karssenberg, Utrecht University, The Netherlands

Rebecca A. Letcher, The Australian National University, Australia

Holger Maier, University of Adelaide, Australia

Gérard Mondello, Groupe de Recherche en Droit, Economie, Gestion de Nice Sophia Antipolis (GREDEG), National Centre for Scientific Research (CNRS), France

Erik Mostert, RBA Centre, Delft University of Technology, The Netherlands

Jaroslav Mysiak, Fondazione Eni Enrico Mattei, Italy

John P. Norton, The Australian National University, Australia

Claudia Pahl-Wostl, University of Osnabrück, Germany

Karin Pfeffer, Free University of Amsterdam, The Netherlands

Dagmar Ridder, University of Osnabrück, Germany

Andrea E. Rizzoli, Istituto Dalle Molle di Studi sull'Intelligenza Artificiale (IDSIA), Switzerland

Paolo Rosato, University of Trieste and Fondazione Eni Enrico Mattei, Italy

J. David Tàbara, Autonomous University of Barcelona, Spain

Marjan van Herwijnen, Free University of Amsterdam, The Netherlands

Marc Vissers, Utrecht University, The Netherlands

Preface

Sustainable development is one of the main guiding principles for our modern societies. Water and sustainable development are closely linked since the provision of water in sufficient quantities and of high quality have important impacts on our environment, society and industry as well as the wellbeing of the next generations.

Nowadays, there are several emerging problems and risks that affect the sustainable management of water resources. Pollution trends and impacts of hazardous pollutants remain uncertain. Diffuse pollution from agricultural practices emerges as a major threat. Water resources and water demands remain unbalanced at various levels. Groundwater abstraction and over-exploitation have serious environmental impacts. Reservoirs, for water storage, flood control, recreation and energy production remain controversial. Climate change will impact on both water availability and demands and the occurrence of extreme events. For instance, only in Europe, the occurrence and severity of floods has increased over the last three decades and represents about half of the material damages to be reimbursed by insurance companies. These problems have not only physical, chemical, biological and ecological dimensions but encompass also important socioeconomic issues, such as legal and regulatory frameworks for water resources management, methods to balance conflicting human and ecosystem demand, financial sustainability of water management systems. This shows the complexity water managers face for the sustainable management of water resources and the need to shift from strong traditional, local and regional water resources management approaches to more integrated river basin approaches dealing with uncertainties in environmental conditions, societal development and global change.

Research plays an important role in the development of truly interdisciplinary, integrative and participative research approaches and methodologies in the area of water management. Over the last years, the principles of integrated water resources management have been widely accepted and various methodological approaches have been developed. However, despite all these efforts, there are still outstanding research questions to be tackled. More effort is therefore needed in order to develop methods, tools and data to integrate climate variability and climate change into integrated water frameworks and to develop qualitative and quantitative techniques and practical tools to incorporate uncertainties and adaptive management into integrated water resources management concepts and practices. Proper attention should be given to sensitivity analysis, uncertainty and vulnerability assessments, institutional and political frameworks, public participation aspects and methods to resolve conflicts in water use between the various sectors. Investigations on the various aspects hampering the linking of specific domain modelling tools which have been developed and used for various purposes, such as different model concept and regimes, scales issues, lack of common data definitions and lack of an appropriate software environment on which various models can be linked, are also needed.

This book constitutes an important contribution to the various concepts, approaches and challenges of integrated management of water resources. It also provides a good insight and understanding of water resources management problems. It is also based on the results of various research projects supported in this field in the context of the European Union's environmental research programmes, highlighting the importance the European Union gives to knowledge generation and the promotion of innovation for sustainable development.

Panagiotis Balabanis and Andrea Tilche
European Commission, Research Directorate-General

PART I

Introduction

1. Integrated Management of Water Resources: Concepts, Approaches and Challenges

Anthony J. Jakeman, Carlo Giupponi, Derek Karssenberg, Matt P. Hare, Anita Fassio and Rebecca A. Letcher

1.1 PURPOSE OF THE BOOK

For more than a decade, sustainability has become a cogent paradigm for the management of natural resources.

Fresh water is generally recognised as the most crucial resource, in part because, at the broadest level, it underpins basic ecosystem functions. But it is also distributed variably over the planet and because of scarcity, lack of financial resources or mismanagement it can fail to meet all competing uses and, as so often occurs in the developing world, it can therefore fail to meet essential human needs.

The challenge for integrated water resource management is to mitigate the inequitable and inefficient distribution of water resources, reduce their vulnerability to excessive demands, and limit the impacts of both land and water-based activities on their quality. This is the context in which Integrated Water Resources Management (defined below) is gathering momentum, accelerated by strong legal and institutional pressures coming into force to guide our management of water for future generations. The necessary interdisciplinary science to assess and inform management of our water resources is, however, less developed.

The purpose of this book is to articulate for researchers, practitioners and water resource managers the concepts and tools required for IWRM, to document how IWRM can be applied to achieve more sustainable socioeconomic and environmental outcomes and to outline some of the challenges ahead.

1.2 THE CONCEPT OF SUSTAINABLE DEVELOPMENT AND THE INSTITUTIONAL PRESSURES ON WATER MANAGEMENT

Before considering IWRM in detail, the concept of sustainable development needs to be discussed since it is the fundamental basis from which IWRM has evolved. Sustainable development was first formalised in the report 'Our Common Future', issued by the UN World Commission for the Environment and Development, in 1987 (WCED, 1987). The Brundtland Report, as it is more commonly known, defined sustainable development as 'development that meets the needs of the present without compromising the ability of future generations to meet their own needs'. This definition highlights the key aspect of sustainability: concern over the impacts on future generations of actions taken today.

Sustainability was subsequently the main theme running through the Rio Declaration of the United Nations Conference on the Environment and Development (UNCED, but better known as the 'Earth Summit') in 1992. The 178 governments attending the Earth Summit signed up to Agenda 21, an ambitious global action plan for achieving sustainable development. This document set out a long-term vision for balancing economic and social needs with the capacity of the earth to provide natural resources. In Agenda 21, sustainable development emerged as a new paradigm of development, integrating economic growth, social development and environmental protection as interdependent and mutually supportive elements of long-term development. Sustainable development also emphasized a participatory, multi-stakeholder approach to policy making and implementation, mobilising public and private resources for development as well as making use of the knowledge, skills and energy of all social groups concerned with the future of the planet and its people.

After the 1992 Earth Summit, hopes were high and expectations were great that the world would take a major step towards sustainable development. Yet in the decade that followed, progress did not match these expectations, as poverty deepened in many areas and environmental degradation continued unabated (CEC, 2001). To renew the commitment to sustainable development, the international community met again in South Africa, in 2002, for the World Summit on Sustainable Development (WSSD). The Summit concluded that most implementation efforts should take place at the local and national level, with national Governments bearing the primary responsibility. The Summit called on all countries to take immediate steps to formulate national strategies for sustainable development, and to begin implementation efforts by 2005. It was recommended that Governments immediately enact and enforce clear and effective laws that support sustainable development, develop and strengthen the necessary infrastructure, and promote public participation.

Water is one of the key issues of sustainable development: current global water challenges and future targets are clearly stated in the Millennium Development Declaration (UN, 2000) – United Nations General Assembly resolution 55/2 – which includes securing equal access to safe drinking water and sanitation in its list of Millennium Development Goals. The Declaration is further strengthened and expanded in the Plan of Implementation of the World Summit on Sustainable Development. The Plan also outlines several key statements related to freshwater and sanitation issues. For example, it states that integrated water resources management and water efficiency plans should be developed by 2005, and that effective coordination among the various international and national bodies should be promoted.

In Europe, the EU has consistently worked towards an ambitious action-oriented plan with clear and measurable objectives, directed at achieving the Millennium Development Goals. The EU Water Initiative was thus established as a key contribution to help achieve the water-related Millennium Development Goals and the targets of the World Summit on Sustainable Development. The EU Water Initiative seeks to make significant progress in poverty eradication and health, in the enhancement of livelihoods, peace and security and in sustainable economic development (EC, 2003a). It marks an attempt to broaden the impact of the principles and best practices advocated by an earlier framework directive of special importance for practitioners of IWRM in Europe: the Water Framework Directive (WFD) (EC, 2000). This Directive, which will be referred to many more times in this chapter and the rest of the book, is one of the main drivers of European water management research and practice as it seeks to establish common institutions and practices, among EU member states, for improving and maintaining surface and groundwater quality in river basins across the continent.

In summary, the principles of sustainable development, since their first elicitation in the Bruntland Report, have had a dramatic worldwide impact in directing development and environmental policies. The next challenge is bringing these new policies into routine practice, by developing new decision making approaches and strategies, and knowledge-based tools for informing decisions.

1.3 THE NATURE OF INTEGRATED WATER RESOURCES MANAGEMENT

As described in the previous section, the main objective of sustainable development is to find a suitable balance between socioeconomic needs and the capacity of the environment to withstand or to buffer potential impacts imposed upon it resulting in an economy, society and environment that are healthy over the long term. At the broadest level, the adjective 'integrated' in IWRM relates to the need to consider this so-called triple bottom line or three pillars of sustainability, as expressed in the definition of IWRM below that is adopted throughout the book:

> Integrated Water Resources Management (IWRM) is a process, which promotes the coordinated development and management of water, land and related resources, in order to maximise the resultant economic and social welfare in an equitable manner without compromising the sustainability of vital ecosystems [GWP-TAC4, 2000].

Integration can also be viewed as having several more specific dimensions (see also ICWE 1992, UNCED 1992, Gijsbers 2000, and Jakeman and Letcher, 2003) as discussed below:

- Integration of issues. Issues is a general term for problems (be they socioeconomic or environmental), specific sustainability outcomes or goals. A typical but by no means exhaustive list from Jakeman et al. (2005) is:
  - the continuing need for new opportunities and new practices in agriculture and other industries, to feed the world;
  - land and river degradation, including salinisation and erosion;
  - surface and groundwater allocation, including allocation for environmental needs;
  - water quality protection;
  - pest management;
  - maintenance of terrestrial and aquatic biodiversity;
  - indigenous and recreational value, and value for other non-extractive uses;
  - equitable management and distribution of resources;
  - changing patterns of settlement and an ageing population;
  - educating the public about the environment;
  - the potential impacts of climate change and climate variability.

IWRM avoids the predilection of treating single issues in isolation and aims for joint treatment of the major issues for the simple reason that these may be in conflict and that trade-offs between their solutions might need to be sought. This issue identification stage then informs the remaining integration aspects in an iterative approach.

- Integration of the parts of a river basin. This naturally follows if issues are being integrated. At the most aggregated spatial level this means relating the effects of different land uses to impacts on the waterways – streams, estuaries, and groundwater systems. It also means contextually selecting indicators of sustainability outcomes whose values are computed at appropriate spatio-temporal scales to compare trade-offs under different scenarios or management options. Trade-offs may be needed not only between and within various socioeconomic and environmental indicators, but also between different parts of a river basin and over different time horizons.

- Integration of major drivers. Outcomes are determined by a range of drivers and system interactions. Drivers can be uncontrollable like climate episodes, longer-term variability and change, or commodity prices and international policies. Controllable drivers are the ones that can be used to effect outcomes. These include instruments such as taxes, subsidies, trading schemes, regulations, public and private investments and education. Both categories of drivers need to be considered for integration.

- Integration of different scientific and engineering disciplines. To deal with the triple bottom line of IWRM, knowledge from a wide range of scientific and engineering fields, such as economics, hydrology and other earth sciences, sociology, psychology and ecology, needs to be targeted and integrated. There will be many methodological and scale issues to consider.

- Integration of people involved or interested in a management problem. This is usually referred to as public participation, which means that all relevant actors or stakeholders, such as government at various levels, industrial groups, environmental sectors and the wider community, are involved in an appropriate way in relevant steps of the solution to a problem in IWRM.

- Integration of models, methods, data and other information. A wide range of methodologies is available that can be used for IWRM. Examples are methods to select stakeholders and to facilitate stakeholder integration, computer and other models to predict possible outcomes of management solutions, methodologies such as multi-criteria analysis to compare and evaluate possible outcomes of management solutions. These methodologies are most powerful when applied in an integrative way, by combining different methodologies in one assessment procedure, albeit with many parts.

- Integration of tools. In the context of IWRM different types of tools may be used and require integration. Examples are monitoring networks, communication means, physical models, and most importantly software tools. The latter may also represent the means for providing the integration of the others. Depending on the problem, user group and resources available this may or may not mean a resultant single piece of software. However it does mean that the development and choice of software to house, visualise, transform data and link models is underpinned by a design. Thus implementation of the design will lead to some product(s) utilising the different components of software in a way that at least illustrates the range of outcomes that are achieved under different management options and under different uncontrollable drivers.

The definition of IWRM given above refers to IWRM as a process. This means that IWRM consists of a set of procedural and cyclic steps that are executed to solve a management problem. Central to this process is a framework, alongside integrated (scenario) modelling, to assess the effects of system drivers on sustainability outcomes.

There are several integration frameworks available and these have been classified by Letcher (in press) as:

- Systems Dynamics (Kuper et al., 2003; Settle et al., 2002).
- Bayesian Networks (Borsuk et al., 2004; Bromley et al., 2005; Rieman et al., 2001).
- Meta-models (Bouman et al., 1999; Bouzaher et al., 1993; Kampas and White, 2002).
- Coupled complex models (Fischer and Sun, 2001; Krol et al., 2001; Merritt et al., 2004).
- Agent-based models (Kaufmann and Gebetsroither, 2004; Hare and Deadman, 2004; Bousquet and le Page, 2004)
- Expert systems (Dai et al., 2004; Marsili-Libelli, 2004)

The integration framework and integrated modelling selected will typically have quantitative and qualitative aspects, the mix varying according to the problem, the disciplines involved and the resources available to perform the assessment.

1.4   INTERNATIONAL APPROACHES TO WATER RESOURCES MANAGEMENT

Internationally, there are many similarities in water resource management approaches and objectives. The following sections briefly summarise examples of such approaches from Europe, the USA, Australia and basins in Africa and Asia.

1.4.1 Europe

As mentioned above, European water resources management is currently being defined and driven by the Water Framework Directive (WFD) (EC, 2000). Its affect is pan-European, since it not only affects the EU member states but also all accession states and those countries that share transboundary waters or have bilateral or multi-lateral agreements with the EU. Broadly speaking, the WFD requires that all partners in a given river basin manage their waters in close cooperation, irrespective of administrative borders according to clear environmental objectives. Based on a river basin approach, it aims at: (a) the provision of a sufficient supply of good quality surface water and groundwater as needed for sustainable, balanced and equitable water use; (b) a significant reduction in pollution of groundwater; (c) the protection of territorial and marine waters; and (d) achieving the objectives of relevant international agreements, including those which aim to prevent and eliminate pollution of the marine environment.

Several key mechanisms are applied to make these aims operational within the Directive. A crucial role is played by the River Basin Management Plan, which is to be produced and updated every six years for each basin. Management objectives are coordinated through a set of targets for so-called good status of both surface and groundwater. These consider both ecological protection, through targets for biological quality, and chemical protection, through a set of minimum chemical quality targets. Good status targets should be achieved by 2015. Other objectives are defined for specific areas, such as bathing or drinking water, where more stringent conditions are required. For groundwater management the basic assumption is that it should not be polluted at all. Management of groundwater includes a prohibition on any discharges to groundwater, a requirement to monitor all groundwater bodies to detect changes in chemical composition, and to reverse any trends caused by anthropogenic pollution. Groundwater quantity is also protected. Another key component of the WFD is the promotion of public participation in river basin management. This participation helps balance the interests of various stakeholder groups and ensures that the Directive is adopted in good faith by Member States, thus ensuring greater enforceability of the Directive's aims and objectives (EC, 2003b).

1.4.2 USA

In the United States, Federal government policy has been developed to support locally based water management groups and a watershed management approach (see, for example, US EPA, 2001). In October 2000, the federal government issued the 'Unified Federal Policy for Ensuring a

Watershed Approach to Federal Land and Resource Management' (Federal Agencies, 2000). This policy supports the watershed or catchment as the basis of management and states that the federal agencies involved will work with 'States, tribes, local governments and interested stakeholders' (Federal Agencies, 2000) to identify and improve the condition of priority watersheds. The use of watershed management plans and water quality targets are also supported.

Regional Watershed Coordination teams, in twelve large river basins, have been developed to improve inter-agency coordination and help leverage resources for basin management. Watershed teams work with local stakeholder and watershed groups to assist with coordination, monitoring and restoration. The US EPA (2001) discusses the status of watershed management in the US and gives many examples of locally based watershed management initiatives. They also identify many of the problems or shortcomings with the practice of watershed management in the USA, including difficulties with partnerships and coordination, monitoring and research, funding, and technical assistance and evaluation.

1.4.3   Australia

In Australia, the Council of Australian Governments (COAG), consisting of the Prime Minister, State Premiers, Chief Ministers and the President of the Australian Local Government Association, endorsed an agreement on sustainable reform of the water industry in February 1994. This agreement was aimed at achieving improved economic efficiency and environmental sustainability of the water industry. COAG supported the need for coordinated action to stop the widespread degradation of natural resources (COAG, 1994), and identified a number of problems with the existing system including: (a) cross-subsidies in the service provision to various groups; (b) impediments to the transfer of irrigation water from low value to high value uses; (c) service delivery inefficiencies; (d) problems in clearly defining roles and responsibilities of many institutions in the water industry; and (e) the need for massive asset refurbishment in rural areas.

The COAG agreement addressed many of these problems. For rural water provision, these included changes to pricing and water allocation. It was agreed that pricing regimes should be 'based on the principles of consumption-based pricing, full cost recovery and desirably the removal of cross subsidies which are not consistent with efficient service, use and provision'. Further, 'where cross-subsidies continue to exist, they be made transparent' (COAG, 1994).

An important part of the COAG process involves the Government consulting the community on aspects of the framework (Russell, 1996). For this reason, and because of the broad nature of the changes required, the initial implementation period for these reforms was set at five to seven years. It was agreed that a full framework should be implemented by the year 2001. Since this time, each of the States involved has moved to implement these reforms, with Integrated Catchment Management and recognition of the need for improved stakeholder involvement in the policy development underlying much of this reform. Additionally, water quality and river flow objectives have been set for most of these catchments and detailed catchment management plans established.

1.4.4　Africa

In Africa significant moves towards IWRM have been made, with policies very similar to those under the EU WFD being implemented. Van Koppen (2003) discusses water reform in Sub-Saharan Africa, and the role that African governments have played in the move towards IWRM. Differences between these countries and others elsewhere, in terms of initiating IWRM, are identified. In particular, the relative abundance of water resources, but scarcity of economic resources to harness the water, is identified as a key difference in the African context.

The Southern African Development Community (SADC), which consists of the governments of Angola, Botswana, Lesotho, Malawi, Mozambique, Namibia, South Africa, Swaziland, Tanzania, Zambia and Zimbabwe, released a protocol on shared watercourses (SADC, 1995, 2000). The objective of this protocol is to 'foster closer cooperation for judicious, sustainable and coordinated management, protection and utilisation of shared watercourses and advance the SADC agenda of regional integration and poverty alleviation' (SADC, 2000). To achieve this objective, this Protocol seeks to foster the introduction of sustainable and equitable utilisation of the shared watercourses by facilitating: (a) the establishment of agreements and institutions for the management of shared watercourses; (b) the harmonisation and monitoring of legislation and policies for planning, development, conservation and allocation of the resources; and (c) research and technology development, information exchange, capacity building and the application of appropriate technologies (SADC, 2000).

Van der Zaag and Savenije (1999) present a comparison of management in the SADC and the EU, finding that there has been a significant convergence between the EU and the SADC concerning the central role of the river basin in management.

Another example of African IWRM is in the Nile River Basin, which is shared by ten countries (Burundi, Democratic Republic of Congo, Egypt, Eritrea, Ethiopia, Kenya, Rwanda, Sudan, Tanzania and Uganda). IWRM is being implemented in the Nile River through the Nile River Strategic Action

Program and the Nile Basin Initiative, which commenced in May 1999 (NBI, 2003). The programme stresses the need to work at local and national levels and focuses strongly on the need for stakeholder involvement.

1.4.5 Asia

An example of IWRM in Asia is the management of the Mekong River Basin, which involves coordination of activities and decisions across Thailand, Vietnam, Laos and Cambodia. This coordination is undertaken through the Mekong River Commission. In 1995 an Agreement was made between countries in the Commission that shifted the focus in the Basin from development of large-scale projects to sustainable development and management of natural resources (MRC, 1995). A Basin Development Plan is in the process of being developed (MRC, 2003). This Plan strongly supports community participation in natural resource management in the basin. The overall approach of the Plan is to achieve basin-wide benefits while taking account of national interests and balancing development opportunities with resource conservation, by implementing broad public participation and efficient knowledge-sharing and capacity building (MRC, 2003).

The Plan is expected to involve themes of environment, human resource development, socioeconomics, poverty reduction, gender equity and public participation (MRC, 2003). Other programmes, including an environment programme, capacity building programme and agricultural, irrigation and forestry programmes are also being undertaken to implement the 1995 Agreement.

1.5 CHALLENGES IN INTEGRATED WATER RESOURCES MANAGEMENT

As the research effort builds in the field of IWRM, old challenges are replaced with new ones. As this book shows, much relevant research is being undertaken, among other things, in terms of developing integrated frameworks, modelling techniques, software platforms and tools, and creating productive links between science, management and the general public. The current research presented, however, raises new challenges. Most of the important issues that will need addressing are presented below.

1.5.1 Science, Integrated Knowledge and Decision Making

It is a fundamental challenge that IWRM calls for a new breed of researchers who are much more interdisciplinary and interested in spending much of their time understanding other points of view and communicating widely. Therefore ways must be found to encourage scientists to be more open-minded towards a broader range of information, knowledge and methods of knowledge representation from different disciplines and stakeholders, while continuing to maintain proper critical standards. Typically paradigms and methods are different between biophysical scientists and social scientists but there are also gaps in shared understanding between some of the major quantitative sciences such as between the earth sciences and economics. Positive contributions are expected from a broader education in systems thinking and in multidisciplinary perspectives and methods.

There is also a clear need for the disciplinary foci of scientists to be sharpened by the management questions. This is a serious but simpler challenge that implies closer and more continuous dialogue between discipline specialists and their clients in natural resource management so that the nature and scale of disciplinary enquiry is more relevant. The research community, as a result, should cooperate with decision makers and jointly develop new application tools framed within the changing needs of the evolving policies. To this end, a new interdisciplinary research community of modellers focused on applying existing scientific knowledge to management problems, and on communicating this knowledge through models, assessments and decision support systems is emerging. This community largely understands the conflicts of time and cost between traditional research efforts and decision making, where research time frames and costs generally exceed the resources available in decision making. This community has the potential to play a valuable communication role linking traditional disciplinary scientists with policy and decision makers, and in transferring key research questions back from real world problems to disciplinary scientists, improving the relevance of research and aiding in the adoption of state-of-the-art science in decision making.

Knowledge acquisition and knowledge generation for IWRM can be accelerated by more systematic testing and comparison of theoretical approaches and methods in case studies. This can be facilitated by more collaborative and strategic science, funded to bring groups together internationally and to execute comparative studies.

More research is needed to manage the wealth of heterogeneous information types (soft, hard, qualitative, quantitative, beliefs, knowledge, expert, non-expert) that is acquired and generated during the course of carrying out IWRM, involving as it does different disciplines, as well as scientists, practitioners and the broad public. Such research needs to include the development of better data mining and navigation techniques for heterogeneous information retrieval to aid quick and efficient access to gathered information, the development of a common approach to quality assurance (see below) for these different information types, and the development of guidelines as to how and when different types should be used in decision making.

1.5.2 Public Participation

In terms of participatory methods, more effort needs to be placed on developing meaningful metrics for evaluating participatory processes. This is needed not only to provide evidence to scientists on whether or not their methods have been successful, as such assessment is also needed to help improve participatory approaches in a rigourous way. Assessment of this nature is also useful in convincing future participants to take part in new processes or to keep current participants actively involves. Additionally, more work is required to develop methods and techniques to integrate participatory processes occuring at different scales of management.

In terms of methods, more effort needs to be placed on developing meaningful metrics for evaluating participatory processes. This is needed not only to provide evidence to scientists on whether or not their methods have been successful, but such assessment is also needed to help improve participatory approaches in a rigourous way. Assessment of this nature is also useful in convincing future participants to take part in new processes or to keep current participants actively involves. Additionally, more work is required to develop methods and techniques to integrate participatory processes occuring at different scales of management.

Simply improving methods and putting in regulations calling for public participation will not be enough, however, to bring about effective public participation in IWRM. As Section 1.4 of this Chapter shows, there are similar approaches to IWRM across the globe. Public participation is a common paradigm and the need for the adequate involvement of stakeholders is clearly stated in all the recent policy documents and regulations. However public participation is not always adequately implemented in water management in practice. Experiences have shown that participation (see Chapter 8; Hare et al., 2003) does not always translate into meaningful new inputs into the traditional management decision-making process. Poor participatory methodology is one cause of such problems, but, crucially, unless there are transparent management procedures in place (e.g., protocols as to how decision makers should use and account for their use of inputs from the public within their decision making) that can guarantee and illustrate that the inputs from public participation are influencing actual decision making, then both decision makers and citizens may end up perceiving public participation simply as a new form of bureaucratic burden, without real benefits for the community.

This may also require new governance institutions to be created. For example, the institution of representative democracy can sometimes restrain public participation in practice, since decision makers who have been voted in, often perceive themselves as already speaking for their community and do not see 'further' public participation as necessary. Also, more participation in decision making requires the sharing of responsibility between decision makers and community. If greater public participation is to be achieved, not only are the methods and technologies described in this book needed, so too are new forms of governance which allow the actual and transparent reallocation of power and responsibility.

1.5.3   Institutions, Science and Ethics

Existing institutions need to be strengthened (e.g., the public funding of research, peer review systems) in order to safeguard the principle of science as an objective servant of decision making, not as a subjective tool of different interest groups. This issue is important to IWRM since, as water issues and conflicts grow in the next decades, water managers are going to face increasing dilemmas. The adversarial approach to using science to promote a particular viewpoint only serves to disconnect the public and the politicians from making the necessary decisions that will be needed to enable the managers to solve them. The integrated assessment community is calling for increased recognition of bias in scientific assessment and honesty in reporting participants, interest groups, results and assumptions underlying scientific investigation. Many research groups are currently advocating an 'evaluation of process' approach to research in which the reporting of research processes and results is more open, including the consideration of the impact of interest groups and their engagement in the research process, as well as the assumptions underlying the research work. Improving the quality of reporting of potential biases in projects, and improving the rigour by which policy relevant science is evaluated will help minimise the problems of politicisation and commercialisation.

1.5.4   New Approaches and Tools for IWRM

Adaptive management (Holling, 1978) and active adaptive management (e.g., Allan and Curtis, 2003) are principles with the potential to improve our management of the environment through learning. In essence, adaptive management is about developing management-revision principles, experiment designs, outcome indicators, and monitoring practices to achieve sustainable management in evolving environments (e.g., STARS 2004). This must include the monitoring and evaluation of active and passive experiments to see what does and does not work and where there are gaps. Examples are improved tools to capture and express qualitative knowledge and approaches to screening and testing a broad range of alternative policies.

New modelling tools should be developed to improve the qualitative differentiation between outcomes under different management options, with at least qualitative confidence; e.g., a particular set of sustainability outcomes or indicator values might be categorised as overall better than, worse than or negligibly different from another set with high, moderate or low confidence. This is enough to facilitate a decision about adopting a policy or initiating a management action to improve outcomes. In particular, Integrated Scenario Modelling (see Chapter 10) can be utilised to differentiate between policies and specify what knowledge or data will clarify the differentiation between various options.

Decision support systems (DSS) can be a useful ally in connecting the interface between science and policy (see Chapter 4). Such tools must find a correct balance between the need for simplicity and ease-of-use for stakeholders, on the one hand, and the implementation of rigorous scientific approaches, on the other. Certainly, transparency of DSS where model limitations and assumptions are clearly acknowledged is essential if trust, engagement and final agreement and adoption of recommendations are to be realised. Moreover, in the future, developers of decision support systems should be less focussed on developing 'one-off' visualisation and interface tools for specific applications, and more focused on extracting generic features which are common to many applications. As far as possible, development of decision support systems should be an investment in learning what is frequently useful, not in generating software that has little capacity for reuse.

1.5.5   Quality Assurance and Uncertainty Management for Credible Models and Decisions

To enhance the credibility and utility of scientific approaches, quality assurance must become mainstream. Quality assurance relates to the development of standards and protocols for model and data reporting and distribution (see e.g., Rykiel, 1996, STARS, 2004). These standards and protocols are required because environmental and natural resource data and models are used to make management decisions, but they often have very large uncertainties or underlying assumptions associated with them (e.g., Anderson and Bates, 2001, Oreskes et al., 1994). In order to ensure models and data are used in an appropriate way, and that decision makers have access to information about the limitations of these models and data sets, reporting standards for model testing, assumptions, appropriate scales and inherent uncertainties must be developed and used. The new models should devote special attention to the management and communication of uncertainty. Although some standard procedures for quantifiying uncertainties in model outputs are available (e.g., Heuvelink, 1998), these have not yet been implemented in modelling tools that are used for decision making, although some first steps have been taken (e.g., HarmonyRib, 2004; Karssenberg and de Jong, 2005).

The key message is that model credibility can be enhanced by a serious two-way modeller-manager dialogue, appropriately rigorous model evaluation tests, sensitivity and uncertainty assessments, and peer reviews of models at their various stages of development (Refsgaard et al., 2005).

1.5.6   IWRM by Doing

In conclusion we have no doubt that good progress is being made in the science of IWRM. And as noted above there is a basic understanding and acceptance of the challenges. As this book shows, the scientific community has been developing a lot of the theory, many useful methods and some convincing applications such as integration frameworks, models for linking outcomes to policy, a deepening understanding of the role and effectiveness of public participation, a practical focus on achieving more sustainable outcomes rather than overly debating what sustainability is, and many concepts and software platforms. There is, however, a general need to accelerate the development and application of integration methods and applications in order to mature such a 'discipline' into a cohesive body of knowledge. In particular there would seem to be much scope for approaches that combine the best features of traditional and novel knowledge-based techniques, with the former based upon existing or hypothesised knowledge, and the latter more on knowledge extraction from fuzzier systems. But substantial advances in managing water resources demand us to systematically accrue the lessons learnt in practical applications and share experiences widely. Only by doing and showing will we handle the complexity and difficulties of integration.

1.6   A BRIEF GUIDE TO THIS BOOK

1.6.1   Outline of the Book

The book structure reflects a general agreement with Gijsbers' claim (Gijsbers, 2000) that the main challenge of water resources management in the coming years is dealing with integration issues. There are many things to be integrated, as discussed in the previous section: the integration of disciplines; the delivery of integrated management solutions that achieve the positive 'triple bottom line' (see Chapter 10) of benefits for the environment, economy and society that underpin concepts of sustainability; the sharing and use of knowledge and information integrated from disparate sources; and the collaborative integration of the public and stakeholder interest groups within water management decision making. This book on IWRM is correspondingly structured to provide the reader with insights into how scientists are designing ways of supporting water managers to meet these diverse challenges of integration.

Part II presents examples of how the different disciplines are combining to provide insights into how to respond to institutional pressures for integrated water management in a way which will provide us with a combination of environmental, economic and social benefits. The Part begins with Mondello, in Chapter 2, providing a first insight into the nature of the triple bottom line of sustainability (i.e. the three pillars of sustainable development: environment, economics, society), with a look at how the economics of markets and trade agreements influence and mould modern water management across the globe, in particular in terms of determining water supply and distribution. By doing so, it raises important questions about how to use economic concepts to achieve both economic efficiency and social equity. Introducing the environmental aspects of IWRM, Ghetti and Giupponi in Chapter 3 explore the interaction of legislative politics and ecology in achieving improved water quality. It first explains the basic concepts of fluvial ecosystems and water quality maintenance within such systems and then moves from the global perspective of Chapter 2 to a more European one by introducing the EU's Water Framework Directive and how managers are responding to its challenge of improving water quality in European river basins.

Part III describes in more detail the water management process and moves on to provide examples of frameworks and software tools for evaluation that can support water managers to represent, integrate and analyse expert and non-expert knowledge, data and model outputs from various disciplines in order to improve management decisions. Methods described, such as multi-criteria analysis, help to evaluate such management decisions according to the three pillars of sustainable development. The Part starts with the Chapter by Giupponi, Fassio, Feás Vàzquez and Mysiak (Chapter 4), focussing on the essentials of decision making in IWRM and providing a framework for supporting managers in their analysis and assessment of management issues. They introduce and explain in broad terms how disparate sources of system and management knowledge can be integrated and structured in conceptual frameworks in order for them to be effectively analysed and assessed. An integrated approach to this is exemplified in the form of the MULINO Decision Support System. This theme of integrated knowledge assessment is made more concrete in the following two chapters in which concepts of multi-criteria analysis are explained and examples of their application are given. Feás and Rosato in Chapter 5 provide a solid introduction to multi-criteria analysis and its various methodologies. By doing so, in partial answer to the question and challenges raised in Part II, they suggest multi-criteria analysis as a way of evaluating and making management decisions that can simultaneously consider, if not meet, the goals of modern IWRM, economic efficiency social equity and healthy environment. In Chapter 6, van Herwijnen and Janssen highlight software tools that can be used to support the various methodologies of multi-criteria analysis and demonstrate how one tool in particular, DEFINITE, can be usefully used to support IWRM.

Part IV illustrates ways of improving collaboration in management and the gathering of knowledge through public and stakeholder participation. Effective participatory methods bring the required knowledge and social capital into the management process. Not only is this required if the evaluation tools are to be used, it also provides inputs for the modelling activities described in Part V.

Part IV poses the question of how collaboration in water management can be increased. In Chapter 7, Mostert introduces the theory, concepts and legislation behind public and stakeholder participation to provide an insight into how more people can be integrated in water management and why they should be. He elucidates on what participation entails, what conditions support it and what benefits it brings to water management. Complementing this, in Chapter 8, Hare, Barreteau, Beck, Letcher, Mostert, Tàbara, Ridder, Cogan and Pahl-Wostl present the reader with an introduction to some practical working methods to support participatory water management. This chapter brings together the experiences of a wide range of participatory water management research scientists from around the globe to give their explanations and critical assessment of using such methods within real world water management processes.

In Part V, it is illustrated how modelling can support integrated water resource management through the formalised representation and exploration of integrated knowledge, information and data, predicting outcomes of possible management scenarios that can be used in the step of evaluation. This part provides reviews of hydrological, ecological, economic and sociological modelling for use in water management. It suggests how integrated knowledge representation and management can be achieved through integrated modelling and how managers can then explore their management options through policy simulation. Fittingly, given the integrative nature of the discipline and the book, the section concludes by looking at how the various techniques of analysis, participation and modelling themselves can be integrated into composite software-based environments to provide support to the manager.

Karssenberg, Pfeffer and Vissers present, in Chapter 9, a concise introduction to the fundamentals of hydrological modelling as a support for water management. In particular they provide an insight into the integration of such models with software referred to as geographical information systems, thus providing a view of how spatial water management planning can be supported. In Chapter 10, Jakeman, Norton, Letcher and Maier then illustrate how integrated modelling can be combined with scenario analysis to support the goals of achieving the positive 'triple bottom line' essential for sustainability. They present proof of the concept in terms of an approach termed Integrated Scenario Modelling and explain its role in three water management cases in Asia and Australasia. The theme of model integration is further taken up by Letcher and Bromley in Chapter 11 by reviewing the wide range of modelling approaches and types of models used in IWRM. The wealth of hydrological, ecological and socioeconomic modelling approaches is reviewed for the reader followed by an analysis of the various frameworks for integration.

Finally, in Chapter 12, Rizzoli and Argent complete the book by exploring how the evolving technology of software component reuse is being applied to develop software management environments that can support the water management process as a whole. Effectively, such environments provide the manager with a platform in which support and methods for the type of analysis, assessment, modelling and participatory activities discussed in this book can be integrated within a composite management system. Such software advances are the seeds of the new generation of IWRM support systems.

1.6.2   How to Get the Most Out of this Book

This book includes work from many scientists, to give the researcher and manager a comprehensive account of current trends in applied research aimed at supporting the full spectrum of activities in IWRM. Hence it provides a snapshot in time of the innovative research being carried out at the start of the twenty-first century. Although this research will certainly be superseded, it will be influencing water management in the coming decades and thus presents a vision of water management in the future. For the manager, this vision is one of what tools they might be able to use to enhance their existing management repertoire and for the researcher, one of how tools for IWRM can be further improved.

A further purpose of the book is to present practical examples, in the form of case studies. Part of the concept of applied research is that new ideas, tools and practices are derived from results of basic research and applied to actual management situations in order for them to be tested. While these situations can never be entirely representative of every management situation, they are an attempt to demonstrate that the ideas and tools can be used by managers. Thus this book provides case studies from around the world to illustrate the ideas and techniques of IWRM so that readers can better judge how they might apply these principles to their own catchments.

While the book has been intended to be read as a whole and cover the full spectrum of IWRM, each chapter has been constructed so that it can be read independently. Should the reader not want to read the book from beginning to end, the following matrix (Table 1.1) acts as a guide to show the various themes, techniques, software and case studies elaborated upon within the various chapters.

Table 1.1   Themes of chapters at a glance

Chapters	2	3	4	5	6	7	8	9	10	11	12
Dimensions of sustainable development											
Environment	·	✓	✓	✓	✓	·	·	✓	✓	✓	·
Economics	✓	·	✓	✓	✓	·	·	·	✓	✓	·
Society/politics/ legislation	✓	✓	✓	✓	✓	✓	✓	·	✓	✓	·
Techniques											
Multi-criteria analysis	·	·	✓	✓	✓	·	·	·	·	·	·
Geographical information systems	·	·	·	·	·	·	·	✓	·	·	·
Scenario development	·	·	✓	·	·	·	✓	·	✓	·	·
Public participation	·	·	·	·	·	✓	✓	·	✓	·	·
Conceptual frameworks	·	·	✓	·	·	·	·	·	✓	·	·
Modelling	·	✓	✓	·	·	·	✓	✓	✓	✓	✓
Software	·	·	✓	·	✓	·	✓	·	·	·	✓
Case study locations											
Europe	·	✓	✓	·	✓	·	✓	✓	·	·	·
Americas	·	·	·	·	·	·	✓	·	·	·	·
Asia	·	·	·	·	·	·	✓	·	✓	·	·
Australasia	·	·	·	·	·	·	✓	·	✓	·	·
Africa	·	·	·	·	·	·	✓	·	·	·	·
Case study themes											
Urban water management	·	·	·	·	·	·	✓	·	·	·	·
Agricultural water management	·	·	✓	·	✓	·	✓	·	·	·	·
Flood management	·	·	·	·	✓	·	·	·	·	·	·
Water quality management	·	✓	✓	·	·	·	✓	✓	·	·	·
Transboundary water management	·	·	·	·	·	·	✓	·	·	·	·

NOTES

1. Examples here represent those papers that have used the framework.

REFERENCES

Allan C. and A. Curtis (2003), 'Learning to implement adaptive management', *Natural Resource Management*, **6**(1), 23–28.

Anderson, M.G. and P.D. Bates (eds) (2001), *Model Validation: Perspectives in Hydrological Science*, Chichester: Wiley.

Borsuk, M.E., C.A. Stow and K.H. Recknow (2004), 'A Bayesian network of eutrophication models for synthesis, prediction and uncertainty analysis', *Ecological Modelling*, **173**, 219–239.

Bouman, B.A.M., H.G.P. Jansen, R.A. Schipper, A. Nieuwenhuyse, H. Hengsdijk and J. Bouma (1999), 'A framework for integrated biophysical and economic land use analysis at different scales', *Agriculture, Ecosystem and Environment*, **75**, 55–73.

Bousquet, F. and C. Le Page (2004), 'Multi-agent simulations and ecosystem management: a review', *Ecological Modelling*, **176**(3–4), 313–332.

Bouzaher, A., P.G. Lakshiminarayan, R. Cabe, A. Carriquiry, R.W. Gassman and J.F. Shogren (1993), 'Metamodels and nonpoint pollution policy in agriculture', *Water Resources Research*, **29**(6), 1579–1587.

Bromley, J., N.A. Jackson, O.J. Clymer, A.M. Giacomello and F.V. Jensen (2005), 'The use of Hugin to develop Bayesian networks as an aid to integrated water resource planning', *Environmental Modelling and Software*, **20**(2), 231–242.

CEC (Commission of European Communities) (2001), 'The European Environment Agency Focuses on EU-Policy in its Approach to Sustainable Development Indicators', Working Paper no. 5.

COAG (1994), 'Communique, Report of the Working Group on Water Resource Policy', Council of Australian Governments.

Dai, J.J., S. Lorenzato and D.M. Rocke (2004), 'A knowledge-based model of watershed assessment for sediment', *Environmental Modelling and Software*, **19**, 423–433.

EC (European Communities) (2000), 'Directive 2000/60/EC of the European Parliament and of the Council Establishing a Framework for Community Action in the Field of Water Policy' (OJ L 327, 22.12.2000).

EC (European Communities) (2003a), 'Water for life – EU Water Initiative', Office for Official Publications of the European Communities, Luxembourg.

EC (European Communities) (2003b), *WFD – Introduction and Overview, European Commission*, downloadable at http://europa.eu.int/comm/environment/water/water-framework/overview.html (last access: April 2005).

Federal Agencies (2000), 'Unified federal policy for a watershed approach to federal land and resource management', *Federal Register*, USA, **65**(202), 62566–72, October 18, 2000.

Fischer, G. and L. Sun (2001), 'Model based analysis of future land-use development in China', *Agriculture, Ecosystems and Environment*, **85**, 163–176.

Gijsbers P. (2000), *Decision Support for the Management of Shared Water Resources*, Delft: Delft University Press.

GWP-TAC4 (2000), 'Integrated Water Resources management, Global Water Partnership', *Technical Advisory Committee Paper,* **4**, Stockholm, Sweden.

Hare, M.P. and P. Deadman (2004), 'Further towards a taxonomy of agent-based simulation models in environmental management', *Mathematics and Computers in Simulation Journal*, **64**, 25–40.

Hare, M.P., R.A. Letcher and A.J. Jakeman (2003), 'Participatory modelling in natural resource management: a comparison of four case studies', *Integrated Assessment*, **2**(4), 62–72.

HarmonyRib (2004), info at http://www.harmonirib.com/ (last access: May 2005).

Heuvelink, G.B.M. (1998), *Error Propagation in Environmental Modelling with GIS*, London: Taylor & Francis.

Holling, C.S. (ed.) (1978), *Adaptive Environmental Management and Assessment*, Chichester: Wiley.

ICWE (International Conference on Water and the Environment) (1992), 'The Dublin statement and report', in International Conference on Water and the Environment: Development Issues for the 21st century, Dublin.

Jakeman, A.J. and R.A. Letcher (2003), 'Integrated assessment and modelling: features, principles and examples for catchment management', *Environmental Modelling and Software*, **18**, 491–501.

Jakeman, A.J., R.A. Letcher, L.T.H. Newham and J.P. Norton (2005), 'Integrated catchment modelling: issues and opportunities to support improved sustainability outcomes', in 29th Hydrology and Water Resources Symposium: Water Capital, Canberra, 20–23 February, 2005.

Kampas, A. and White, B. (2002), 'Emission versus input taxes for diffuse nitrate pollution control in the presence of transaction costs', *Journal of Environmental Planning and Management*, **45**(1), 129–139.

Karssenberg, D. and K. de Jong (2005), 'Dynamic environmental modelling in GIS: 2. Error propagation modelling', *International Journal of Geographical Information Science*, **19**(6), 623–673.

Kaufmann, A. and E. Gebetsroither (2004), 'Modelling self-organization processes in socio-economic and ecological systems for supporting the adaptive management of forests', in C. Pahl, S. Schmidt and A.J. Jakeman (eds), *iEMSs 2004 International Congress: 'Complexity and Integrated Resources Management'*, International Environmental Modelling and Software Society, Osnabrück, Germany, June 2004.

Krol, M.S., A. Jaeger, A. Bronstert and J. Krywkow (2001), 'The Semi-arid Integrated Model (SIM), a regional integrated model assessing water availability, vulnerability of ecosystems and society in Brazil', *Physics and Chemistry of the Earth (B)*, **26**(7-8), 529–533.

Kuper, M., C. Mullon, Y. Poncet and E. Benga, (2003), 'Integrated modelling of the ecosystem of the Niger river inland delta in Mali', *Ecological Modelling*, **164**, 83.

Letcher, R.A. (in press), 'Integrative frameworks for natural resource management', *Environmental Modelling and Software*.

Marsili-Libelli, S. (2004), 'Fuzzy prediction of the algal blooms in the Orbetello lagoon', *Environmental Modelling and Software*, **19**, 799–808.

Merritt, W.S., B.F.W. Croke, A.J. Jakeman, R.A. Letcher and P. Perez (2004), 'A biophysical toolbox for assessment and management of land and water resources in rural catchments in Northern Thailand', *Ecological Modelling*, **171**, 279–300.

MRC (1995), 'Agreement on the cooperation for the sustainable development of the Mekong River Basin', Mekong River Commission, downloadable at: http://www.mrcmekong.org/pdf/95%20Agreement.pdf (last access: May 2005).

MRC (2003), 'Basin Development Plan', Mekong River Commission, downloadable at: http://www.mrcmekong.org/programmes/bdp/bdp.htm (last access: May 2005).

NBI (2003), 'International Consortium for Cooperation on the Nile – Nile Basin Initiative', Nile Basin Initiative, info at: http://www.nilebasin.org/ (last access: May 2005).

Oreskes N., K. Schraderfrechette and K. Belitz (1994),'Verification, validation, and confirmation of numerical-models in the earth-sciences', *Science*, 263, 641–646.

Refsgaard, J.C., H.J. Henriksen, W.G. Harrar, H. Scholten and A. Kassahun (2005), 'Quality assurance in model based water management – review of existing practice and outline of new approaches', *Environmental Modelling and Software*, 20(10), 1201–1215.

Rieman, B., J.T. Peterson, J. Clayton, P. Howell, R. Thurow, W. Thompson and D. Lee (2001), 'Evaluation of potential effects of federal land management alternatives on trends of salmonids and their habitats in the interior Columbia River basin', *Forest Ecology and Management*, 153, 43–62.

Russell, L. (1996), 'Appendix I. Current Commonwealth and State Organisations, Policies and Programs. Managing Australia's Inland Waters', Department of Industry, Science and Tourism: Canberra, 111–121.

Rykiel, E.J. (1996), 'Testing ecological models: The meaning of validation', *Ecological Modelling*, 90, 229–244.

SADC (1995), 'Protocol on Shared Watercourse Systems, Southern African Development Community', downloadable at: http://www.sadc.int/index.php, ref.: 28/08/1995 (last access: May 2005).

SADC (2000), Revised Protocol on Shared Watercourse Systems, Southern African Development Community, downloadable at: http://www.sadc.int/index.php, ref.: 7/08/2000 (last access: May 2005).

Settle, C., T.D. Crocker and J.F. Shogren (2002), 'On the joint determination of biological and economic systems', *Ecological Economics*, 42, 301–311.

STARS, (2004), Network for Sustainable Terrestrial, Aquifer and Riverine Systems, info at http://stars.net.au (last access: May 2005).

UN (United Nations) (2000), 'United Nations Millennium Declaration. Resolution adopted by the General Assembly on 18 September 2000 (A/Res/55/2)', New York: UN.

UNCED (United Nations Conference on Environment and Development) (1992), *Agenda 21, United Nations General Assembly*, New York: UNCED.

US EPA (2001), *Protecting and restoring America's watersheds: Status, trends, and initiatives in watershed management*, United States Environmental Protection Agency, June 2001.

Van der Zaag, P. and H. Savenije (1999), 'The management of international waters in EU and SADC compared', *Physics and Chemistry of the Earth*, 24, 579–589.

Van Koppen, B. (2003), 'Water reform in Sub-Saharan Africa: what is the difference?', *Physics and Chemistry of the Earth*, 28, 1047–1053.

World Commission on Environment and Development (WCED) (1987), *Our Common Future*, Oxford: Oxford University Press.

PART II

New Challenges for Water Management

2. Policy Setting for Sustainable Water Management: GATS Rules and Water Management Systems

Gérard Mondello

2.1 INTRODUCTION

Nowadays, scientists recognise that fresh water resources are being exhausted, polluted, and overexploited.[1] However, and maybe paradoxically, in physical terms, the same quantity of water is being exchanged, following a natural cycle of evaporation and precipitation. Human activities and water policies have heavily impacted on the regularity of this natural cycle and, as a consequence, on the quality and the quantity of water available for human use. To ensure the sustainability and efficiency of water use in the future, a programme of Integrated Water Resource Management (IWRM)[2] should be implemented without delay.

IWRM recognises two important, but potentially conflicting, aims. The first one is based essentially on the ethical and moral ideal of providing free and fair access to water resources for every human being. The second aim recognises that IWRM must follow sound economic practices. Recent studies of water management have concluded that the quantity and quality of water must be dealt with in an integrated way, for example, it must consider how efficient allocation and distribution can also be made equitable (see, for instance, Spulber and Sabbaghi, 1997; Shirley, 2002). However, when faced with the harsh realities and complexities of this much debated subject, it quickly becomes apparent that it is far simpler to write about IWRM than to successfully implement it in the real world.

Whatever the level of economic development in a country, the management of the water system raises the same basic questions. These are: what should be the right price of fresh water and how should it be determined? How to achieve an acceptable water quality? What are the necessary investments to meet the future needs of the population? One of the dilemmas facing governments is that water may be considered both as a private and/or a public good. For instance water may be owned by a private entity, which considers it as a commodity that can be bought and sold for profit. But, because it is essential to life, water also has the features of a public good which must be available to all members of the community. This conflicting status is at the root of many controversial views about water management, and will reappear in many of the discussions in this chapter.

IWRM depends highly on the institutional and international context in which local Governments are moving.[3] For instance, since the beginning of the1980s, a lot of countries have changed their local water management from public to private as the privatisation process gains ground. Furthermore, International Institutions such as PNUD, World Bank, FAO, etc. are financing an increasing number of developing countries for targeted water management projects. As a consequence, a wide range of different organisations – international and national institutions, public and private firms – are interacting together more and more. Local water management is becoming a competitive industry regulated by the rules of private industry. Water firms are becoming more and more multinational and companies are providing services at all levels of water treatment, conveyance and disposal. Hence, there is an increasing need for the legal framework of the World Trade Organisation (WTO) for an international referee. In this direction, the General Agreement on Trade and Services (GATS) of WTO is being called to regulate the water services industry.

Under GATS commitments, the privatisation and introduction of competition into the water services industry is a complex undertaking. It is worth noting that this includes both the supply and treatment of drinking water, and also collection and treatment of sewage. It is also worth noting that the privatisation of water services may be analysed under the 'Agreement on Government Procurement' (AGP) which is a specific agreement under the aegis of WTO.

To narrow the scope of this chapter, we will focus our discussion on fresh water management for urban use. However, with the exception of the developed countries in the northern hemisphere, water is often physically scarce, and its allocation creates conflicts between different users. This issue has been exacerbated by the increasing pollution of groundwater and rivers caused by agricultural and industrial activities. It is therefore difficult to discuss urban water use without some consideration of the agricultural and industrial users within the system as well. In section two of this chapter the specificity of economic water management will be analysed, and we will discuss the importance of Institutions in this area. Then in section 3 the consequences for water management will be studied, in particular the adoption of GATS rules and commitments. In light of the trend for privatisation, an analysis of how IWRM may be implemented will also be addressed.

2.2 INSTITUTIONAL FRAMEWORKS AND IWRM

Until recently, in most countries water supply was managed according to public criteria. Water infrastructures (urban, agricultural, industrial) were centrally owned and publicly managed. In the beginning of the 19th century, France resorted to private concessions and opened the road for privatisation of urban water management. Initially only Paris, Lyon and Marseille were involved.[4] The privatisation scheme was essentially similar to the modern 'Build, Own, Operate, Transfer' (BOOT) system.[5] A private entity received a franchise to finance, design, build and operate a facility (and to charge users fees) for a specified period, after which ownership was transferred back to the public sector. By the end of twentieth century, this system had been established all around the world. The demographic pressure, the increasing level of urbanisation, the ageing of the water distribution system, and conflicts between water users, have all led to governments being forced to modernise, fully or partially, their water systems. Privatisation has been seen as a short cut to reach this goal.

2.3 TECHNOCRATIC AND CENTRALISED MANAGEMENT OF WATER

In a recent paper, David Zilberman (2003) states that water systems are more and more complex and, as a consequence, several important institutions responsible for the design and implementation of water projects and the conveyance of water have emerged. Considering the Californian example, he distinguishes 'water project management agencies' that are led only by government authorities[6] because of the high cost of implementing major water projects. Because of its bureaucratic structure, the 'water project' is managed by the State, and their responsibility includes management of the project, collection of the fees and allocation of the water. In addition, the State may have several units that are responsible for key facilities, such as the conveyance canals and pumps. Similar management structures exist in Europe. In France, for instance, six major basin Agencies manage the water collection, treatment and allocation for the 22 Regions within the country. All of them depend on the French Ministry of Environment. These agencies are at the top of the water allocation process. Their aim is to share the water resource between the different users: irrigation, urban needs, industry, etc. while maintaining a high level of water quality. This last objective is supported by a specific tax/subsidies scheme as an incentive to improve water quality by introducing new technologies.

The way public water utilities are being managed is being questioned more and more. For instance, one may ask whether their management should be under private or public criteria. The problem is hard to solve because some countries have too little water, or no scope for additional supplies without massive technological and financial inputs. Others have adequate supplies, at least for the short term, but manage their reserves poorly. The integrated use and management of storm waters, wastewater, groundwater and water supply (total urban water cycle) is yielding a range of social, economic and environmental benefits. But all these systems call for investments, and the technical and economic resources may be hard to find locally. As a consequence, the privatisation of water management will continue for a long time and will not be easily reversible as such.[7]

Today, three main alternatives exist for fresh water distribution. Firstly, in the United Kingdom the entire basin system has been privatised. This means that the whole infrastructure, from the top of the system (collection and storage of water) to the bottom (treatment and distribution to individual users) is shared between private companies. Secondly, France and most other European Countries allow their municipalities to delegate for a fixed time period, the management of their water and sewage systems to specialised private companies. Thirdly, there are a large number of the remaining systems that are still publicly managed and could stay in public hands indefinitely because of insufficient income prospects.

2.4   THE NECESSITY FOR BETTER WATER MANAGEMENT: HABITS CHANGE

Two kinds of pressure induce the local authorities to change the way they manage water. The first one is due to the population growth and water needs in urban areas. These are striking phenomena that affect both developing and developed countries. For developed ones, even if population growth is weak, urban water demand is being driven by increasingly sophisticated uses (for example tourism, and other kinds of leisure activities which require increased use of water). The second pressure is induced by the alteration of water quality due to either the scarcity of water in arid zones or because of an intensive agriculture that depletes and pollutes the groundwater with pesticides and fertilisers.

2.4.1   Changing Local Management Water Systems

Until recently water management was essentially confined to local and national boundaries. Trans-boundary questions were raised only when the resource had to be shared among two or several areas. However, since the

1980s, local water management has become increasingly international. The reason for this trend is mainly twofold. Firstly, there has been an international trend towards privatisation across all sectors of the economy, and water management is no exception. Secondly, there are a growing number of large multi-national companies that possess a broad range of engineering and management skills, and they are successfully competing for work on a worldwide basis. Because of this international trend, water management involves more and more private criteria. Increasingly, water is being marketed like any other commodity, and its allocation and pricing are being controlled by the economic forces of supply and demand.

The consequences of traditional and publicly owned water management are well known: prices of water are subsidised and their level is well below the true management costs of collecting, treating and distributing the water. Hence, in most countries, large cities have been forced to modernise their local water utility. This is becoming an absolute necessity because of their inefficiency (ageing infrastructure, new regulations and water standards, etc.). Furthermore, the privatisation process may be explained because these cities want to keep their population free from diseases and unhealthy conditions due to old pipe networks (using lead for instance). This is particularly true for fresh water supply systems. Consequently, potable water markets are developing (Becker, 1994). The change is not only technological. It also requires the transfer of a high level of knowledge and this cannot be undertaken without resorting to international private corporations and without institutional changes.[8]

2.4.2 Changing Water Systems: The Role of Intensive Agriculture

The trend to water privatisation may also be explained by the increasing incidence of water conflicts between users for agricultural, urban and industrial purposes.[9] Two main factors, sometimes closely linked, are involved. The first one is quite well known and is associated with water scarcity and population growth. All countries in the Saharan and sub-Saharan regions of Africa as well as the southern Mediterranean countries are faced with this dilemma. Similar problems are occurring in the Middle Eastern countries (Becker 1994, 2003). The second factor has been caused by changes in agricultural practices.[10] As Scheierling (1995) and Bergman and Pugh (1994) show, agricultural water pollution is becoming a major concern, not only in developed regions such as the European Union (EU), but also in many developing countries. This is due to the intensification of agriculture (the increasing use of fertilisers and pesticides,[11] and the specialisation and concentration of crop and livestock production).

As a consequence, urban areas are being faced with the prospect of less water and water of poorer quality. This is particularly true for the large cities of South America, Africa and Asia. Institutional changes for improving municipal water management are then needed. These changes cannot be undertaken on bilateral relationships only. The question is then to know whether GATS may fulfil this task.

2.5   THE GENERAL AGREEMENT ON TRADE AND SERVICES (GATS) IN THE WATER SECTOR: INSTITUTIONAL AND STRUCTURAL CHANGES

The GATS is a set of multilateral rules and commitments covering Government activities which affect trade in services. First adopted in 1994, the GATS includes a commitment to negotiate further liberalisation starting in 2000. The GATS covers all services with two exceptions; services provided in the exercise of governmental authority, and in the air transport sector and all services directly related to the exercise of traffic rights. GATS is twofold – the framework agreement containing the rules, and the national schedules of commitments in which each Member specifies the degree of access it is prepared to guarantee for foreign services suppliers. Water services are included in GATS.

GATS commitments cannot be reversed; once a WTO member has agreed to a commitment, the decision cannot be reversed. This is part of the 'lock in' effect that GATS is liable to produce,[12] and applies equally to water services.

2.5.1   GATS on Water: General Features

The aim of GATS is to remove any restrictions and internal government regulations in the area of service delivery that are considered to be 'barriers to trade'. If a service is to be supplied on a permanent or regular basis (for example, cleaning of roads or household waste collection) or for the capital works (construction of buildings), it can either be purchased on a one-off basis, hired (consultancy) or provided through concessions. Each country lists specific commitments on service sectors and on activities within those sectors. The commitments guarantee access to the country's market in the listed sectors, and they spell out any limitations on market access and national treatment. The commitments contain the negotiated and guaranteed conditions for conducting international trade in services. If a recorded condition is to be changed for the worse, then the government has to negotiate compensation with affected countries. The commitments can be improved at any time by further liberalisation. The General Agreement on Trade in Services (GATS) can be expanded to include all public services.

This fact caused some anxiety within the international community. A country's sovereignty seemed to be threatened. For instance, clause (c) says that:

> If a service is provided on a non-commercial basis but in competition with other suppliers or on a commercial basis but without competition, it is not a service supplied in exercise of governmental authority.

Article 1, Paragraph 3 of the GATS defines the scope of the agreement as follows: (b) 'services' includes any service in any sector except services supplied in the exercise of governmental authority; (c) 'a service supplied in the exercise of governmental authority' means any service which is supplied neither on a commercial basis, nor in competition with one or more service suppliers. As Shrybman (2001) points out, the wording of the clauses in Article 1:3 means that they are open to interpretation. This creates legal uncertainty about government decisions and means they are always under threat of being sued by companies or other governments.[13] For instance, one interpretation is that the municipal water management system must be assessed as a whole, despite any commercial or competitive nature of its individual parts, and that management provide services 'in the exercise of governmental authority'. However, it could just as easily be interpreted that if any aspect of the service being provided is operating commercially and/or in competition with another provider, the GATS rules apply. In this case, the public service role provided by the municipality would not enter into the equation. The problem is that we simply do not know how the clauses in question would be interpreted in the event of a challenge. Tuerk, Holland and Granger (2003, p. 21) recall that:

> (. . .) when focusing on water as a natural resource (as well as wetlands and ecosystems), the scope of services sectors that affect water resources and that may become subject to the various GATS disciplines is significantly broader than just water services providers.

Hence, a close examination of the original GATS legal texts shows that the set of water services covered by the GATS is quite large. It includes: (a) water service providers and wastewater treatment providers, (b) water infrastructure services (the water treatment plants, and pipe networks, etc.), (c) water-demanding services (all services around the supply of water for the energy sector or transport services), and (d) water-polluting services.

2.5.2 GATS and the Water Question: An Ongoing Process

Due to general concerns about the ramifications of the GATS rules, the WTO released a publication (WTO, 2001) providing more precise details of the aims and scope of the GATS. In respect to water distribution and all other public services, the following policy options are open to all WTO members:

- To maintain the service as a monopoly, public or private;
- To open the service to competing suppliers, but to restrict access to national companies;
- To open the service to national and foreign suppliers, but to make no GATS commitments on it;
- To make GATS commitments covering the right of foreign companies to supply the service, in addition to national suppliers.

However, it is well known that, until now, no GATS members have made direct commitments on water distribution. This, however, may be challenged by the 'Agreement on Government Procurement' (AGP). That agreement is an extension of the WTO commitments on trade and services. In particular, in article 10 of the AGP, it states that:

> To ensure optimum effective international competition under selective tendering procedures, entities shall, for each intended procurement, invite tenders from the maximum number of domestic suppliers and suppliers of other Parties, consistent with the efficient operation of the procurement system. They shall select the suppliers to participate in the procedure in a fair and non-discriminatory manner.

This article leaves little space for divergent interpretation. Hence, once governments agree to the AGP terms they will be forced to abide by them. No matter what the goals and objectives of the public sector are, their public tenders will have to abide by the terms of the agreement. Water management will not be an exception. Once municipalities are defined as a service provider then it would be discriminatory to distinguish between private and municipal providers. Municipalities could be forced to compete with foreign corporations in providing these services, under the principle of free trade. This fact could have detrimental effects on local businesses.[14] Privatisation and liberalisation may actually make things worse where private companies have no obligation to ensure access to services for all sections of the community or to ensure basic safety standards.

Proponents of GATS are very much convinced that water privatisation and the institution of the global water market will benefit rich and poor alike. However, more and more civil society organisations have also become aware of the implications and have voiced their objections to water services being put under legally binding trade agreements like GATS. These objections cover two main issues. As stated above, GATS may help the private sector, especially large multinational companies, to expand their operations all over the world. On a positive note, this could lead to the transfer of more efficient technologies to developing or less developed countries. But from experience, without any independent control, water privatisation may create many new problems. When corporations sell water for profit, the quality, access and safety of water supplies may be endangered and the future of water resources threatened. Most countries are well aware of this dilemma. For instance, at the beginning of 2003, European Union trade negotiators were using the services negotiations of the World Trade Organisation (WTO) to open up other countries' water sectors for the benefit of Europe's private sector water industry. The European GATS negotiators want to be sure that drinking water is included in the GATS agreement because they have large companies like Suez Lyonnaise des Eaux and Generale des Eaux, a division of Vivendi SA, and Thames Water which are involved in privatising municipal water services around the world. The privatisation process of the water system in the United States (U.S.) has commenced.[15] As a consequence, this will prevent the U.S.A from maintaining public service 'monopolies'. The local distribution of drinking water has previously been a municipal function. However, there are increasing demands that these systems be privatized, as has already occurred in France and Great Britain. This would oblige the U.S. government to give large EU water companies, such as Vivendi, Suez Lyonnaise and Thames Water, the right to buy up or otherwise operate for profit the more than 60 000 U.S. municipal water service providers now in existence. If the U.S. commits water services, to the proposed GATS rules, any federal, state or local authority which regulates water management for the purposes of protecting water quality, or providing universal access at the expense of open competition or full privatisation, could be challenged for creating 'barriers to trade' in the powerful and binding dispute resolution system of the WTO. A government might be forced to demonstrate that the regulation of a private provider was necessary and that no other 'less trade-restrictive measure' could be taken to accomplish the same objective in order to maintain it.

2.6 EQUITY, EFFICIENCY AND FAIRNESS: THREE PRINCIPLES UNDERLYING IWRM

Until recently, even in developed countries, economic efficiency criteria for urban water management were not a priority. Most of the water utilities were public and locally owned and their management was direct, for example, the municipality could be directly involved (as in France or Spain)[16] or a local public utility managed the water system (Germany). As a result, because of a lack of focus on economic considerations (costs, efficiency, etc.) most of the urban water was supplied on the basis of social equity. Fresh water was cheap because it was highly subsidized. Furthermore the water supply sector was far from being competitive because of the employment of a great number of low qualified employees; and also because water and sewage networks were old and in need of heavy investments. As a consequence of this bad management, outbreaks of waterborne disease occurred in some systems. For instance, Esrey (1996) used epidemiology of small children in urban areas of developing countries to demonstrate the need for an improvement of both water supply and sewage systems.

The question that most countries were faced with was: how to cope with the necessity to improve or renovate the water system as a whole while improving efficiency and equity.[17] Privatisation has been a key word for achieving the goals of providing and sanitising water. Essentially, however, urban water management has the features of a natural monopoly. This is due to the fact that a water supply network cannot easily be shared by several operators. Hence, a monopoly is not necessarily an inefficient alternative for local water management. Furthermore, very large investments in infrastructure are required, and these will only be worthwhile if long-term operating contracts are also granted. As a consequence, once an operator wins the project, it gains control of the water system for a long time. Indeed, a positive return on investment generally needs around fifteen years and, generally, the contracts are signed for an even longer period.

Equity in price is another important challenge. For instance, in France an extensive survey was conducted by the French Institute for the Environment (IFEN) and the Ministry of Agriculture's Department of Statistics (SCEES) among 5000 local authorities covering the financial year 1998. The survey revealed a wide variation in the prices paid by consumers for water. In 90 per cent of French municipalities (communes), water costs between €0.85 and €2.8 per cubic metre (see for instance Nowak, 1995, or Rebeix, 2001a). This variation in prices had many reasons including different methods used for organising and managing the system for drinking water distribution, and variable geophysical conditions. It depends also on whether users are in a densely populated area or scattered across rural areas. In the drinking water sector, management by private companies is most common, with only small rural municipalities managing their water services directly. Management of drinking water distribution is delegated to the private sector where municipalities are grouped together and also in densely populated areas.

From a theoretical point of view, the viability of privatisation of water services requires that conditions for fair and free competition are institutionally organized. This involves gathering a significant number of competitors (firms) and allocating the water management system on a competitive basis. A well organised bid-auction system may meet this requirement. This auction system gives the right to operate the water utility under a management contract, lease or concession. In other words, a periodic auction has to be held. Fairness in competition with an equal access to information for all agents has to be guaranteed by some independent institution. However, local water systems can be very complex and the requirements for fair competition are very difficult to fulfil. Following definitions provided by the World Bank, four kinds of competitive pressure are possible in water and sanitation provision:

- Direct competition in the supply of services, sometimes referred to as 'competition in the market';
- Competition for the right to supply water and sanitation services (through concession or other contracts), often referred to as 'competition for the market';
- Competitive pressures deriving from markets for the capital with which new investments are financed;
- Comparative, or 'yardstick,' competition, in which the performance of suppliers in different cities is compared.

Each of these items may assist Governments with full or partial privatisation of their water and sanitation system. However, it is quite difficult to define how to fulfil both efficiency and equity requirements. Even if the World Bank defines quite precisely how to manage the privatisation scheme, economic criteria that ensure the efficiency of the process are lacking. Under the GATS rules and commitments, it seems that most countries react in a similar manner. If a country has developed an efficient industry that uses the latest technologies, it will accept favourably the GATS terms. In contrast, it will be reluctant to endorse the agreement if the sector is economically weak and using outdated technology. That is why many countries have kept their water monopolies, even if they are inefficient. Paradoxically, this situation occurs much more often in the developed countries than in the developing ones.

2.7 PRIVATISATION AND INTERACTION IN THE ECONOMIC-ECOLOGICAL SYSTEM

Water pollution is a by-product of agricultural, industrial and urban activities and must be viewed in the broader context of water resource management. Protection of the local water cycle is a high priority environmental aim. However, the setting of policies to meet this requirement may conflict with a country's commitments under GATS. The emerging conflict between national protection priorities for health and environment and the WTO rules is a well-known issue.[18]

The rules specified in GATS have repercussions for a whole range of sectors that are undergoing, or considering, privatisation. For instance, one may quote GATS article XVI[19] that prohibits certain types of policies which could induce quantitative limitations (articles (a) to (e)). A discussion on this issue is provided by Tuerk, Holland and Granger (2003, p. 31) who state:

> Thus, assuming that a WTO member had made commitments in sectors that cover economic activities such as deviating or extracting water, environmental laws that put overall caps on the amount of water to be extracted or to be deviated could be considered limits on the total quantity services output.

This argument applies to all measures that could be regarded as quantity protection, even those that might reduce the risk of over-exploitation.[20]

It should be made clear that the previous argument does not mean that GATS prohibits all quantity regulation of water. However, it does appear that once a country has accepted GATS commitments for some services linked with water management, then it is likely that some conflict with GATS rules will occur. For instance, the conflict could originate from claims that the tendering of large contracts is not sufficiently open to international competition or there is a lack of international firms in the national market.

2.8   THE SCOPE AND AIMS OF A PUBLIC POLICY UNDER PRIVATE CONSTRAINTS

Public regulators no longer have the luxury of choosing whether they manage the economics of urban water systems under public or private rules (Boyer, Patry and Tremblay, 1999). Indeed, urban water privatisation is an ongoing process and every country is (or will be) faced with this issue. Furthermore, the acceptance of GATS commitments will induce irreversible choices towards private management. Hence, to deal with the benefits (or the losses) of this process it is useful to compare the new system with the older system of publicly owned water authorities. However, the exercise is not so simple. In France, the report of the Cour des Comptes (1997) compared performances of public and private water systems and showed that both of them generated market failures.[21] The main failures of direct management by the French municipalities were bad coordination between municipalities, low productivity of workers, badly oriented investment and poor quality of water. On the other hand, the failures of the private system included high water prices, the risk of corruption and delays in large infrastructure investments.

There are a number of arguments used by the opponents of GATS rules and full privatisation. These arguments use facts and observations drawn from privatisation experiments that have already occurred in some countries. However, to reach a more accurate conclusion about the performance of the GATS privatisation process some deeper economic analyses are necessary. It should be noted that even in the most advanced countries of the world, there is concern about the implications of GATS and the privatisation of water services. The arguments used by opponents include:

- Privatisation will result in a rise in water prices and tariffs (see for instance the study of Alcazar, Abdala and Shirley (2002) about the Buenos Aires Water Concession that shows that a municipal water system working with the same opaque tariff system as in France);
- Mitigated effects on population welfare because of low improvement in water quality;
- Loss of control by the State over water investments when long-term contracts renegotiations are due;
- Massive lay-off of workers.

Hence, the question facing local governments is how they might exercise control on water management in such a way that the above-mentioned effects can be avoided.

2.9 MANAGING POTABLE WATER UNDER IWRM RULES

One of the challenges being faced by water managers is how to ensure social equity. The price of water needs to be carefully structured so that all members of the community can afford the minimum volume of water required by each household, regardless of their financial or social status (Alcazar, Abdala and Shirley 2002). On the other hand, pricing structure must also cover the marginal long-term cost of the whole water infrastructure, including the collection, storage, treatment and supply systems. The road to privatisation generally commences with private industry finding rental opportunities in the water management sector. However, all this needs to be managed carefully or the market failures predicted by opponents to the GATS rules might become a reality.[22]

We will recall that, ideally, IWRM will achieve two key objectives. The first is the social imperative of ensuring all members of society gain access to a minimum quantity of water to maintain their health. The second objective is to preserve the quality of water resources on a long-term basis, for both present and future generations.

2.9.1   Fresh Water Management as a Natural Monopoly

The distribution of water obeys the theoretical rules of a natural monopoly. In fact, the water sector can be characterised as a 'double' natural monopoly. The first element relates to the fact that towns and cities have only one water distribution network that cannot easily be shared and is expensive and inefficient to duplicate. This corresponds to the traditional definition of a natural monopoly. The second element relates to the patent protected technological advances in water management.

•   The statute of public utility requires that the supplier of the service satisfies total demand and guarantees a certain level of continuity and reliability. The pricing rules associated with public utilities have to be respected too. Concerning water and sewage, this is especially important because of the necessity to preserve equity in access for present and later generations. Concession of water management raises the profile of these ethical considerations because it involves the introduction of market mechanisms into the system.

The delegation process involves only partial privatisation. The whole infrastructure remains in the hands of the public sector (either the State or the municipality). Furthermore, the mechanism is temporary because the delegation is limited contractually in time. Delegation is becoming more controversial because of some highly publicised scandals and the generally higher prices that accompany it, which are seen as an index of the inefficiency of delegation. The municipalities and their delegated firms are facing increased pressure for better services and lower prices. Regulatory norms and environmental constraints are making it necessary to undertake costly new investments (see for instance Clark and Mondello, 2000a and 200b). They create temporary technological monopolies, which reinforce the natural monopoly structure. Water pricing is a political problem, with social and economic aspects. Under the older management systems where water management was controlled by the Municipality or State (see for instance Tietenberg, 1992), the prices charged by water distribution utilities were too low, perhaps because water is considered an essential commodity.[23]

2.9.2   Organising Competition Under GATS Rules

Under the proposed GATS rules, not only will governments face added pressures to deregulate and privatise their water systems, but once a city's water services have been taken over by a foreign-based corporation, efforts to take these services back into public hands will trigger severe economic penalties under the WTO. That point raises some questions about the investment level that a large city (or a state) may be willing to undertake to improve its skills and knowledge in water management (labour training, acquiring new technologies, etc.) with the aim of managing its own water system some time in the future.

These issues must be considered when setting water tariffs and determining the level of investment in infrastructure. Water utilities throughout the world are facing several constraints. The first, as noted above, is the necessity to ensure adequate water for members of the community, without excluding any sub-groups (such as the poorest ones). A second constraint is how to cope with different kinds of water scarcity (geographical, linked with quality, etc.). A third constraint is how to meet the international requirement of maintaining free competition among international private firms for the management of the local water utilities.

In fact, stronger international competition can often result in better management of the water system. Hence, a strong organisation of competition infrastructure is needed to give the country a real negotiation power. The aim of this organisation is to avoid collusion and allocate efficiently the water public service. As shown by McAffe and McMillan, (1987, 1988), or Laffont and Tirole (1993), bid auctions are considered as the most efficient pricing system when allocating natural monopolies to private operators. However several conditions about information, the number of competitors and the method of bidding, have to be met to make the allocating system efficient.[24]

2.10   CONCLUSION

Nowadays, one cannot study water management sustainability and its implementation process without a reference to the institutional frameworks in which most countries are moving. The trend towards privatisation is slow but steady. This will occur even if GATS negotiations do not succeed. Furthermore, a full assessment of benefits and impacts of the privatisation process probably cannot occur for many years to come, and so it is difficult to dispute. That means essentially, that the supply of water for all kinds of uses (urban, agriculture, industrial, tourism, etc), its purification process, the sewage system, etc. have to be dealt with globally and under economic efficiency criteria. However, because water is essential to life and has no substitute, managing water systems purely by market forces may lead to unfair situations from an ethical and moral point of view. Nobody can be excluded from free access to fresh water, and both equity and economic efficiency must be jointly considered for the sake of both present and future generations.

In the future, because of their high capacities, large private companies will be called to play a growing and major role in the international water sustainability debate. Implementing IWRM depends on several factors. Firstly, the negotiation power of countries and large cities dealing with private companies; secondly, the willpower to negotiate favourable conditions; and thirdly the power of international institutions to enforce moral and ethical considerations. Final agreement on the terms of the WTO services, especially on water, is still an ongoing process. IWRM will have to be taken into account inside the main institutional features of the General Agreement on Trade and Services.

NOTES

1. The oceans contain 96 per cent of the Earth's water, experience 86 per cent of planetary evaporation, and receive 78 per cent of planetary precipitation, and thus represent a key element of the global water cycle. Because evaporation concentrates salt in the surface of the ocean, increasing evaporation rates cause detectable spikes in surface ocean salinity levels. In contrast, salinity decreases generally reflect the addition of fresh water to the ocean through precipitation and runoff from the continents. Relatively large-scale, rapid oceanic changes put into evidence by Curry, Dickson and Yashayaev (2003) suggest that recent climate changes, including global warming, may be altering the fundamental planetary system that regulates evaporation and precipitation and cycles fresh water around the globe.
2. For a complete description of what IWRM consists of, see Giupponi et al.'s contribution in this book (Chapter 4).
3. See in this book Mostert's paper (Chapter 7) for an analysis of the importance of institutions in water management.
4. See for instance Lorrain (1995) for an historical analysis of this movement.
5. See for instance Soler (2003) for a full analysis of the Catalan case in Spain, and Boyer et al. (1999) for a more analytic survey of the Quebec case.
6. That is to say the Federal Government through the Army Corps of Engineers and Bureau of Reclamation and also the California State government.
7. See Boyer, Patry and Tremblay (1999) for a precise analysis of the delegation process.
8. See for instance in this book Ghetti and Giupponi's contribution for a more complete assessment (Chapter 3).
9. See for instance Gleick's works on the matter in 1994 and 1998.
10. See for example Dinar and Zilberman (1991).
11. From 1970 to the mid-1980s, inorganic nitrogen use on agricultural land grew by 42 per cent in the Netherlands and by 135 per cent in the United Kingdom. Owing to the incentives provided by the CAP, inorganic nitrogen use in the four member countries reached relatively high levels, compared with non-Community countries. For instance, in 1985, nitrogen use intensity in Germany was about five times, and in the Netherlands more than ten times, higher than in the United States.
12. See for example Tuerk, Holland and Granger (2003).
13. See for instance Landes and Posner (1987) and the associated literature for the importance of tort laws as an incentive to postpone projects under liability laws.
14. For instance, the NGO, South Asia Watch on Trade, Economics and Environment (SAWTEE), has found that domestic firms in South Asia are unable to compete with multinationals once privatisation and liberalisation is introduced. The incoming firm can sometimes negotiate amazing deals with the local government anxious for inward investment. In Argentina, a water consortium was awarded a 95-year contract, leaving local firms with little hope of ever competing in the future.

15. Under the 'progressive liberalisation' programme of the General Agreement on Trade in Services (GATS), the EU has targeted the water sectors of 72 other WTO member countries for liberalisation – including developed, developing and least developed countries alike. The EU is demanding that the US fully commit its drinking water and sewage services under the 'GATS-2000' talks.

16. See for instance Soler (2003), who shows that water management in Spain is submitted to a non-uniform geographical and seasonal distribution of water resource, worsened by the non-uniform allocation of demand (mainly irrigation and urban). Spain has a very long tradition in public water management (first water law in 1879). The recently approved changes in the former Spanish Water Law, limiting water rights and introducing water markets, the new and expected Hydrological National Plan and the European Framework Directive, reinforce the opportunities of the private sector to enter, giving financial resources, technological advances and quick answers to new social concepts in water management procedures.

17. For instance, considering the French situation, as Rebeix (2001b) shows, the total length of main piping used to distribute drinking water in France is 800 000 km (20 times the Earth's circumference). In 1998, the volume of drinking water distributed was estimated to be 5.6 billion (bn) m^3 but only 4 bn m^3 was actually charged via water bills. Over 28 per cent of water distributed is thus either lost through leakages or not accounted for. The mains system is particularly extensive in terms of length in rural areas. Replacing old pipes is a problem: the replacement rate was only 0.6 per cent in 1998. This situation is nothing exceptional, and occurs throughout Western Europe.

18. For instance we may recall the opposition between the EU and the USA about the interpretation of the precautionary principle under the WTO rules against cattle hormones.

19. GATS art. XVI:

> In sectors where market-access commitments are undertaken, the measures which a Member shall not maintain or adopt either on the basis of a regional subdivision or on the basis of its entire territory, unless otherwise specified in its Schedule, are defined as:
> - limitations on the number of service suppliers whether in the form of numerical quotas, monopolies, exclusive services suppliers or the requirement of an economic needs test;...
> - Limitations on the total value of service transactions or assets in the form of numerical quotas or the requirement of an economic needs test;
> - Limitations on the total number of service operations or on the total quantity of service output expressed in the form of numerical quotas or the requirement of an economic needs test;
> - Limitations on the total number of natural persons that may be employed in a particular service sector or that a service supplier may employ in the form of numerical quotas or the requirement of an economic needs test;
> - Measures which restrict or require specific types of legal entity or joint venture through which a service supplier may supply a service; and
> - Limitation on the participation of foreign capital in terms of maximum percentage limit or foreign share holding or on the total value of individual or aggregate foreign investment.

20. For a more comprehensive analysis see Tuerk, Holland and Granger (2003, p. 30 onwards).

21. They are very close to the definition of Bator (1958).

22. Encouraging the private sector to supply water for commercial uses could lead to less water being available for public uses like public drinking water and wildlife protection. Also, if big commercial users get water from private sources, public water supplies will have to carry more of the public infrastructure costs, leading to higher rates. For instance, it is interesting to follow the study of the US position on water privatisation in which negotiators are still figuring out how to respond. They know there is a controversy in the US about having GATS cover water. US corporations would like limited coverage in areas where they are competitive with the European corporations. Advocates for environment and justice do not want water covered in GATS at all. The US is looking for a compromise position. They are likely to propose that GATS 'carve out', for example, it excludes transportation of bulk

water across international borders by private companies. This would be good from the perspective of citizens and organisations who believe water is a right and not just another commodity to be supplied by the market for profit. They have also suggested limiting the application of GATS in the US to commercial applications. Unfortunately, this approach does not deal with the fact that other countries might have a harder time resisting the pressure from large companies to put public water systems on their schedule of commitments. If a country does this and later realizes it made a mistake, it could be too late to change course.

23. For instance, this is no longer true in France where only the user is charged (and not the tax-payer). The mean price in France is around €2 by cubic meter. The bill includes about two thirds for supply of drinking water and one third for wastewater cleaning and pollution prevention. With respect to new European regulations, safeguarding of water resources will become more and more expensive in the near future, implying a yearly increase of costs in the range of 2 to 5 per cent.

24. See for example M. Mougeot and F. Naegelen (1997), McAffe and McMillan (1987) and (1988), Hendricks and Porter (1989), Bontemps (1995), Carey (1993).

REFERENCES

Alcazar, L., M. Abdala and M. Shirley (2002), 'The Buenos Aires Water Concession, in thirsting for efficiency: the economics and politics of urban water system reform', in Mary M. Shirley (ed.), *Thirsting for Water*, The World Bank, New York: Pergamon.

Bator, F.M. (1958), 'The anatomy of market failure', *Quarterly Journal of Economics*, **72** (August), 351–79.

Becker, N. (1994), 'The Value of Institutional Change in Moving from Central Planning to a Market System: Implications from the Israeli Water Sector', *Fondazione Eni Enrico Mattei working paper*, **16.94**, Milan.

Becker, N. (2003), 'Water pricing, its effects and proposed reforms: the Israeli experience', *International Journal of Public Administration*, **26**(3), 247–263

Bergman, L. and D.M. Pugh (1994), *Environmental Toxicology, Economics and Institutions, The Atrazine Case Study*, Dordrecht: Kluwer Academic Publishers.

Bontemps, P. (1995), *Contrôle de la Pollution en Présence d'Asymétries Informationnelles*, Thèse, Paris X Nanterre.

Boyer, M., M. Patry and P.J. Tremblay (1999), *La Gestion Déléguée de l'Eau: Les Enjeux*, Montreal: Cyrano, pp. 1–52.

Carey, R. (1993), 'Reservation price announcement in sealed bid auction', *Journal of Industrial Economics*, **61**(4), 668–680.

Clark, E.A. and G. Mondello (2000a), 'Water management in France: delegation and irreversibility', *Journal of Applied Economics*, **3**, 325–352.

Clark, E.A., and G. Mondello (2000b), 'Resource management and the mayor's guarantee in French water allocation', *Environmental and Resource Economics*, **15**, 103–113.

Cour des Comptes (1997), 'La Gestion des Services Publics Locaux d'Eau et d'Assainissement', éditions du *Journal Officiel*, January, 1997, Paris.

Curry R., R. Dickson and I. Yashayaev (2003), 'A change in the freshwater balance of the Atlantic Ocean over the past four decades', *Nature,* **426**, 826–829.

Dinar A. and D. Zilberman (eds) (1991), *The Economics and Management of Water and Drainage in Agriculture*, Norwell MA: Kluwer Academic Publishers.

Esrey, S.A. (1996), 'Water waste and well-being: a multicountry study', *American*

Journal of Epidemiology, **143**, 609–21.

Gleick, P.H. (1994), 'Water, war, and peace in the Middle East', *Environment*, **36**(3).

Gleick, P.H. (1998), 'Water and conflict', see Chronologies A and B, in P.H. Gleick (ed.), *The World's Water 1998–1999*, Washington DC: Island Press, pp. 105–135.

Hendricks, K. and R. Porter (1989), 'Collusions in auctions', *Annales d'Economie et de Statistiques*, **15–16**, 217–30.

Laffont, J.-J. and J. Tirole (1993), *A Theory of Incentives in Procurement and Regulation*, Cambridge, MA: M.I.T. Press.

Landes, W. and R. Posner (1987), *The Economic Structure of Tort Law*, Cambridge MA: Harvard University Press.

Lorrain, D. (1995), *Gestion Urbaines de l'Eau*, Paris: Economica.

Margat J. (1992), *L'Eau dans le Bassin Méditérranéen, Situation et Prospective, Les fascicules du Plan Bleu*, Paris: Economica.

McAffe, R.P. and J. McMillan (1987), 'Auctions with a stochastic number of bidders', *Journal of Economic Theory*, **43**, 1–19.

McAffe, R.P. and J. McMillan (1988), *Incentives in Government Contracting*, Toronto: University of Toronto Press.

Mougeot, M. and F. Naegelen (1997), 'Marchés publics et théorie economique: un guide de l'acheteur', *Revue d'Economie Politique,* **107** (January), 1–31.

Nowak, F. (1995), *Le Prix de l'Eau*, Paris: Economica.

Oates, W.E. (1992), *The Economics of the Environment*, Aldershot, UK and Brookfield, US: Edward Elgar.

Rebeix, G. (2001a), 'Eau potable: diversité des services... grand écart des prix', *Les données de l'environnement, Eau,* IFEN, April.

Rebeix, G. (2001b),'800 000 km de conduites pour distribuer l'eau potable', *Les données de l'environnement, Eau,* IFEN, November-December.

Scheierling, S. (1995), 'Overcoming agricultural pollution of water: the challenge of integrating agricultural and environmental policies in the European Union', *World Bank Technical Paper*, **269**, Washington.

Shirley, M. (ed) (2002), *Thirsting for Efficiency: the Economics and Politics of Urban Water System Reform*, Amsterdam, London and New York: Elsevier Science, Pergamon.

Shrybman, S. (2001), *An assessment of the impact of the general agreement on trade and services on policy*, programs and law concerning public sector libraries, Toronto, downloaded from http://www.caut.ca/english/issues/trade/GATS.pdf (last access: December 2001).

Siebert, H. (1995*), Economics of the Environment: Theory and Policy*, Berlin: Springer Verlag.

Solanes, M. (2002), 'Water: Rights, Flexibility and Governance: A Balance that Matters?', Economic Commission for Latin America and the Caribbean of the United Nations.

Soler M. (2003), 'Water privatisation in Spain', *International Journal of Public Administration*, **26**(3), 213–246.

Spulber, N. and A. Sabbaghi (1997), *Economics of Water Resources: From Regulation to Privatization*, Boston: Kluwer Academic Press.

Tietenberg, T.H. (1992), *Environmental and Natural Resource Economics,* 3rd edition, New York: Harper Collins.

Tuerk, E., R. Holland and S. Granger (2003), 'GATS, Water and the Environment, Implications of the General Agreement on Trade in Services for Water Resources', *CIEL and WWF, International Discussion Paper*, Oct. 2003.

WTO (2001), 'GATS facts and fiction' downloadable at http://www.wto.org/ english/tratop_e/serv_e/gats_factfiction_e.htm (last access: April 2005).

Zilberman, D. (2003), 'Water marketing in California and the West', *International Journal of Public Administration*, **26**(3), 291–315.

3. Water Policies and the Integrated Management of Surface Waters: An Ecological Approach

Pier Francesco Ghetti and Carlo Giupponi

3.1 BACKGROUND

On 22 December 2000, the Water Framework Directive (WFD) was published in the Official Journal of the European Communities (EC, 2000). The WFD is generally considered one of the most important pieces of legislation issued at the European level in the last decade, for its ambitious aim of establishing 'a framework for the protection of inland surface waters, transitional waters, coastal waters and groundwaters' (Dir. 2000/60/EC, art. 1) for all Member States, which should enable the EU to achieve a 'good status' of surface and groundwaters, through a common implementation process expected to last for 15 years. The WFD has catalysed the attention of the scientific community and provided a strong momentum for rethinking the principles and the methods of water management not only at the European level.

The promotion of 'sustainable water use based on long-term protection of available water resources' (art. 1b) is one of the main objectives and the approach adopted considers water bodies as components of ecosystems that should be managed at the level of 'river basin districts'.

The emphasis is on a systemic approach that integrates biological and chemical aspects, with the consideration of the 'quantitative status' of water bodies, together with the delineation of districts based on hydrological and geomorphological features instead of the more usual administrative units. This brings the European water policy into the field of environmental sciences and, in particular, enforces the role of an ecological approach to water management. The integration of such an environmental approach with the economic (art. 9) and sociological (art. 14) ones, should provide the ground for the three pillars of sustainable development to be equally considered in the future.

Interest in the European WFD is not limited to that continent, because the EU has consistently worked to bring the approach developed for the Directive into the international context and, in particular, in the context of the international agreements related to sustainable development (see also the Introduction of this volume). The EU 'Water Initiative' (EC, 2003) is a key reference, in which the European approach is described as contributing to the implementation of the 2002 World Summit on Sustainable Development agreements and helping achieve the water-related Millennium Development Goals (MDGs). Water is seen as a key element for the implementation of sustainable development and as a catalyst for peace and security worldwide. In particular it is seen as a means for achieving the ambitious targets of the MDGs in terms of poverty eradication and health and in the enhancement of livelihoods (EC, 2003). It is also worth mentioning that in terms of the timing of policy implementation, the targets set for the WFD and the MDGs have the year 2015 as the most important deadline.

It is therefore of interest for this book to examine how the integrated approach for water resources management, which is more or less unanimously proposed by international agreements and policies, can find a robust scientific basis. Having dealt with the economic issues in the previous chapter, this section attempts to provide a brief overview of the main issues of the ecology of surface waters. Specific focus is on water quality issues (section 3.2), and the role of ecology in integrated water resources management (section 3.3). A European perspective is then presented, with particular reference to the EU Water Framework directive (section 3.4). Finally, a discussion of the WFD implementation in Italy is presented as a case study (section 3.5).

3.2   ECOLOGY OF SURFACE WATER AND QUALITY ISSUES

3.2.1   The Water Cycle: Natural and Artificial Components of the Same System

The natural water network functions as a 'circulatory system' of a region, collecting the water in a capillary manner and transporting it downstream. But it also works as an 'excretory system', collecting natural residues and human refuse and, like the nephrons of a kidney, it filters and processes these substances, recovering what is needed and offloading downstream what is not.

It should never be forgotten that the natural surface and groundwater bodies that supply the basic necessity for life and production must be available in adequate amounts, compatible timing, and must have precise quality requisites. On the other hand, it should also be remembered that even if we keep defining water as a natural resource, in all the areas of the globe with significant presence of humans, the biogeochemical cycle of water takes place in artificial contexts and flows through human activities and artefacts, so that an 'artificial cycle' is superimposed, and in some cases completely substitutes the natural one.

This becomes more serious when the watercourse loses its ecological resistance and resilience to human pressures and is no longer able to recover, becoming nothing more than a sewer for polluted waters. The usual strategy for coping with such a problem was to seek cleaner waters further away or deeper underground and so the artificial water network lengthens, creating further impact on the self-purification capacities of natural ecosystems.

In recent years, water management plans have been developed to ensure sufficient water supplies are available for the ever-increasing human demands. Analysing these plans shows that most investments are for the construction of infrastructure such as aqueducts, dams, water treatment plants, channelling and other hydraulic works. Many of these have been necessary, as pointed out in the previous chapter, but tend to solve individual problems rather than considering the whole aquatic system. Each aquatic environment has its own carrying capacity, which refers to the ability to constantly restore its water quality characteristics despite the effects of external pressures. However, when polluting loads and other human pressures overstep the carrying capacity of the aquatic ecosystem, they degrade and progressively lose their natural potential for self-purification (see Figure 3.1 for a visual comparison between natural and artificial watercourses).

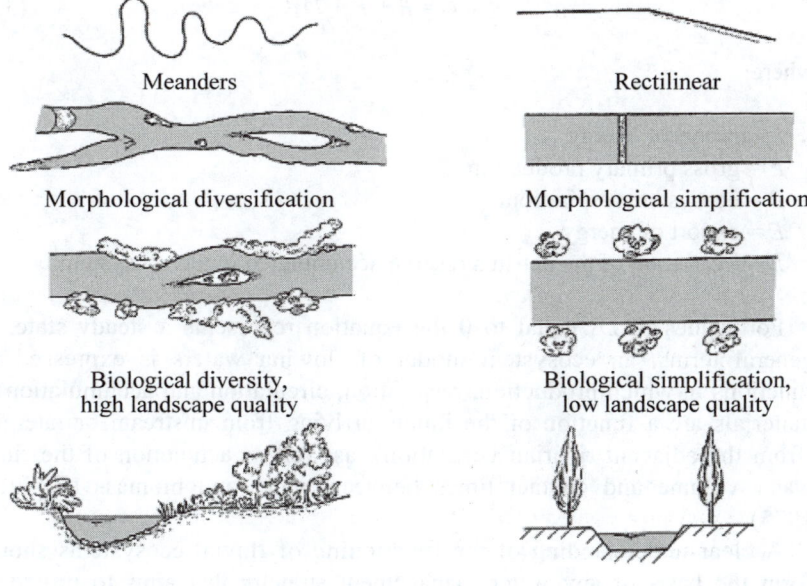

Meanders	Rectilinear
Morphological diversification	Morphological simplification
Biological diversity, high landscape quality	Biological simplification, low landscape quality

Source: Ghetti (1997) modif.

Figure 3.1   Natural and artificial watercourses

It seems clear that water managers tend to forget that the river environment, under natural conditions, constitutes the most efficient and least costly purifier. New policy documents, such as the WFD, seem to recognise this problem and identify the acquisition of 'good ecological status' of water bodies as the main target of water management strategies in the coming years. The challenge is to introduce sound ecological knowledge into the practice of IWRM.

3.2.2   Watercourses as Open Ecosystems

A watercourse is constantly affected by fluxes of material and energy that arrive from upstream and are transported downstream, representing a typical example of an open ecosystem. Energy enters both as radiant energy and in the form of reduced carbon compounds from any part of the basin upstream. The input of organic material drained from the basin can be in a dissolved form, in particles or unrefined.

A watercourse is an environment that reaches a steady state when the ecosystem respiration and loss of energy downstream are balanced by the external inputs and internal production. Fisher and Likens (1973) described this as follows:

$$I + P = R + E + Ds \tag{3.1}$$

where:

I = import of energy
P = gross primary production
R = ecosystem respiration
E = export of energy
Ds = variation of the detritus reserve accumulated in the ecosystem.

For values of Ds equal to 0 the equation represents a steady state. In general terms, an ecosystem model of flowing waters is expressed by functions in which production, respiration, circulation and accumulation of materials are a function of the inputs arriving from upstream or laterally (from the adjacent riparian vegetation), as well as a function of the flow, water volume and contact times between water and biomass (Whitton, 1975).

A clear understanding of the functioning of fluvial ecosystems should form the basis of any water management strategy that aims to provide a healthy river system for the future.

3.2.3 Processes of Self-Regulation and Self-Purification in a Watercourse

Along the longitudinal profile of a watercourse the quality of the ecosystem, and in particular of the waters and sediments, is defined by the state of equilibrium between mass gains and losses: there is self-purification when the losses are higher than the gains. If this negative mass balance is repeated downstream, from one tract to the next, a final state of low mass and energy turnover is created due to the impoverishment of the medium. These conditions occur in nature as a tendency to restore the environment to the characteristic metabolic efficiency of that river type.

What is described above depends on a series of factors: (a) the type and amount of biomass that can actively metabolise the available matter in the stream; (b) the biomass geometry and transport factors of the substrate (e.g. time of contact between biomass and water); (c) the type and quantity of available compounds; and (d) the physical and chemical characteristics of the water (e.g. turbulence, temperature, pH, dissolved oxygen concentration, etc.).

The main processes that occur in the river ecosystem are:

- particle sedimentation;
- chemical processes: pH reaction, redox processes, adsorption, precipitation;
- biochemical processes: dissimilation of organic and inorganic compounds metabolised by organisms;
- loss of volatile substances into the atmosphere;
- chemical and biochemical oxidation in the sediment.

The riparian zone (Figure 3.2) also contributes to the self-purification process (Ghetti, 1999). The terrestrial and semi-aquatic vegetation of the

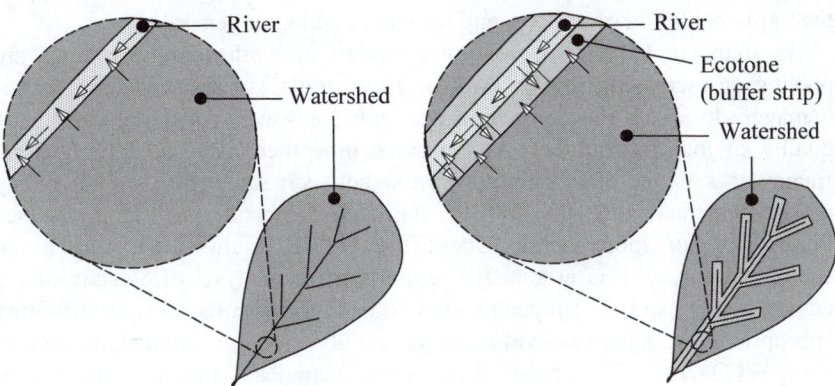

Figure 3.2   River basins, ecotones and watercourses

riverbanks has a direct influence on the aquatic communities by shading, and the consequent regulation of the temperature of the water (in particular the summer maximum), and the addition of organic matter. It also functions as a filter or buffer zone with its capacity to retain and transform appreciable amounts of nutrients draining from the surrounding area. Given that the loads of nutrients into watercourses from non-point sources are relevant, and that the status of receiving waters is often altered by human intervention, thus limiting their self-purification capacity, the importance of preserving and re-naturalising riparian belts appears obvious. Therefore, in terms of both policies and management, water bodies must be considered to be complex ecological systems made up of interacting aquatic and terrestrial ecosystems.

3.3   BRINGING THE ECOLOGICAL PERSPECTIVE INTO THE PRACTICE OF WATER MANAGEMENT

3.3.1   The Ecological Perspective in IWRM

Ecology is the science that studies the relationships between the organisms (living bodies) and the physical environment. In the context of the management of water resources, ecology can thus contribute specifically in two directions:

- by providing the systemic approach;
- by supporting the dynamic analysis of human and natural components.

The intrinsic complexity of interacting – and often conflicting – human-environmental systems is reinforced by the natural and spatial diversity of catchments. Therefore, IWRM is quite a challenging issue and Chapters 4 and 5 of this book deal specifically with those methodologies that can support the implementation of policies and decision making in general.

As stated in Chapter 4, computer models and information systems are playing an increasing role in IWRM. These tools can assist water resource managers to assess the competing demands for water, while preserving the quality of the environment. At the same time there is a need for general frameworks to facilitate communication between scientific experts, policy makers and managers, the DPSIR[1] approach being one such example (see Figure 4.3 for more details about the DPSIR framework). Clearly an ecological approach is crucial for supporting the analysis of *S* (state of the environment) and *I* (impacts) and thus fundamental for determining appropriate responses that will achieve a reduction in environmental harm, or using WFD terminology, preserve the 'good ecological status' of water bodies. Chapter 4 provides details about the transformation of the DPSIR into a

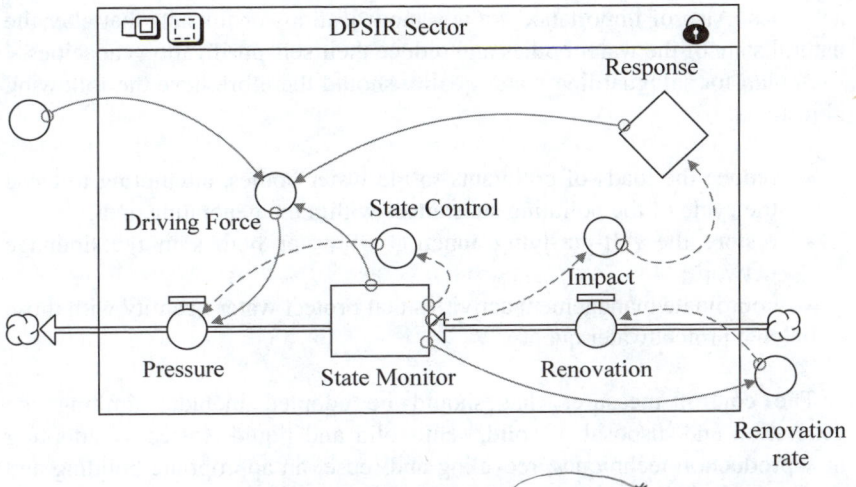

Figure 3.3   The ecological approach to IWRM, within the DPSIR framework

framework for dynamic Integrated Assessment Modelling (IAM) and evaluation procedures. This chapter will focus on how the ecological approach can be brought in the DPSIR framework as a whole. Figure 3.3 provides a schematic presentation of how the usual DPSIR chart (see Figure 4.3) can be represented by adopting the systemic and dynamic approach adopted in ecology.

Having recognised the nature of the watercourse as an ecosystem, with its own metabolism as described in equation 3.1, within the DPSIR approach water managers should identify the most suitable and efficient strategies to facilitate the maintenance of a natural equilibrium status, which should, by definition, coincide with the policy objective of the 'good ecological status'.

However, a condition of natural equilibrium is rather unrealistic in most watercourses, because of human activities (*D's*) and their pressures (*P's*). Therefore, the role of water managers should be to make efficient use of the available technologies (e.g. flux regulation, oxygenation, etc.) to activate those responses (*R's*) that may enhance the natural potentials of the watercourse to counteract the human impacts (*I's*). The ecological approach may thus provide the instruments and background for implementing IWRM in a system dynamic context.

3.3.2   Principles for the Safeguarding of Water Resources

The management of water bodies to protect their ecological and chemical qualities, requires action that addresses a series of factors, starting with the causes of point and diffuse source pollution from civil, industrial and farming activities. Also of importance are any modifications or impacts that alter the natural state of the water bodies and reduce their self-purification capacities.

A plan for safeguarding water quality should therefore have the following objectives:

- reduce the loads of pollutants to the water bodies, attempting to close the cycle of the polluting substances within the generating area;
- restore the self-purifying function of water bodies in the drainage network;
- coordinate management activities that protect water quantity with those that protect water quality.

The control measures that should be adopted include: limiting the generation and disposal of solid, semi-solid and liquid wastes by adopting new production techniques, recycling and reuse; an appropriate building and management policy for treatment plants that takes into account the carrying capacity of the water bodies into which the treated waste is dumped; the compatible and controlled reuse of treated (or untreated) water for irrigating crops; and the treatment by phyto-remediation plants of wastes from disperse civil settlements or small industries. In addition, control measures are necessary that will improve the self-purification capacities of water bodies. such as increasing the transport time of the water before it reaches the end user, or using reservoirs to store peak flows. The use of existing wetlands should not be overlooked, or the development of new ones with the multiple function of reserve tanks, irrigation basins, phyto-purification systems and leisure areas. Last but not least, the conservation or replanting of vegetation along watercourses can limit the effects of diffuse polluting loads (Ministero dell'Ambiente, 1997; Autorità del Bacino del Fiume Po, 2000).

3.4   INTEGRATED WATER RESOURCES MANAGEMENT IN THE EUROPEAN CONTEXT

3.4.1   A Brief History

The European Union's (EU) approach to the management of water resources has evolved since the early 1970s, culminating recently in the Water Framework Directive (2000/60/EC). Several trends have marked the development of these policies and are important background information for the interpretation of the current approach. Firstly, the privatisation of the water sector in many European countries has changed pricing systems and institutional structures for the management of public water supplies.

Secondly, the internationalisation of markets has led to changes in the scale of economic activities and as a result the intensity of water use in some sectors. Also, growth in tourism has increased the demand for 'pristine' water bodies for recreational purposes. Finally, an ideological shift from a focus on 'government' to new concepts about 'governance' has led to a re-examination of political processes and in some cases to a redistribution of power between centralised and local authorities within the structure of national governments (Kaika, 2000). These trends have brought about an increased and more varied demand for water resources and the appearance of new actors who now play a role in water resource management and require innovative policy approaches.

Early EU water legislation was initially formulated around priority issues and focussed on water quality, with a single sector approach, such as preserving public health or protecting the environment. Aubin and Varone (2004) identify two generations of water directives, between 1972 and 1998. In the first set of instruments the definition of water quality standards is based on human needs, and minimum quality requirements are defined for surface waters destined for drinking water, bathing water and fishing. Methods for monitoring and analysis are prescribed, hazardous substances are defined, and emission standards are based on 'best available technologies'.

In the second generation of directives, there is an intensification of efforts to improve and protect water quality in the EU territories and, as a consequence, in the period from 1991 to 1998, new directives were issued addressing urban wastewater, agricultural pollution and industrial emissions, with a focus on emission standards (Aubin and Varone, 2004). However, this approach to water policy legislation has been widely criticised as piecemeal and inconsistent, often lacking in clear identification of aims and methods (Foster et al., 2000).

Inconsistent implementation of the various directives throughout the EU has compounded these problems, and it is notable that Member States are fairly frequently penalised for failure to comply with the EU legislation that regulates the management of water resources, such as in the case of the Nitrate Directive (91/676/EEC). In some instances it seems that it may even be more convenient for a Member State to pay the penalties instead of bearing the cost of complying with the requirements of a directive.

3.4.2 The EU Water Framework Directive

This new Directive has been designed to solve some of the more persistent problems that impede the realisation of EU environmental objectives, and it can be interpreted as an attempt to establish a coherent legislative framework for the protection and improvement of the water environment within the context of achieving sustainable development. It may also represent a crucial step in ensuring an effective structure for the application of the existing directives that address water management in Europe. In fact, eight of these directives will be repealed in two phases over thirteen years, leaving the WFD as the primary legislative instrument.

The Directive is the result of over ten years of work, and took almost five years to complete from the time its establishment was proposed. It is more than seventy pages long and consists of 26 Articles and eleven Annexes. The integrated approach adopted is, as previously mentioned, both innovative and ambitious, and foresees long lists of actions and obligations that could be very challenging for the majority of Member States.

The main innovative features of the WFD can be summarised in relation to four disciplinary fields (Giupponi et al., 2002):

- territorial aspects, in particular concerning the introduction of the river basin as the geographical unit for water management;
- sociology, for the emphasis placed on public participation processes in policy and decision making;
- economics, given that water users bear the true cost of water resources (full cost recovery principle);
- ecology, for the emphasis given to the integrated approach for defining the status of water bodies and the combined approach for the control of pollution.

The first and, more especially, the fourth point, are of most interest in the present work.

Concerning the territorial aspects, Articles 3, 5, 11 and 13 are relevant, which change the geographical focus of water management from the traditionally used administrative boundaries, to the more practical hydrological unit of the river basin.[2] Member States are required to describe their national territories in terms of individual river basins and assign them to river basin districts, so determining the new management units that will be the basis for future planning, monitoring, reporting and the organisation of water management institutions (international in the case of transboundary basins) responsible for water protection. This redefinition of Member States' territorial management is a technical requirement that is an important prerequisite to a series of other obligations, and will form the basis for assigning the rights and responsibilities associated with water management. Member States are thus obliged to nominate a competent authority for each river basin district, which will be responsible for the management in accordance with the Directive. In some countries the existing institutional structure will map onto this new territorial concept without too much disruption. In others, the administrative infrastructure will have to be significantly modified.

The first major task for these new authorities will be to develop the fundamental tool for river basin management, the River Basin Management Plan (RBMP) (Article 13). These plans must be drawn up on the basis of information collected in a comprehensive survey aimed at determining the current status of the river basin by examining physical and geographical characteristics, industrial activities, human populations and their activities in the basin, a review of the environmental impact of human activity and an economic analysis of water usage (Chave, 2001). The overall objective of RBMPs is to achieve 'Good Ecological Status' for the water bodies within the basin through a 'Programme of Measures'. The definition of environmental objectives will be described in terms of ecological and chemical quality of surface waters and the quantitative and chemical status of groundwater, with reference to their current status. Relevant to the water quality issue is the establishment of a combined approach that permits the use of both the traditional Emission Limit Value (ELV) and the Water Quality Objective (WQO) approaches (Chave, 2001).[3] Good status for individual water bodies will also depend on their type and their geographical location in Europe.

While water quality has been the clearly articulated objective of EU water policy for over thirty years, the WFD introduces a more holistic approach to the assessment of the status of water resources, where it is considered as part of a wider ecological system. This is reflected in the definition of Ecological Status provided in Annex V of the Directive and which includes criteria for biological, hydromorphological and physico-chemical elements of water quality. Article 4 directs Member States to make the programme of measures specified in River Basin Management Plans operational in order to achieve the environmental objectives that have been set for individual water bodies. This article provides for the classification of water bodies as 'artificial' or 'heavily modified' which will lead to the definition of environmental objectives that focus on 'good ecological potential'.

Rivers are further categorised in accordance with the schemes provided in Annex II: two alternative systems are provided: System A is simpler and based on the identification of the eco-region to which the river belongs (15 in total in Europe), depending on the altitude, size and geology; System B requires the identification of latitude and longitude instead of eco-region and provides a long list of physical and chemical factors (energy of flow, transport of solids, etc.).

Member States must assess the status of four categories of water bodies: rivers, lakes, transitional waters and coastal waters. In order to reach the minimum requirements of the Directive, substantial monitoring will be required to assess these waters in terms of the parameters set out and to classify each water body as having high, good, moderate, poor or bad status. The criteria for this classification process are given in Annex V of the WFD.

3.4.3   Some Criticisms from an Ecological Perspective

As stated earlier, the overall objective of the WFD is to achieve 'Good Ecological Status' for all water bodies within each basin. However, the implementation of this objective creates a series of challenges.

Firstly, the water quality policy aims (correctly) at meeting standards for each water body that should be typical of 'that type under undisturbed conditions', thus requiring that a 'reference environment' be identified for every water body type. This can sometimes be very difficult, both because of the difficulty in finding similar environments in good condition and because of the specific needs of highly detailed hydrobiological studies requiring teams of experts who are not always available. Application of the WFD will therefore also require notable investments in terms of research and training of personnel engaged for its knowledge, control and management.

Despite the fact that the process of full implementation is relatively long (15 years), it is clear that, at least in some countries, an initial transition phase will be necessary, based mainly on reference indicators which can be applied using fairly simple methods that are already in use.

Another problem concerns the two methods of classifying rivers. System A is schematic, but too generic: very different (and therefore not comparable) environments can be classified as being of the same type. System B is more descriptive if the various optional factors are utilised and can allow different river types to be represented better. Nevertheless, some items should be revised: e.g. the siting by latitude and longitude is not appropriate for large geographical areas such as river basins. A geographical indication of the hierarchical administrative type would be better: State–Region–Province–Local Council (Fabiani and Mussapi, 2002).

For 'heavily modified and artificial water bodies' (with modifications that would not allow recovery of their original state), the recovery of 'Good Ecological Potential' is required, and can be derived from a comparison with natural water bodies with similar characteristics (ecological potential). This definition can however be difficult to apply. Take for example a hydroelectric dam: to what type of natural water body could this be assimilated? Not a lake because of the short exchange times, not a watercourse because the water is still and the chemical activity and sedimentary contents alter. Furthermore the communities of organisms are entirely specific. In some countries, Italy for example, another problem with the application of these definitions occurs when rivers have been transformed into artificial watercourses (regulation, channelling, remodelling of banks, occupation of the flood bed, dyke construction, canalisation, capturing and releases, etc.). In these cases the task of definition becomes extremely complex and it is difficult to make comparisons with natural water bodies possessing similar characteristics.

In some cases (e.g. for wetlands) the management criteria revert to the concept of simple 'protection', but this seems too limiting. Instead, it would be worth adopting the concept of 'functional management' through appropriate plans that coordinate the uses so that they are 'supportable and compatible' with the functioning of each environment.

3.4.4 Plans and Programmes for the Safeguarding and Reclaiming of the Waters

It is clear that member states must arm themselves with a strategy for local implementation of the Directive, aimed at obtaining water bodies with 'Good Ecological Status' by 2015. This strategy can be summarised in a sequence of five stages, i.e. information, prevention, control, planning and intervention. Translated into planning terms, the measures for reclaiming water bodies in the light of the WFD can be described as follows:

- information on the structure and natural functioning of the different water bodies;
- preventative protection measures;
- control networks for evaluating water quality evolution and functioning of the water bodies in relation to the quality aims;
- identification and planning of the safeguarding and reclamation measures;
- reclamation interventions.

The first stage is probably the most precise of the water resource management procedures.

Because the new Directive sets an objective of a 'Good Ecological Status' for each water body, it becomes essential to understand what 'normal or natural functioning' would be for the various types of water body. It would at least be useful to know this state of functionality for some 'reference types' to be used as models. This requires very demanding research (in terms of both time and costs) conducted by teams of experts who can make these assessments, to avoid repeating the mistakes made in the past of introducing quality standards in the regulations (often using only concentrations of the various chemicals) based on literature sources that are totally unsuitable and unrealistic for the different situations.

A sound environmental policy must first of all include actions for protecting at least those environments that still conserve high quality conditions. As said, these environments can be used as references for applying the WFD and must also be protected under the principle that prevention is better than the cure, in both environmental and economic terms.

The identification and planning of measures for the safeguarding and reclamation of water bodies must take into account the involvement of local stakeholders and the policy makers involved at the different institutional levels. In European countries the alteration of water bodies can generally be traced to a combination of causes attributable to the push for economic development. But it is the loss of these high quality resources that has aroused conflicts between different users and renewed interest in regaining them. It is therefore quite unlikely that the reclaiming process can take place without detailed planning of control measures, in terms of defining resources, organisation, times, and their political, economic and social effects. This requires long-term management plans for both the quality and quantity of the water resources and aquatic ecosystems. The WFD foresees drafting of the RBMP within nine years of its publication and also periodic revisions (every six years).

The set of reclamation measures can be taken in the wide sense as the set of actions and decisions aimed at the reclamation, including the works planned for solving specific environmental problems (a water treatment works, an aqueduct, a fish ladder, a riverbank, a basin to provide water for agriculture, etc.). The specific set of measures chosen from the list of possible ones contributes to the RBMPs, in particular to part 7, which includes a summary of the programme(s) of measures adopted (Annex VII). Of particular importance is the role of an adequate monitoring system to evaluate the effects of the control measures, and also monitor any impacts that propagate up or downstream.

A sound management policy of the water resources cannot exist without considering the entire range of problems in an integrated way and, in particular, the question of the quantity and quality of the waters under the effect of the various human pressures. An example of this dichotomy is the potential conflict between water concessions and the guarantee of a minimum streamflow. Other examples are the management of hydraulic works and the self-purification capacity of the rivers themselves, or the reclamation of agricultural land while protecting the remaining wetlands. This leads back to the crucial theme of managing the natural and artificial water cycles in such a way that they are in harmony with the natural functioning of the riverine ecosystems and that the waters are not just flowing, but also constantly regenerating.

3.4.5 Monitoring, Indicators and Indices for Assessing Water Status

Monitoring comes specifically within the actions of control and, according to the WFD (Annex V, 1.3), can be of three types:

- surveillance: to provide information to supplement and validate the impact assessment of water bodies, contributing to the design of future monitoring systems and the assessment of long-term changes;
- operational: to establish the status of water bodies at risk and assess changes resulting from the adoption of the programme of measures;
- investigative: to supplement operational monitoring programmes, as yet not established, in order to identify the reasons for failure to achieve the WFD objectives, and to ascertain the magnitude and impacts of accidental pollution.

Monitoring is focussed towards the space and time dimension of controls, thus requiring constant organisation and an efficient strategy for implementing control measures. The latter must be managed at a river basin level and be customised on a case-by-case basis, even if they must also be comparable with data at a more general level. Water quality monitoring must include a set of physical, chemical, microbiological and biological parameters. It must go beyond the exclusively hygiene-health point of view that in previous decades characterised water quality control.

The objective of the measures must be to assess if the water body or, better, the ecosystem, can preserve and constantly regenerate the resources needed for human activities. This is in accordance with the environmental objectives that are based on achieving and maintaining the 'Good Ecological Status' and therefore the functional quality of the aquatic ecosystems. All this involves the need to use indicators and indices in the monitoring methods that can represent the ecological status and therefore the 'functioning method' or 'metabolism' of the various ecosystems. 'Good Ecological Status' is nothing more than the 'State of Health' of the different ecosystems, which can represent their functioning level with respect to the conservation and regeneration of the quality of the waters, sediments and biota. If this is the main principle of the monitoring foreseen by the WFD, a lot of effort must be made in the next few years to develop suitable ecological indicators and indices of the functioning of the different ecosystems, and to form research groups and personnel who can provide these data.

In recent years biological-ecological monitoring has become an integral part of the quality control of running waters worldwide. Within this context two main lines can be identified: the setting up and application of biological indices and biological surveys of water quality.

Quality surveys are aimed at evaluating the environmental risk of individual substances or mixtures and include alarm or early-warning tests, toxicity, bioaccumulation, biodegradation and trophic tests. These can be done in the laboratory on groups of individuals of the same species, or individuals of different species representative of the different susceptibilities and trophic levels (multiple test). Or they can be done directly in the field using specific apparatus that isolates the sample species or portions of the environment (microcosms).

Biotic indices are based on the study of species or groups of species (partial communities) in nature, with a clear preference for the macro-invertebrate communities (see De Pauw et al., 1992 and Ghetti, 1997 for details). Indices based on other components of the community could also be useful, such as macrophytes, fishes, or on the study of the global river environment. The WFD cites most of these approaches – however, it generally does not mention standard methods to adopt given the current absence of CEN/ISO standards.

An ideal strategy for biological monitoring involves a general index, applicable on a vast scale and on a sufficiently wide number of types and a series of indices more aimed at the definition of the specificity of the problem and typology to be monitored. The general index would have the scope of allowing standard classification of the overall quality of the different environments (considering the distance from the Good Ecological Status of the environment), while the more specific indices would have the aim of increasing knowledge on the nature of a particular form of pollution or a particular type of alteration.

3.5   A POLICY IMPLEMENTATION CASE IN ITALY

3.5.1   Italian Policies on the Quality Management of Internal Waters

The date that officially signals the start of interest of the Italian legislator in the management of water resources quality coincides with the publication of the Law 139/76 (known as 'Legge Merli'). This recognised the need to impose a limit on the progressive degradation occurring in the inland surface and groundwaters and coastal waters due to the enormous economic development in Italy after the last war, which paved the way for the consumer society and, in parallel, waste. With the Merli Law, intense activity began for treating civil and industrial discharges and, although there was much confusion between the State, Regions, Provinces and Local Councils over responsibility, some good results were obtained.

The advent of the Law 183/89 (known as 'Legge Galli') represented, 13 years later, a great novelty in Italian environmental policy, with the setting up of the national, inter-regional and regional River Basin Authorities. These had the task of planning water and land management within the territorial ambits of the hydrographical basin, bringing all the responsible institutions around the same table. Unfortunately, the results achieved so far, and the future prospects, are not very encouraging, due to conflicts between competing Ministries, regional and local jealousies in terms of responsibilities, the lack of secure funding, and the incapacity of the often gargantuan bureaucracies that have managed them. The opportunities have not yet been fulfilled, and the foundations of a new water quality policy have not yet been fully set.

The Law 152/99 anticipated the Directive 2000/60/CE and was in some aspects a second turning point in the management policy of surface and groundwater bodies in Italy. One of the main innovations of this law was that of adopting a philosophy of prevention and reclamation of the water bodies based on 'quality objectives' specific to each water body depending on the seriousness of the problem and the territory it was located in. This orientation, new at a European level and methodologically correct, nevertheless requires the formation of a new culture of resource planning, environmental surveillance and methods of gathering and processing the environmental data.

Law 152/99 attempted to implement this approach to water resource management on two different levels, through the River Basin Authorities and the creation, at local level, of Optimal Territorial Areas (Goria and Lugaresi, 2004). Unfortunately, this reform is still a long way from being a success because the complexity of the decentralisation process has once again generated institutional conflicts.

3.5.2   Implications and Directions for the Application of the 'Water Framework Directive' 2000/60/CE in Italy

From the above it is clear that Italy has arrived at the application stage of the European Directive with experience derived from the important work done for the initial execution stage of Law 152/99. In general the implementation process of the WFD in Italy presents a situation fairly typical of the history of water resource management in the country: good laws exist, but the application is partial because of a series of chronic problems, such as a serious lack of information on the status of the different aquatic environments and the conflicts between a large number of administrative bodies with overlapping responsibilities.

At present in Italy the system that comes closest to the functions foreseen for river basin districts is that of the Basin Authorities, enacted by Law 183/89. However, these authorities are currently in a state of crisis in terms of organisation, motivation, results and institutional relations with the Regions and the State. They also need to be integrated with new functions and the organisation and management restructured.

The criteria foreseen by the WFD for defining 'Good Ecological Status' on the basis of reference types used as models, poses a problem in Italy where there is limited ecological information available, in particular for transitional waters, coastal waters and ground waters. This will require a lot of research effort and careful protection of those ecosystems that still have a high natural value and can therefore act as reference models.

In Italy, despite some indices of quality having been applied for years, in particular to the fluvial environments, there has been a considerable delay in the setting up and standardising of these indices based on particular components of the community (e.g. phytoplankton, macrophytes, phytobenthos, fish), especially in environments like transitional waters, coastal areas and lakes. There is also inadequate transfer of information from the research groups to the operators distributed across the territory. Another relevant question in Italy is the number of water bodies that are completely or partly artificial, which under the WFD should be inventoried and require a case-by-case definition of their relative 'Ecological Potential'.

The existing monitoring network of water bodies in Italy is not sufficiently systematic, with some thoroughly studied areas (and types of environment) and others lacking even basic information. These data are also at times difficult to compare with one another, due to the lack of national co-ordination of the criteria and methods used. It will therefore be essential, at least in terms of guidelines, to collect this information on the whole territory and define uniform criteria for data gathering and interpretation. Also, the organisation of registers of effluent discharges, areas at risk, water balances and resource availability differs widely from area to area, depending on the attention the different administrations have paid to their management.

The WFD Directive calls for the attention of the political and civic world on the crucial subject of the safeguarding of water resources and aquatic ecosystems that can guarantee their constant regeneration. Given that everything must be achieved with finite resources it is necessary to set up a strategy for defining precise priorities and an efficient implementation plan that should include:

- reorganisation of the central structures and those distributed over the territory assigned to the management of both the quantity and quality of the waters;
- the promotion and coordination of research to gain knowledge that can improve management of the aquatic environments and water resources for the different types of use;
- the involvement in these actions of all the many institutions and structures that today operate on the territory and occupy themselves with particular aspects of water use.

3.6   CONCLUDING REMARKS

The most recent water policies have ambitious aims, which are absolutely necessary to achieve the safeguarding and utilisation of water resources under the perspective of sustainable development. The new stance places the protection and reclamation of aquatic environments at the centre of water management to guarantee the constant availability of this resource. This is a Copernican revolution that radically alters the perspective for guaranteeing water availability, passing from an era during which the search was always for new sources in order to sustain development, to one in which it has to be acknowledged that water is only a partially renewable resource, distributed in an unequal way in space and time. It must therefore be managed in a sustainable way, encouraging all those processes that allow adequate amounts of water to be available today and in the future, when needed and of a quality that can guarantee specific uses, including environmental ones (e.g. minimum vital flow).

The European legislators have made enormous efforts to standardise approaches to water resource management. Analysing the results of these efforts in the light of the various local situations, however, we can ask ourselves whether this will be possible and if it makes sense. There are many difficulties in the application and, going into the contents of the regulations in more detail, for example in the proposed classification methods, the question appears unresolved of balancing the trade-off between the need to include extremely detailed and complex systems that can consider the whole range of existing situations, against the need to standardise and simplify. In some cases there is an impression that the results could be banal or insignificant (for example, application of the two systems for classifying water body types), requiring adaptations to the local situations, which are in contrast with the efforts of uniformity and co-ordination of the directive itself.

Looking at the prospects for implementation of the WFD, in the light of the past history of water policy, various reasons for scepticism emerge, which are linked to the high application costs and the ambitious aims. The role given to standardised physical, chemical and biological parameters add more challenges to the usual implementation problems due to socioeconomic and cultural diversity. Only a robust ecological perspective, based upon the systemic approach, can provide the ground for a correct interpretation of the general principles in the various environmental and socioeconomic contexts and for making the general fulfilment of the 'Good Ecological Status' of water bodies to be feasible within a decade.

NOTES

1. DPSIR stands for Driving Force – Pressure – State (of the environment) – Impact – Response (EEA, 1999).
2. According to Article 2(13) of the WFD, a river basin is an 'area of land from which all surface run-off flows through a sequence of streams, rivers and, possibly lakes, into the sea at a single river mouth, estuary or delta'.
3. The Emission Limit Value (ELV) approach is typical for dealing with point sources of pollution and provides reference to the regulatory standards defined for the substances that are discharged. The main drawback to this approach is a lack of flexibility for the emission standards to be adjusted in relation to the effect on the immediate environment. So, although this method is relatively easy to implement, the results may be too lax to achieve environmental goals or too stringent to allow the full potential of human activities. Furthermore, when the source of pollution is diffuse, as is the case for many farming activities, the ELV has limited applicability. The Water Quality Objective (WQO) approach consists of identifying the receiving watercourses in terms of their use, along with the degree of water purity required for those purposes. The objective is then to achieve the standards described for water quality, and the methods of control may be extended beyond imposing emission limits. Clearly, the monitoring required for this approach must be more extensive in order to assess results and to consider factors other than the discharge of pollutants that can influence water quality, such as the self-purification properties of the water body or the amount of dilution available (Chave, 2001).

REFERENCES

Aubin, D. and F. Varone (2004), 'The evolution of European water policy: towards integrated resource management at EU Level', in I. Kissling-Näf and S. Kuks (eds), *The Evolution of National Water Regimes in Europe*, Amsterdam: Kluwer Academic Publisher.

Autorità di Bacino del Fiume Po (2000), *Il Po Fiume d'Europa: riflessioni e proposte sulle strategie di pianificazione*, Parma: AdBFP.

Chave, P. (2001), *The EU Water Framework Directive: an Introduction*, Cornwall: IWA Publishing.

De Pauw, N., P.F Ghetti., P. Manzini and R. Spaggiari (1992), 'Biological assessment methods for running waters', in P.J. Newman (ed.), *Ecological Assessment and Control*, Brussels: C.C.E., pp. 217–248.

EC (European Communities) (2003), *Water for Life – EU Water Initiative*, Luxembourg: Office for Official Publications of the European Communities.

EC (European Communities) (2000), *Directive 2000/60/EC of the European Parliament and of the Council Establishing a Framework for Community Action in the Field of Water Policy* (OJ L 327, 22.12.2000).

EEA (European Environmental Agency) (1999), *Environmental Indicators: Typology and Overview*, Copenhagen: European Environment Agency.

Fabiani, C. and R. Mussapi (2002), 'Il monitoraggio dello stato di qualità ambientale dei corpi idrici nella legislazione nazionale e comunitaria: acquisizioni ed esigenze', in *L'Indice di Funzionalità Fluviale (IFF). Il caso di studio del Ticino e le altre esperienze italiane*, Milan.

Fisher, S.G. and G.E. Likens (1973), 'Energy flow in Bear Brook, New Hampshire; An integrative approach to stream ecosystem metabolism', *Ecological Monographs*, **43**, 421–439.

Foster, D., A. Wood and M. Griffiths (2000), *The Water Framework Directive*

(2000/60/EC) – *an Introduction*, downloaded from http://www.defra.gov.uk/ environment/water/wfd/index.htm (last access: April 2003).

Ghetti, P.F. (1997), *Indice Biotico Esteso (E.B.I.). I macroinvertebrati nel controllo della qualità degli ambienti di acque correnti. Manuale di applicazione*, Trento: Agenzia Provinciale per la Protezione dell'Ambiente, Provincia di Trento.

Ghetti, P.F. (1999), 'Le reti ecologiche: struttura e funzione', in Provincia di Milano, *Atti del Seminario Reti Ecologiche in Aree Urbanizzate*, Milan: Franco Angeli Edizioni, pp. 19–21.

Giupponi, C., V. Cogan and I. La Jeunesse (2002), 'EU water policy: research developments and new management tools', in *Proceedings of the 8th Joint Conference on Food, Agriculture and the Environment*, downloadable at http://agecon.lib.umn.edu (last access: April 2005).

Goria, A. and N. Lugaresi (2004), 'The Evolution of the Water Regime in Italy', in I. Kissling-Näf and S. Kuks (eds), *The Evolution of National Water Regimes in Europe*, Amsterdam: Kluwer Academic.

Kaika, M. (2000), *Creating the European Water Framework Directive. Achieving Sustainable and Innovative Policies through Participatory Governance in a Multi-level Context: Interim report on water supply*, University of Oxford, School of Geography and the Environment.

Ministero dell'Ambiente (1997), *Relazione sullo Stato dell'Ambiente*, Rome: Istituto Poligrafico e Zecca dello Stato.

Whitton, B.A. (1975), *River Ecology*, Oxford: Blackwell Scientific Publications.

PART III

Supporting Decision Making

4. Sustainable Water Management and Decision Making

Carlo Giupponi, Anita Fassio, Jacobo Feás Vàzquez and Jaroslav Mysiak

4.1 DECISION MAKING IN WATER RESOURCES MANAGEMENT

Human society is always interacting with water, land and air, the natural resources of the earth. In particular:

> Water is essential to all life, all ecosystems and all human activity. Wisely used, water means harvests, health, prosperity and ecological abundance for the peoples and nations of the earth. Badly managed or out of control, water brings poverty, disease, floods, erosion, salinisation, waterlogging, silting, environmental degradation and human conflict.

This quote from the World Water Council's Constitution (WWC, 1996) illustrates the essential role of water in our world. Water is a basic element for human survival; it is an important production factor in our economy, particularly in agriculture, and it is the habitat of a wide range of species.

As stated in the Introduction to this book, the IWRM approach, firmly bounded in the sustainability concept, stresses the need to view water resources in a holistic way, in which socioeconomics and environmental sciences should find integration. But water management must not rely only on robust and integrated scientific knowledge, it also needs to be supported by clear policy and regulatory frameworks and needs to be put in practice by means of adequate tools. The sustainable use of water resources, as defined in a number of policies and regulations, requires coherent and efficient tools that can assist decision making. For the purposes of this work, a useful definition of decision making which leaves enough room for interpretation, while remaining accurate, is the classical definition by Simon (1957): 'Decision making is the process of choice that leads to action'. Thus, decision making tools are all those instruments (methods, guidelines, software, etc.) that can facilitate the implementation of the IWRM principles, as described in policy documents and regulations.

One of the fundamental documents for framing IWRM in the broader concept of sustainable development is Agenda 21, signed by 178 governments at the Earth Summit in Rio de Janeiro in 1992. Chapter 8 of Agenda 21 aims at improving or restructuring the decision-making process so that consideration of socioeconomic and environmental issues is fully integrated and a broader range of public participation is assured. Integrated decision making was also discussed in Chapter 18 of Agenda 21 where the rationale for the sustainable development and the management of freshwater resources is clearly articulated. As already anticipated in the Introduction, the key elements of water resource management for sustainable development are integration (of disciplines, of approaches, and of tools), collaboration and participation (of all the actors involved), and the sharing of knowledge and information (Gijsbers, 2000).

Decision making should, therefore, involve the integration of different perspectives and objectives, and be prepared to manage trade-offs or priority setting between these objectives where necessary, by carefully assessing them in an informed and transparent manner, according to societal objectives and constraints (Van der Zaag 2001). IWRM again provides the reference for policy- and decision-making approaches providing joint consideration of the physical water system, and the societal functions and demands for water (Bogardi, 1994) (Figure 4.1).

Like environmental planning in general, IWRM is usually characterised by the involvement of numerous decision makers operating at different levels and the very large number of stakeholders with conflicting preferences and different value judgements (Lahdelma et al., 2000). This makes decision making in the context of IWRM a very complex issue because it requires a broad integration with other sectors such as environment, energy, industry, agriculture and tourism.

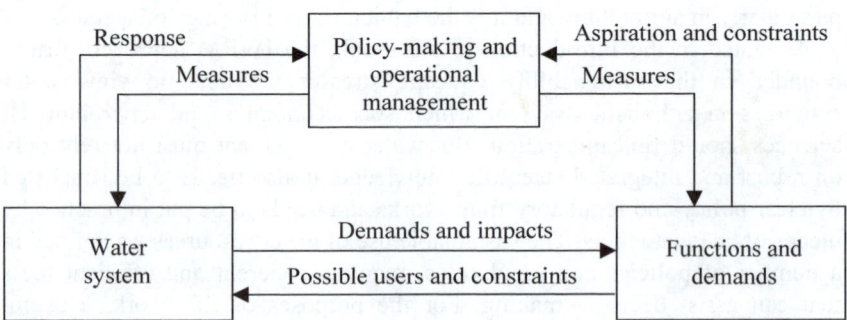

Source: Bogardi (1994).

Figure 4.1   Concepts of integrated water resources management

Adequate methodologies and tools therefore become necessary in order to measure how a specific policy meets the objectives established by the various actors, to identify and understand the possible conflicts that may arise between these actors and, finally, to design possible paths and courses of action to arrive at a sustainable solution.

The need for adequate methodologies and tools calls for a strong role to be played by science and research. The commitments made by the scientific community at the 2002 World Summit on Sustainable Development was in fact to make science more policy-relevant. Relevancy can be improved by placing more emphasis on social aspects of sustainability, by addressing the uncertainty of the scientific process by using common languages that are understandable to stakeholders, and by customising environmental assessments so that they are relevant to the local conditions and issues of a basin (ICSU, 2002).

As previously pointed out, environmental problems, and in particular those related to water resources, are usually very complex and therefore the decision-making process requires detailed background information from environmental, economic and social disciplines. Moreover, there is quite often a dramatic gap between those who analyse and provide disciplinary expertise and those who decide, not only in the knowledge but also in the aims, the way of thinking and the language (Luiten, 1999).

From the above it should be clear that bringing water resources management within the principles of sustainable development (SD) is a very complex issue, which can be supported by the scientific and methodological approaches of IWRM. The next section provides a concise presentation of such an approach in water resources management, and is based on the integration of information into adequate conceptual frameworks, analysis and assessment tools.

4.2 INFORMATION, CONCEPTUAL FRAMEWORKS, ANALYSIS AND ASSESSMENT TOOLS IN SUPPORT OF DECISION MAKING

Four major steps can be identified in the evaluation process of policies and decision making in terms of their contribution to sustainable development (Figure 4.2). The first step relates to the identification of a wide array of indicators and measures available for monitoring development and environmental change. These indicators can, and should, vary depending upon place and scale. The second step deals with conceptual frameworks, which provide powerful insight and organising qualities. The third involves specific forms of analysis that rely on indicators that are best selected through

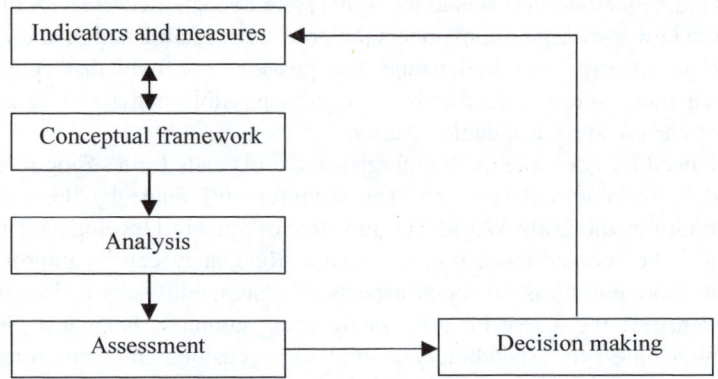

Figure 4.2   Four steps in knowledge and decision making for IWRM and sustainable development

the use of sound conceptual frameworks. Finally, all these steps contribute to a fourth one: sustainability assessment.

Throughout this chapter, each step will also be referred to as a 'tool' for assessing the effects and effectiveness of policy measures. Such tools are closely related to one another: indicators and measures are the pillars, as assessment and communication are their main function. Conceptual frameworks are ordering mechanisms that help organise indicators logically, for instance in cause-effect-response chains. Based on this information, analysis helps gain information and insight and contributes to the assessment of policy makers' decisions through specific and comprehensive decision support tools.

In an IWRM perspective, the above mentioned tools act as guiding instruments for decision making, involving the sustainable development, management, protection and use of freshwater resources. IWRM can be regarded as the vehicle that makes the general concept of sustainable development operational for the management of freshwater resources. Since it adopts an holistic approach, information is needed on the state of the economy, society and water resources, but their mutual relationship must be analysed, and impacts of proposed measures assessed, in order to make informed decisions.

4.2.1   Indicators

The 1992 Earth Summit recognised the important role that indicators can play in helping countries make informed decisions concerning SD. This recognition is articulated in Chapter 40 of Agenda 21 which calls on governments at the national level, as well as international, and non-government organisations, to develop and identify Indicators of Sustainable Development (ISDs) that can provide a solid basis for decision making at all levels.

ISDs can allow better communication and accessibility to information by bridging the gap between the producer and user of information, i.e. between the information available through scientific resources and the need of information for decision making (Boisvert et al., 1998). Indicators can provide crucial guidance for decision making in a variety of ways. They can translate physical and social science knowledge into manageable units of information that can facilitate the decision-making process. They can provide an early warning, sounding an alarm in time to prevent economic, social and environmental damage. They are important tools to communicate ideas, thoughts and values, and as one authority said, 'We measure what we value, and value what we measure' (UNCSD, 2001). A crucial role of ISDs is to provide a means of measuring, monitoring and reporting on progress towards sustainability, which is still an open problem both for the academia and the decision makers.

This process-oriented logic characterises SD: experts have to rely on information that allows them to judge on a regular basis whether or not the current evolution is to be considered as a contribution to 'stay' or to 'get' on a sustainable path. As such, SD requires constant feedback for evaluation and, as a consequence, decision making is also becoming more process-orientated (Bauler and Hecq, 2000).

Therefore, it becomes important to assess effects (ex-ante) and effectiveness (ex-post) of policy measures: effects imply that a policy has an impact on the outside world. The process of identifying effects is based upon scientific and social observation and analysis. Assessing effectiveness judges whether and how far the observed effects of a policy satisfy the explicit objectives, and this involves comparing intention with performance (EEA, 2001). In order to assess whether policies are working and to fine-tune them in order to reach the ultimate objective, feedback information for policy-makers and methodological approaches are needed.

Indicators are being classified in different ways, on the basis of the purpose they serve. The European Environmental Agency (EEA) distinguishes five categories of indicators (EEA, 1999). The first category (Descriptive indicators) answers the question: 'How are pressures on the environment, and how is the quality of the environment, developing?' Examples are indicators referred to in Chapter 3 for assessing water status. The second category includes EEAs Performance indicators that answer the follow-up question: 'And is that relevant?' The third category, which can be found in between the environment and the economy circle, are Eco-efficiency indicators, answering the question: 'Have we become more efficient in our economic processes?' The fourth category, Policy-effectiveness indicators, may provide answers to the question: 'What has been the effect of policy?', and clarify what the structural changes in the economy or in the production processes, and in the (environmental) decision making, have lead to. Finally, a fifth category of indicators (Total welfare indicators) is connected with the question: 'And are we on the whole better off?', which asks for a balance between economic, social and environmental progress.

Thinking in terms of questions to be answered, and trying to identify the proper questions for solving problems, helps in identifying the most suitable indicators. Formalising these questions helps to get a good balance in the indicator sets. Combining relevant indicators into a composite index reveals the available evidence in a much more convincing fashion than just using individual indicators (ICSU, 2002). With such purposes in mind, analytical frameworks structure a collection of indicators and communicate their application. These are discussed in the following paragraph.

4.2.2   Conceptual Frameworks

As stated in the previous paragraph, there should be a clear structure that communicates to policy-makers how each piece of information is related to the various policy processes. To achieve this, frameworks that structure a collection of indicators and communicate their application are being developed.

In general, different analytical levels require different frameworks. That is to say, depending on the detail of analysis and the purpose of the monitoring, different frameworks provide the proper support and help.

Three commonly used frameworks that can help 'think at the scales that matter and act at the levels that count' (Vasishth and Sloane, 2002) are listed below (Segnestam, 2002):

1. Input-Output-Outcome-Impact framework, which is used in the monitoring of the effectiveness of projects. Indicators are structured in terms of inputs, outputs and the overall project objectives;
2. UNCSD's framework based on environmental (or sustainable development) themes, in which indicators are organised according to Major Areas, Themes and Sub-themes 'to support policy-makers in their decision-making at a national level' (UNCSD, 2000);
3. Driving Force–Pressure–State–Impact–Response (DPSIR) framework for environmental reporting and monitoring at regional, national and international levels.

The DPSIR derives from other models developed in recent years: the PSR (Pressure–State–Response) model adopted by the Organisation for Economic Co-operation and Development (OECD, 1994) for its environmental performance reviews, and the DSR system (Drivers–State–Response) proposed by the Commission on Sustainable Development of the United Nations (UN, 1997). The models have been extended by EEA (EEA, 1999) to cover the causes (driving forces) and the impacts on the environment. The DPSIR framework is now also used by Eurostat for the organisation of the environmental statistics. The DPSIR framework will now be presented in detail for the purpose of the present work.

The DPSIR framework is widely used to structure indicators to allow for a holistic and multi-dimensional view of causal relationships. Within the DPSIR framework, indicators are used to assess the interaction between man and his environment. The integrated set of indicators is used by the decision maker to simplify the complex interlinking between human actions and the co-existing ecological, economic and social states. A graphical presentation of the scheme is reported in Figure 4.3: Driving forces (D) are the underlying causes which lead to environmental pressures (e.g. human demands for agricultural land, energy, industry, transport and housing); D's lead to Pressures (P) on the environment (e.g. the exploitation of resources deriving from human demands), which in turn affect the State (S) of the environment. This refers to the quality of the various environments (air, soil, water, etc.) and their consequent ability to support the demands placed on them (e.g. supporting human and non-human life, supplying resources, etc.). Changes of S may have an Impact (I) on human health, ecosystems, biodiversity, amenity value, financial value, etc., which may be expressed in terms of the level of environmental harm. Finally, Responses (R) demonstrate the efforts of society (e.g. politicians, decision makers) to solve the problems (e.g. policy

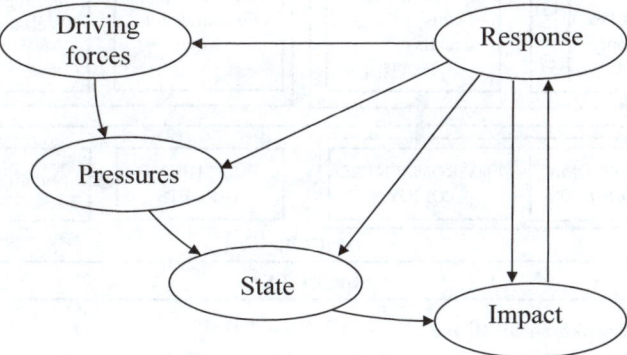

Figure 4.3   DPSIR framework

measures, planning, actions in general).

The framework is broadly accepted, and many countries find it useful for state of environment reporting. Core lists of environmental issues, and of relevant pressure–state–response indicators, have been developed by several organisations, building on initial work by the OECD. Italy, for example, publishes a national state of the environment report every two years using this framework, and is setting up a national monitoring system along the same lines. Several applications of the DPSIR approach have been proposed for the management of water resources, as in the example reported in Figure 4.4.

Conceptual frameworks may remarkably support a correct identification and use of indicators, first of all because they facilitate their categorisation and the identification of their mutual relationships. The EEA proposes the combination of the five categories of environmental indicators mentioned in

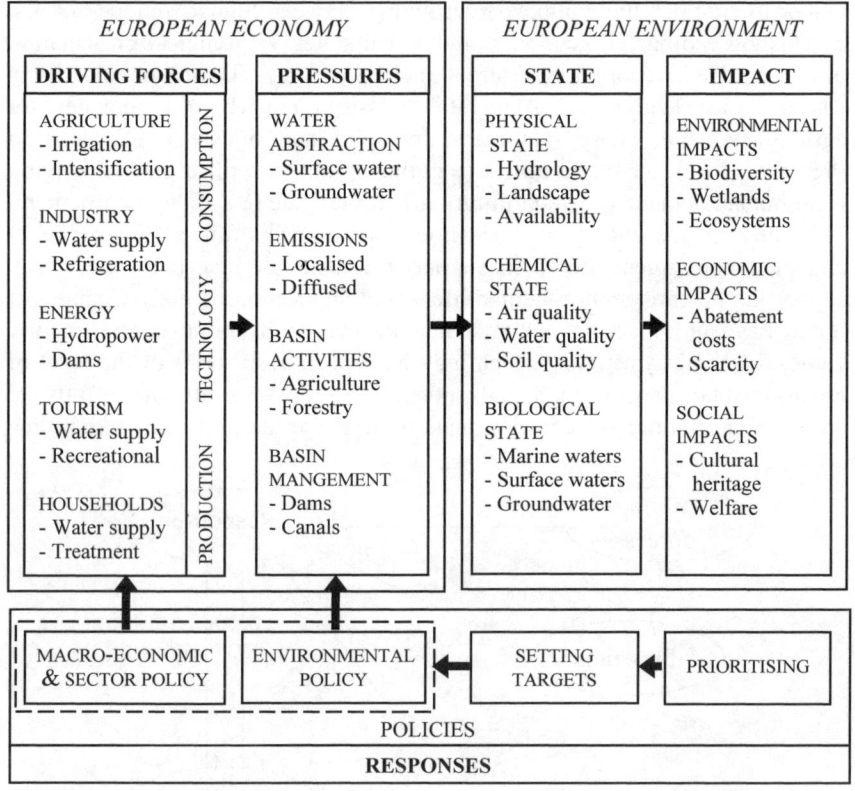

Source: Adapted from NERI, 1997.

Figure 4.4   DPSIR framework applied to water management

paragraph 2.1 with the DPSIR framework (CEC, 2001):

> For problems that are in the beginning of their policy life cycle, that is, in the stage of problem identification, indicators on the state of the environment or on impacts play a major role. They will be mainly descriptive indicators, which identify alarming developments in the state of the environment. State indicators that may give rise to policy reactions can be those that describe the sudden decline of a particular species or of surface water quality. This function of state indicators is thus limited in time: as soon as a problem is recognised politically, the attention shifts to pressure and driving force indicators. In the next and longer stages of the policy cycle (formulation of policy responses, implementation of measures and control) performance indicators of the changes in driving forces and pressures, are the most used since policymakers focus on what they can influence. Eco-efficiency and policy effectiveness indicators are used to support and document the policy decisions and the level of acceptance and uptake of measures and also as tools to measuring the degree of meeting the stated objectives, with the involvement of stakeholders. Finally, in the control phase of the policy cycle, state indicators can be used again to monitor the recovery of the environment.

A framework for organizing the selection and development of indicators is essential. Nevertheless, it must be recognised that any framework, by itself, is an imperfect tool for organising and expressing the complexities and inter-relationships encompassed by SD. Ultimately, the choice of a framework and a core set of indicators must meet the needs and priorities of users, including national experts, civil society groups and decision makers. Indicators can therefore be considered as a basis for analysis, to be integrated into a wider assessment framework.

4.2.3   Analysis Methods and Tools

Analysis goes a step further, synthesising information to produce useful outcomes for improved decision making. Such technical tools help identify and apply existing knowledge to the challenges of SD, identifying gaps, and filling them through research. In this context, the main analytical methodologies are introduced.

When indicators have been selected and structured in a manner that facilitates their interpretation, analysis may follow. Analytical tools for such a purpose range from physical models, such as mathematical models (for example basin scale hydrologic modelling), and Geographical Information Systems, to various forms of economic analyses, such as cost benefit analysis, risk-benefit analysis, or multi-criteria analysis methods.

Modelling involves the process of using precise and typically mathematical descriptions of the system inputs, outputs and processes to simulate the present, past or future aspects of the system. Prediction and the ability to try out some different 'what if?' scenarios are essential to understand past and current developments, to anticipate the future and to evaluate policy strategies. Integrated Assessment Modelling (IAM) links the mathematical representations of different components of natural and social systems (see Jakeman et al., Chapter 10 and Letcher and Bromley, Chapter 11) at local, regional or global level. As Risbey et al. (1996) stress, IAM is more than just a model building exercise, it is also a 'methodology that can be used for gaining insight over an array of environmental problems spanning a wide variety of spatial and temporal scales'.

Today, powerful modelling tools with Geographical Information Systems (GIS) interfaces can be utilised to analyse the effect of possible measures such as changes in land use, water usage and water abstraction, or point and diffuse pollution. With respect to the construction and application of environmental models, a GIS can be used to import the spatial data needed for modelling, to manage the data in a database, process the data and to visualise the models' inputs and outputs. The most recent software technologies even merge GIS and modelling functionality using an environmental modelling language embedded in the GIS (see Karssenberg et al., Chapter 9).

Analyses of sustainability are not limited to physical sciences and economics. Dalal-Clayton in his resource book on *Sustainable Development Strategies* (Dalal-Clayton and Bass, 2002), draws attention to the importance of stakeholder analysis in SD: people, groups or institutions who have specific rights and interests in an issue that the strategy seeks to address. Such analysis, strongly supported by all the documents about SD, consists of the objective identification of stakeholders in the transition to SD, their interests, powers and relations. As a continuous process, it needs to involve those people who have an interest but might not otherwise have come forward. Mostert in Chapter 7 treats the topic of public participation and demonstrates its importance in IWRM.

From the above it becomes clear that the decision process in IWRM needs to analyse the multiple disciplinary viewpoints referring to the various objectives, judgement values and constraints. Several techniques are proposed in literature for supporting decision/policy-makers in exploring and evaluating their choices, and quite often they belong to the broad category of multi-criteria analysis methods (see Feás Vàzquez and Rosato, Chapter 5). These methods are based on a model, which associates an index of attractiveness to each policy/decision option, depending on its estimated impacts and on the subjective values of those who evaluate it. In general terms, MCA methodology unfolds into a series of stages:

1.   Problem structuring, that is the analysis of the concerns of a unit and the selection of the indicators that measure the impacts of policy options;

2. Model building, which is the construction of the value index, which serves to state the attractiveness of a policy option for a policy unit;
3. Elaboration of recommendations that represent the interpretation of the evaluation in terms of guiding the behaviour of the policy unit in the decision process.

When dealing with integrated water management, the main problems generally arise at the beginning of the decision process because of the difficulty of having an overall perspective of the problem and a deep understanding of all the issues involved. The structuring of a decision-making process seems to be the most valuable and essential part of the MCA methodology, in that it can provide a useful basis for developing further the decision process by means of assessment methods and tools.

4.2.4 Assessment Methods and Tools

Ensuring the implementation of SD requires the further development and packaging of appropriate 'tools' that can aid project and programme development, and assist the setting of policy frameworks. Moreover, the evaluation of proposed policies or decisions in general may require tools integrating the various monitoring and analysis tasks. Therefore, conceptual frameworks providing adequate information in the form of indicators, combined with analytical tools to analyse cause-effect links and correlations, should be further integrated into assessment tools. The incorporation of appropriate instruments into an integrated tool is fundamental to the implementation of SD.

Assessments may guide, support, monitor and evaluate policies and decision making that seek actions supporting SD. Different assessment approaches and tools were developed in the past aimed at supporting the development and implementation of various typologies of actions, some of which are briefly introduced below.

Impact assessment is a planning approach that provides detailed documentation on environmental and social impacts, adverse effects and mitigation alternatives. It is a process to improve decision making and to ensure that the measures under consideration are environmentally and socially sound and sustainable. Impact assessment now includes a broad suite of different techniques, including environmental impact assessment (EIA), social impact assessment (SIA), cumulative effects assessment (CEA), environmental health impact assessment (EHIA), risk assessment, strategic environmental assessment (SEA) and biodiversity impact assessment (BIA) (Donelly et al., 1998).

Impact assessment relates to a process rather than a particular activity. It provides information on the environmental, social and economic effects of proposed activities and is a mechanism by which information can be presented clearly and systematically to decision makers. For these reasons impact assessment can provide the basis for a correct approach to the concept of sustainability assessment (SA), the fourth step in which the process for implementing IWRM culminates, as reported in Figure 4.2. According to the level and the scale at which SA is performed, two methodologies could be of particular interest: environmental impact assessment (EIA) and strategic environmental assessment (SEA). Within the context of impact assessment methodologies, EIA has conventionally been applied at a project level. It represents a limited response to the challenges of sustainable development (Dalal-Clayton and Bass, 2002). Within the context of EIA, Multi-criteria analysis methods help in selecting options based on objective functions including weighted goals of the decision maker, with explicit consideration of constraints and costs.

In an IWRM perspective, EIA plays a central role in acquiring information on the social and environmental implications – including water resources implications – of development programmes and projects, identifying the measures necessary to protect the resource and related ecosystems and then ensuring that such measures are implemented. The IWRM approach implies that sectoral developments are evaluated for possible impacts on the water resource and that such evaluations are considered when designing or prioritising development projects. EIAs are not only concerned with impacts on the natural environment but also with effects on the social environment. Hence, the EIA includes cross-sectoral integration of project developers, water managers, decision makers and the public, and provides a mechanism or tool to achieve this.

It is increasingly evident that many of the environmental problems associated with development projects arise from insufficient attention being given to environmental issues at higher levels of policy-making. SEA has thus emerged in the last decade as a more proactive, integrated approach that addresses the causes of unsustainable development, which were previously promoted by government macro-economic policies, investment, trade and development programmes, energy and transport plans, and so on (Dalal-Clayton and Bass, 2002) (Figure 4.5).

Sadler and Verheem (1996) have defined SEA as

A systematic process for evaluating the environmental consequences of proposed policy, plan or programme initiatives in order to ensure they are fully included and appropriately addressed at the earliest appropriate stage of decision-making on par with economic and social considerations.

SEA is therefore a cross-sectoral tool (like EIA), relevant in the area of water resources management as well, that should be seen as a decision-aiding

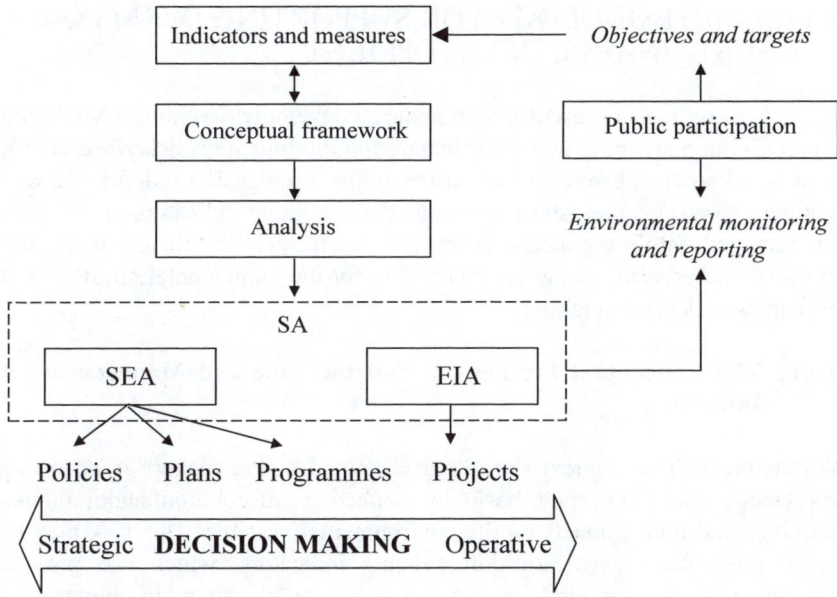

Figure 4.5   Sustainability assessment approaches within the context of the process of knowledge and decision making for IWRM and sustainable development

rather than a decision-making process; it is a flexible 'tool for forward planning' to be applied at various stages of the policy-making cycle (Sadler, 1998). Under this broad perspective, SEA encompasses assessments of both broad policy initiatives and more concrete programmes and plans that have physical and spatial references (Dalal-Clayton and Bass, 2002).

Within the broadest context of methodologies for SA, the need for operational tools to put them into practice may be solved by Decision Support Systems (DSSs), which are assessment tools that provide useable knowledge at an appropriate point of the decision-making process, and at an appropriate level of precision.

A DSS is a computer-based instrument that facilitates the processing, analysis and presentation of information. It helps decision makers to identify which information is relevant at any given time in the policy-making process. With this information, the quality of the policy-making process can be enhanced. On the one hand, a DSS assists with policy analysis by forecasting of future contexts, design and screening of alternatives, impact assessment, and comparing and ranking alternatives. On the other hand, a DSS involves more process-like actions such as communication or interactive and participative decision-making processes.

4.3 A METHODOLOGY FOR SUPPORTING IWRM FOR SUSTAINABLE DEVELOPMENT

The following pages present a methodology developed within the MULINO Project (Giupponi et al., 2004) for integrating the four steps described above, in which knowledge relevant to sustainability science is used for decision making in IWRM. The next paragraphs describe how indicators and indices (i), managed within a conceptual framework (ii), can be utilised in specific forms of analysis (iii) and assessments (iv), for the implementation of IWRM principles in decision making.

4.3.1 The Conceptual Framework and the Role and Management of Indicators

Within the IWRM context the initial task of decision makers is acquiring knowledge about the river basin by collecting information about human activities and their impacts on the environmental systems. This task may be based upon the identification of suitable indicators, which can provide concise quantification and temporal monitoring of the main human and environmental variables.

The whole process should be then formalised within a conceptual network, in this case based upon the DPSIR approach. In a conceptual framework for natural resources management, and in particular to IWRM, the Impacts describe the existing problems arising from the change detected in State variables, which affects their economic value, environmental function and social role. The level of the responses has to be related to the magnitude of the impacts. These different responses need different planning processes, and different decision makers could be involved. The different planning levels could be policies, plans, programmes and projects, from macro to micro level. As previously mentioned, as far as water resources are concerned, the spatial level is usually defined by the physical boundaries of the hydrological subdivisions of the land: river basins and sub-basins. Nevertheless, various levels of response may be identified for local, regional and national decision makers. For instance, local decision makers (e.g. municipal water administrators) do not deal with responses at the Driving forces level with sector policies. Instead, they may act with plans on Pressures, or with specific projects affecting the state of the environment. Conversely, the higher level policy-making bodies usually act on Driving forces and Pressures, having fewer possibilities to deal directly with environmental conditions, or State. In any case a coordination effort may be required in order to produce an efficient response.

A crucial aspect of applying the DPSIR approach to the principles of decision making in IWRM is the transformation of a static reporting scheme in a dynamic framework for integrated assessment. The next two paragraphs present how Integrated Assessment Modelling (IAM) combined with Multi-Criteria Decision Methods (MCDMs) can provide support for analysis and assessment procedures.

4.3.2   Methods of Analysis: Modelling and Evaluation

The implementation of IAM in the DPSIR framework is approached by focusing on the DPS part of the conceptual framework. These three elements were considered as formalisations of driving variables, model parameters and outputs, respectively. In the case of water pollution models, for instance, Ds represent the forcing variables ruling the behaviour of the simulated system (i.e. the catchment). Ps may be represented by parameters that express the rate of pollution processes and Ss are the output variables quantifying the dynamic evolution of the catchment system, as affected by the pollution sources and processes. Integration of models may occur at various levels and in different ways and thus relationships could be expressed by parallel one-to-one flows, or one-to-many (e.g. one activity affecting various environmental compartments), or many-to-one (e.g. various sectors affecting the same environmental indicator), or even many-to-many, in the case of multi-sector integrated models.

In the context of environmental decision making, IAM can thus support the identification of the correct Responses by providing sets of indicator values derived from simulations. Several model(s) runs are needed in which every run is parameterised to represent the expected consequences for one option in turn, within the set of alternative responses to be examined. However, a crucial step is needed: the development of a set of evaluation indices, targeted in particular to evaluate Impacts derived from the State indicators. Evaluation procedures may be implemented by focussing on the link between S and I and between I and R by adapting concepts and methods derived from the literature about Multi-Criteria Decision Methods, and in particular Multi-Attribute Methods (Hwang and Yoon, 1981). Within this disciplinary context a preliminary phase of Problem Structuring is targeted towards the identification of those factors to be considered for choosing between previously defined alternative response options. These factors are expressed as indicators derived from output variables of IAMs or monitoring activities and used to fill the cells of the Analysis Matrix (AM). The step between the quantification of State variables in the AM and the identification of Impact evaluation indices can be conceptualised as the conversion of the AM into an Evaluation Matrix (EM), which expresses the estimated impacts (see Figure 4.6).

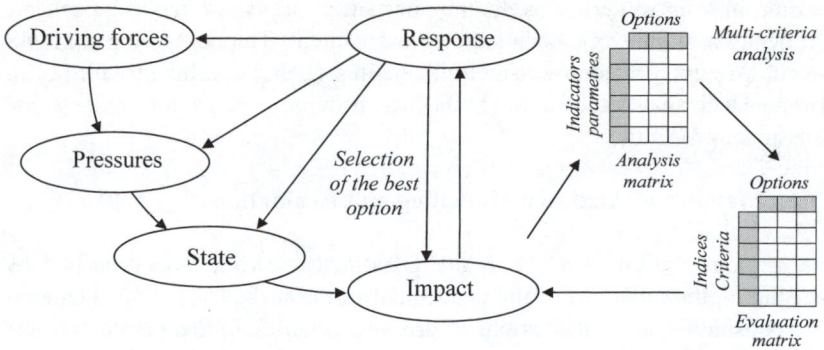

Figure 4.6   Implementation of MCA techniques within the DPSIR framework

This step is realised by means of normalisation procedures and value functions, allowing respectively the comparison of multidimensional indicators/factors and the expression of judgements to convert their scales into evaluation criteria, specific to the decision in question. The standardisation procedure simply transforms any arbitrary data range to a standard interval which represents the degree to which a decision objective is matched by every possible value of the indicators stored in the AM. The value function is in practice a mathematical representation of human judgements. The way the performances of the alternatives are translated into value scores is controlled by the decision maker's preferences. Weights are usually applied to evaluation criteria to contribute to making explicit the preferences of the decision maker.

Having identified the impacts, the decision maker has to apply decision rules to the values stored in the EM to determine the preferred option, and therefore filling the gap between I and R. In the simplest case the rule can be expressed by the weighted sum of values stored in the columns of the EM. Various iterations are possible at this step to refine the selection of the preferred response by considering the results of the sensitivity analysis, refining the weights, or choosing alternative decision rules. Parallel procedures are also possible in multi-stakeholder group decision making.

4.3.3   Assessment Methods: a Dynamic and Integrated DPSIR-DSS Tool

Many decision support systems have been developed to address the problems of water resource management (Mysiak et al., 2002). DSSs can improve the quality of decision making by combining the capabilities of geographical information systems, database technology, modelling techniques and optimisation procedures into one computerised system. Furthermore, openness about how decisions are reached is greatly facilitated using a DSS in which effects of alternative development policies can be explained and their impacts assessed in a form which can be comprehended by the non-expert. Similarly, a DSS is ideally suited to answering questions arising from policy changes on water resources by providing the understanding of the processes involved, evaluating the consequences and delivering advice.

The main objective of the MULINO project was to improve decision making in sustainable water resource management at the catchment scale, in compliance with the recently released Water Framework Directive, WFD (EC, 2000). In accordance with the WFD, the DSS developed by the project integrates hydrological and socioeconomic approaches in order to assist water authorities in the management of water resources.

Converting the DPSIR framework in a dynamic environment through the implementation of IAM procedures, posed no problem until the issue of multidisciplinary integration was touched upon. When social and economic considerations were brought into the IAM environment, the DPSIR approach was limited by its static environmental monitoring and reporting.

Two main alternative solutions were examined in order to expand the DPSIR context to social and economic issues. The first solution consisted of reconsidering the definition of State by broadening its meaning to include socioeconomic indicators. The second consisted of maintaining the restrictive environmental meaning that focuses socioeconomic analyses on the D component. Pros and cons were evident for both solutions. The first allowed a more explicit representation of causal links and processes within the catchment, but lost coherence with the original – or at least the common – terminology, while the second was more coherent but probably less effective in representing the territorial system (the catchment or river basin) and the decisional process.

The second solution was adopted because it was considered sound, from a theoretical viewpoint, to represent causal links between social and economic drivers and the state of the environment through the DPS chains, thus restricting socioeconomic aspects to the origin of the chain. For example, social indicators of driving force, such as 'Unemployment rate', can be included in a model assessing environmental impacts in a given territorial context. This is valid for analysis conducted at broad territorial scale in particular. With this in mind, in contrast with some interpretations of the DPSIR framework, it was also considered useful to include within D indicators non-socioeconomic drivers such as climate change. This solution required an expansion of the IAM environment to not only deal with D-P-S chains, but also with 'within D' modelling, in the cases where the responses determine dynamic processes modelled within the socioeconomic systems.

This is true, in particular for applications conducted at broader scales, where responses at the D level are considered in the form of new policies or regulations. Feedback effects of environmental changes in this context are possible in two ways: (i) by closing the DPSIR cycle, or (ii) by internal DPS loops. Both are consistent with the framework presented herein.

A key issue is to guarantee the possibility of feeding decisional matrices with social, economic and environmental criteria, to allow decisions to be taken in a perspective of SD. This aspect was tackled by allowing D and P indicators to be considered as decision factors within the AM.

For the sake of concreteness, the application of the methodology described above to a pilot study in the area of the Venice Lagoon Watershed (VLW, north-east Italy) is presented in the next section. The mDSS tool (Giupponi et al., 2004), in which the methodology developed by the MULINO project has been implemented, has been applied to support a recent decision problem of a water management authority (the Destra Piave Reclamation Board) in the Vela catchment.

4.4   A PILOT STUDY APPLICATION IN THE VENICE LAGOON WATERSHED

The Venice Lagoon and its watershed form an environmental system of approximately 2500 km^2, where historical and recent cities, large and medium-small industrial districts and intensive agricultural activities coexist within a peculiar natural area. The drainage basin consists of a low-gradient floodplain with a surface of about 2000 km^2. It is drained by water courses with different hydraulic regimes (natural, mechanical, alternate mechanical). About 40 per cent of the basin surface is below mean sea level and is under reclamation by pumping machines. The pollution discharged into the Venice Lagoon by streams and canals flowing through the catchment represents a substantial contribution to the overall pollution budget of the Lagoon and is a major environmental issue.

In Italy public funds are made available by specific national and regional regulations in order to support the realisation of initiatives for the abatement of pollutant loads that travel from the catchment into the lagoon. To apply for those funds, local agencies in charge of water management can present suitable projects targeted at reducing diffuse pollution in the drainage basin. One of the recipients of such funds are the Land Reclamation Boards, public administrative bodies made up of all the private individuals who live or have economic activities in a given territory requiring water management (defined according to hydrological and administrative criteria). Their main task is that of managing the water distribution system, protecting the territory from floods, and managing and maintaining the public infrastructure for land reclamation and irrigation.

The pilot study for mDSS focuses on the choice among alternative environmental engineering operations, such as revitalising and re-naturalising water courses, in order to reduce non-point source pollution (agricultural and other sources) of surface waters.

The Vela Catchment, 100 km^2 in size, is located in the Venetian floodplain. In the north, along the spring belt, soils sit on a deep geologic layer of gravel, while the southern part of the catchment is characterised by deep alluvial soils with various textures. From the hydrologic point of view, the area is thus characterised by varying natural vertical flows of water to the aquifer and a dense surface network of natural rivers and artificial canals. Some areas drain naturally while others, mainly located in the southern part where low lying lands dominate, drain mechanically by means of pumping plants. Intensive crop production (mainly maize), livestock production and fragmented urban areas not yet adequately served by waste water treatment plants act as main driving forces affecting water quality of the Vela catchment, substantially contributing to the overall pollution budget of the Lagoon.

In the problem-formulation phase (Conceptual Phase), once the exploration of available indicators for Driving forces, Pressure and State is concluded, DPS chains representing the problem's underlying cause-effect relationships are constructed (Table 4.1). Some chains are incomplete, in particular those related to the socioeconomic drivers that are relevant for the decision but do not provide significant environmental consequences.

At the end of this phase the problem is described in a cognitive and structured way (DPSI) and the area of interest and relevant database inspected. The Impact, that is the problem for which a Response is needed, in this case stands in general as the degradation of the Lagoon's ecosystem.

In the Design Phase, for the sake of simplicity, only three options were selected to present the MULINO approach and mDSS, out of an original list of twelve alternative projects:

1. Excavation of a tributary, the Meolo River, in order to increase water retention time (EXCAV_MEO). Rivers have the natural capability of diminishing pollutant contents through dilution, deposition and absorption processes, as well as through purification with microbes;

2. Plantation of a buffer strip of trees along the riverbank of one of the main rivers of the catchment, the Vallio River, to improve the phytoremediation effect (BUFF_VALLIO). Vegetation filter strips have been identified as a best management practice that has the potential to remove substantial amounts of sediments and nutrients from cropland and urban runoff;

Table 4.1   DPS chains for the Vela catchment

Driving force indicators (D)	Pressure indicators (P)	State indicators (S)
Urban settlements (inhabitants/km^2)	Urban net emission of BOD5 (t/yr)	BOD/COD in rivers (mg/l)
Impermeable (developed) areas (ha)	Loads of hazardous substance to water bodies by sector (tHS/yr)	Hazardous substances (pesticides) in rivers (µg/l HS)
Irrigated land (ha)	Use of water for irrigation (m^3/yr)	N uptake with crop irrigation (t/yr)
Buffer strips (ha)	Drainage water interception by vegetation (m^3/yr)	N uptake with buffer strips (t/yr)
		Nitrate concentrations in water bodies (mg/l)
Use of nitrogen fertilisers in agriculture (kg/ha/yr)	Nitrogen balance: total surplus from fertilisers and manure applications (kg/ha/yr)	Flooding damages (MEur)
Land reclamation by pumping machines (m^3/yr)	Hydraulic risk: return time (yr)	Self-remediation of water bodieN retention (t/yr)
Land reclamation by drainage network (m^3/yr)	Total discharge of nitrogen (t/yr)	Water retention time (hrs)
Land reclamation by drainage network (m^3/yr)	Surface water drainage (mm/yr)	
Social conflicts (index)		
Bureaucratic pressure (index)		
Variation of social welfare (index)		
Local legislation (index)		
Public investments (MEur)		
Maintenance costs (Eur/yr)		

3. Redirection of the discharge of an area (153 ha) from the Vallio River into the Candellara Canal, that flows outside the lagoon (DIV_CANDE). This option prevents a certain amount of nutrients flowing into the Lagoon.

The first two operations are mainly intended to increase the capacity of water courses in terms of self-purification, in-stream storage and retention times to obtain a reduction in diffuse pollution. The third simply diverts a certain amount of pollutants away from the Lagoon (Figure 4.7).

Environmental engineering projects such as revitalising and re-naturalising water courses have a good capacity of reducing pollution loads. But they can also have other functions such as upgrading the farming landscape and improving the recreational use of rural areas. The decision-making process is therefore complicated by this multi-functionality that operates in the territory and that combines hydraulic engineering, natural resources management, recreational activities, etc.

A set of appropriate decisional criteria, ranging from environmental impact indicators to expressions of political will, were subsequently chosen from the list of indicators used to build the DPS chains. The selection of the criteria was aimed at determining a scale of preferences that consider the objectives and functions of the Board and that reflect those stated in the regional regulations. For instance, criteria that reflected a possible change in the irrigation availability were considered important.

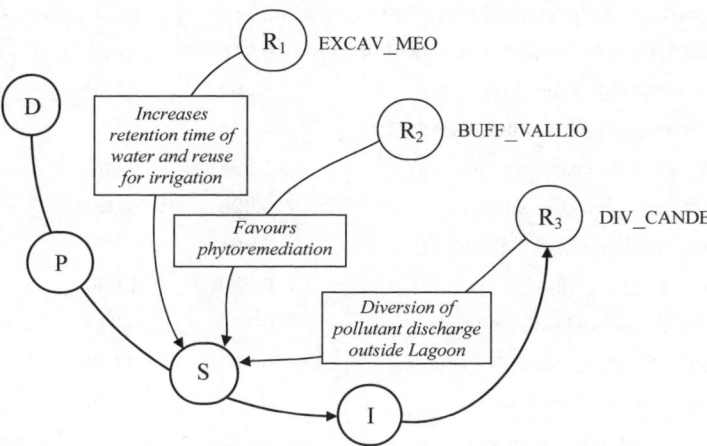

Figure 4.7   Set of alternative responses that may improve the water quality of the Vela catchment

The estimation of resulting changes of indicator values lead to the effectiveness assessment of the three alternative options: first the performances of each criteria were calculated and stored in the Analysis Matrix (Table 4.2). Then each criterion score was translated into a value score that made explicit, through appropriate value functions, the DM's preferences, and therefore the degree to which the main goal was matched by each alternative option. These operations led to taking the decision process a step further: the Choice Phase.

As previously stated, decision problems involve criteria of varying importance. Criterion weights, that provide information on the relative importance of the considered criteria, were assigned. A vector of weights was obtained using the procedure of pair-wise comparison implemented in the software, using the judgements expressed by the Board's technical staff. The reduction of hydraulic risk, the irrigation value and the financial constraints resulted in being the most important parameters for the ranking of the alternative projects.

Once the weights are defined, the evaluation criteria are aggregated by means of a specific decision rule. This is the procedure by which criteria are

Table 4.2   Analysis matrix built with criterion indicators extracted from the DPS chains reported in Table 4.1

Criteria	BUFF_VALLI	DIV_CANDE	EXCAV_MEO
D: Impermeable (developed) areas (ha)	2.716	0.000	0.000
D: Use of nitrogen fertilisers in agriculture	0.876	0.004	1.171
S: Water retention time (hrs)	3.500	0.000	3.000
S: Self-remediation of water bodies: N ret	0.338	9.839	0.170
S: N uptake with crop irrigation (t/yr)	1.664	0.000	33.281
S: N uptake with buffer strips (t/yr)	15.000	0.000	0.000
D: Urban settlements (inhabitants/km^2)	2.005	0.000	0.000
D: Social conflicts (index)	0.000	1.000	0.000
D: Bureaucratic pressure (index)	0.132	0.075	0.034
D: Variation of social welfare (index)	0.067	0.127	0.057
D: Maintainance costs (Eur/yr)	0.042	0.079	0.074
D: Local legislation (index)	0.032	0.167	0.085
P: Use of water for irrigation (m^3/yr)	100.000	0.000	2 000.000
P: Hydraulic risk: return time (yr)	0.022	0.149	0.072
D: Public investments (MEur)	300.000	250.000	200.000

selected and combined to arrive at a single final score for each option, and by which evaluations are compared. The Simple Additive Weighting (SAW) method was the first chosen for testing mDSS. Using the preferences expressed by the Board, DIV-CANDE (diversion of the discharge of part of the catchment through the Candellara canal with outlet outside the Lagoon) resulted in being the most suitable option. A sensitivity analysis carried out on the results of the SAW decision rule enabled the exploration of the options' performances. It was observed that a small increase in the weight of 'Nitrogen uptake with buffer strips' (from 0.04 to 0.14), lead to a change in the option's rank order by reversing the best with the second best option (BUFF_VALLIO). Therefore, the choice of the option recommended by the SAW method using the Board's criterion weights was neither very robust nor stable, and this can be observed by the very similar value of the overall performances.

The Order Weighting Average (OWA) required a second set of (order) weights that allow one to control the trade-off level between criteria and that describing the risk behaviour of the decision maker. The order weights are not assigned to the criteria, but to the position of the rank order defined by the criterion values of an option. According to this, the first order weight is assigned to the criterion with lowest outcome value and the last order weight to the criterion with highest outcome value for an option. To test the method, five sets of order weights were applied to the 15 criteria:

1. The order weights [0, 0, 1] assign extreme importance to the five highest criterion scores (0.2 each). This yields an aggregation operator with a moderate degree of trade-off between criteria and a high degree of Orness (absence of compensation between criteria with good and bad performances), representing the most risk-taking behaviour;
2. The order weights [0,1,0] assign extreme importance to the five middle-ranked criterion scores. This yields an aggregation operator with a moderate degree of trade-off, as well as of ANDness (compensation) and ORness;
3. The order weights [1, 0, 0] assign extreme importance to the five lowest criterion scores. This yields an aggregation operator with a moderate degree of trade-off between criteria and a high degree of ANDness, representing the most risk-adverse solution;
4. The order weights [0.5, 0, 0.5] assign same importance to the highest and lowest criterion scores (0.1 each). This yields an aggregation operator with substantial trade-off and a moderate degree of ANDness and ORness;
5. The order weights [0.33, 0.33, 0.33] apply equal importance to all criterion scores (a weight of 0.066 each) and thus do not change the existing ranking order: the result is equivalent to that of the SAW rule, for which full trade-off is allowed.

As a result (Table 4.3), the option DIV_CANDE is the preferable one in most of the cases and EXCAV_MEO the least desirable. BUFF_VALLIO stands up as the best option in the case of a risk-averse behaviour. This is due to the fact that greater significance is given to criteria related to the self-purification capacity value of the options.

The Ideal point methods order a set of alternatives on the basis of their separation from the ideal and negative-ideal solutions. The ideal solution represents a hypothetical alternative that consists of the most desirable level of each criterion across the options under consideration. The negative-ideal solution consists of the least desirable level of the options' performance. The best alternative is the one closest to the ideal point and most distant from the negative-ideal solution. TOPSIS (Technique for Order Preference by Similarity to Ideal Solution) is one of the most popular compromise methods. This method's outcome is different from those of the previously-presented decision rules, as it indicates BUFF_VALLIO as the best option, confirming the very close performance of two of the three options (as demonstrated also by the sensitivity analysis). Furthermore the TOPSIS method goes beyond the simple closeness to the ideal solution by considering the closeness to the less desirable solution as well.

In view of testing every capability of the software, a simulation of group decision making was also performed. A parallel assignation of weights was carried out with a group of students simulating an environmentalist group: higher weights were assigned to criteria relevant for the environment and the landscape (e.g. nitrogen uptake through buffer strips). In general criteria linked to the processes involving a natural reduction of nitrates were assigned higher weights.

As a result, the SAW method gave the plantation of buffer strips along the Vallio river (BUFF_VALLIO) the best ranking score. The level of problem understanding and preferences of the two groups considered were different, but assuming they were willing to come up with a compromise solution, the very simple group decision-making capability of mDSS helped in finding a common final solution. The Borda technique is a very simple algorithm implemented in

Table 4.3　Final scores resulting from application of different sets of order weights in the OWA rule

Order weights	DIV_CANDE	BUFF_VALLI	EXCAV_MEO
[0, 0, 1]	0.086	0.074	0.07088
[0, 1, 0]	0.0204	0.0099	0.00876
[1, 0, 0]	0.00016	0.0	0.0
[0.5, 0, 0.5]	0.043	0.03708	0.03544

mDSS, which assigns ranks to decision alternatives based on the rationale that the higher the position of an alternative plan on the voter's list, the higher the rank assigned. DIV_CANDE is the compromise solution in this case.

CONCLUSIONS

The literature review indicated that there is a clear need for methodologies and tools to put sustainable development principles into practice, in which decisions and choices are assessed in terms of their sustainability, not only over the long term, but also with regards to their day-to-day contribution to sustainable development.

This may also be described in terms of the implementation of an integrated framework allowing decision makers to choose first and then to monitor the process induced by their decisions. IWRM falls within this domain, thus requiring ad hoc approaches tailored to the specific needs and peculiarities of water resources.

The development of environmental policies has led to the need to utilise the wealth of data and scientific knowledge that has become available and can support integrated water resources management. Various methods and tools, such as modelling, environmental impact assessment and decision support, can provide rational insight into the system's behaviour and the problems addressed. However, integration remains a difficult issue.

The four-step process described above may help cope with the problem mentioned above, focussing in particular on:

1. The complexity of the decision making process that is typical of IWRM;
2. The large amounts of multi-sectoral and multidisciplinary information;
3. The need for efficient communication between the scientific and policy sectors and between decision makers and the stakeholders.

The DPSIR scheme proved to be sufficiently broad to allow the formalisation of the whole procedure of decision making in the context of sustainable water management, but a great number of analyses are necessary to develop an integrated and dynamic DSS tool upon that basis. The resulting methodology, and the application tool presented above, combined the innovative potentials of IAM and MCA approaches, with the effective communication potential of the well-known DPSIR approach.

REFERENCES

Bauler, T. and W. Hecq (2000), 'On the usability of indicators for sustainable development', in Third Biennial Conference of the European Society for Ecological Economics, Vienna, 3–6 May 2000.

Bogardi, J.J. (1994), 'The concept of integrated water resources management as a decision making problem in multicriteria decision analysis', *Water Resources Management*, Paris: International Hydrological Program, Unesco.

Boisvert, V., N. Holec and F. Vivien (1998), 'Economic and Environmental Information for Sustainability', in S. Faucheux and M. O'Connor (eds), *Valuation for sustainable development: methods and policy indicators*, Cheltenham: Edward Elgar, pp. 99–119.

CEC (Commission of European Communities) (2001), 'The European Environment Agency Focuses on EU-Policy in its Approach to Sustainable Development Indicators', Working Paper no. 5.

Dalal-Clayton, B. and S. Bass (2002), *Sustainable Development Strategies: A Resource Book*, London: National Strategies for Sustainable Development.

Donelly, A., B. Dalal-Clayton and R. Hughes (1998), *A Directory of Impact Assessment Guidelines*, (2nd edition), London: International Institute for Environment and Development.

EC (European Communities) (2000), 'Directive 2000/60/EC of the European Parliament and of the Council Establishing a Framework for Community Action in the Field of Water Policy' (OJ L 327, 22.12.2000).

EEA (European Environmental Agency) (1999), *Environmental Indicators: Typology and Overview*, Copenhagen: European Environment Agency.

EEA (European Environmental Agency) (2001), *Reporting on Environmental Measures: are We Being Effective?*, Copenhagen: European Environment Agency.

Gijsbers, P. (2000), *Decision Support for the Management of Shared Water Resources*, The Netherlands: Delft University Press.

Giupponi, C., J. Mysiak, A. Fassio and V. Cogan (2004), 'MULINO-DSS: a computer tool for sustainable use of water resources at the catchment scale', *Mathematics and Computers in Simulation*, **64**, 13–24.

Hwang, Ch. L. and K. Yoon (1981*), Multiple Attribute Decision Making: Methods and Applications*, Berlin: Springer Verlag.

ICSU (International Council for Science) (2002), 'Making Science for Sustainable Development More Policy Relevant: New Tools for Analysis', *ICSU Series on Science for Sustainable Development*, No. 8.

Lahdelma, R., P.Salminen and J. Hokkanen (2000), 'Using multicriteria methods in environmental planning and management', *Environmental Management*, **26**(6), 595–605.

Luiten, H. (1999), 'A legislative view on science and predictive models', *Environmental Pollution*, **100**, 5–11.

Mysiak, J., C. Giupponi and V. Cogan (2002), 'Challenges and Barriers to Environmental Decision Making: A Perspective from the Mulino Project', proceedings from the 8th EC-GI & GIS Workshop, ESDI – A Work in Progress, Dublin (Ireland), July 3–5, 2002.

NERI (National Environmental Research Institute) (1997), *Integrated Environmental Assessment on Eutrophication*, Technical Report n. 207, Denmark.

OECD (Organization for Economic Cooperation and Development) (1994), *Environmental Indicators*, Paris.

Risbey, J., M. Kandlikar and A. Patwardhan (1996), 'Assessing integrated assessments', *Climatic Change*, **34**, 369–395.

Sadler, B. (1998), 'Institutional Requirements for Strategic Environmental Assessment', paper to Intergovernmental Forum, organised by the Ministry for the Environment,

Christchurch, New Zealand, 25 April 1998.

Sadler, B. and R. Verheem (1996), *Strategic Environment Assessment: Status, Challenges and Future Directions*, The Netherlands: Ministry of Housing, Spatial Planning and the Environment, and the International Study of Effectiveness of Environmental Assessment.

Segnestam, L. (2002), 'Indicators of Environment and Sustainable Development', *Environment Department Papers*, **89**, Washington DC, USA: The World Bank.

Simon, H.A. (1957), *Administrative Behaviour,* 2nd edition, London, UK: MacMillan.

UN (United Nations) (1997), 'From theory to practice: Indicators for sustainable development', New York: UN, Division for Sustainable Development.

UNCSD (United Nations Commission on Sustainable Development) (2000), 'Report of the Consultative Group to Identify Themes and Core Indicators of Sustainable Development', 6–9 March 2000, New York: UN.

UNCSD (United Nations Commission on Sustainable Development) (2001), 'Indicators of Sustainable Development: Framework and Methodologies, Commission on Sustainable Development', Ninth Session, 16–27 April 2001, Background Paper No. 3, New York: UN.

Van der Zaag, P. (2001), 'Principles of Integrated Water Resources Management, WaterNet module IWRM 0.1', 1st draft; June 2001, IHE Delft & Department of Civil Engineering, University of Zimbabwe.

Vasishth, A. and D. C. Sloane (2002), 'Returning to ecology – an ecosystem approach to understanding the city', in Michael J. Dear (ed.), *From Chicago to LA – Making Sense of Urban Theory*, London: Sage Publications.

WWC (World Water Council) (1996*), Constitution of the World Water Council*, 14 June 1996, Marseille, France.

5. Multi-Criteria Decision Making in Water Resources Management

Jacobo Feás Vàzquez and Paolo Rosato

5.1 INTRODUCTION

Water management is one of the main issues for human development. Water can be considered the most important primary good, and is very closely related to social and economic development. Water is generally a limited resource that must be managed efficiently for its conservation and future uses, but must also be distributed with equity.[1]

Water is a natural resource that has always played a strategic role in both social and economic development although this role differs with reference to both space and time. It is extremely difficult to generalise the problems concerning water management, which are specific and depend on the physical, economic and social characteristics of the considered context. In other words, it is not easy to find a common model to manage water resources in Africa and the Far East or in the Venetian Plain. Furthermore, water is an economic enigma: a human right, a production factor and a luxury good. Therefore, many issues must be taken into account in water management. The most important is the multipurpose use of water. Water resources are used for multifunctional purposes and managed by different water institutions with different final objectives. In fact, together with the consolidated civil and production function of water, it plays a protection function for the environment and a recreational function for which demand is rapidly increasing.

The different water uses and the many relationships with surface and groundwater systems are represented in Figure 5.1. In general, five different uses of water can be considered: for generating energy, irrigation in agriculture, drinking water for humans, production for industry and for recreational services. The inflows represent water demands for each use that are usually in conflict because of scarcity and the impacts of some uses on water quality. The outflows represent the wastewater returned to the system, more or less polluted. All flows (in and out) are highly dependent on one another. The multi-functionality of the scarce water resources makes it

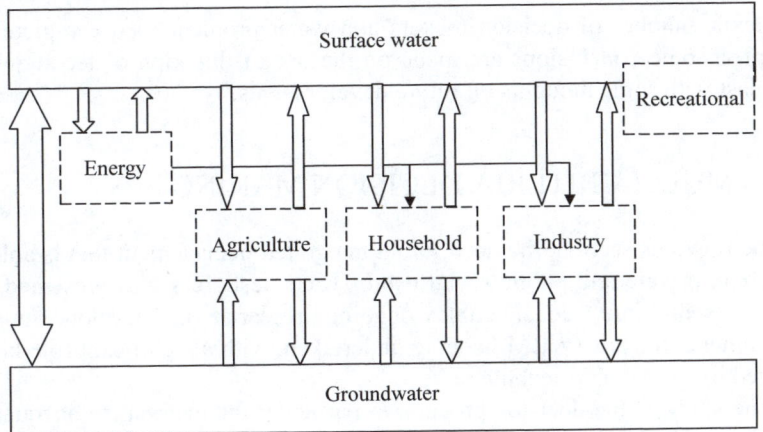

Figure 5.1 Water uses

extremely difficult to satisfy all the demands, and generates a great deal of conflict in use priorities. These conflicts are exacerbated by population growth (particularly in areas where water scarcity is rife) and by the growing importance of industrial versus agricultural production and by the growing social sensibility for the protection of the environment.

For these reasons, a global and sustainable perspective for integrated water resources management is strongly required and a lot of effort has been made in recent years to establish the basics for adequate integrated water resources management (EU Water Framework Directive, 2000).

The necessity to pursue an integrated water resources management by the public authorities produces a strong demand for operational tools in order to support decisions in this difficult task. In recent years, many advances have been made in technical tools for modelling water resource problems, and multi-criteria decision making (MCDM) procedures are widely considered very useful in challenging conflicts related to water management. This usefulness relies on the logical structure of the valuation procedures and on the common language developed for defining and discussing complex water problems. It is also a useful tool for communication purposes, between those who have to make the decisions and those who are affected by the decisions. Finally MCDM easily includes in the decision-making process the effect of uncertainties that often characterises water management problems.

This chapter illustrates the MCDM approach in integrated water resources management (IWRM). Firstly, a brief description of the basic terms and concepts in MCDM is presented and the most popular multi-criteria decision analysis methods are illustrated. A survey is presented of the different methodologies applied to water resources management within different contexts, number of decision makers and water problems. To complete the chapter, some conclusions are made on the use of this kind of technique in the past with some thoughts on future developments.

5.2   MULTI-CRITERIA DECISION MAKING

In the previous section, the need for an integrated management that is able to combine private and public/social use of water resources was presented. At the present time, considerable ongoing research to develop support instruments for this IWRM is being undertaken, with a significant role being played by the MCDM technique.

The study of the decision process, in particular the methods to adequately understand and represent the structure of preferences of a decision maker in order to find a satisfactory decision, has led, in the last twenty years, to the elaboration of an operational research methodology based on multiple objectives and criteria. There are many applications of these methodologies in natural and other resources management.

There is no generally accepted taxonomy of the different multi-criteria decision analysis methods. In the present chapter, we define MCDM as a general term to identify various formal approaches, which take into account explicitly multiple criteria in helping decision makers (Belton and Stewart, 2002). Other terms are widely used by different authors to identify similar concepts: multi-criteria analysis, multi-criteria decision aid, and so on.

In the study of the decision process in complex environments, the terms 'multiple objectives', 'multi-attributes', 'multi-criteria', 'multi-dimensional', and so on, are used frequently. In many cases, they are considered synonyms because a universal definition has not yet been found. The term MCDM has been therefore used to cover all the general methodologies.

In order to understand the structure of MCDM models and not just the context in which they are or may be used, it is worth evaluating the terminology adopted. This is because recent methodological developments have highlighted a further need to define more precisely the terms currently in use. In fact, most of the key words that will be identified have similar meanings and are often used indifferently. Therefore, apart from creating confusion, this can also lead to a wrong analysis of the methodologies.

Zeleny (1982) proposed a reference for use of the terminology, together with Romero and Rehman (1989) and Goicoechea et al. (1982). This collection of definitions is useful and interesting because it also helps in the classification of the various current developments in MCDM. Terms like decision variable, attribute, objective, target or goal that need a clarification are presented below.

- Decision variable: decision variable represents the lever on which the decision maker operates. Thereby it represents all the aspects within which the user decides to act. In IWRM, the main decisional variables are water quantity allocated in different uses, water quality standards required, and so on.
- Attribute: The attribute is a parameter that represents any particular aspect of a given problem assumed by the decision maker to make their decision (income, savings, employment, debt, pollution level, and so on). It is objectively determined and normally expressed as a mathematical function of the decisional variables.
- Objective: The objective is the direction (min or max) that the decision maker chooses to follow for a certain attribute (that is to maximise a specific output as profit or minimise pollution, and so on).
- Target: The target is the value set by the decision maker as a reference point for the attribute chosen.
- Goal: The goal is the expected level of the chosen attribute that the decision maker aims to achieve with their decision (that is amount of water for irrigation, nitrate levels in water, and so on).

The definitions provided above may cause some confusion. In fact the distinction between some of them, seemingly obvious, is sometimes ambiguous – in particular that between goal and target and even more so between objective and goal. On the other hand, the definition of these terms in the specialist literature is not univocal; in Goicoechea et al. (1982), goal and target are synonyms whilst the term objective frequently has a more general connotation and goal reassumes the definition of objective and target. It should therefore be stressed that the aforementioned definitions permit a more rigorous classification of MCDM methods according to the characteristics of the decisional process.

Various problems are encountered in MCDM, which for our analysis can be divided into two main categories:

1. Multi-objective decision making (MODM);
2. Multi-attribute decision making (MADM).

In both categories, the user can take into consideration more, conflicting, evaluation criteria for which units of measurement differ. In the MODM methods, the decision process concerns the identification of the best choice within an infinite set of alternatives, defined by the constraints of the problem. In MADM methods, instead, the method guides the decision makers among a finite set of decisional alternatives.

On a general level, as observed in Rehman and Romero (1993), the existence of multiple objectives in the decision process brings about a fundamental qualification of the utility function that, contrary to the neo-classical economic analysis, is based on more factors. This is shown in the following optimisation model:

$$Max\, U = u[C_k] \quad \text{with} \quad C_k = f_k\,(\vec{x}) \quad \text{and} \quad \vec{x} \in X \qquad (5.1)$$

where

U is the total utility of the decision maker to maximise;

u is the function that expresses the utility with respect to the k decisional criteria;

C_k represents the criteria (attribute/objective);

$\vec{x}$ is the vector of the decisional variables.

The set X identifies the region of feasible solutions that is continuous in MODM problems (infinity alternatives); in this case, the objective of the decision maker is to identify the best solution to the problem. However, in MADM problems this region is represented by a discrete set of vectors of decision variables, each representing a predefined alternative solution and the objective of decision maker is to create a ranking (see Figure 5.2). In Table 5.1 (Hwang and Yoon, 1981, modified), the main characteristics of the two approaches are shown. In the next paragraphs, some of the most popular methods for both approaches are illustrated. The objective is not to present an exhaustive
description of the models, just some basic concepts to understand the different perspectives to assist decision-making problems.

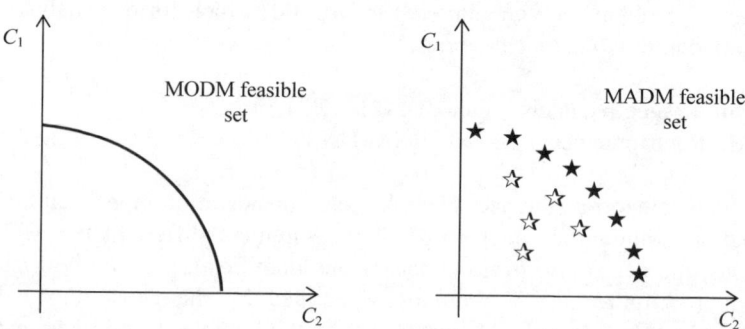

Figure 5.2   Feasible sets in MODM and MADM

Table 5.1 MADM versus MODM

	MADM	MODM
Criteria	attributes	objectives
Objectives	implicit	explicit
Attributes	explicit	implicit
Constraints	inactive	active
Alternative	finite, discrete	infinite, continuous
Use	selection, evaluation	design

5.2.1 The Multi-objective Approach

The multi-objective approach is a development of traditional mathematical programming models of which much of the structure is retained. Research into methods for scientifically tackling decisional processes has often used mathematical programming because, by organising the information coherently with the theory, it can be used to formalise the operational reality in a mathematical model able to represent the pursuing of the chosen objectives. Obviously, the representation of reality has to be 'stylised' but, with its rational structure, it can provide the analyst with a good simulation of the economic facts and an acceptable approximation of the decisional processes (Hazell and Norton, 1986). MODM methods support decisional problems in which the decision space is continuous and the objectives are established for each of the criteria. No predefined set of solutions exists in these models, so the process seeks to discover the best option.

Traditional mathematical models are based on the assumption that the decision maker formulates choices with respect to a well-defined parameter. In fact, these models generally take the form of the classical linear programming model, that is:

$$\max/\min Z = \sum_{i=1}^{n} c_i x_i \quad \text{with} \quad \sum_{i=1}^{n} a_{ji} x_i \le b_j \qquad x_i \ge 0 \qquad (5.2)$$

where:

c_i = contribution of the ith decision variable to the optimisation of the objective function;

x_i = decision variable;

a_{ij} = use level of the jth resource to accomplish one unit of ith decision variable;

b_j = availability of the jth resource.

The problem is therefore solved by finding the vector $\vec{x}$ that optimises (max or min) Z according to the availability of resource b_j. This approach assumes that the decisional rule is to optimise just one parameter (Z).

This assumption greatly reduces the interpretative potentials of the linear programming model, as the decision maker does not usually make a choice based on just one parameter, but refers to a multi-criteria utility function. It is worth stressing that if a choice must be made on the basis of just one objective it is not an economic choice but more a technical question of measurement and research (Zeleny, 1982). The decisional problem arises when there is more than one conflicting objective to be pursued contemporarily and reasonable compromises must be identified.

Therefore, based on this assumption, the solving of a linear programming model cannot be taken as an optimisation of the allocation of a given supply of resources but rather as a method of searching for the combination that guarantees the best performance with respect to a given objective. The problem therefore is to make a decision with regard to more than one conflicting decisional parameter.

Consistently with the definition of terms given in the previous section, we can have a decision maker who:

1.   operates with more than one conflicting objective (without an expected level for the relative attributes);
2.   decides on the basis of a given number of conflicting goals.

In the former case the technique to use is multi-objective programming (MOP) and related developments (compromise programming), aimed essentially at identifying efficient solutions with respect to the objectives expressed by the decision maker. In the latter case, goal programming (GP) is adopted on the basis of which the decisional problem is resolved by finding the solution closest to the set of goals stated by the decision maker.

Multi-objective programming

The MOP techniques are used when the decision maker tries to achieve a set of objectives at the same time, but satisfactory levels are not established. The MOP seeks to solve the simultaneous optimisation of several goals under a set of constraints, linear and non-linear. The method identifies a set of efficient solutions.[2] With such a formulation, it is obvious that it is not possible to identify just one optimal solution to achieve all the objectives at the same time.

On the basis of this assumption, the structure of the MOP model remains as follows:

$$EFF\,[\,f\,(\vec{x})\,] = [\,f_1\,(\vec{x}),\,f_2\,(\vec{x}),\,...,f_n\,(\vec{x})\,] \quad \text{with} \quad \vec{x} \in X \quad (5.3)$$

where *EFF* is the 'search for efficient solutions' and *n* are the objectives to be pursued.

Efficient solutions can be identified in different ways. The most widely used are the weights method, constraints method and methods for estimating the non-dominated set (non-inferior set estimation method, NISE). Their diffusion is essentially due to the fact that they can be applied using the standard simplex algorithm.

In the weights method, the functions expressing the different objectives are combined in a single objective function through the application of weights. These weights are initially attributed arbitrarily. The model has the following structure:

$$\max/\min \sum_{i=1}^{n} w_i f_i(\vec{x}) \quad \text{with} \quad \vec{x} \in X, w_i \geq 0 \tag{5.4}$$

The set of efficient solutions are generated by parameterising the weights w_i. For each set of weights, an efficient solution is generated; obviously, the precision with which the set is produced depends on the size of the steps with which the weights are varied reciprocally. The smaller the step, the higher the number of efficient solutions there are and the better the approximation.

The constraints method uses a model in which one of the objectives is set in the objective function, while the others are transformed into constraints:

$$\max/\min f_j(\vec{x}) \quad \text{with} \quad f_i(\vec{x}) \leq L_i, \ x \in X, \ i \neq j \tag{5.5}$$

The set of efficient solutions is generated by parameterising the constraints L_i. This method guarantees the efficiency of the solutions produced only if the parameterised constraints are limiting in the optimisation process. Also in this case, the precision with which the efficient set is generated depends on the size of the steps with which the constraints are parameterised. In the search for the set of efficient solutions with both weights and constraints methods, a sensitivity analysis, which can identify the variations to give to a weight or constraint to vary the solution, can be enormously useful.

From what has been described above, it can be deduced that there are essentially two, partly interrelated, weak sides to the MOP. The first is the huge amount of computation due to the large number of iterations necessary to identify the set of efficient solutions. The second is the decision maker's possible uncertainty when faced with the high number of efficient solutions. There is a need to identify methods for reducing the number of efficient solutions to simplify both the calculation phase and/or the decisional one. Compromise programming (CP) is probably the most widely used method and will be presented in the following paragraph.

Compromise programming

Compromise programming (CP) was proposed by Zeleny (1973) as a method for pruning the set of efficient solutions consistently, with the preferences of a rational decision maker who attempts to make a decision.

The basic assumption is that the decision maker aspires to come as close as possible to the solution that they consider ideal (see also next section). In order to model this tendency an objective function must be defined and this is the measure of the distance between the set of efficient solutions and the ideal one. Obviously at this point it is not important to define a geometric function (Euclidean) of the distance but rather a relation that simulates the attitude of the decision maker as precisely as possible.

A generalisation of the concept of distance in n dimensions (criteria) between an ideal solution and an efficient feasible solution is represented by the following equation:

$$\overline{DI}_p = \left[\sum_n | i_n - d_n |^P \right]^{1/p} \tag{5.6}$$

where:

i_n is the ideal solution;
d_n is the efficient feasible solution from which a different measure for each value of p can easily be obtained and which, for p equals 2, the Euclidean distance is obtained.

Two of the infinite values of DI_p appear to be especially interesting for simulating the decision maker's preferences, that is those corresponding to $p = 1$ and $p = \infty$. For $p = 1$, the distance is given by the algebraic sum of the absolute value of the gaps with respect to n dimensions. For $p = \infty$ it can be demonstrated that the distance is equal to the maximum deviation among the n dimensions.

From the above equation, it is simple to deduce that DI_1 is the maximum value of the distances that can be considered, while DI_∞ is the minimum.

Using metrics 1 and ∞ it is possible to simulate the two extreme attitudes of a rational decision maker: on the one hand, the one who takes into consideration all deviations with respect to the ideal solution in a weighted additive way; on the other hand, the one who is careful to limit what becomes the maximum deviation each time. It should be noted that, to compare deviations expressed with different dimensions, preventive normalisation becomes necessary. This can be done in different ways, usually with respect to the maximum interval of variation given by the difference between the best and the worst performance for each criterion.

The CP model can then be written as:

$$\min \overline{DI}_1 = w_n \frac{i_n - f_n(\vec{x})}{i_n - a_n}, \quad \vec{x} \in F$$

$$\overline{DI}_\infty, \quad w_1 \frac{i_1 - f_1(\vec{x})}{i_1 - a_1} \le \overline{DI}_\infty, \dots, w_n \frac{i_n - f_n(\vec{x})}{i_n - a_n} \le \overline{DI}_\infty, \quad \vec{x} \in F \tag{5.7}$$

Solving the model according to the two above metrics, the set of efficient solutions can be reduced, thus simplifying the choice for the decision maker. It is also possible to reduce significantly the number of computer elaborations, as it is not necessary to identify the whole set of efficient solutions, but just the extreme points (pay-off matrix).

The solutions obtained on solving formula 5.7 identify the so-called compromise set, within which, given the assumptions carried out, the decision maker should choose. However, the compromise set of solutions is often quite large and so the problems of choice arise again. Regarding this, Zeleny (1974) suggested a procedure (displaced ideal method) through which it is possible to reduce the compromise set coherently with the decision maker's preferences. This is based on the fact that, although it is reasonable to assume that the decision maker has the ideal solution as a point of reference, it cannot be assumed that the interval of variation, considered admissible for each decisional criteria, has the dimensions of the difference between the best and worst solution. In other words, it is possible that the decision maker does not consider acceptable solutions implying a reaching of a significantly higher level in the minor objectives to that identified by the worst solution. These minimum levels in attaining goals are introduced in the model for the calculation of a new pay-off matrix and, consequently, for the redefinition of the space within which to search for compromise solutions. A new compromise set, smaller than the original one, will be obtained through this redefinition. The process can continue with successive reductions of the admissible interval until the compromise set allows the decision maker to make his choice. Obviously, this is an iterative process that alternately involves both analyst and decision maker.

Goal programming

Goal Programming (GP) was probably the first method introduced in the field of multi-objective decision making (Charnes et al., 1955). The GP simulates a decisional process that tries to satisfy several predetermined objectives at the same time. In GP, the decision maker introduces their preferences by establishing satisfactory values for each criterion. The search for the optimal solution is through minimising the difference between the achievement of objectives within constraints and the expected values. These differences are represented and quantified by deviational variables, which can be positive or negative.

The first step in the formulation of a GP model is the identification of the set of criteria to adopt as decisional parameters. An objective value or goal (b_i), considered satisfactory by the decision maker, must then be defined for each attribute. It is also necessary to specify if that goal must be reached precisely, if it can be exceeded or if some level of non-reaching is admissible.

At this point, the deviational variables for each defined goal are introduced, these can be positive (p_i) or negative (n_i). They represent the deviation in the reaching of a given goal. If the deviation is positive, and the goal therefore exceeded, the positive deviational variable p_i represents the excess. If it is negative, the variable n_i represents the deficit. Obviously, given that positive and negative deviations cannot coexist for the same objective, at least one of the deviational variables must be nil. If the goal is fully reached, both variables are nil (Romero, 1991).

Based on this, the pursuing of the generic i^{th} goal can be expressed by the following equation:

$$f_i(\vec{x}) + n_i - p_i = b_i \qquad (5.8)$$

where $f_i(\vec{x})$ is the function expressing the value of the ith attribute as a function of the decisional variables $\vec{x}$. Now, if the decision maker wants the value b_i of the ith attribute to be reached from below (for example a given income level), it is necessary to minimise the negative deviation n_i. On the contrary, if the wish is that the goal is reached from higher values (for example a given pollution level), then it is necessary to minimise the positive deviation p_i. Lastly, if the decision maker hopes that a particular defined goal will be balanced, then the term to be minimised will be the sum of $n_i + p_i$. In substance, the main characteristic of GP is the search for the optimum solution through minimising the differential between the level achieved with the solutions $f_i(\vec{x})$ and the expected levels b_i.

The solving procedure can be done in different ways, in relation to the structure of the decision maker's preferences. Decision makers can pursue their goals simultaneously, although with different intensity, or they can attribute an absolute priority to some of them. In the former case, the variant of GP defined weighted goal programming (WGP) is adopted, while the lexicographic goal programming (LGP) version is used in the latter.

The WGP assumes all the goals simultaneously and summarises them in a single objective function. Through this 'compound' objective function, we attempt to minimise the weighted sum of the normalised deviations. Obviously, normalisation is necessary for comparing criteria expressed in different unit measures, while the weights are applied coherently with the relative importance given by the decision maker to the various goals. If the objective function and the equation of the constraints are linear, the model can be solved with the simplex method.

The LGP variant of GP uses the concept of absolute priority. In this case, the goals are ranked according to a scale of priorities, and it is assumed that attaining those with a given priority level will take precedence over achieving those with lower levels. Therefore, in an LGP model, attaining goals belonging to high-level priorities will be pursued first, and only subsequently, those of a lower level will be taken into consideration. In summary, the model is solved first by taking the top priority as objective function. The attainment level of related goals is then introduced as a constraint for the next step, where the objective function is the priority immediately below, and so on until all priorities have been used. The final solution is the definitive one.

The WGP and LGP are traditionally considered the two main variants of GP. But many other approaches to MODM, developed subsequently and commonly held to be alternatives to GP, have been revealed on further examination as being specific forms of GP, at least from the algebraic point of view (that is CP).

5.2.2 The Multi-attribute Approach

The MADM methods face decisional problems with a finite number of solutions. MADM guides the choice between n predetermined discrete alternatives $(A_1, A_2, ..., A_n)$ through their valuation with regard to a discrete number k of attributes $(a_1, a_2, ..., a_K)$, for which each alternative has a given performance index, called attributes (a_{ij}). This score can also be interpreted as the result of a function of the relative vector of decision variables referring to each n alternative $(i = 1, 2, ..., n)$, or otherwise:

$$a_{ij} = f_j(x_i) \quad \text{for} \quad j = 1, ..., k \tag{5.9}$$

These scores (see Figure 5.3 and 5.4) can generally be represented by both quantitative and qualitative attributes. Alternatives and criteria can therefore be related through an evaluation matrix (Goicoechea et al., 1982), the structure of which is shown in Figure 5.5 (see page 113). In some cases, the evaluation matrix already offers a clear ranking of the alternatives. For example, having to select just one alternative, the score of an alternative is the best for all attributes that can occur. It is then a case of absolute Paretian dominance that solves the problem of choice in a simple and unequivocal way (Voogd, 1983).

The identification of Paretian dominated alternatives can be useful for

Figure 5.3   Matrix of alternatives and decision criteria

	A_1	A_2	...	A_n
a_1	a_{11}	a_{12}	...	a_{1n}
a_2	a_{21}	a_{22}	...	a_{2n}
...	...	...	...	...
a_k	a_{k1}	a_{k2}	...	a_{kn}
$\vec{a}$	$\vec{a}_1$	$\vec{a}_2$	...	$\vec{a}_n$

Figure 5.4   Matrix of alternatives and decision variables

	A_1	A_2	...	A_n
x_1	x_{11}	x_{12}	...	x_{1n}
x_2	x_{21}	x_{22}	...	x_{2n}
...	...	...	...	...
x_m	x_{m1}	x_{m2}	...	x_{mn}
$\vec{x}$	$\vec{x}_1$	$\vec{x}_2$	...	$\vec{x}_n$

reducing the number of columns in the evaluation matrix in the case (more frequent) where the scores do not identify a clear ranking of the examined options.

Many methods can support the choice among defined and Paretian efficient alternatives, to maximise the decision maker's utility. Although these methods share the same basic information (the evaluation matrix), they differ substantially in terms of quantity and quality of the information required.

The most popular procedures are:

1.   value functions (Keeney and Raiffa, 1976);
2.   Analytic Hierarchy Process – AHP (Saaty, 1980);
3.   outranking methods (Nijkamp and van Delft, 1977; Roy, 1985).

These procedures differ by the method with which the preferences are derived and represented in the decision-making process.

The value functions methods
The value functions approach is a very popular type of procedure supported by a wide theoretical base that guarantees internal coherence. Moreover, being the very first MADM technique used, there is a great deal in literature that demonstrates its validity in real cases (Beinat, 1997).

This method attempts to obtain a true value for each alternative, which represents the preferences and value judgements of the decision-maker. To obtain this value, a value function is first identified for each considered criterion and the relative importance of each criterion in the global value. The choice is made by identifying the criterion which maximises the multi-attribute value function $f(\vec{a})$ where $\vec{a}$ represents the vector of the attributes. The final choice is made by identifying the alternative that maximises the multi-attribute value function.[3]

In the widely used, simplified method with uni-dimensional functions, the a_{ik} scores are normalised from the natural scale into a conventional scale, from 0 to 1, representing the value associated with each impact. On this scale, the first value indicates a situation of minimum utility and 1 indicates the maximum satisfaction for the decision maker.

$$v_{ij} = f_j(a_{jk}) \quad \text{for} \quad i = 1, 2, ..., n \quad \text{and} \quad j = 1, 2, ..., k \quad (5.10)$$

which when applied to the values in Table 5.3, leads to the construction of a new matrix. This matrix can allow the alternatives to be ranked using, for example, the 'worst case' criterion. This consists of applying a 'max min' logic to minimise the risk of opting for alternatives with low utility levels, even for a single attribute. The minimum value for each alternative is then selected and used to rank the alternatives (Colorni and Laniado, 1989). Many MADM techniques require further information from the decision maker, that is an expression of the importance or priority of the different attributes. This means defining a vector in which a weight w_j, usually scalar, is associated to each of the j attributes so that:

$$\sum_{j=1}^{k} w_j = 1 \quad (5.11)$$

Now a new matrix can be obtained of the 'weighted values' z_{ij}, multiplying each value in 5.10 by the relative weight, v_{iz}.

$$z_{ij} = v_{ij} \cdot w_j \quad \text{for} \quad i = 1, 2, ..., n \quad \text{and} \quad j = 1, 2, ..., k. \quad (5.12)$$

Returning briefly to the 'max min' ranking, the ranking procedure seen before can be applied using data from 5.12, which here is identified as a 'weighted worst case' (Colorni and Laniado, 1989).

Finally, on the 'weighted value' matrix an aggregation procedure must be applied to obtain the final ranking. With the aggregation procedure, a real value (s) is identified that expresses the agreement, or value, deriving from opting for a given alternative. The ranking of the alternatives is implicitly determined by the transformation of the problem from multi-attribute in 'mono-attribute'. For example, a cardinal value is associated with each alternative using the summation of the weighted values of that alternative, or (Voogd, 1983):

$$s_i = \sum_{j=1}^{k} z_{ij} \quad \text{for} \quad i = 1, 2, ..., n \qquad (5.13)$$

The alternative that maximises the overall preferences of the decision maker is the one presenting the maximum value *s*.

There are no substantial criticisms of the value function approach and, in fact, it is often even called the 'exact method' of MADM. The only real problem is the assigning of the value function. This is why, faced with the possibility of using a sophisticated but complicated model, less elaborate but more flexible methods are chosen, such as the two described below.

The hierarchic analysis

The Analytical Hierarchy Process – AHP (Saaty, 1980), as one of the value functions methods, is based on the assumption that the decision makers may always express their preferences. Therefore, it is possible to represent the relative importance and an overall score to each attribute. AHP is one of the most widely applied MADM methods but also one of the more criticised by specialists.

Within AHP, the valuation decision process is faced through different steps, dividing the overall decision problem into several less complex ones, which have easier solutions. The first phase of the analysis defines the objective of the choice, the criteria for valuating the achievement of the objective (attributes), and the alternatives amongst which the choice must be made. Moreover, the structure of the decision maker's preferences must be analysed and formalised in order to evaluate the trade-off between the options. In the next recapitulation phase, the most satisfactory alternative must be decided by ranking on the basis of the criteria determined in the previous phase.

The analysis and recapitulation phases are resolved on the basis of a decomposition principle, pair-wise comparisons and hierarchical composition. The first principle, by means of a breakdown of the problem, leads to the definition of a structure that allows ranking the information of the reciprocal relations of the aspects which influence the final choice. The procedure can be carried out bottom-up or, more often, top-down. The structure of breakdown is organised by specifying, in order, the global objective (super-criterion), valuation criteria (attribute), sub-criteria (parameters) and the alternatives. Figure 5.5 illustrates a four-level hierarchy relating to the choice between three alternatives according to three criteria: first level – alternative selection; second level – criteria of choice (attributes); third level – parameters expressing each attribute; fouth level – alternatives.

The decomposition task, as well as providing an overview of all the aspects that may determine a decision, prepares the ground for the subsequent

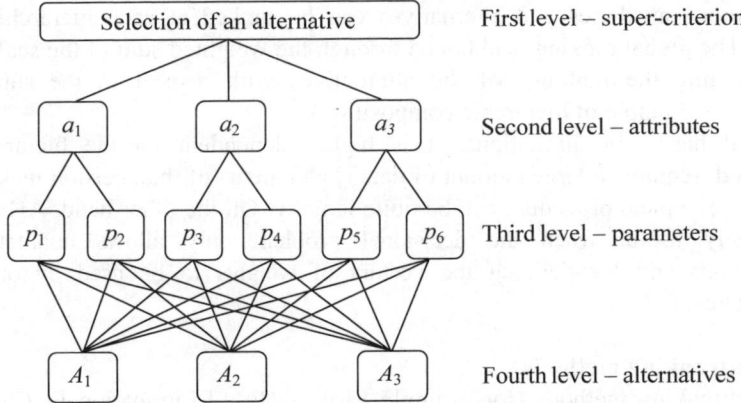

Figure 5.5   The structure of hierarchic analysis

valuation based on the principle of pair-wise comparisons. So the decision maker can concentrate on solving many small, partial problems, and then summarise the global solution, instead of having to consider contemporarily all aspects of the problem.

The global preference of the decision maker is reached starting from the preferences expressed between the pair-wise comparisons:

1.   among the alternatives with reference to one parameter at a time;
2.   among the parameters with reference to each attribute;
3.   among the attributes with reference to the super-criterion.

The pair-wise comparisons are organised in square matrices, positive and reciprocal, where the numbers represent the decision maker's preference for the element reported in the row regarding the one reported in the column. The pair-wise comparisons require a suitable scale to represent preferences among alternatives, parameters and attributes. Referring to psychological studies on 'indistinguishability classes', Saaty (1980) proposed a scale of values that can translate qualitative comparisons into quantitative terms. This scale of relative importance covers an interval of values from 1 (equal importance) to 9 (extreme importance) and also defines the reciprocal values of the precedents because, for example, when a preference intensity of 3 is assigned to one aspect compared to another, then the latter has a preference intensity that is the reciprocal of the former (1/3). The scale proposed by Saaty (1/9–9) is not the only one in the literature. Other authors have proposed more restricted (1/5–5) or wider scales (0–100). Starting from the pair-wise comparisons data, eigenvectors are calculated according to which parameters, attributes and alternatives can be ranked at each hierarchical level. The global ranking is obtained through the weighted sum of the scalars representing the rankings of the alternatives with respect to the super-criterion (principle of hierarchic composition).

AHP has some limitations: it is highly dependent on the hierarchy assumed, requires a large amount of data (judgements of the decision maker) and the complete procedure can be quite lengthy. On the other hand, AHP is extremely useful when the decisional problem only allows qualitative evaluations and for defining the vectors of weights to be used by other procedures.

The outranking methods

The outranking methods (for example ELECTRE – ELimination Et Choix TRaduisant la rEalité) have been developed in France (Roy, 1985) and are based on the concept of outranking and concordance/discordance analysis. These methods are based on a pair-wise comparison between every pair of alternatives being considered, trying to identify when one alternative 'outranks' another, which means that it is at least as good as the other. The objective is to eliminate the alternatives that are dominated by the others.

The concept of outranking (Roy, 1974) implies that one alternative A outranks another B when, starting from the decision maker's preferences, enough arguments can be found to say that A is at least as good as B (concordance), and there are not enough arguments against that (discordance). The different outranking methods differ in the way this definition is formalised. Given two alternatives, there are three possibilities as a result of their comparison: $A_i > A_j$ or $A_i < A_j$: one outranks the other ($A_i \uparrow A_j$ or $A_i \downarrow A_j$); $A_i = A_j$: the alternatives are indifferent ($A_i \ I \ A_j$); A_i and A_j are incomparable ($A_i \ S \ A_j$).

Based on this idea, outranking methods generally involve two consecutive steps:

1. construction of an outranking relation of the decision maker's preferences: defining concordance and discordance indices;
2. exploitation (using assignment procedures) of the outranking relation depending on the nature of the problem to be solved: combining the concordance and discordance indices.

There are several ways to define the concordance and discordance index. The concordance index used in ELECTRE I can be defined as follows:

$$c_{ij} = \sum w_k \quad \text{with} \quad c_{ij} = \left\{ k : v_{ki} \geq v_{kj} \right\} \quad (5.14)$$

where k is the set of criteria for which alternative i is equal or preferred to alternative j. The index takes values between 1 and 0: value 1 when A_i is better than A_j for all criteria and value 0, when A_i is worse than A_j for all criteria.

The discordance index is calculated by the maximum difference for which i is dominated by j, divided by the maximum difference in absolute value between performances obtained in i and j.

$$d_{ij} = \frac{\max_{k \in D_{ij}} (v_{kj} - v_{ki})}{[\max (v_{kj} - v_{ki})]} \quad \text{with} \quad D_{ij} = \{ k: v_{ki} < v_{kj} \} \quad (5.15)$$

If alternative i is better than alternative j on all criteria, the discordance index is 0. When the alternative i is worse than alternative j in all criteria the discordance index is 1.

The information contained in the concordance and discordance matrices can lead to a ranking of the alternatives using different methods. A possible approach to attain a ranking of the alternatives on the basis of concordance and discordance matrices is the 'weak dominance' approach (Colorni and Laniado, 1989). The method is based on the assumption that, in comparing two alternatives A_i and A_j, the first dominates the second in the 'strong' or Paretian sense if $c_{ij} = 1$ (all aspects favour A_i) and $d_{ij} = 0$ (no aspect is contrary to A_i). In the case of weak dominance, the Paretian conditions are 'relaxed' through the definition of 'thresholds' of concordance S_c and discordance S_d, respectively. On the basis of these thresholds, A_i weakly dominates A_j if at the same time:

$$c_{ij} \geq S_c \quad \text{and} \quad d_{ij} \leq S_d \quad (5.16)$$

The cardinal and complete ranking of the n alternatives is achieved through a progressive relaxing of the two thresholds, that is reducing S_c and increasing S_d. This ranking does not provide a measurement of the overall performances of the alternative, but makes a judgement on the easiness of excluding it from the analysis, being weakly dominated. ELECTRE I leads to the identification of two subsets of the n alternatives, those which can surely be ignored and those which require further study. It is not therefore a matter of better alternatives, but of alternatives, which remain in play based on some considerations. Within this context the thresholds are intended as the minimum value of satisfaction (S_c) and maximum value of dissatisfaction (S_d) that the decision maker can tolerate. From application of the two thresholds to the two matrices, ELECTRE I determines a relation of outranking (preference) between the alternatives through a graphic analysis, and from this reaches the identification of incomparable alternatives on which to acquire further information. The version II of the ELECTRE method, based on the same logic, reaches a cardinal ranking of the alternatives (Goicoechea et al., 1982) determining the relationship of outranking based on two pairs of thresholds, one associated with a 'weak' value and one with a 'strong' value. Two outranking graphs (strong and weak) are thus created, from which one final average graph is worked out. This latter is then used to create two rankings of the alternatives, one descending (best vs. worst) and one ascending (worst vs. best), to derive a final ranking that combines both.

ELECTRE I and II are based on the idea of 'true criteria', which implies that any differences in performance between two criteria are considered as differences in preferences. However, it is not sometimes so easy to determine clearly the preferences when two performances are very close. For that purpose ELECTRE III uses 'quasi-criteria', defining two thresholds (preference and indifference) introducing the concept of 'weak' and 'strong' preferences. As in ELECTRE II, ELECTRE III is used for ranking problems, but in this more sophisticated method some fuzzy information is introduced by the definition of the preference and indifference thresholds when comparing alternatives against a specific attribute. The concordance and discordance indices are also based on this parameter, obtaining two complete pre-orders, ending in a weighted ranking of the alternatives.

Based on ELECTRE III, other versions have been developed for challenging specific problems. ELECTRE TRI is used for classification problems where the objective is to assign the alternatives in more than three categories (acceptable, indeterminate and unacceptable). ELECTRE IV has been developed for specific situations where the decision maker is unable or does not wish to specify the criteria weights. This method uses the same procedure as ELECTRE III, but the outranking is defined by referring directly to the performances of the alternatives (Belton and Stewart, 2002).

Another popular outranking method is PROMETHEE. This method (Brans and Vincke, 1985), like ELECTRE III, is based on weighted outranking relations. The differences between performances for each criteria are measured using different preference functions which describe the intensity of the preference of an alternative *a* over alternative *b*.

The PROMETHEE method can be described in the following steps. The first step consists of building the evaluation matrix by defining the alternatives and the criteria against which they will be evaluated (the criteria can be measured in different units and scales). The next step involves the specification of the preference structure (by introducing generalised criteria) to remove scaling effects. From this point, PROMETHEE specifies the dominance relation by building a multi-criteria preference index that represents the strength of the assumption that one alternative is preferred to the others and creating an associated outranking graph that represents the weakness of the assumption.

$$\pi(a,b) = \sum_{j=1}^{n} w_j P_j(a,b) \tag{5.17}$$

This dominance index is summarised in two index flows that represent both how an alternative is preferred over the others and how the others are preferred over this alternative:

$$\phi^+(a) = \sum_{b \in A} \pi(a,b) \text{ inflows: how } a \text{ is preferred over others} \tag{5.18}$$

$$\phi^-(a) = \sum_{b \in A} \pi(a,b) \text{ outflows: how the others are preferred over } a \tag{5.19}$$

The exploitation for decisional aid differs depending on the version of the method. PROMETHEE I provides a partial ranking of the alternatives where the best one has ϕ^+ and the lower ϕ^-. In PROMETHEE II a complete pre-order is derived from the net flow of each alternative (inflows–outflows) $\phi(a) = \phi^+(a) - \phi^-(a)$. Other more sophisticated versions have been developed (Promethee III, Promethee IV and Promethee V) to tackle more complicated problems, in particular those with a stochastic component.

5.2.3   Fuzzy Sets

One of the main problems in applying MCDM in integrated water resources management is the quality of information available. Sometimes the effects over a long period of WRM cannot be identified and this makes it more difficult to analyse the consequences, such as the environmental effects of building a dam. Many hydrological models have been developed to simulate certain aspects of water problems but in general they are too rough to represent all the effects of a certain decision. In integrated water resources management, the uncertainty and vagueness of the information has to be taken into account. On the other hand, decision makers normally encounter a lot of problems to identify precisely their preferences. Fuzzy sets is a way to model vagueness and imprecision.

The fuzzy set, introduced by Zadeh (1965), cannot be considered as model in itself, but as a tool that, in given circumstances, could be very helpful in MCDM. The fuzzy approach underlies the fact that, in the real world, decision makers cannot normally define their preferences within a precise (crisp) logic, and provide an explicit way to represent the vagueness of the decision maker's mind and real word aspects.

Formally a crisp set $A \subset X$, can be represented in terms of a membership function $I_A(\vec{x})$, such that for any object $\vec{x} \in X$, $I_A(\vec{x}) = 1$ if $\vec{x} \in A$, otherwise $I_A(\vec{x}) = 0$. Given the set of alternatives A that dominates an alternative b, for $\vec{x} \in X$, the alternatives are $\vec{x} \in A$ or $\vec{x} \notin A$.

The fuzzy set approach replaces the indictor function of a set by a membership function that represents up to what level we can say that $\vec{x} \in A$, what is $0 \leq \mu_A(\vec{x}) \leq 1$. Normally in the real world when we have to establish our preferences, we are more fuzzy than 'crisp' in our judgements. When we use qualitative variables, the outranking concept, establishing goals or aspiration levels of the value function, the use of fuzzy sets is very helpful. All the most common MCDM approaches, such as AHP, ELECTRE, Goal Programming, and so on, have their fuzzy version (Fuller and Carlsson, 1996).

5.3   A SURVEY OF MULTIPLE CRITERIA DECISION MAKING APPLICATIONS IN WATER RESOURCES MANAGEMENT

In this survey, we present the main contributions on the application of MCDM techniques in the last ten years in the most important journals related with MCDM and WRM. This study is not meant to be exhaustive, and just a small number of articles have been analysed. For that reason other interesting papers have been omitted in this analysis. In any case, our objective is to present a general outlook of the last applications of MCDM in the field of WRM, evidencing the integration aspects. A summary of the articles analysed is presented in the appendix.

In MCDM there is not a common framework regarding the models to apply to support the decision-making process. Different researchers with different backgrounds use the multi-criteria methods according to their needs in alternative ways. In addition, different types of problems are faced under different circumstances. Many MCDM techniques and applications have been developed in the field of water resources management. Earlier examples can be found in Haimes et al. (1974), where the use of the surrogate worth trade-off method as a decision tool in water resources planning is discussed, Cohon and Marks (1975) who presented an early review of multi-objective programming techniques, and in Goicoechea et al. (1982).

In WRM, a broad type of problem can be encountered. The different nature of the problems motivates the different MCDM methodologies used and it is difficult to find the most suitable technique for a specific problem or type of problems. In fact, there are no strict relationships between methods and problems. Furthermore, the selection of MCDM techniques depends also on the availability of information and their quality.

Regarding the main problems faced in the different analyses (see Table 5.2), water scarcity is dominant in the survey. Water scarcity is one of the main problems currently in the Mediterranean area and developing countries, especially in the Middle East where the low levels of water resources combined with high rates of population increase become serious constraints to development. However, applications normally consider more than a single issue because of the interrelation with the other major problems related with water. In that sense Al-Shemmeri et al. (1997) and Jaber and Mohsen (2001) face the problem of water scarcity management in Jordan from an integrated perspective. Other papers also present problems related to water quality. Quality in surface water affected by agriculture are analysed by Heilman et al. (1997) or affected by wastewater planning in Kholghi (2001). Shafike et al. (1992) describe problems in groundwater contamination management and Woldt and Bogardi (1992) consider groundwater monitoring system design. Other examples in flood control can be seen in Tkach and Simonovich (1997) and Janssen et al. (2005), where the MCDM are combined with GIS tools, or in transboundary contexts as in Özelkan and Duckstein (1996).

An interesting question that arises from the survey is the fact that most of the analysis attempts to assist decision makers from a strategic perspective because of the evolution of the water problem issues in a global perspective (see Table 5.3). MCDM, initially developed for operational analysis, has evolved also to become a very useful tool in strategic planning and management. Specific examples in river basin planning can be found in Pouwels et al. (1995) and Hamalainen et al. (2001). In some problems, normally at operative level, only quantitative information derived from technical data was analysed, also using hydrological models (Prathapar et al., 1997). In other cases, mainly at strategic level, politicians and other non-

Table 5.2   Distribution of the papers by type of problem

Type of problem	Paper	%
Water scarcity	17	40
River basin management	8	19
Reservoir management	8	19
Water quality	6	14
Flood control	1	2
Power generation	1	2
Transboundary	1	2
Total	*42*	*100*

technical decision makers need to express their preferences and their points of view using qualitative information as well. At a strategic level, some non-commensurable criteria were also found using qualitative data in order to assess the impact of each alternative against each criterion, as in De Marchi et al. (2000) where the impact of the different policy options presented in the analysis are constructed based on qualitative scales.

In most of the papers the feasible set of solutions is discrete (see Table 5.4). Some authors have used a combination of methodologies starting from a continuous set of alternatives to develop a discrete set to be analysed in a second step, as in Ko et al. (1992) and Ridgley et al. (1997) where continuous methods are applied to identify non-dominated solutions and then discrete methods are used to select the preferred one. Regarding the type of context where MCDM methods were applied, most of the problems deal with the selection of the best alternative from predefined courses of action or a ranking of them. For example in reservoir management (Mahmoud et al., 2002) the choice of different management alternatives is made from a list of alternatives previously selected regarding technical feasibility. Continuous applications include Prathapar et al. (1997) and Bazzani et al. (2005) where the objective is to identify the optimal combination of crops regarding their water consumption, Heilman et al. (1997) where the effects of the quality of pollutants and economic returns are evaluated on different management systems, and Lee and Wen (1997) where the optimal solution is derived from the pollution assimilative capacity and the cost of treatment of wastewater.

One of the main problems in applying MCDM techniques is to identify a feasible set of alternatives as was explained in the previous section, for

Table 5.3   Distribution of the papers by decision context

Decision context	Paper	%
Strategic	30	71
Operational	12	29
Total	*42*	*100*

Table 5.4   Distribution of the papers by type of set of alternatives

Set of alternatives	Paper	%
Discrete	29	69
Continuous	11	26
Mixed	2	5
Total	*42*	*100*

example in water allocation where the alternatives are implicitly defined as a combination of decision variables subjected to a certain number of constraints. In this case, the objective of the analysis would be the selection of the best alternative from an infinite range of possibilities. In IWRM, considering water as a scarce resource, the main constraints are the quantity of water for different purposes and the quality of water under standards depending on the final use of the water. This kind of analysis is usually done at operational level; examples can be found in Harboe (1992) and Ko et al. (1992) related to reservoir management, and Shafike et al. (1992) and Woldt and Bogardi (1992) in groundwater management.

The identification of a set of alternatives could be seen not only as a final analysis, but as a preliminary step for the evaluation analysis. In some examples (Ko et al., 1992; Gupta et al., 2000) both type of analysis have been done, where a set of alternatives, subjected to constraints of quantity or environmental protection, has been identified in a first step. In the second step, the selection of the best alternative from those defined in the previous one is included.

Following the classification of MCDM analysis proposed in a previous section of this chapter, both main categories of methods, MODM and MADM, are used in the same proportion (see Table 5.5). Moreover, several articles present comparative studies of the different methods with the aim of identifying the methodology that satisfies the specific characteristics of the problems presented. Some papers have emphasised the problem to find the appropriate technique to be applied in different cases as in water scarcity in Raju and Pillai (1999) where five different MCDM techniques were used to rank alternative policies in an irrigation area in Spain, reservoir management in Mahmoud et al. (2002) where also five different multi-criteria evaluation methods are compared for fish migration in the Red Bluff diversion dam, or river basin planning in the Flumen Monegros irrigation area in Spain (Raju et al., 2000).

Most of the MODM methods (see Table 5.6), that were initially developed to be applied in continuous problems, have been adapted for discrete problems. Within the MODM methods, Compromise Programming is the most widely used (Shafike et al., 1992), sometimes combined with fuzzy sets (Woldt and Bogardi, 1992).

Table 5.5   Distribution of the applications by type of methods

Type of method	Applications	%
MODM	28	47
MADM	32	53
Total	*60*	*100*

The MADM techniques were applied mainly at strategic level where some qualitative information was required (see Table 5.7). Examples can be found in Roy et al. (1992) with the analysis of the priority order in the use of a new water supply system. Within the MADM, there are four techniques that have been used in higher percentage: Value Functions, AHP , ELECTRE and PROMETHEE. Within the MADM methods, PROMETHEE is the most used (31 per cent), followed by AHP and then ELECTRE. All of them have available computer software that facilitates their use. A good example of PROMETHEE application can be found in Al-Shemmeri et al. (1997) where the decision making process is presented using a combination of techniques in the identification of the alternatives in strategic planning in Jordan. Other examples are Abu-Taleb and Mareschal (1995), also in Jordan, and Al-Kloub et al. (1997). Within other outranking applications different versions of ELECTRE are applied like ELECTRE I-II (Harboe, 1992), ELECTRE III (Roy et al., 1992; Bella et al., 1996) or ELECTRE-TRI (Raju et al., 2000). Some other MADM like AHP are all widely used (Qureshi et al., 1999; Jaber et al., 2001; Tongplew and Varawoot, 2003).

In all the cases analysed, the decision makers were always associated with public agencies. The problem of stakeholders' involvement has been studied in depth in some papers, as in De Marchi et al. (2000) where the preferences of the various actors involved are analysed in a municipality problem in Sicily, and in Hamalainen et al. (2001) where a framework for support of a multi-stakeholder decision process is described.

Table 5.6   Distribution of the applications by MODM methods

MODM method	Applications	%
MOLP	7	25
Compromise Programming	13	46
Goal Programming	8	29
Total	*28*	*100*

Table 5.7   Distribution of the applications by MADM methods

MADM method	Applications	%
Value functions	6	19
AHP	9	28
ELECTRE	7	22
PROMETHEE	10	31
Total	*32*	*100*

5.4 CONCLUSION

Since the first developments in Operations Research at the beginning of the last century, several MCDM methods have been developed and applied to water-related problems. In general terms, it is possible to affirm that integrated water resources management can be considered as a multi-criteria decision making problem itself. The first applications to water management in the 1970s were oriented to operational decision contexts with highly structured problems to be solved by just one decision maker. The evolution towards a more integrated approach in water management has imposed an evolution of the methods to assess water measures management under this new paradigm.

The use of MCDM has now been extended from operational to strategic level. At the strategic level, it becomes more difficult to find a well-defined problem and most of the criteria are non-commensurable. For this reason, methods applied also need to be able to take qualitative data into account.

A great number of multi-criteria methods have been applied over the last years in different situations and for different purposes in the field of integrated water resources management. The strongest argument for use of the methods was their ability to give better comprehension of the water problems and the possibility to explore conflicting points of view. It seems that recently more effort has been put into the application of existing methods than into the development of new ones. In general, many achievements have been obtained from these applications but also some problems have arisen.

The first group of problems relates to the information available. Some contributions tried to overcome the merely technical data perspective by including socioeconomic aspects in a more integrated manner. Nevertheless, the lack of suitable information for the evaluation process seems, at the moment, to be the most relevant problem, sometimes because of the randomness of future situations or the incomplete knowledge of experts. In general, uncertainty about the possible effects of alternative courses of action is also very high. For this reason, several applications have included the use of fuzzy sets in their applications.

The second group of problems refers to the transparency of the decision-making process in IWRM. Decision makers, normally politicians without a quantitative background, have difficulties accepting complicated methods even if they have a user-friendly software interface. If the algorithms used are too complicated to be understood by the decision maker, the decision-making process is seen as a black box, and the results can create some distrust and rejection within a decision group.

Thirdly, public administrations, whose responsibility is to make decisions in water management, are not experienced in applying this type of MCDM methodology. Sometimes thorough studies about alternatives within complex water resources problems are required, but this raises conflict with restrictions in cost and time that characterise administrative procedures. The public administration is conscious that the mono-criterion approach is not sufficient anymore to assess water resources problems, but on the other hand applying multi-criteria decision analysis in the real world can become difficult from the institutional point of view.

Finally, decision-making problems normally imply the existence of a group of decision makers with different conflicting points of view. Hence, Group Decision Making is becoming of more and more interest along with methodologies that allow more interactive and collaborative analyses of the alternatives, as well as the risk associated with each of them.

The trend in the last few years seems to emphasise the use of less complex MCDM methods instead of more sophisticated ones. The reason is that, in most cases, integrated water resources management implies public decisions at the strategic level that normally are undertaken by politicians without a technical background in water resources or in multi-criteria methods. The less complex MCDM methods can be used in this situation as they facilitate a higher level of transparency in the process.

In any case, a comprehensive framework for analysing policies and prioritising options to guide the decision-making process around integrated water resources management is needed. This framework needs to highlight the importance of structuring the problems, the use of understandable technical data combined with value judgments with an active participation of all the actors involved in the whole process.

NOTES

1. See Chapter 1 for a comprehensive discussion on policy issues related to water management.
2. A solution is Pareto-efficient if is not possible to identify an alternative solution which, within the set of those feasible, along with an improvement with respect to one objective, would not also imply a worsening of at least one other (Romero, 1991).
3. Although the terms 'value' and 'utility' are frequently used as synonyms (as in this chapter), it should be specified that, more accurately (Keeney and Raiffa, 1976), value functions are used for deterministic data, while utility functions are used in stochastic situations.

REFERENCES

Abu-Taleb, M.F. and B. Mareschal (1995), 'Water resources planning in the Middle East: application of the PROMETHEE V multicriteria method', *European Journal of Operational Research*, **81**, 500–511.
Al-Kloub, B., T. Al-Shemmeri and A. Pearman (1997), 'The role of weights in multicriteria decision aid, and the ranking of water projects in Jordan', *European Journal of Operational Research*, **99**(2), 278–288.

Al-Shemmeri, T., T. Al-Kloub and A. Pearman (1997), 'Computer aided decision support system for water strategic planning in Jordan', *European Journal of Operational Research*, **102**(3), 455–472.

Arondel, C. and P. Girardin (2000), 'Sorting cropping systems on the basis of their impact on groundwater quality', *European Journal of Operational Research*, **127**, 467–482.

Bazzani, G.M., S. Di Pasquale, V. Gallerani, S. Moranti, M. Raggi and D. Viaggi (2005), 'The sustainability of irrigated agricultural systems under the Water Framework Directive: first results', *Environmental Modelling and Software*, **20**, 165–175.

Beinat, E. (1997), *Value Functions for Environmental Management*, Dordrecht: Kluwer Academic Press.

Bella, A., L. Duckstein and F. Szidarovszky (1996), 'A multicriterion analysis of the water allocation conflict in the upper Rio Grande Basin', *Applied Mathematics and Computation*, **77**, 245–265.

Belton, V. and T.J. Stewart (2002), *Multiple Criteria Decision Analysis: An Integrated Approach*, Boston: Kluwer Academic Publishers.

Bender, M.J. and S.P. Simonovic (2000), 'A fuzzy compromise approach to water resource systems planning under uncertainty', *Fuzzy Sets and Systems*, **115**(1), 35–44.

Berbel, J. and A. Rodriguez-Ocaña (1998), 'An MCDM approach to production analysis: An application to irrigated farms in Southern Spain', *European Journal of Operational Research*, **107**, 108–118.

Bogardi, I. and L. Duckstein (1992), 'Interactive and multiobjective analysis embedding the decision maker's implicit preference function', *Water Resources Bulletin*, **28**(1), 75–88.

Brans, J.P. and P. Vincke (1985), 'A preference ranking organization method: the PROMETHEE method for multiple criteria decision making', *Management Science*, **31**, 647–656.

Cain, J.D., K. Jinapala, I.W. Makin, P.G. Somaratna, B.R. Ariyaratna and L.R. Perera (2003), 'Participatory decision support for agricultural management. A case study from Sri Lanka', *Agricultural Systems*, **76**, 457–482.

Chang, N., C.G. Wen and S.L. Wu (1995), 'Optimal management of environmental and land resources in a reservoir watershed by multiobjective programming', *Journal of Environmental Management*, **44**, 145–161.

Chang, N., C.G. Wen, Y.L. Chen and Y.C. Yong (1996), 'A grey fuzzy multiobjective programming approach for the optimal planning of a reservoir watershed. Part A: Theoretical development', *Water Resources*, **30**(10), 2329–2334.

Chang, N., C.G. Wen, Y.L. Chen and Y.C. Yong (1996), 'A grey fuzzy multiobjective programming approach for the optimal planning of a reservoir watershed. Part B: Application', *Water Resources*, **30**(10), 2335–2340.

Charnes, A., W.W. Cooper and R. Ferguson (1955), 'Optimal estimation of executive compensation by linear programming', *Management Science*, **1**, 138–151.

Cohon, J.L. and D.H. Marks (1975), 'A review and evaluation of multiobjective programming techniques', *Water Resources Research*, **11**, 208–220.

Colorni, A. and E. Laniado (1989), 'Sistemi di supporto alle decisioni per la valutazione di Impatto Ambientale', in INEA, *Problemi economici nei rapporti tra agricoltura e ambiente, Atti del XXV Convegno SIDEA*, Bologna: Il Mulino, pp. 123–139.

De Marchi, B., S.O. Funtowicz, S. Lo Cascio and G. Munda (2000), 'Combining participative and institutional approaches with multicriteria evaluation. An empirical study for water issues in Troina, Sicily', *Ecological Economics*, **34**, 267–282.

Dhillon, J.S., S.C. Parti and D.P. Kothari (2001), 'Fuzzy decision making in multiobjective long-term scheduling of hydrothermal system', *Electrical Power and Energy Systems*, **24**(2001), 19–29.

EC (European Communities) (2000), 'Directive 200/60/EC of the European Parliament and of the Council of 23 October 2000 establishing a framework for Community action in the field of water policy', *Official Journal of the European Communities*, L **372**(43), 1–73.

Fuller, R. and C. Carlsson (1996), 'Fuzzy multiple criteria decision making', *Fuzzy Sets and Systems*, **78**, 139–153.

Goicoechea, A., Hansen, D.R. and L. Duckstein (1982), *Multiobjective Decision Analysis with Engineering and Business Applications*, New York: John Wiley & Sons.

Goicoechea, A., E.Z. Stakhiv and F. Li (1992), 'Experimental evaluation of multiple criteria decision models for application to water resources planning', *Water Resources Bulletin*, **28**(1), 89–102.

Gómez-Limón, J.A. and J. Berbel (2000), 'Multicriteria analysis of derived water demand functions: a Spanish case study', *Agricultural Systems*, **63**(1), 49–72.

Gupta, A.P., R. Harboe and M.T. Tabucanon (2000), 'Fuzzy multiple-criteria decision making for crop area planning in Narmada river basin', *Agricultural Systems*, **63**, 1–18.

Haimes, Y.Y., W.A. Hall and H.T. Freedman (1974), 'Multiobjectives in water resource system analysis: the surrogate worth trade off method', *Water Resources Research*, **10**(4), 615–623.

Hamalainen, R.P., E. Kettunen, M. Marttunen and H. Ehtamo (2001), 'Evaluating a framework for multi-stakeholder decision support in water resources management', *Group Decision and Negotiation*, **10**(4), 331–353.

Harboe, R. (1992), 'Multiobjective Decision Making Techniques for Reservoir Operation', *Water Resources Bulletin*, **28**(1), 103–110.

Hazell, P.B.R. and R.D. Norton (1986), *Mathematical Programming for Economic Analysis in Agriculture*, New York: Macmillan Publishing Company.

Heilman, P., D.S. Yakowitz and L.J. Lane (1997), 'Targeting farms to improve water quality', *Applied Mathematics and Computation*, **83**(2–3), 173–194.

Hwang, C.L. and K. Yoon (1981), *Multiple Attribute Decision Making: Method and Applications*, Berlin: Springer-Verlag.

Jaber, J.O. and M.S. Mohsen (2001), 'Evaluation of non-conventional water resources supply in Jordan', *Desalination*, **136**, 83–92.

Janssen, R., H. Goosen, M.L. Verhoeven, J.T.A. Verhoeven, A.Q.A. Omtzgt and E. Maltby (2005), 'Decision support for integrated wetland management', *Environmental Modelling and Software*, **20**, 215–229.

Keeney, R.L. and H. Raiffa (1976), *Decisions with Multiple Objectives: Preferences and Value Tradeoffs*, New York: John Wiley & Sons.

Ko, S.K., D.G. Fontane and J.W. Labadie (1992), 'Multiobjective optimization of reservoir systems operation', *Water Resources Bulletin*, **28** (1), 111–129.

Kholghi, M. (2001), 'Multi-Criterion Decision-Making Tools for Wastewater Planning Management', *Journal of Agricultural Science and Technology*, **3**, 281–286.

Lee, C.S. and C.G. Wen (1997), 'Fuzzy goal programming approach for water quality management in a river basin', *Fuzzy Sets and Systems*, **89**, 181–192.

Lee, Y.W., I. Bogardi and J.H. Kim (2000), 'Decision of water supply line under uncertainty, *Water Resources*, **34**(13), 3371–3379.

Mahmoud, M.R., H. Fahmy and J.W. Labadie (2002), 'Multicriteria Siting and Sizing of Desalination Facilities with Geographic Information System', *Journal of Waterway, Port, Coastal and Ocean Engineering*, **128**(2), 113–120.

Nayak, R.C. and R.K. Panda (2001), 'Integrated Management of a Canal Command in a River Delta using Multi-Objective Techniques', *Water Resources Management*, **15**, 383–401.

Nijkamp, P. and A. van Delft (1977), *Multi-Criteria Analysis and Regional Decision-Making*, Leiden: Martinus Nijhoff Social Science Division.

Özelkan, E.C. and L. Duckstein (1996), 'Analysing water resources alternatives and handling criteria by multi criterion decision techniques', *Journal of Environmental Management*, **48**, 69–96.

Pouwels, I.H.M., H.G. Wind and V.J. Witter (1995), 'Multiobjective decision-making in integrated water management', *Physics and Chemistry of the Earth*, **20**(3–4), 221–227.

Prathapar, S.A., W.S. Meyer and J.C. Madden (1997), 'SWAG MAN options: A hierarchical multicriteria framework to identify profitable land uses that minimize water table rise and salinization', *Applied Mathematics and Computation*, **83**(2–3), 217–240.

Qureshi, M.E. and S.R.Harrison (2001), 'A decision support process to compare Riparian revegetation options in Scheu Creek catchment in North Queensland', *Journal of Environmental Management*, **62**, 101–112.

Qureshi, M.E., S.R. Harrison and M.K. Wegener (1999), 'Validation of multicriteria analysis models', *Agricultural Systems*, **62**, 105–116.

Raj, A.P. and D.N. Kumar (1998), 'Ranking multi-criterion river basin planning alternatives using fuzzy numbers', *Fuzzy Sets and Systems*, **100**, 89–99.

Raju, S. and C.R.S. Pillai (1999), 'Multicriterion decision making in river basin planning and development', *European Journal of Operational Research*, **112**, 249–257.

Raju, S., L. Duckstein and C. Arondel (2000), 'Multicriterion analysis for sustainable water resources planning: a case study in Spain', *Water Resources Management*, **14**, 435–456.

Rehman, T. and C. Romero (1993), 'The Application of the MCDM Paradigm to the Management of Agricultural Systems: Some Basic Considerations', *Agricultural Systems*, **3**, 239–255.

Ridgley, M., D.C. Penn and L. Tran (1997), 'Multicriterion decision support for a conflict over stream diversion and land-water reallocation in Hawai', *Applied Mathematics and Computation*, **83**(2–3), 153–172.

Romero, C. (1991), *Handbook of Critical Issues in Goal Programming*, Oxford: Pergamon Press.

Romero, C. and T. Rehman (1989), *Multiple Criteria Analysis for Agricultural Decisions,* Amsterdam: Elsevier.

Roy, B. (1974), 'Critères multiples et modelisation des preferences – l'apport des relations de surclassement', *Revue d'Economie Politique*, **1**, 1–44.

Roy, B. (1985), *Méthodologie Multicritère d'Aide à la Décision*, Paris: Economica.

Roy, B., R. Slowinski and W. Treichel (1992), 'Multicriteria programming of water supply systems for rural areas', *Water Resources Bulletin*, **28**(1), 13–31.

Saaty, T.L. (1980), *The Analytic Hierarchy Process*, New York: McGraw-Hill.

Shafike, N.G., L. Duckstein and T. Maddock (1992), 'Multicriterion Analysis of Groundwater Contamination Management', *Water Resources Bulletin*, **28**(1), 33–42.

Thongplew, K. and V. Varawoot (2003), 'Multicriteria decision making for multireservoir water allocation during shortage: a case study of upper Mun basin', Fourth Regional Symposium on Infrastructure Development in Civil Engineering, 3–5 April 2003, Bangkok, Thailand.

Tkach, R.J. and S.P. Simonovic (1997), 'A new approach to multi-criteria decision making in water resources', *Journal of Geographic Information and Decision*

Analysis, **1**(1), 25–43.

Voogd, H. (1983), *Multicriteria Evaluation for Urban-and-Regional Planning*, London: Pion Limited.

Woldt, W. and I. Bogardi (1992), 'Ground water monitoring network design using multiple criteria decision making and geostatistics', *Water Resources Bulletin*, **28**(1), 45–62.

Zadeh, L.A. (1965), 'Fuzzy sets', *Information and Control*, **8**, 338–353.

Zeleny, M. (1973), 'Compromise programming', in J.L. Cochrane and M. Zeleny (eds), *Multiple Criteria Decision Making*, Columbia: University of South Carolina Press.

Zeleny, M. (1974), *Linear Multiobjective Programming*, Berlin: Springer-Verlag.

Zeleny, M. (1982), *Multiple Criteria Decision Making*, New York: McGraw Hill.

APPENDIX

n.	Authors	Year	Problem	Strategic	Operational	Fuzzy	MOLP	Compr. Prog.	Goal Prog.	Value function	AHP	PROMETHEE	ELECTRE
1	Roy, B., Slowinski, R., Treichel, W.	1992	WATER SCARCITY	✓				✓					✓
2	Shafike, N.G., Duckstein, L., Maddock, T.	1992	GROUNDWATER QUALITY		✓	✓		✓					✓
3	Woldt, W., Bogardi, I.	1992	GROUNDWATER QUALITY		✓								
4	Bogardi, I., Duckstein, L.	1992	RESERVOIR MANAGEMENT		✓								
5	Goicoechea, A., Stakhiv, E.Z., Li, F.	1992	WATER SCARCITY					✓					✓
6	Harboe, R.	1992	RESERVOIR MANAGEMENT		✓			✓	✓				✓
7	Ko, S.K., Fontane, D.G., Labadie, J.W.	1992	RESERVOIR MANAGEMENT					✓	✓	✓			
8	Chang, N., Wen, C.G. Wu, S.L.	1995	RESERVOIR PLANNING	✓							✓		
9	Pouwels, I.H.M., Wind, H.G., Witter, V.J.	1995	RIVER BASIN PLANNING	✓									
10	Abu-Taleb, M.F., Mareschal, B.	1995	WATER SCARCITY	✓		✓						✓	
11	Chang, N., Wen, C.G., Chen, Y.L., Yong, Y.C.	1996	RESERVOIR PLANNING	✓			✓						
12	Özelkan, E.C., Duckstein, L.	1996	TRANSBOUNDARY		✓								
13	Bella, A., Duckstein, L., Szidarovszky, F.	1996	WATER SCARCITY			✓		✓				✓	
14	Al-Shemmeri, T., Al-Kloub, T., Pearman, A.	1997	WATER SCARCITY		✓			✓					
15	Prathapar, S.A., Meyer, W.S., Madden, J.C.	1997	GROUNDWATER SCARCITY		✓		✓					✓	
16	Heilman, P., Yakowitz, D.S., Lane, L.J.	1997	WATER QUALITY		✓		✓						
17	Lee, C., Wen, C.	1997	WATER QUALITY	✓									
18	Ridgley, M., Penn, D.C., Tran, L.	1997	RIVER BASIN PLANNING	✓		✓		✓	✓		✓		
19	Tkach, R.J., Simonovic, S.P.	1997	FLOOD CONTROL	✓					✓				
20	Al-Kloub, B., Al-Shemmeri, T., Pearman, A.	1997	WATER SCARCITY	✓									
21	Raj, P.A., Kumar, D.N.	1998	RIVER BASIN PLANNING				✓		✓				
22	Berbel, J., Rodriguez-Ocaña, A.	1998	WATER SCARCITY	✓									
23	Raju, S., Pillai, C.R.S.	1999	RIVER BASIN PLANNING	✓							✓	✓	✓
24	Qureshi, M.E., Harrison, S.R., Wegener, M.K.	1999	RIVER BASIN PLANNING								✓	✓	✓

Column groups: **MADM** = ELECTRE, PROMETHEE, AHP, Value function; **MODM** = Goal Prog., Compr. Prog., MOLP.

APPENDIX (continued)

n.	Authors	Year	Problem	ELECTRE	PROMETHEE	AHP	Value Function	Goal Prog.	Compr. Prog.	MOLP	Fuzzy	Operational	Strategic
				MADM	MADM	MADM	MADM	MODM	MODM	MODM			
25	Arondel, C., Girardin, P.	2000	GROUNDWATER QUALITY	✓								✓	
26	Raju, S., Duckstein, L., Arondel, C.	2000	WATER SCARCITY	✓	✓				✓				✓
27	Bender, M.J., Simonovic, S.P.	2000	RIVER BASIN PLANNING	✓					✓				✓
28	Gupta, A.P., Harboe, R., Tabucanon, M.T.	2000	WATER SCARCITY				✓			✓			✓
29	De Marchi, B., Funtowicz, S.O., Lo Cascio, S., Munda, G.	2000	WATER SCARCITY								✓		✓
30	Gómez-Limón, J.A., Berbel, J.	2000	WATER SCARCITY						✓		✓		✓
31	Lee, Y.W., Bogardi, I., Kim, J.H.	2000	WATER SCARCITY								✓		
32	Jaber, J.O., Mohsen, M.S.	2001	WATER SCARCITY					✓					✓
33	Hamalainen, R.P., Kettunen, E., Marttunen, M., Ehtamo, H.	2001	RIVER BASIN PLANNING							✓		✓	✓
34	Nayak, R.C., Panda, R.K.	2001	WATER SCARCITY	✓						✓	✓		✓
35	Dhillon, J.S., Parti, S.C., Kothari, D.P.	2001	POWER PRODUCTION		✓			✓			✓		✓
36	Qureshi, M.E., Harrison, S.R.	2001	RIVER BASIN PLANNING		✓	✓							
37	Kholghi, M.	2001	WATER QUALITY		✓		✓				✓		
38	Mahmoud, M.R., Fahmy, H. Labadie, J.W.	2002	RESERVOIR MANAGEMENT		✓		✓						
39	Cain, J.D., Jinapala, K., Makin, I.W., Somaratna, P.G., Ariyaratna, B.R., Perera, L.R.	2003	WATER SCARCITY										✓
40	Thongplew, K., Varawoot, V.	2003	RESERVOIR MANAGEMENT										✓
41	Janssen, R., Goosen, H., Verhoeven, M.L., Verhoeven, J.T.A., Omtzgt, A.Q.A., Maltby, E.	2005	RESERVOIR MANAGEMENT			✓	✓					✓	
42	Bazzani, G.M., Di Pasquale, S., Gallerani, V., Moranti, S., Raggi, M., Viaggi, D.	2005	WATER SCARCITY					✓					

130

6. Software Support for Multi-Criteria Decision Making

Marjan van Herwijnen and Ron Janssen

6.1 INTRODUCTION

Few decisions have a single objective. The very idea of making decisions suggests the need for considering multiple aspects and achieving a successful blend of performances. Management of water resources is no exception to this general rule. Multiple stakeholders participate in management of water resources. This results in multiple objectives to be considered by any decision maker involved in water management. Examples are:

- Selection of a management strategy for a freshwater lake. Objectives are water quality, water quantity, biodiversity, recreational quality, residential quality, cost, etc.;
- Selection of a flood management strategy. Objectives are risk of flooding, biodiversity, visual quality, land use and cost;
- Selecting a strategy for river basin management. Objectives are water quality, flood risks and navigation, but also visual quality of the landscape and biodiversity.

Because water is in many cases a public good, the decision maker is often a public body. This public body must take into account the interest of a multitude of stakeholders and has to be able to justify its decisions. The decision maker evaluates a set of alternatives, which represent the possible choices. The objectives to be achieved drive the design (or screening) of these alternatives and determine their overall evaluation. Attributes are the measurement rods for the objectives and specify the degree to which each alternative matches the objectives. Factual information and value judgements jointly establish the overall merits of each option and highlight the best solution.

The problems described above involve a set of alternatives that are evaluated on the basis of conflicting objectives. An objective is a statement about the desired state of the system under consideration. For any given objective, one or more different attributes are used to measure the performance in relation to that objective. These attributes are usually measured on different measurement scales. Multi-criteria analysis (MCA) can be used to address these types of problems. Multi-criteria analysis can be classified in a number of ways. A convenient distinction is that between discrete and continuous multi-criteria methods (Janssen, 1992, p. 53; Malczewski, 1999, p. 84). Continuous multi-criteria methods are intended to search for the best alternative among an infinite or very large set of feasible alternatives. These methods can be seen as a natural extension of linear and mathematical programming, Continuous multi-criteria methods can consider several objective functions simultaneously. Discrete multi-criteria methods are developed to analyse and rank a finite, moderate, small and discrete set of alternatives. Discrete multi-criteria methods compare and rank a discrete and finite set of alternatives. For practical reasons this chapter deals with discrete multi-criteria methods only.

The next section elaborates on the need to use software to effectively support the evaluation of MCA problems in practice. Then two case studies demonstrate the use of decision support software. The first case study describes the various steps of an evaluation procedure and how software can be used to support these steps. The final case study shows the use of graphical evaluation and how the results can be communicated to the stakeholders.

6.2   SOFTWARE FOR MULTI-CRITERIA ANALYSIS

Multi-criteria methods combine factual information with policy priorities. Therefore, they not only support decision making with multiple objectives but also discussions and negotiations between stakeholders involved in the decision process. Belton and Stewart (2002, p. 281) state that for the effective conduct of MCA good supporting software is essential. In this way the facilitator, analyst and decision maker are free from the technical implementation details, and are able to focus on the fundamental value judgments and choices. Although it is possible to set up macros in a spreadsheet to achieve this, it is more convenient to make use of specially designed software. This software should be visual and interactive to facilitate communication about the problem and the evaluation of the results. Interactive software permits information on evaluations, impact scores, priorities and other parameters to be easily entered and changed. Effective visual tools can be used to display the results back to the decision makers, for example by using a graphical presentation of a value function or of an aggregated evaluation result. These visual tools can help to create a better understanding of the issues.

MCA software tools can be subdivided into four groups:

1. Problem structuring for discrete choice problems;
2. Discrete choice problems;
3. Discrete group choice problems; and
4. Discrete spatial choice problems.

Most decision support systems assume that a problem is already structured (cause-effect relationships are known, evaluation criteria are specified, alternatives under evaluation are well described, etc.). But in practice this assumption is the exception rather than the norm. Therefore, a number of software tools are available to support the structuring of discrete choice problems (group 1). If a discrete choice problem is structured, many software tools are available to support the evaluation of the problem. Most of these tools were originally designed for individual support, or group support in which the group shares one single set of information (group 2). Lately, a number of developments have taken place in the field of real group systems. A group system allows more than one user to independently input their own evaluations and provides facilities for synthesising and displaying this information. Group systems can therefore be used to support discussions in stakeholder sessions (group 3). Another development taking place in the field of multi-criteria decision support is the integration of spatial data. Systems that allow space-dependent input data, incorporate spatial multi-criteria evaluation tools and can display the information and results spatially, are called spatial decision support systems (see also Herwijnen, 1999 and Uran, 2002). Most of these systems are tailor-made for one specific problem. But tools to support general discrete spatial choice problems can sometimes be found in specific procedures incorporated in a GIS (group 4).

Table 6.1 shows a list of software tools that could be used to support MCA in practice. Only off-the-shelf commercial software is presented. Software mainly available for academic use is not included. Note that the list is not complete and will, of course, rapidly be outdated. Other listings of MCA software can be found in Belton and Stewart (2002, pp. 345–350) and at http://www.lionhrtpub.com/orms/surveys/das/das.html.

For practical reasons this chapter focuses on software for discrete choice problems. Most software tools to support discrete choice problems from this list are designed around one multi-criteria technique. Because the objective of this chapter is to illustrate a range of methods, the software package DEFINITE is used to demonstrate the use of decision support software.

Table 6.1   MCA software

Package	Short description
Group 1. Problem structuring for discrete choice problems	
Decision Explorer 3.2	Qualitative data analysis, linking concepts through cognitive or cause maps (http://www.banxia.com)
Mind Manager 4.0	Structures complex situations through organising ideas and concepts, graphical visualisation with icons, graphics, colours and multimedia (http://www.mind-map.com)
Group 2. Discrete choice problems	
Criterium DecisionPlus 3.0	Value function model based on trade-off analysis (http://www.infoharvest.com)
DEFINITE 3.1	Multi-attribute value functions including options for imprecise preference information, cost-benefit analysis, outranking (http://www.definite-bosda.nl)
ELECTRE III-IV	Outranking relations using pseudo-criteria (http://www.lamsade.dauphine.fr/english/software.html#el34)
HIPRE	Multi-attribute value functions with imprecise preference information (http://www.hipre.hut.fi)
Hiview	Multi-attribute value functions (http://www.enterprise-lse.co.uk)
Logical Decisions 5.1	Multi-attribute value functions and AHP (http://www.logicaldecisions.com)
MacBeth	Multi-attribute value functions in an additive value model using qualitative judgements (http://www.m-macbeth.com/Msite.html)
VISA	Multi-attribute value functions, graphical interaction and presentation (http://www.simul8.com/visa.htm)
Group 3. Discrete group choice problems	
Team Expert Choice	AHP, pair wise comparisons (http://www.expertchoice.com)
VISA Groupware	Multi-attribute value functions (http://www.simul8.com/visa.htm)
Web-HIPRE	Multi-attribute value functions and AHP (http://www.hipre.hut.fi)
Group 4. Discrete spatial choice problems	
Idrisi 3.1	A GIS that includes the following decision support procedures: WEIGHT (AHP), MCE (Boolean combination, weighted linear combination or ordered weighted average), RANK (rank order the cells) and MOLA (allocate pixels to multiple objectives) (www.clarklabs.org)
EMDS	Ecosystem Management Decision Support; combines ArcGISTM, NetWeaver and Criterium DecisionPlus (http://www.fsl.orst.edu/emds)
Ilwis	Integrates spatial multi-criteria analysis in GIS using raster maps as criteria or locations as alternatives (http://www.itc.nl/ilwis)

6.3 FROM PROBLEM DEFINITION TO REPORT: SOLVING THE ALGAE PROBLEM IN GRAND ANSE, GRENADA

The first case study[1] is used to illustrate the four steps of an evaluation: Step 1: Problem definition; Step 2: Multi-criteria analysis; Step 3: Sensitivity analysis; and Step 4: Report. Figure 6.1 shows part of the main menu of DEFINITE including the first three steps.

With its abundant natural resources, outstanding beaches and the near shore coral reefs, Grand Anse in Grenada is the typical Caribbean paradise. Unfortunately, the coral reefs are at high risk due to near shore development, pollution and sedimentation. Parts of these problems are caused by the lack of a sewage system for solids. Most liquid waste is sent totally untreated into the sea, which causes high nutrient levels, algal growth, diminishing quality of corals, fish mortality and finally a decline of tourism and less income (see Figure 6.2).

Figure 6.1   Main menu: steps of an evaluation procedure

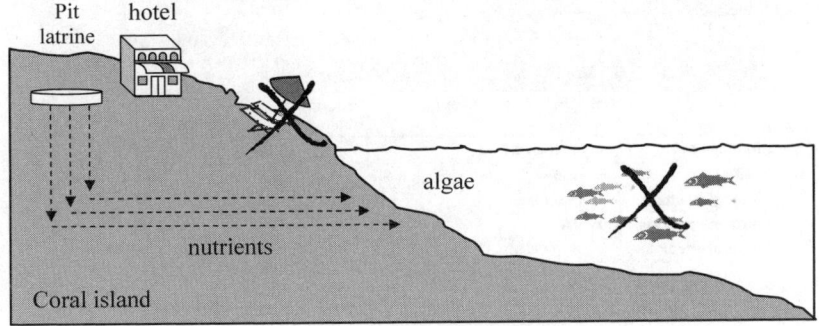

Figure 6.2   Problem chain in Grand Anse caused by the lack of a sewage system for solids

6.3.1   Step 1: Problem Definition

Step 1 involves:

1. Definition of alternatives: identify the policy alternatives which are to be compared with each other;
2. Selection and definition of criteria: identify the effects or indicators relevant for the decision; and
3. Assessment of scores for each alternative: assign values to each effect or indicator for all alternatives.

Definition of alternatives

Generating a complete set of relevant alternatives is a complex task. Political reasons, bad practice or the pressures of time may lead to an incomplete set. This can cause substantial delay because external pressure may force the decision maker to include additional alternatives at a later stage of the process. The effects table of 'Solving the algal problem in Grand Anse' is shown in Figure 6.3. The effects table includes three alternatives to deal with the algal problem:

1. Filtering: sewage is filtered before discharge;
2. Secondary treatment: connection of several households and commercial properties to the sewage system and the upgrading of the sewage plant to secondary treatment;
3. Tertiary treatment: connection of all households and commercial properties to the sewage system and the upgrading of the sewage plant to tertiary treatment.

	C/B	Unit	filtering	secondary treatment	tertiary treatment
financial costs	●	million G$	5.09	10.33	15.23
welfare	●	index	1.1	3.2	8.4
ecological effect	●	species	19	24	31
participation rate	●	%	41.16	27.44	13.72
cultural effect		--/+++	--	-	+

Figure 6.3   Problem definition: the effects table of 'Solving the algal problem in Grand Anse'

Selection and definition of criteria

The choice of decision criteria is a very important step in the MCA process. The criteria are specifications of the impacts that will be taken into account in the decision. The criteria must be unambiguous, and it must be possible to measure their performance with reasonable accuracy. The three alternatives to deal with 'Solving the algal problem in Grand Anse' are evaluated against five criteria:

1. Financial costs: these costs, measured in Grenada $, cover investment costs and maintenance costs;
2. Welfare: an index measuring the welfare of the people in Grand Anse;
3. Ecological effects: the ecological quality of the sea and its marine life, measured in number of fish species;
4. Participation rate: willingness of people to obey the new rules, measured as a percentage;
5. Cultural effects: possibility of preserving cultural practices.

Assessment of scores for each alternative

Scores can be assessed in many ways. Examples are simulation models, laboratory tests, direct measurement and expert judgment. Impact scores can be measured on a quantitative scale such as ratio, interval or monetary scale, or on a qualitative scale such as an ordinal, +++/--- , or binary scale. A +++/--- scale is useful to score expert judgment. In 'Solving the algal problem in Grand Anse' the criterion 'Cultural effect' is measured on a ---/+++ scale; the other four on a quantitative scale. Figure 6.3 shows this in the third column. The second column indicates whether a criterion is a benefit criterion (the higher the better) or a cost criterion (the lower the better).

6.3.2 Step 2: Multi-Criteria Analysis

Multi-criteria analysis is the second step in this evaluation procedure. The purpose of Step 2 is to derive a ranking of the alternatives. To do this the scores must be standardized to make them comparable, and weighted to determine the relative importance. The three elements of multi-criteria analysis are:

1. Standardisation;
2. Weighting; and
3. Ranking.

Standardisation

If the performances of the criteria are measured on different measurement scales (e.g. costs in million G$ and ecological effects in number of species), they must be standardised to a common dimension or dimensionless unit before the criteria can be combined. There are several ways to standardise the criteria. The simplest procedure involves scaling the performance according to the relative distance between zero and the maximum performance, called maximum standardisation. This means that for each criterion the alternative with the best effect receives a value of one and all other alternatives receive a value between one and zero according to the following formula:

$$\text{Benefit effect: } \frac{\text{Score}}{\text{Highest score}} \tag{6.1}$$

$$\text{Cost effect: } 1 - \frac{\text{Score}}{\text{Highest score}} \tag{6.2}$$

Alternatively, the performance can be scaled according to the relative position on the interval between the lowest and highest performance. This can be done using the following formula:

$$\text{Benefit effect: } \frac{\text{Score} - \text{lowest score}}{\text{Highest score} - \text{lowest score}} \tag{6.3}$$

$$\text{Cost effect: } 1 - \frac{\text{Score} - \text{lowest score}}{\text{Highest score} - \text{lowest score}} \tag{6.4}$$

It is also possible to specify for every effect an ideal or goal value and a worst value, and then scale the scores between these two values. This is called goal standardisation. A meaningful worst value can, for example, be the score in a reference year in the past. Goal values can sometimes be deducted from policy documents or environmental standards. In this case study all criteria are standardised using maximum standardisation. The linear value function linked to this standardisation is shown in Figure 6.4.

Although in practice the relationship between a criterion score and its value (utility) is usually more complex, a linear standardisation is often an acceptable approximation if the range of the scores is not too large. In those cases where a linear approximation is not acceptable, other, non-linear, standardisation or value functions should be used. An example of an S-shaped value function is presented in Figure 6.5.

In Figure 6.5 the range of standardisation is between ten and 35 species. The shape of the value function is in this case based on interviews with experts (Beinat, 1997). The value of filtering is low for criterion 'ecological effects'. Secondary treatment shows a substantial improvement. Tertiary treatment achieves the maximum value. The shape of the curve is dependent

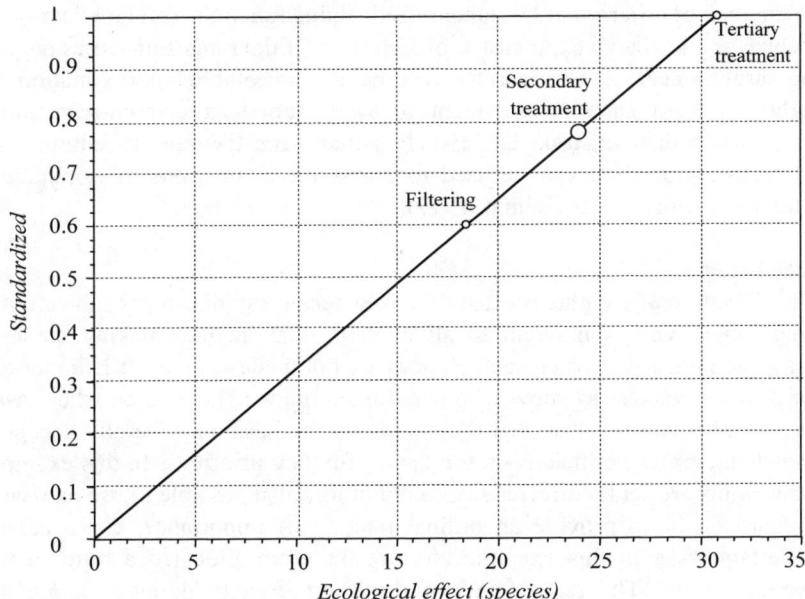

Figure 6.4   Linear standardisation of the ecological effects (number of species)

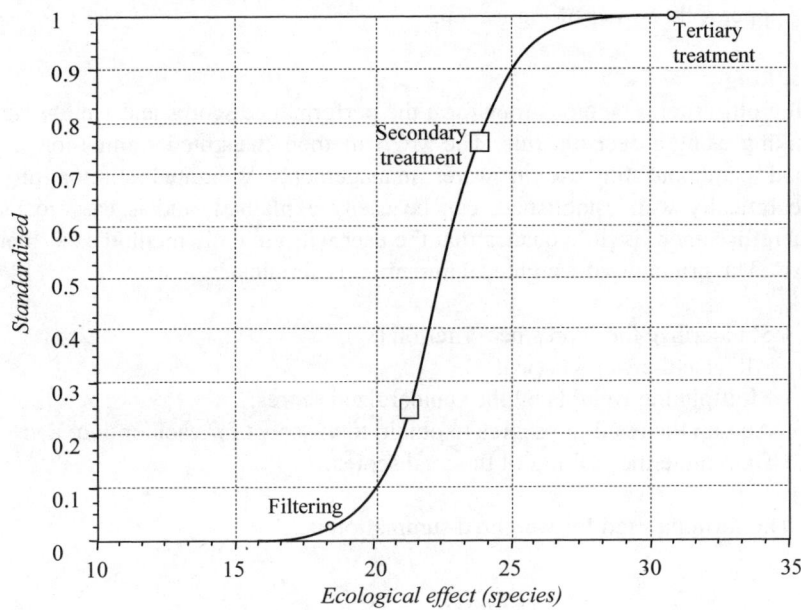

Figure 6.5   Standardisation of the ecological effects (number of species) using an S-shape value function

on the type of criterion to be standardised. Value functions can be linear or S-shaped, and also convex, concave or free form. If the ranges of scores are not too large, linear standardisation will be an acceptable approximation of reality in most cases. Assessment of value functions and corresponding weights is a difficult task. DEFINITE includes the EValue procedure. This interactive procedure can be used to assess these functions by conducting interviews with experts (Beinat, 1997).

Weighting

The allocation of weights is often criticised because it introduces subjectivity. This subjectivity is inherent to all methods that include making choices. Criticism is justified when such choices are not made explicit. It is important for decision makers to know who determined the weights and on what basis. The weights can be attributed by experts on the basis of generally accepted knowledge or by politicians on the basis of policy priorities. In this example the weights are set by direct assessment but it is also possible to use pair-wise comparison or to provide an ordinal ranking of importance. Costs are an important issue in this example and are therefore allocated a third of the overall weight. The remaining two thirds are equally divided among the remaining four criteria: welfare, ecological effects, participation rate and cultural effects. The distribution of the weights is shown in the pie chart in the upper right corner of Figure 6.6.

Ranking

All multi-criteria methods transform the performance scores and weights to a ranking using a decision rule. The MCA method 'weighted summation' is a good candidate for use in water management. Weighted summation is theoretically well established, can be easily explained, and is easy to use. Therefore, there is little chance that the user will view the method as a 'black box'. The principle of weighted summation is simple:

1. Standardize the scores per criterion ($\hat{s}_{ij}$);
2. Allocate the weights (w_i);
3. Multiply the weights by the standardized scores;
4. Add up the resulting scores to obtain total scores for each option; and
5. Determine the ranking of the total scores.

The formula used for weighted summation is:

$$\text{score}(a_j) = \sum_{i=1}^{N} w_i \cdot \hat{s}_{ij} \qquad (6.5)$$

where:

A is the set of alternatives with a_j (j = 1, ..., *M*);
C is the set of effects with c_i (i = 1, ..., *N*);
s_{ij} is the score of alternative a_j for effect c_i,
$\hat{s}_{ij}$ is the standardized score of alternative a_j for effect c_i,
w_i is the weight of effect c_i.

Figure 6.6 shows the results of weighted summation. It is clear that for the Grand Anse, the filtering option ranks first, followed by tertiary and secondary treatment. The stacked bars represent the total scores of the three alternatives and also show weighted contribution of each criterion to these totals.

The difficulty with weighted summation does not lie in the calculation but in choosing a good standardization method (the way in which the scores are converted to a common denominator) and in the setting of the weights. A disadvantage of the method is that it is less suitable for processing qualitative data. However, in practice the pluses and minuses used for qualitative

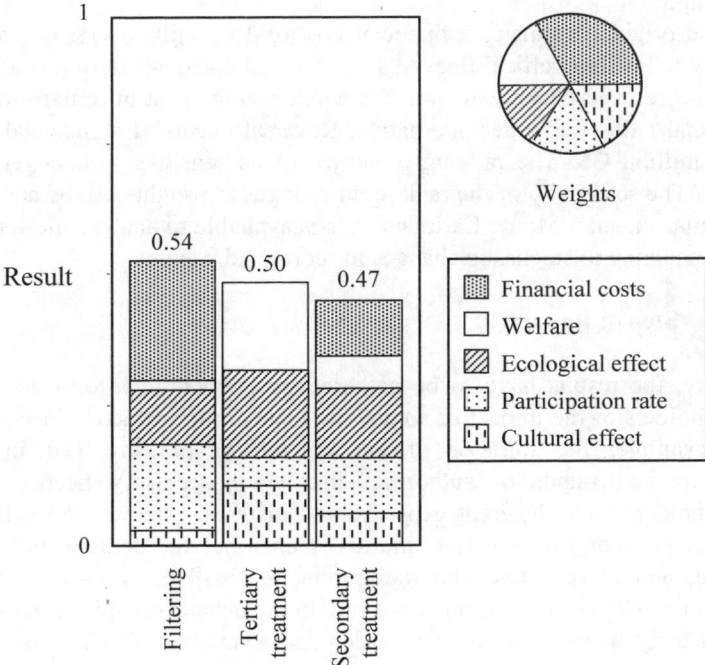

Figure 6.6 Multi-criteria analysis: ranking, evaluation scores and weights

assessments are often derived from underlying classes of quantitative data and can therefore be treated as quantitative information. Weighted summation is the simplest and most used form in multi-attribute utility theory. Other non-linear, multiplicative or multi-linear utility functions are proposed in the extensive literature on utility analysis (Keeney and Raiffa, 1976; Keeney, 1992 and French, 1988). In addition to weighted summation, other multi-criteria methods are available in DEFINITE: the ELECTRE 2 method (Roy 1973), the Regime method (Hinloopen and Nijkamp, 1990) and the Evamix method (Voogd, 1983). See Janssen (1992) and Janssen and Munda (1999) for a description of all these methods.

6.3.3　Step 3: Sensitivity Analysis

Next, the sensitivity of the ranking to uncertainties in scores and weights is analysed. This is a vital step in MCA. Varying weights and scores can check the sensitivity of the results individually or through the use of Monte Carlo Analysis. This provides insight into the significance of the results (see also Herwijnen et al., 1995). The ranking of alternatives is dependent on the scores and weights. Changes in scores or weights may therefore change the ranking.

The original estimate, a financial cost of 15.3 million G$, is marked in Figure 6.7 with a vertical line. At 15.3 the total score of filtering is above the total score of tertiary treatment. A reduction in the cost of tertiary treatment will make this the better alternative. Reversal occurs at a financial cost of 11.3 million G$. The ranking is shown to be sensitive to changes in this score. The sensitivity of the ranking to changes in weights can be analysed in a similar manner. Monte Carlo analysis is available to analyse the sensitivity of the ranking to stochastic changes in scores and weights.

6.3.4　Step 4: Report

Finally, the results have to be gathered in a report to inform all relevant stakeholders of the impact of an activity. The group of stakeholders include, for example, the initiator of an activity, people involved in public participation rounds or authorities that grant necessary licences. These stakeholders have different expertise and different interests. To achieve its task of providing information, the MCA must be well documented, easy to repeat, and as objective and transparent as possible. Well-conducted and presented MCAs play an important role in the debate around the activity and are usually appreciated by all participants (Janssen, 2001). This example provided a tour through the four evaluation steps.

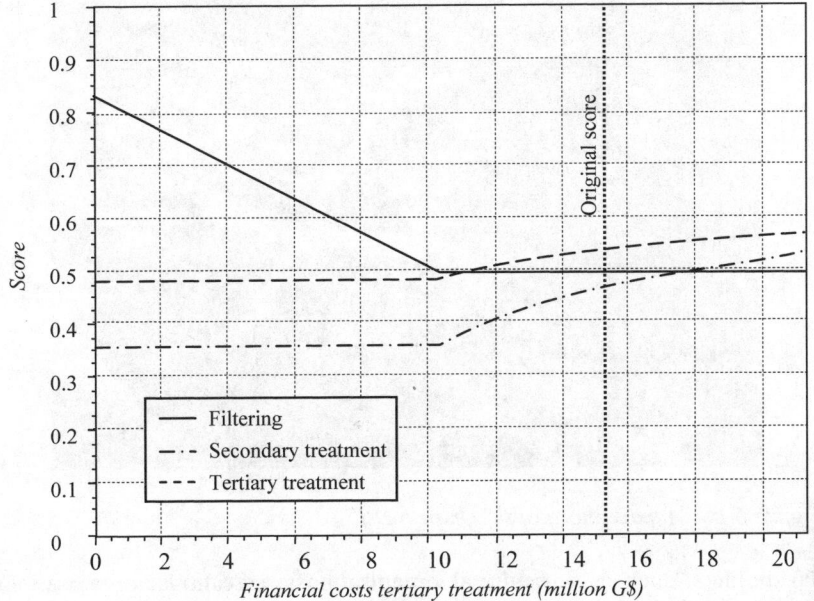

Figure 6.7   Sensitivity analysis: sensitivity of the ranking for changes in the financial costs of tertiary treatment

6.4   PRESENTATION OF RESULTS: WATER MANAGEMENT OF THE JISPERVELD

DEFINITE includes a number of graphical procedures. Some of these can be used to present the results. Water management of the Jisperveld[2] is used as a case study to demonstrate how results of multi-criteria analysis can be presented. The Jisperveld is an area of about 2 500 ha, north of Amsterdam. The area consists of small lots of drained peat land within a network of ditches and shallow lakes (Figure 6.8). The area is mainly in (extensive) agricultural use and internationally important as a habitat for meadow birds. The outer belts of the area and land parcels connected to houses are private. Water levels are controlled in the area. Changes in water regimes are proposed (National Policies, Water Framework Directive) which will have great influence on the performance of agriculture, nature, residential and recreation opportunities.

Policy makers are faced with complex decisions about future land-use in these fen meadow areas. A process of discussion and negotiation with stakeholders and institutions in the area has already started. Different

Figure 6.8   Aerial photo of the Jisperveld

stakeholders, such as agricultural organisations, recreational organisations, nature conservation organisations and provincial/regional authorities, each have their own ideas about the future land use. Three alternatives are identified for the Wormer- en Jisperveld:

1. Modern fen-meadow: this is the current situation with 'counter-natural' water management. The area can be used for (extensive) agriculture;
2. Historic fen-meadow: management aimed at a more natural water level fluctuation. Agriculture is still possible, however less intensive than in the modern peat pasture scenario;
3. Dynamic mire: water levels will fluctuate between 40 cm above soil surface in winter and more or less at the soil surface in summer. The area is not suitable for agriculture any more.

Figure 6.9 shows the objective tree for this example. The tree shows that twelve indicators are used to describe the performance of the alternatives grouped according to five objectives: (1) water quality; (2) water quantity; (3) climate; (4) biodiversity and (5) socioeconomic. The icon in front of the criteria shows the measurement scale: in this case all criteria are measured on a ratio scale. A tree structure like this is recommended if the effects table includes more than ten criteria. The tree in this example has two levels. Any number of levels can be specified in DEFINITE. However, for ease of presentation two levels are recommended. The tree structure is used to assign weights to criteria within each objective and to assess the weights between objectives.

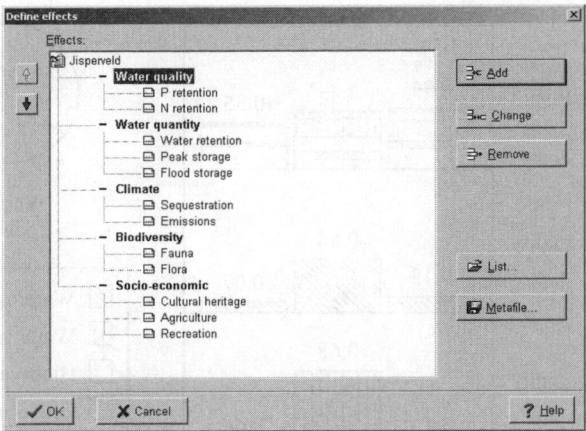

Figure 6.9   The objective tree of the Jisperveld

Weighted summation is used to rank the alternatives (Janssen et al., 2001). The overall performance of the alternatives is presented in Figure 6.10. The pie chart to the right of Figure 6.10 shows the weights of the objectives that were used to derive this ranking. The weight of climate change is low (0.10) because the relative importance of the Jisperveld for this objective is small. The remaining 0.90 were equally divided among the three remaining objectives: water, biodiversity and socioeconomic. The water objective includes both water quality and water quantity. Because of the importance of the Jisperveld for water storage, water quantity was given a weight of 0.2 and water quality a weight of 0.1. The stacked bars represent the weighted contribution of each objective to these totals. It is clear that using the weights described above, the 'historic fen meadow' alternative ranks first, closely followed by 'dynamic mire'. The difference in total scores of these two alternatives with the 'modern fen meadow' alternative is substantial. Figure 6.10 also shows that the 'dynamic mire' alternative scores best on water quality, water quantity and climate. The high score on these three objectives compensates for the slightly lower score on biodiversity and the much lower score on socioeconomic. DEFINITE has other graphical techniques available. For example a scatter diagram could be used to analyse further the conflict between economy and environment.

Assessment of weights is to some extent subjective and political. This is particularly true for weights of the objectives. From the perspective of local enterprise, socioeconomic criteria should receive a higher weight. On the other hand, from the perspective of nature conservationists, biodiversity should receive a higher weight. DEFINITE has a procedure to explore systematically the relations between political perspectives and the ranking of

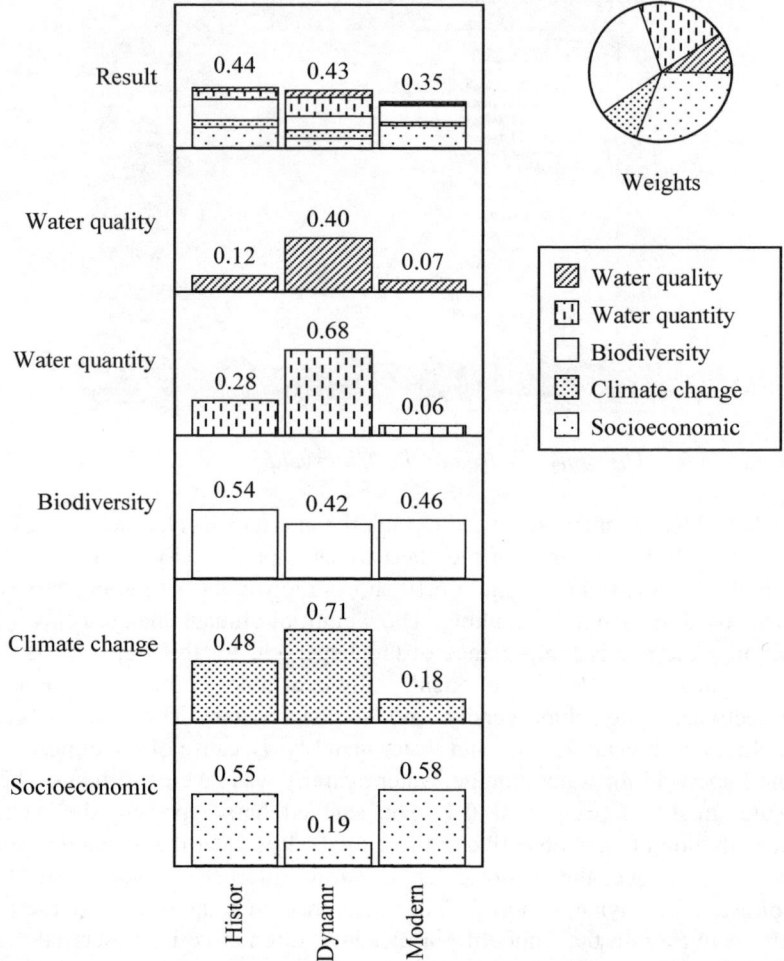

Figure 6.10   Total scores and scores per objective of the alternatives

the alternatives. To do this each perspective is translated into a set of weights. It is clear that thorough consultation with all stakeholders is required to specify these perspectives.

The rankings presented in Figure 6.11 are linked to perspectives, each emphasising a particular interest in the decision. In each row priority is given to one objective: in the first row a weight of 0.5 is given to water quality, the second row to water quantity, etc. Figures like Figure 6.11 are useful to demonstrate the relation between political priority and preferred choice.

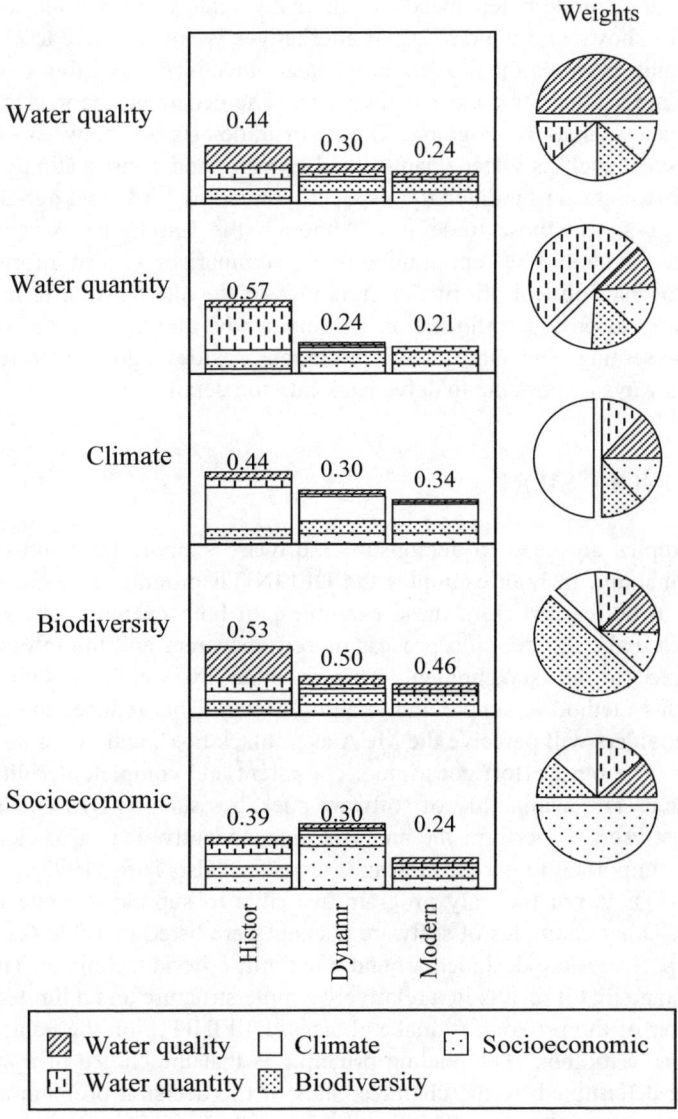

Figure 6.11   Total scores of the alternatives using various perspectives on objective weights

In this example the 'dynamic mire' alternative ranks first if priority is given to water quality, water quantity, climate and biodiversity. However, this alternative ranks last if priority is given to socioeconomic. Except for socioeconomic, the 'modern fen meadow' alternative ranks last for all weights. Figure 6.11 shows that the ranking of alternatives is not sensitive to changes of the weights between the four environmental objectives. In all four cases the 'dynamic mire' alternative clearly ranks first. The debate on the management of fen-meadow areas is on-going. The main trade-offs are between climate related issues, such as water quantity and climate, and conservationists that put a high weight on biodiversity, especially meadow birds and agriculture. Figure 6.11 shows these trade-offs. Although the last figure is relatively complicated, it should be kept in mind that it summarises a lot of information in order to link political priorities to rankings of the alternatives. In practice the best way to provide information will always be a mixture of the various ways of presenting. The aggregated information provides a good overview but it should always be possible to delve back into the detail.

6.5   CONCLUSION

Two examples are used to demonstrate software support for multi-criteria decision making. In both examples the DEFINITE program is used. A few lessons can be learned from these examples. In both examples the role of MCA is to make the decision process more transparent and the information manageable for all stakeholders. This is done by weighted summation because this method is simple and straightforward. This reduces the chance that stakeholders will perceive the MCA as a 'black box', and therefore reject its results. The most effort goes into a consistent and complete definition of the problem. The availability of software packages such as DEFINITE will allow most users to perform the analysis independently. It is also clear that graphs are important to get the message across (see also Tufte, 1997).

DEFINITE is not the only program available to support discrete choice problems. Other examples of software packages are listed in Table 6.1. Most software packages are designed around one multi-criteria technique. This has the advantage that it results in a relatively simple structure and a limited need for the user of the program to make choices. DEFINITE, on the contrary, is designed as a toolbox. The leading principle is that the choice of a method should be determined by the characteristics of the decision problem and by the preferences of the user. This results in a relatively large program with many options. To prevent users from getting lost in the detail, the program is based on simple step menus. These menus guide the user step by step through all the necessary procedures of the program.

Sustainable management of water resources usually includes many stakeholders and is based on multiple conflicting objectives. The available information is usually extensive and a mixture of quantitative and qualitative data. Putting a monetary value on this information is in many cases not possible. Therefore it requires an approach that highlights the relevant trade-offs and provides a good means of communication with the stakeholders. As shown by the various case studies in this chapter, multi-criteria analysis suits these requirements well, especially when incorporated into a software tool. Only then, can the facilitator, analyst and decision maker focus on the fundamental value judgments and choices.

NOTES

1. The example presented is based on a case study conducted by Cesar et al. (2003).
2 . The example presented is a case study conducted as part of EVALUWET project (European Valuation and Assessment tooL sUpporting Wetland Ecosystem legislaTion). A full description of the case study can be found in Janssen et al. (2005). The EVALUWET project was funded under the EU 5th framework programme: energy, environment and sustainable development (contract no: EVK1-CT-2000-00070).

REFERENCES

Beinat, E. (1997), *Value Functions for Environmental Management*, Dordrecht: Kluwer Academic Publishers.

Belton V. and T.J. Stewart (2002), *Multiple Criteria Decision Analysis: An Integrated Approach*, Dordrecht: Kluwer Academic Publishers.

Cesar, H., P. van Beukering and G. de Berdt Romilly (2003), 'Mainstreaming Economic Valuation in Decision Making: Coral Reef Examples in Selected CARICOM-countries', ARCADIS/CEEC Consultancy Report to the Latin America and Caribbean Socially and Environmentally Sustainable Vice-Presidency (LCSES) of the World Bank for the Caribbean Planning for Adaptation to Global Climate (CPACC) Project, Washington DC: World Bank (June 30).

French, S. (1988), *Decision Theory: An Introduction to the Mathematics of Rationality*, Chichester: Ellis Horwood Limited.

Herwijnen, M. van (1999), *Spatial Decision Support for Environmental Management*, PhD dissertation, Amsterdam: Vrije Universiteit.

Herwijnen, M. van, P. Rietveld, K. Thevenet and R. Tol (1995), 'Sensitivity analysis with interdependent criteria for multi criteria decision making', *Multi Criteria Decision Making*, 4(1), 57–70.

Hinloopen, E. and P. Nijkamp (1990), 'Qualitative multiple criteria choice analysis, the dominant regime method', *Quality and Quantity*, 24, 37–56.

Janssen, R. (1992), *Multiobjective Decision Support for Environmental Management*, Dordrecht: Kluwer Academic Publishers.

Janssen, R. (2001), 'On the use of multi-criteria analysis in environmental impact assessment in the Netherlands', *Journal of multi-criteria decision analysis*, 10(2), 101–109.

Janssen, R. and G. Munda (1999), 'Multi-criteria methods for quantitative, qualitative and fuzzy evaluation problems', in J.C.J.M.v.d. Bergh, (ed.) *Handbook of Environmental and Resource Economics*, Cheltenham, UK and Brookfield, US:

Edward Elgar, pp. 1000–1012.

Janssen, R., M. van Herwijnen and E. Beinat (2001), *DEFINITE for Windows. A system to support decisions on a finite set of alternatives* (Software package and user manual), Institute for Environmental Studies (IVM), Amsterdam: Vrije Universiteit.

Janssen, R., H. Goosen, M. Verhoeven, J.T.A.Verhoeven, N. Omtzigt and E. Maltby (2005), 'Decision support for integrated wetland management', *Journal of environmental modelling and software*, **20**, 215–229.

Keeney, R.L. (1992), *Value-Focused Thinking*, Cambridge: Harvard University Press.

Keeney, R.L. and H. Raiffa (1976), *Decisions with Multiple Objectives; Preferences and Value Trade Offs*, New York: Wiley.

Malczewski, J. (1999), *GIS and Multi-Criteria Decision Analysis*, New York: John Wiley & Sons, Inc.

Roy, B. (1973), 'How outranking relation helps multiple criteria decision making', in J.L. Cochrane and M. Zeleny (eds), *Multiple criteria decision making*, Columbia: University of South Carolina Press, pp. 179–201.

Tufte, E.R. (1997), *Visual Explanations: Images and Quantities, Evidence and Narrative*, Cheshire, Connecticut: Graphics Press.

Uran, O. (2002), *Spatial Decision Support Systems for Coastal Zone and Water Management*, PhD-thesis, Amsterdam: Vrije Universiteit.

Voogd, H. (1983), *Multi-Criteria Evaluation for Urban and Regional Planning*, London: Pion.

PART IV

Participation

7. Participation for Sustainable Water Management

Erik Mostert

7.1 INTRODUCTION

Numerous international declarations mention public participation as essential for integrated water resources management. Probably the best known is the Dublin Statement, second principle, which reads, 'water development and management should be based on a participatory approach, involving users, planners and policy-makers at all levels' (Dublin Statement, 1992). In addition, many international conventions and regulations contain public participation requirements, such as the Aarhus Convention on Access to Information, Public Participation in Decision-making and Access to Justice in Environmental Matters and the EU Water Framework Directive (EC, 2000; Ebbesson, 1998; REC, 1999; Kakebeeke and Bouman, 2000; UN-ECE, 2000; Drafting Group, 2002).

Despite this official recognition, there is no consensus on the practical meaning of public participation. While some see public participation as a means of empowering people and enhancing democracy, others see it mainly as a marketing tool for the water managers. Still others are simply against public participation. Not surprisingly, the public participation requirements of many international declarations and conventions are not implemented (for example, REC, 1998).

This chapter provides a short introduction to public participation in water management. It discusses the concept and the different types of public participation, the goals of public participation and the cultural context. It also discusses participatory research and social learning. In addition, the organisation of participatory processes and water users' associations are discussed in detail, as well as public participation in large international river basins, the European Water Framework Directive and the level at which to organise public participation. The chapter concludes with nine public participation principles.

7.2 WHAT IS PUBLIC PARTICIPATION?

Public participation can be defined as direct involvement of the public in decision making. The most complete form of participation is decision making by the public, usually through some form of water users' association. In this case, the public assumes complete responsibility for some or all water management functions within a certain area, along with financing. Water users' associations are especially important in some developing countries, but they also exist in many developed countries.

The second form of public participation is participation in decision making by government. This includes informal participation, such as lobbying and demonstrations, as well as participation that is initiated or supported by government. The latter includes consultation processes (such as public commenting periods, surveys and interviews), small-group discussions (such as design workshops, focus groups and citizen juries) and large meetings (such as public hearings, search conferences and open space technology; see also Chapter 8). This chapter focuses on these more formal types of public participation.

Table 7.1 presents the different levels of participation. This table is based on Arnstein's 'ladder of citizen participation' (Arnstein, 1969) and subsequent variations (Roberts, 1995; Connor, 1997; Creighton, 2000; Edelenbos, 2000; IAP2, 2001). Arnstein focused on power issues and emphasized that many forms of so-called 'citizen participation' do not give any real influence to

Table 7.1   Levels of public participation

Level of participation

---

1. *Information supply*
   The public is provided with or has access to information. On its own this is not genuine public participation, but it is a prerequisite for it.
2. *Consultation*
   The public can react to plans or their views are actively solicited.
3. *Co-thinking*
   Real discussions take place between the public and government.
4. *Co-designing*
   The public actively contributes to policy development, for example, through design workshops.
5. *Co-decision making*
   The public shares decision making powers with government.
6. *Self control*
   The public performs tasks independently, for example, through water users' associations.

---

the public. Table 7.1 also reflects other aspects of public participation, such as social learning that may result from public participation.

Unfortunately there is no standard terminology. Where this chapter uses the term public participation, other writers use the term 'public involvement.' They reserve public participation for participation levels above consultation (for example, Roberts, 1995). Moreover, the meaning of 'public' is not fixed. In this chapter public means all non-governmental stakeholders. It includes all individuals, groups, organisations and associations with an interest or 'stake' in an issue, either because they will be affected or because they may have some influence on its outcome, or simply because they are interested. Many writers, however, distinguish between public participation and stakeholder participation. They reserve 'public participation' for participation by the unorganised 'general' or 'broad public', sometimes including public interest groups (for example, REC, 1999). By 'stakeholder participation' they mean participation by well-organized and recognised interest groups and other influential actors, sometimes including government bodies.

A somewhat different distinction is between public participation as participation by representatives of the 'general interest' and stakeholder participation as participation by representatives of specific interests. Often these two distinctions – individual versus organised participants and general versus specific interests – are combined. This can only be done if one assumes that individual citizens always represent the general interest and organised groups always represent specific interests.

The confusion with terminology cannot easily be solved since it reflects (and hides) substantive differences of opinion. For instance, a narrow interpretation of 'public participation' will be attractive for people who believe that participation by individual citizens can counterbalance the influence of well-organised partial interests. A broad interpretation will be attractive for people who believe that there is no such thing as 'the general interest', that citizens represent different mixes of specific interests and that these interests can be best represented by organised interest groups.

7.3 PARTICIPATORY GOALS

Public participation can be organised for different reasons (Pateman, 1970; Delli Priscolli, 1978b; Roberts, 1995; Webler and Renn, 1995; Budge, 1996; Woerkom, 1997; DETR, 2000). First, public participation can result in better-informed and more creative decision making. It helps to ensure that all relevant interests are heard. Important information can become available, new perspectives can be presented and creative solutions can be developed.

Secondly, public participation can result in more public acceptance or even 'ownership' of the decisions, resulting in less litigation, fewer delays and generally better implementation. Partly, this is the result of better-informed and more creative decision making, but often it is simply the result of having the public involved in the process.

Public participation can also promote more open and integrated government. To get better-informed decisions and more public acceptance, government should treat any comments from the public seriously and should not be preoccupied with its own internal problems.

Moreover, public participation can enhance democracy. Many see public participation as a democratic right of the citizens and therefore as a goal in itself. Public participation may also instil more democratic attitudes in the participants (Pateman, 1970; Budge, 1996).

Finally, public participation can result in social learning. Social learning could be described as learning by groups – authorities, the public and experts together – to manage issues in which all members have a stake. It is the ultimate goal of public participation.

If public participation is not well organised, it can result in limited and unrepresentative response from the public, ill-informed responses and the public participation process being hijacked by certain groups. Moreover, if public input is not taken seriously and if the promises of public participation are not fulfilled, the public may get disillusioned. This can result in less-informed decisions, less trust in government, less public acceptance, more implementation problems and less social learning (Assetto and Mumme, 2000; Edelenbos, 2000). In addition, it reduces the chances of effective public participation in the future.

7.4　THE CONTEXT OF PUBLIC PARTICIPATION

Public participation is not simply a technique for obtaining desirable outcomes. It also reflects the natural and socioeconomic conditions, ideology and culture. In The Netherlands, for example, water users' associations were established in the Middle Ages to undertake large-scale flood protection works. Government did not have the means to do this: the only solution was for the landowners in the flood-prone areas to combine forces and organize themselves. In the 19th century – the classical liberal era – some limited forms of public participation were introduced as a form of legal protection against government. In the 1960s and 1970s, public participation received renewed attention as a result of a broader social movement towards more democracy (Enserink et al., 2003; Mostert, 2003a).

To understand national differences, the concept of culture can be useful.

BOX 7.1

The Parrett Catchment – an Example of a Participatory Process

The River Parrett Catchment lies in South-west England and covers an area of 1665 km^2. The floodplain forms a significant part of the Somerset Levels and Moors, an area of international importance for wildlife. From January 2000 to March 2002 a participatory process was conducted in the catchment as part of the Wise Use of Floodplains (WUF) project, an EU Life Environment funded project. Twenty-seven participatory workshops were held to encourage stakeholders to share views and address problems jointly. For each workshop some 85 stakeholders were invited, of which some 40 attended. The workshops were managed through facilitative leadership; with the help of group management techniques, stakeholders were helped to work together in a non-conflict environment.

The objectives outlined through this process were:

1. Generating new options for the sustainable management of flood events and water levels on the floodplain;
2. Testing methods to assess the economic, social and environmental costs and benefits of the different options;
3. Finding out how the English and European policies need to be changed to promote sustainable catchment management;
4. Disseminating the results across Europe;
5. Commissioning research to provide up-to-date facts and information to advance the debate.

The project built up ownership and trust. It raised awareness of catchment management issues and provided a means of accessing local knowledge and expertise. It can be regarded as an investment as it involved early identification of issues and consensus building. Tangible results include the following:

1. A statement of the consensus between all stakeholders, which forms the basis for a vision for the future management of the catchment and floodplain;
2. Eleven potential components for an Integrated Flood Management approach and a detailed analysis of these components;
3. Initiation of a productive dialogue on finding a new balance between agriculture and environmental interests;
4. Practical sustainability indicators to monitor the effectiveness of changes in water and land management.

The costs of organising the public participation process are estimated at €30 000 (salary costs of project officer/facilitator), plus minor expenses for workshops of approximately €150–180 for each event (hire of the venue, catering for participants).

Source: Cuff, 2001; Drafting Group, 2002.

Culture can be defined as the dominant patterns of emotion, thought and action in a group (Thompson et al., 1990; Hofstede, 1991; Faure and Rubin, 1993). Using survey material from 1970, Hofstede (1991) has identified five dimensions in which national cultures differ: power distance, individualism, masculinity/femininity, uncertainty avoidance and long or short timeframe. How countries score on these dimensions can have important implications for public participation (see Table 7.2).

Table 7.2   Dimensions of national cultures and possible implications for public participation

Dimension*	Implications for public participation
POWER DISTANCE Degree to which members of a culture expect and accept (or totally reject) power differences	In countries with a large power distance, the authorities will not embrace public participation. Introducing public participation may require strict regulations. The public is likely to be passive or cynical, so extra efforts are needed to mobilise them. A good option might be to organize public participation through local institutions that are close to the people.
INDIVIDUALISM Degree to which members of a culture see themselves primarily as an individual or primarily as a group member	In 'collectivist cultures', not losing one's face is an important concern. In the event of conflict, intermediaries could be employed to facilitate concessions without losing face (Cohen, 1993). Methods such as gaming may conflict with the dignity of authorities. Public participation methods developed in individualist cultures such as the USA involving an open discussion of differences may not work.
MASCULINITY Degree to which members of a culture are expected to be assertive and competitive	In 'masculine' cultures with an adversarial culture, such as the USA, public participation could be used to prevent litigation. Adversarial methods, such as citizen juries involving cross-examination of witnesses, and voting fit very well in such a culture. In 'feminine' cultures consensus-based methods may be more appropriate (Armour, 1995).
UNCERTAINTY AVOIDANCE Degree to which members of a culture feel uncomfortable with unknown or unpredictable situations	Countries with much uncertainty avoidance may have difficulties with the unpredictable character of participatory processes and are liable to organise public participation only at a very late stage in the process. Both government and the public may function more effectively with a detailed public participation work plan (Dienel and Renn, 1995). Research results could be the basis for discussions. In countries with little uncertainty avoidance, research should be the object of discussion in order to prevent technical controversies (Jasanoff, 1990; Linnerooth-Bayer, 1995).
TIMEFRAME Short-term versus long-term orientation	No implications identified.

Note: * Hofstede, 1991.

Hofstede's theory has been heavily criticized (for example, McSweeney, 2002). His concept of a stable national culture that determines behaviour may result in so-called 'sophisticated stereotyping' (Osland and Bird, 2000). An alternative approach is to see culture as a set of context-specific behavioural patterns or 'scripts'. The specific context determines which script is used. For example, the USA is generally quite egalitarian, but in a work context executives can behave very autocratically (Osland and Bird, 2000).

Not all members of a nation have the same scripts (or knowledge or emotions). Companies, disciplines and all sorts of groups can have their own culture, which may have more in common with the culture of their counterparts abroad than with the culture of other groups in their own country (see the cultural theory of Thompson et al., 1990; Verweij, 2000). Culture may change as different groups gain prominence, contexts change and new scripts develop (on Japan: Faure, 2001).

Attention to culture is essential when organizing public participation in international basins or considering the adoption of public participation approaches developed in a different context. But it is also time consuming and requires an open and self-critical attitude. Despite the limitations of Hofstede's theory, it provides useful hypotheses (Osland and Bird, 2000).

7.5 PARTICIPATION AND RESEARCH

Modern water management generally involves a lot of research. If water management is to be participatory, the research supporting water management should also be participatory. The research results should be available to the different public groups and be presented in a way that is understandable for them. Moreover, the public should have a say in what exactly is researched and how. Finally, the public may participate in the research itself.

What is studied and how, is usually decided by the agency funding the research and the experts conducting the research. Many policy choices, however, are already made in the research phase. Some alternatives receive attention while others do not and certain effects are studied while others are not (Collingridge and Reeve, 1986; Frankena, 1988; Jasanoff, 1990).

Presentation of the results is related to the legal issue of access to information, to communication and dissemination strategies and to the skills of experts in explaining results in an understandable way. These are not neutral issues. For instance, what information should remain confidential? How does one deal with the fact that research results are never completely certain? And how are the results presented? Positive effects can be discussed in more detail than negative results or vice versa. Summaries are necessarily selective. The choice of illustrations can convey a strong but implicit message, and so on. In principle, the presentation should be 'balanced', but it is difficult to say what that exactly means in a specific case.

Genuine participatory water management requires that the public is involved in the research as well. Ideally, water management research should contribute to social learning. The experts should see themselves not as providers of objective truths, but as facilitators and resource persons for both the authorities and the public. They should be receptive to information from the public and to hear their concerns. The authorities should be receptive to research and to the concerns of the public (for example, Scheer, 1996). The public should ideally go through the same thought process and be exposed to the same information and arguments as the researchers and the authorities.

The research skills of the public are usually quite limited, but the public can be involved in setting the terms of reference and the research methods and results can be discussed with them. If models are used, the assumptions adopted should be made explicit and the models themselves should be sufficiently flexible to accommodate the dynamic character of participatory processes (Loucks, 1990; Ubbels and Verhallen, 2000). Moreover, the public can provide data and help to monitor compliance with regulations. In the EU, for instance, environmental NGOs play an important role in controlling compliance with EU regulations (Roller, 2003).

There is often confusion among researchers between participation in decision making and participation in research. Participation in decision making requires some participation in the research that supports the decision making, but they are not the same. Many, especially academic research projects have no direct link with management and decision making, even when they are meant to be policy-relevant. Involving members of the public in this kind of research may help the researchers to do better research, but as a matter of principle there should be benefits for the public as well (Pahl-Wostl and Ridder, 2004). The research may have an indirect, long-term impact on policy, the participants may learn a lot about the issues at stake and the participation may be an opportunity for them to meet other participants, all of which might be important benefits for them. In any case, potential participants should know what to expect.

7.6   SOCIAL LEARNING

7.6.1   The Social Learning Concept

The ultimate objective of public participation is social learning (Craps et al., 2003; Thaillieu et al., 2003). Social learning usually means learning from others (one-way) or from each other (two-way), as opposed to individual learning. In this chapter, social learning means all this and more. As used in this chapter, social learning refers to the growing capacity of social entities to perform common tasks, such as the management of a water resource. Put differently, social learning is learning together to manage together.

A fundamental idea behind social learning is that water management is both a social-relational activity and a technically complex task. It is a social-relational activity because information, funds, competencies and other resources are spread over many different actors, including non-governmental actors. Together they have to come to some kind of agreement. Yet, water management is also a technically complex task. It involves problem definition, information gathering, development and selection of alternatives, implementation and evaluation. Both aspects of water management are inseparable: problem definitions, information gathering, the development of alternatives and so on are the result of interactions between individuals and groups with specific backgrounds, experiences, interests, communication channels and hierarchical positions.

To start a social learning process, people first need to realize that they are interdependent and organise themselves around the issue at stake. Next, they should start interacting – exchange information, discuss, negotiate, etc.

7.6.2   Three Social Learning Principles

Social learning requires that the stakeholders not only reflect on the best means to reach their goals (single-loop learning), but also on the goals themselves and on their relationship (double-loop learning). Perhaps their goals are not the best to achieve what they really want. In any case, reflection on the goals creates more space for agreement and more possibilities for win-win solutions (compare the concept of principled negotiations: Fisher and Ury, 1981).

A very simple example is the following. Two people want to go on holiday together. One wishes to go to Norway and the other to Spain. If the two do not reflect on their goals, only a few solutions are possible and none is satisfactory. Either the one or the other has to give in or they compromise (for example, they go to The Netherlands, which is located in between Norway and Spain) and then nobody is really happy. However, it might be the case that the one wants to go to Norway because of the mountains and the other to Spain because of the nice weather. If they come to realize this, many more options become available, such as Greece and the Azores, where you have both.

Reflection on goals requires open communication and this requires that people reflect on how they react to and influence each other. Quite often, people do not discuss possible differences openly. Instead, they use two strategies: unilateral control of the issue at hand and unilateral protection of self and others from problematic information. Potentially embarrassing information is not stated and face-saving moves are often made. Opinions are not illustrated but instead presented as obviously correct and solutions are proposed in a way that discourages inquiry into their merits. These strategies trigger or reinforce similar strategies by the other parties involved. The overall results are defensive relationships, less valid information, limited public testing of ideas and fewer alternatives from which to choose.

Argyris and Schön (1996) give many more details on these kind of processes. Their main interest is to promote more double-loop learning in potentially embarrassing situations, but they confess that they do not yet have the solution. Perhaps it is not really possible to change behaviour in potentially embarrassing situations and more may be achieved from promoting an atmosphere in which fewer situations are experienced as embarrassing.

Reciprocity, the second principle for social learning, is essential for arriving at and sustaining joint or coordinated action. The participants need to realize that they are interdependent and cannot effectively exercise unilateral control. Next, they have to act upon this, consider the interests of the others, give information as well as receive and reciprocate any favours to them. This can benefit all those involved.

Respect of diversity is the third prerequisite for social learning. All participants need to acknowledge that the other participants may have different interests, views and information. These differences may create problems that need to be addressed, but they can also be a source of strength. Different views and information can complement each other and different interests can provide opportunities for mutually beneficial exchanges (Vansina and Thaillieu, 1997).

7.6.3   Leadership and Facilitation

Leadership and facilitation are important aspects of public participation. Because of the interdependencies, traditional leadership does not work. Telling others what has to be done only triggers resistance, position taking and win-lose negotiations instead of integrative, reflexive win-win bargaining. Ideally, there should be a neutral facilitator without a high stake in the outcome, but such a facilitator may be difficult to find.

7.6.4   Representation

Learning is best achieved in small groups that interact directly, such as working groups or river basin commissions (Wenger, 1998). However, the number of people involved in water management is huge and they all need to be reached somehow. Different forms of representation may be needed, for example, local NGOs can be represented in national NGOs, that can be represented in international NGOs that can be represented in an international river basin commission. The representatives need to represent the needs and concerns of their community correctly and stay in close contact with their community to maintain their trust. They also need sufficient freedom to interact effectively with the other representatives in the new community. In addition, different media may need to be used, such as the mass media to interact with public opinion and the journal of an environmental NGO to reach their members. Key principles for the interactions with the broader public – who in the end may prove to be very influential – are openness, transparency and fostering trust.

7.7 ORGANISING PUBLIC PARTICIPATION

Public participation comes in many forms and shapes. It can have significant benefits and may ultimately lead to social learning, but if it is not organised well it may be counterproductive. The key question is how to organise it? The preceding sections have shown that it should be organised in a culturally sensitive way and that the principles of social learning, such as reflexivity, reciprocity and respect of diversity, should be applied. This section will address some issues that need to be addressed when setting up participatory processes.

7.7.1 The 'Public' and the Purpose of Public Participation

A basic issue in public participation is the identification of the different stakeholders. They need to be identified beforehand for two reasons. Firstly, they must be actively approached to avoid limited or unrepresentative response. Secondly, when public participation methods are used that can only accommodate a limited number of participants, the 'right' participants need to be selected.

Four criteria can be used for identifying the different stakeholders:

1. Do they possess relevant information or new points of view?
2. Can they actively contribute to the development of new policy or projects? Do they have special skills?
3. To what extent will their interests be affected? Are all affected interests represented in proportion to their importance?
4. Can they obstruct decision making or frustrate implementation?

The criteria to be used depend upon the benefits sought and the level of public participation envisaged. Criteria 1 and 2, for instance, are especially relevant for improving the quality of decision making and with respect to the public participation levels 'discussion' and 'co-designing'. Criterion 3 is crucial for improving co-decision making and self-control, while criterion 4 is essential if implementation problems are to be prevented.

In practice a fifth criterion is often used: are the potential participants likely to oppose the pertinent plan or project? Excluding such opponents from participating ensures a very smooth public participation process, but may create serious problems later on and is in fact more likely to increase the level of opposition. Moreover, it precludes the possibility of real social learning.

7.7.2   Stakeholder Analysis

Identifying the different stakeholders usually requires some form of stakeholder analysis (IIAV, 2000; Hermans and Timmermans, 2001). This should include gender analysis to account for the role of women in water management. Stakeholder analysis may consist of the following elements:

1. An identification of the issues at stake, including intangibles and issues related to the informal economy, and their historical development;
2. A preliminary analysis of the relevant physical system or systems (basin, sub-basin, irrigation system, etc.) and the use made of these systems;
3. An analysis of the relevant institutional structure, including the responsible organizations, the management tools available and relevant standards;
4. The identification of the various government and non-government stakeholders (organisations, groups, individuals, including the 'general public');
5. An assessment of the perceptions and resources of the different government and non-government stakeholders, including their goals and interests, their perception of the relevant systems, their perception of each other, their information needs, the time and money they have available, their level of education, their technical expertise and their communication skills.

Stakeholder analysis along these lines is helpful in determining the scope of public participation (see below) and mobilising the different stakeholders. It could be discovered, for example, that some segments of the public lack sufficient financial resources for attending meetings. Their travel costs might then be reimbursed and other forms of financial support might be offered (Roberts, 1995).

7.7.3 Roles and Rules

Before public participation can begin, the roles of the different parties should be clear. These can range from merely listening, to answering questions, participating in the discussions, designing policy and actually taking decisions. The assigned roles should reflect the intended level of public participation and the capacities and expectations of the different stakeholders. For some public participation methods, specific rules may be needed, for instance with respect to speaking time, voting and deadlines for submitting documents.

7.7.4 Process Managers and Project Organization

A role of particular importance is that of process manager, who is responsible for designing the process, facilitating meetings and liaising with the various government bodies involved. Appointing a staff member from the lead government agency as process manager would facilitate follow-up and promote the integration of public participation in the daily routine of that agency. However, there are also many advantages with the appointment of an external process manager. Process managers should ideally be impartial with respect to the initiative at hand and should certainly be perceived as such. Moreover, they should have public participation expertise. These criteria are usually much easier to meet in the case of an external process manager. A third alternative is to appoint an internal process manager, but also hire an independent public participation professional to support the process manager and facilitate meetings (Delli Priscolli, 1978a; Mostert, 2001).

The process manager should have sufficient administrative support for organising meetings, sending notifications to the media, processing written comments and similar activities. In addition, a steering committee may be created in which the different government bodies involved are represented. This would be a good forum for discussion on the level and purpose of public participation, the roles and rules and follow-up (Creighton, 2000).

7.7.5 Scope

Another topic on which the different government bodies involved must agree is the scope of public participation: what can be debated and what cannot? The various legal and political constraints must be taken into account, including existing international obligations. Stakeholder analysis is useful in determining what these constraints are and how hard they are.

It is essential to give the public some advance information on the scope to ensure that their expectations are appropriate. They can then focus on those aspects that are open for discussion and will not get disillusioned later on. It also allows the public to press for a broader scope or decide not to participate at all, if they consider the scope to be too narrow.

7.7.6   Timing

Public participation may be conducted during different phases of the policy process. If it is implemented too late, new alternatives cannot be considered without causing serious delays. Many concerns of the public may not be addressed and public participation is less likely to result in better decisions and more public acceptance. On the other hand, if public participation starts early in the policy process, it may be difficult to generate public interest. Plans in this phase are often quite vague and the potential consequences for the general public may not be fully appreciated. A way out of this dilemma might be to target different stakeholders at different phases: in the early phases only (semi-) professional NGOs and large companies might be involved and in later phases small NGOs, small companies and individual citizens may be involved as well.

7.7.7   Choice of Methods

The final issue to be decided is the choice of public participation methods. This choice should reflect the level of participation envisaged, since methods for providing information or for consulting the public differ quite a lot from methods for promoting real discussion. Secondly, the cultural context should be considered (see Table 7.2). A third consideration is the phase in the policy process. Methods with little structure such as 'open spaces' may be appropriate in the early phases for exploring issues. More structured meetings may be appropriate when concrete proposals are tabled and decisions have to be taken.

Moreover, the type of public concerned is important. Large formal meetings such as public hearings easily intimidate persons that are not well educated or have poor verbal skills and tend to favour middle-class participants (Webler and Renn, 1995). Methods that require a lot of time and attention from the participants favour large and well-organised stakeholders and may result in a 'participation burn-out'. Too many separate public participation processes – often the result of a sectoral, non-integrated approach to government – have the same effect (Roberts, 1995).

Finally, the demands made on the organisers should be considered. Some public participation methods require skilled facilitators. Others require a large number of administrative staff and large expenses for printing, mailing, advertising and rental of premises. All necessary resources must be assessed in advance and made available. Where sufficient resources cannot be made available, methods requiring fewer resources should be chosen.

7.7.8 An Outline of the Public Participation Process

Effective public participation requires a great deal of preparation and much follow-up. Step one is the initiation phase, in which all government bodies have to agree on the purpose of public participation (level, effects aimed for). A process manager should be appointed during this phase. Some preliminary consultations on the public participation process may be held with, for instance, large NGOs.

Step two is to conduct a stakeholder analysis and develop a process design. The process design should pay attention to the purpose of public participation, the scope (what may or may not be discussed), the different stakeholders, the role of policy research, the project organisation, the roles of the different parties, the phasing of the process and the public participation methods to be used. The process design should make clear what the public can expect. The public should be involved in the development of the process design as public participation can only be successful if the public supports the process.

The actual public participation process could start with a 'kick-off meeting', where the proposed participatory process is presented and discussed with the public. The next steps depend very much on the process design. The public participation process should be flexible enough to cope with new and unforeseen developments. However, expectations that have been raised should be respected. Major changes therefore require the agreement of all individuals and organisations that have invested time and effort in the process.

Sooner or later decisions will have to be taken, such as the adoption or approval of a plan. Depending on the level of participation, the different stakeholders may or may not be directly involved. In all cases their input should be taken seriously and they should receive feedback.

Participatory processes should be completed with an external and an internal evaluation. External evaluators who were not involved in the process can identify points for improvement that internal evaluators may miss. However, the parties involved should also make their own evaluation as well in order to learn from the experiences gained.

7.8 INTERNATIONAL RIVER BASINS AND THE SCALE ISSUE

7.8.1 Public Participation: At What Scales?

Public participation in international river basins poses special challenges. By definition, different states are involved, often with different political systems, water management systems, cultures, languages, levels of development, goals and interests. The number of potential participants is huge and distances are large. Moreover, upstream and downstream interests frequently conflict.

In many international river basins, river basin organizations have been established (Mostert, 2003b). Where these exist, public participation can be organised both nationally and at the international level. Public participation at the national level is of prime importance since usually most decision-making powers remain at this level. Yet, public participation at the national level can only be meaningful if decisions have not been predetermined at the international level.

At the international level the public may participate in different capacities. NGO representatives may participate in river basin organisations as observers, advisers, members of national delegations or as full members in their own right. In addition, river basin organisations could actively disseminate information and organise, for example, opinion polls.

Public participation in river basin organisations can be problematic if it means that each and every step of the process immediately becomes public. This would seriously reduce the potential for exploring possible solutions (Mastenbroek, 1996; Mostert, 2000; Marty, 2001). However, NGOs can agree to respect the confidentiality of the negotiations. They have already participated in some international negotiations, such as the preparations for the UN-ECE protocol on environment and health.

Nationally, the public may be involved in the ratification and implementation of international agreements and in the preparation of these agreements. Public participation events could be organised at the national level, but also at the regional or even local level. Especially at the national level, public participation will have to work through representatives. If many local events are organised, it may be possible to involve individual members of the public as well. However, organising public participation at this level will be much more complex and expensive. Whatever the level at which public participation events are organised, the different states must coordinate their public participation efforts. To ensure proper follow-up, public participation in all basin states should preferably be synchronised and the results should be communicated to the appropriate authorities in the other basin states.

7.8.2 Experiences at the International Level

Experience with public participation at the international level is limited, but it does exist. The North American international bodies and the Rhine and the Danube commissions are most active (Bouman, 1999; Milich and Varady, 1999; Assetto and Mumme, 2000; Mostert, 2003b). They have very informative websites, publish a large number of reports, which can usually be obtained free of charge or at low cost, and often hold consultations.

Moreover, international NGOs have observer status and actively participate in the plenary commission and/or in various subsidiary bodies. NGOs are often involved in national preparations for the meetings of the commission and in the implementation of its decisions.

7.8.3   The European Water Framework Directive

The issue at which level or levels to organise public participation has become especially acute in the European Union. On 22 December 2000, the EU published the Water Framework Directive (2000/60/EC). The key objective of the directive is to achieve 'good water status' for all European waters by 2015. The backbone of the Water Framework Directive is a system of river basin management. Member States are obliged to identify their national and international river basins and assign these to so-called 'river basin districts'. For all districts, six-yearly river basin management plans and programmes have to be developed. Moreover, several supporting assessments and continuous monitoring are required (see also Chapter 3).

Public participation will play a key role in the implementation of the WFD. The WFD contains four public participation requirements:

1. All EU Member States have to encourage the active involvement of all interested parties in the implementation of the WFD.
2. Member States have to ensure three rounds of written consultation in the river basin management planning process.
3. The reactions of the public need to be collected and considered seriously.
4. On request, access has to be given to background information.

Additional forms of public participation may be needed to reach the ambitious environmental goals of the WFD and ensure its success.

To support the implementation of the WFD, the European Commission and the Member States have established different working groups to prepare guidance documents. The Drafting Group on public participation (Drafting Group, 2002) has dealt explicitly with the scale issue. The approach proposed is to first identify the main issues and their geographical scale, in co-operation with the main stakeholders, and then identify the relevant stakeholders that could make a contribution. Next, public participation should be organised as close to the relevant stakeholders as possible, given the budgetary and staffing constraints. The (first) results of the public participation exercise should be communicated as soon as possible across different scales and between relevant units at the same scale. Finally, follow-up should be reported not only at the river basin level, for example, in the river basin management plan, but also at the level that public participation was organised because many details may be lost at the river basin level. The input of all participants needs to be acknowledged.

In principle any level of public participation is possible at any scale, even at the international river basin level. The main issue is to find, for each issue, the right combination of stakeholders, scale, public participation level and methods (Drafting Group, 2002).

7.9   WATER USERS' ASSOCIATIONS

Until now, this chapter has concentrated on 'Western' public participation; involvement of the public in decision making by government. However, in many developing countries public participation primarily means water users' organisations. These are organisations of water users that execute management tasks, especially in irrigation schemes. From the 1970s onwards they have been established to reduce costs for government and improve service delivery and efficiency. They now exist in many countries, for instance the Philippines, Senegal, Turkey, Egypt, Kenya, South Africa, Argentina, India, Pakistan and Bangladesh (Pradhan, 1996; Meinzen-Dick, 1997; BUET, 2003; Hamid et al., 2004). In addition, in countries such as Nepal and Indonesia traditional farmer-managed irrigation systems exist.

Information on the performance of water users' associations in irrigations schemes is limited. A number of conditions have to be met if they are to be a success (Meinzen-Dick, 1997):

1.   The benefits for the farmers should exceed the costs (which include cash payments to the association, labour, other in-kind contributions and the 'transaction costs' of attending meetings and settling disputes). Usually only well-functioning systems can be transferred to the users successfully. Moreover, parts of the system that remain under government control, such as the primary channel, should be functioning well. The benefits of the system should be distributed over all those who have to contribute to its functioning: if the local elite appropriates most of the benefits, the system is likely to collapse.

2.   The farmers need to get organised. This could be coordinated by the local elite, if they are willing to share the benefits and can maintain trust. External agencies can be involved as well.

3.   The irrigation authorities should be willing and able to move beyond adversarial or paternalistic relationships with the farmers. Farmer participation may threaten the opportunities for rent seeking and may even threaten the jobs of the staff under the management transfer programmes. Farmers may distrust the irrigation authorities.

4. An effective legal and institutional framework should be put into place. For example, water users' associations should be allowed to maintain their own bank account.

Water users' associations have also been established for purposes other than irrigation, such as flood protection and drainage (the Dutch waterboards) and maintenance of river banks (the German Wasser und Bodenverbände) (Ven, 1993; CHO, 1998; Ijjas and Szlávik, 1998; Krämer and Jäger, 1998). These associations could reduce the burden on government budgets and improve efficiency and service delivery. Bringing together the different stakeholders on an equal basis may promote social learning – provided all stakeholders are represented and the different social learning principles are observed. Decision-making and financing by the water users themselves may prevent economically and environmentally harmful over- and undersupply of infrastructure and may ensure proper maintenance. Water users' associations can be especially useful if the government is undemocratic or ineffective or if it lacks the necessary finances. However, mechanisms should be put in place to address upstream-downstream conflicts and conflicts between different water use sectors (Ostrom, 1990; Dinesh Kumar, 2000).

7.10 CONCLUSIONS

Public participation comes in many forms and shapes. It is essential for integrated water resources management. The question is: what type of public participation is best? There is no general answer to that. It depends on the cultural context, the issues at stake, the types of stakeholders, and the relationships between the stakeholders, the authorities and the experts. Yet, a number of general principles apply:

1. *Take public input seriously*: trying to 'sell' a project by means of public participation may be counterproductive.
2. *Learning but not copying from other countries and cases*: methods developed in one context are not necessarily appropriate in another context.
3. *Participatory water management research*: participatory water management requires that the supporting research is participatory too (but participatory research without a link to management or other benefits for the participants may not be such a good idea).
4. *Social learning*: public participation should promote interactions between all stakeholders, based on the principles of reflexivity, reciprocity and respect of diversity.

5. *Careful preparation*: participatory processes need to be prepared carefully. Beforehand, the relevant stakeholders need to be identified, agreement needs to be reached concerning the purpose, scope and level of public participation, everybody's roles and the rules to follow need to be discussed and a process design needs to be prepared.
6. *Neutral facilitation*: an independent convenor/ facilitator usually works better than one with a stake in the outcomes.
7. *Feedback*: report on follow-up to the participants.
8. *Public participation at multiple scales*: public participation should be organised at all scales where important decisions are made, as close to the relevant stakeholders as possible.
9. *Water users' associations are an option*: sometimes handing over responsibility to the public is a better option than just involving the public.

ACKNOWLEDGEMENTS

This chapter uses some parts from previous work by the author (Mostert, 2003c; Mostert, 2003a; Mostert, 2004). It is largely based on research that is being carried out as part of the HarmoniCOP-project (Contract no EVK1-CT-2002-00120). The author is indebted to the European Commission, who funded the HarmoniCOP project, to the stakeholders that have been involved and to all colleagues in the project. Moreover, the author benefited a lot from discussions in the European Drafting Group on Public Participation.

REFERENCES

Argyris, C. and D. Schön (1996), *Organizational Learning II. Theory, Method and Practice*, Reading, MA: Addison-Wesley.
Armour, A. (1995), 'The Citizens' Jury Model of Public Participation', in O. Renn and T. Webler (eds), *Fairness and Competence in Citizen Participation: Evaluating Models for Environmental Discourse*, Dordrecht, Boston: Kluwer Academic, pp. 175–187.
Arnstein, S. (1969), 'A ladder of citizen participation in the USA', *Journal of the American Institute of Planners*, (8)**3**, 216–224.
Assetto, V.J. and S.P. Mumme (2000), 'Decentralization, public participation and transboundary water management in Hungary and Mexico', in J. Gayer (ed.), *Participatory Processes in Water Management (PPWM); Proceedings of the Satellite Conference to the World Conference on Science* (Budapest, Hungary 28–30 June 1999), Paris: UNESCO, pp. 41–60.
Bouman, N. (1999), 'Public Participation in International River Basin and Lakes Management', Background paper prepared for the UNEP – UNECE – Netherlands initiative to develop guidelines on public participation in river basin management.

Budge, I. (1996), *The New Challenge of Direct Democracy*, Cambridge, MA: Polity Press.

BUET (2003), *Water Management: Institutional and Legal Framework for Flood Control, Drainage and Irrigation Systems. Report BUET-DUT Linkage Project Phase III: Capacity Building in the Field of Water Resources Engineering and Management in Bangladesh*, Dhaka: Bangladesh University of Engineering and Technology.

CHO (1998), *Water in the Netherlands*, Delft: Netherlands Hydrological Society.

Cohen, R. (1993), 'An advocate's view', in G. Faure and J.Z. Rubin (eds), *Culture and Negotiation: The Resolution of Water Disputes*, Newbury Park, CA: SAGE Publications, pp. 22–37.

Collingridge, D. and C. Reeve (1986), *Science Speaks to Power: the Role of Experts in Policy Making*, New York: St. Martin's Press.

Connor, D.M. (1997), *Public Participation: A Manual, How to Prevent and Resolve Public Controversy*, Victoria, BC: Development Press.

Craps, M., E. Van Rossen, S. Prins, T. Taillieu, R. Bouwen and A. Dewulf (2003), 'Social learning and water management: Lessons from a case study on the Dijle catchment', in *Proceedings of the Connections Conference on 'Active Citizenship and Multiple Identities'*, Leuven , September, pp. 418–429.

Creighton, J.L. (2000), 'Tools and techniques for effective public participation in water resources decision making', in J. Gayer (ed.), *Participatory Processes in Water Management (PPWM); Proceedings of the Satellite Conference to the World Conference on Science,* Budapest, Hungary 28–30 June 1999, Paris: UNESCO, pp. 147–166.

Cuff, J. (2001), *Participatory Processes: A tool to assist the wise use of catchments; A guide based on experience, Wise Use of Floodplains Project report*, downloadable at: http://www.floodplains.org.uk/technical.htm (last access: May 2005).

Delli Priscolli, J. (1978a), 'Implementing public involvement programs in federal agencies', in S. Langton (ed.), *Citizen Participation in America: Essays on the State of the Art*, Lexington, MA: Lexington Books.

Delli Priscolli, J. (1978b), 'Why the Federal and Regional Interest in Public Involvement in Water Resources Development', *IWR Working Paper*, **78**(1), Fort Belvoir, VA: U.S. Army Engineers Institute for Water Resources.

DETR (2000), *Public Participation in Making Local Environmental Decisions; The Aarhus Convention Newcastle Workshop; Good Practice Handbook*, London: Department of the Environment, Transport and the Regions.

Dienel, P.C. and O. Renn (1995), 'Planning cells: a gate to fractal mediation', in O. Renn and T. Webler (eds), *Fairness and Competence in Citizen Participation: Evaluating Models for Environmental Discourse*, Dordrecht, Nl and Boston, US: Kluwer Academic, pp. 117–140.

Dinesh Kumar, M. (2000), 'Institutional framework for managing groundwater: A case study of community organisations in Gujarat, India', *Water Policy*, **2**(6), 423–432.

Drafting Group (2002), 'Guidance on Public Participation in Relation to the Water Framework Directive; Active involvement, consultation, and public access to information, Prepared in the Framework of the Common Implementation Strategy of the European Commission and the EU Member States', downloadable at: http://forum.europa.eu.int/Public/irc/env/wfd/library (last access: May 2005).

Dublin Statement (1992), 'The Dublin Statement and Report of the Conference', International Conference on Water and the Environment: Development issues for the 21st century, 26–31 January 1992, Dublin, Ireland.

Ebbesson, J. (1998), 'The notion of public participation in international environmental law', *Yearbook of International Environmental Law*, **8**, 51–97.

EC (2000), 'Directive 2000/60/EC of the European Parliament and of the Council Establishing a Framework for Community Action in the Field of Water Policy' (OJ L 327, 22.12.2000).

Edelenbos, J. (2000), *Proces in vorm; Procesbegeleiding van interactieve beleidsvorming over lokale ruimtelijke projecten*, Utrecht: Uitgeverij LEMMA.

Enserink, B., D. Kamps and E. Mostert (2003), 'Public Participation in River Basin Management in the Netherlands; (Not) Everybody's concern', Delft: RBA Centre, Delft University of Technology, downloadable at: http://www.harmonicop.info (last access: May 2005).

Faure, G. and J.Z. Rubin (eds) (1993), *Culture and Negotiation: The Resolution of Water Disputes*, Newbury Park, CA: SAGE Publications.

Fisher, R. and W. Ury (1981), *Getting to Yes: Negotiating Agreement Without Giving In*, Boston: Houghton Mifflin.

Frankena, F. (1988), 'The emergent social role and political impact of the voluntary technical expert', *Environmental Impact Assessment Review*, **8**(1), 73–82.

Hamid, A., A.S. Qureshi and K. Mahmood (2004), 'Managing water through user participation: a case study from Pakistan Punjab', in J.G. Timmerman et al. (eds), *Information to Support Sustainable Water Management: From Local to Global Levels. Proceedings Monitoring Tailor-Made IV*, Lelystad: RIZA, pp. 111–119.

Hermans, L. and J. Timmermans (2001), 'Actoranalyse voor integraal waterbeheer', *H2O*, **34**(3), 19–21.

Hofstede, G. H. (1991), *Cultures and Organizations: Software of the Mind*, London, New York: McGraw-Hill.

IAP2 (2001), 'IAP2 Public Participation Toolbox', downloadable at: http://www.iap2.org/displaycommon.cfm?an=5, (last access: May 2005).

IIAV (2000), *Gender 21; Women's Recommendations to the 2nd Ministerial Conference on Water*, Amsterdam: IIAV.

Ijjas, I. and L. Szlávik (1998), 'Country Report from Hungary', in *Water Resources Management in the Czech Republic, Hungaria, Lithuania, Slovenia*, Hennef: GFA.

Jasanoff, S. (1990), *The fifth branch: science advisers as policymakers*, Cambridge, MA: Harvard University Press.

Kakebeeke, W. and N. W. M. Bouman (2000), 'The Aarhus Convention: Application of the convention principles to European water regimes', in J. Gayer (ed.), *Participatory Processes in Water Management (PPWM); Proceedings of the Satellite Conference to the World Conference on Science* (Budapest, Hungary 28–30 June 1999), Paris: UNESCO, p. 249–256.

Krämer, R.A. and F. Jäger (1998), 'Germany', in F.N. Correia (ed.), *Water Resources Management in Europe: Institutions, Issues and Dilemmas*, Rotterdam: Balkema, Vol. 1, pp. 183–325.

Linnerooth-Bayer, J. (1995), 'The Varresbecker Bach Participatory Process: An Evaluation', in O. Renn and T. Webler (eds), *Fairness and Competence in Citizen Participation: Evaluating Models for Environmental Discourse*, Dordrecht, NL and Boston, US: Kluwer Academic.

Loucks, D. P. (1990), 'Analytical Aids to Conflict Management', in W. Viessman and E. T. Smerdon (eds), *Managing water-related conflicts: the engineer's role. Proceedings of the Engineering Foundation Conference, Sheraton Santa Barbara, Santa Barbara, California*, November 5–10, 1989, New York: American Society of Civil Engineers, pp. 23–37.

Marty, F. (2001*), Managing international rivers : problems, politics and institutions*, Bern and New York, US: Peter Lang.

Mastenbroek, W. F. G. (1996), *Onderhandelen*, Utrecht: Spectum/ Marca.

Meinzen-Dick, R. (1997), 'Farmer participation in irrigation; 20 years of experience and lessons for the future', *Irrigation and Drainage Systems*, **11** (2), 103–118.

Milich, L. and R.G. Varady (1999), 'Openness, Sustainability and Public Participation; New Designs for Transboundary River-Basin Institutions', *Journal of Environment and Development*, **8** (3), 258–306.

Mostert, E. (2000), 'The management of International River Basins: How can the public participate?' in J. Gayer (ed.), *Participatory Processes in Water Management (PPWM); Proceedings of the Satellite Conference to the World Conference on Science* (Budapest, Hungary 28–30 June 1999): Paris: UNESCO, p. 61–76.

Mostert, E. (2003a), 'The Challenge of Public Participation', *Water Policy*, **5** (2), 179–197.

Mostert, E. (2003b), 'Conflict and co-operation in international freshwater management; A global review', *Journal of River Basin Management*, **1** (3), 1–12.

Mostert, E. (2004), 'Public participation and social learning for river basin management', in J.G. Timmerman, H.W.A. Behrens, F. Bernardini, D. Daler, P. Ross, K.J.M. van Ruiten and R.C. Ward (eds), *Information to support sustainable water management: from local to global levels. Proceedings Monitoring Tailor-Made IV*, Lelystad: RIZA, pp. 103–109.

Mostert, E. (ed.) (2003c), 'Public Participation and the European Water Framework Directive; A framework for analysis, Inception report of the HarmoniCOP project', downloadable at: http://www.harmonicop.info (last access: May 2005).

Mostert, E. et al. (2001), 'Open planning vereist integrale aanpak; Verslag van de NVA studiedag op 21 november', *Het Waterschap*, 201–203.

Osland, J.S. and A. Bird (2000), 'Beyond sophisticated stereotyping: Cultural sensemaking in context', *Academy of Management Executive*, **14**(1), 65–77.

Ostrom, E. (1990), *Governing the Commons: the Evolution of Institutions for Collective Action*, Cambridge, UK and New York, US: Cambridge University Press.

Pahl-Wostl, C. and D. Ridder (2004), 'Participatory integrated assessment in local level planning', in J.G. Timmerman, H.W.A. Behrens, F. Bernardini, D. Daler, P. Ross, K.J.M. van Ruiten and R.C. Ward (eds), *Information to support sustainable water management: from local to global levels. Proceedings Monitoring Tailor-Made IV*, Lelystad: RIZA, pp. 129–139.

Pateman, C. (1970), *Participation and Democratic Theory*, Cambridge: Cambridge University Press.

Pradhan, T.M.S. (1996), *Gated or Ungated Water Control in Government-built Irrigation Systems*, Wageningen: Wageningen University.

REC (1998), Doors to Democracy, Szentendre: Regional Environmental Center.

REC (1999), *Healthy Decisions; Access to Information, Public Participation in Decision-making and Access to Justice in Environment and Health Matters*, Szentendre: Regional Environmental Center.

Roberts, R. (1995), 'Public involvement: from consultation to participation', in F. Vanclay and D. A. Bronstein (eds), *Environmental and Social Impact Assessment*, Chichester, UK and New York, US: J. Wiley.

Roller, G. (2003), 'The role of EU institutions and the influence of citizens in the enforcement of EU environmental law', *ELNI Review*, **1**, 7–12.

Scheer, S. (1996*), Communication Between Irrigation Engineers and Farmers; The Case of Project Design in North Senegal*, Wageningen: Wageningen University.

Thaillieu, T., R. Bouwen, M. Craps, A. Dewulf and S. Prins (2003), *Multiorganizational Collaboration in River Basin Management and the Social Learning Concept,*

MOPAN Conference, Glasgow, June 2003.

Thompson, M., R. Ellis and A.B. Wildavsky (1990*), Cultural Theory*, Boulder, Colo.: Westview Press.

Ubbels, A. and J.M. Verhallen (2000), *Suitability of Decision Support Systems for Collaborative Planning Processes in Water Resources Management*, Lelystad: RIZA.

UN-ECE (2000), *The Aarhus Convention: An Implementation Guide*, New York, US and Geneva, SW: United Nations.

Vansina, L. and T. Thaillieu (1997), 'Diversity in collaborative task systems', *European Journal of Work and Organizational Psychology*, **6**(2), 183–199.

Ven, G.P. van de (1993), *Man-made lowlands*, Utrecht: Matrijs.

Verweij, M. (2000), *Transboundary Environmental Problems and Cultural Theory: The Protection of the Rhine and the Great Lakes*, New York: Palgrave.

Webler, T. and O. Renn (1995), 'A Brief Primer on Participation: Philosophy and Practice', in O. Renn and T. Webler (eds), *Fairness and Competence in Citizen Participation: Evaluating Models for Environmental Discourse*, Dordrecht, NL and Boston, US: Kluwer Academic, pp. 17–33.

Wenger, E. (1998), *Communities of practice: learning, meaning, and identity*, Cambridge, UK and New York, US: Cambridge University Press.

Woerkom, C.V. (1997), *Communicatie en Interactieve Beleidsvorming*, Houten, NL and Diegem, BE: Bohn Stafleu Van Loghum.

8. Methods for Stakeholder Participation in Water Management

Matt P. Hare, Olivier Barreteau, M. Bruce Beck, Rebecca A. Letcher, Erik Mostert, J. David Tàbara, Dagmar Ridder, Valerie Cogan and Claudia Pahl-Wostl

8.1 INTRODUCTION

This chapter, by way of case studies, illustrates the variety of participatory methods that can and are being applied to carry out participatory water management activities around the world. To understand which participatory method to apply to any given participatory management context is not straightforward. Participatory methods may work in some contexts and not so well in others. A good analysis and understanding of when participatory methods can be best applied are important. This chapter develops such an analysis based on the assumption that, in practice, methods are selected to match a set of four participatory management criteria: a) the particular management stage to be supported; b) the goal of participation; c) the desired level of participation; and d) the type of stakeholders involved (see Hare et al., 2003). Five case studies are thus categorised according to these criteria and critiques their application of particular methods in order to help readers to identify methods that may be suitable for their own participatory management contexts and to copy the successes of previous research, whilst avoiding the pitfalls.

In Chapter 7, Erik Mostert introduced the concept of public and stakeholder participation in water management. He explained what participatory water management can be, gave reasons for why it is being promoted, defined different levels of participation and provided some principles for the design of such participatory processes. This chapter complements the previous one by providing more details about particular methods used to actually carry out participatory water management. In Section 8.2 of this chapter, 'Participatory methods in water management', a framework for considering participatory methods is presented and placed in the context of water management. Section

8.3, 'Participatory processes, methods and evaluation techniques', then goes on to introduce selected participatory methods that are highlighted in the case studies presented in Section 8.4 'Case studies'.

The case studies in Section 8.4 represent a snap-shot in time of research work being done on participatory water management and have been compiled from the experiences of various experts in the discipline. These case studies are in no way intended to be a comprehensive list, yet they are intended to represent research from different continents, each of which adopts its own approach. They therefore serve as a broad starting point for the interested manager and researcher from which to find out more about research into participatory water management.

Following the case study descriptions, Section 8.5, 'Conclusions: lessons to be learnt from the studies', derives lessons about the strengths and weaknesses of the methods as reported by practitioners in the field. Rather than being an assessment of the methods in isolation, this critique is of the methods as they are used in the context of the particular case studies. It also notes the difference between direct participation in water management decision making and participation in the water management research. It is important for the reader to bear in mind that the emphasis of the cases in this chapter lies more on the research side.

In the appendix at the end of the chapter, 'Handbooks on participation', a brief critique of participatory management handbooks is presented, which, together with an extensive list of references, provides the reader with sources for further learning about the subject.

8.2 PARTICIPATORY METHODS IN WATER MANAGEMENT

The use of participatory methods in all or some of these management stages has been a goal of Integrated Assessment and management for some time (Rotmans, 1998; Renn et al., 1995; Kasemir et al., 2003). However, which types of participatory methods should be used to support water management? To answer this question, one needs to consider the following four criteria: the management stage to be supported; the level of participation; the organisers' intended (top-down)[1] goals of participation; and the types of participant that need to become involved (see Table 8.1).

8.2.1 Management Stages

Water management involves various linked stages of activities. The framework provided by the Social Learning Group (2001) to analyse environmental

Table 8.1   Instances of the four criteria

Levels of participation[2]	Management stages[3]	Participant types[4]	Participatory goals
Information supply	Problem and goal identification	Broad public	Greater acceptance of policy
Consultation	Monitoring	Organised stakeholder	Social learning
Co-thinking	Option assessment		Elicitation of local knowledge into management process
Co-designing	Strategy formulation		Increased democracy
Co-decision making	Implementation		Conflict reduction
Self-control	Evaluation		

policy processes related to global change can also be useful to identify the activity stages which occur within the water policy domain. These stages are:

1. Problem and goal identification: What is the problem?
2. Monitoring: What is happening?
3. Option Assessment: What could be done?
4. Strategy formulation: What should be done?
5. Implementation: What is being done?
6. Evaluation: How well are we doing?

Participation of stakeholders can occur in all of these different stages of the policy process. Furthermore, different actors might play a greater role in some of these phases, and also might need different resources or channels to participate. Additionally, in the case of water management there are other important activities such as the development and validation of models and decision support systems which support the six activities above and which in turn may require participation.

8.2.2   Levels of Participation

The levels of participation considered in this chapter are those that are aimed for under the EU Water Framework Directive (WFD – see Chapter 3). In the terminology of Mostert (see Chapter 7), these represent the first four levels: information supply, consultation, co-thinking and co-designing (co-decision making and self-control are not envisaged since responsibility for decision remains with the responsible authorities).

8.2.3   Goals of Participation

The goals for participation (Mostert, Chapter 7; Pretty, 1995; Glicken, 2000; van Asselt et al., 2001; van der Sluijs and Kloprogge, 2001; Cooke and Kothari, 2001; Pahl-Wostl, 2002a) are seen in terms of improving the decision making process through social learning, the elicitation and use of local knowledge, increased democracy, conflict resolution and, arguably most importantly from a manager's point of view, greater public and stakeholder acceptability of management decisions.

8.2.4   Participant Types

Here the distinction between public and stakeholder participants is adopted which reserves 'public participation' for participation by the unorganised 'general' or 'broad public' and 'stakeholder participation' for 'participation by well-organised and recognised interest groups and other influential actors, sometimes including government bodies' (Mostert, Chapter 7).

8.2.5   Selecting Methods

The selection of methods also requires knowledge about the methods that are available and which are best used for which purpose. The knowledge available is not yet comprehensive. Even in such countries where participatory management methods have a comparatively long history of practice (e.g. Australia), it is unclear to practitioners how to match 'what we want from participation and the many ways in which people can participate' (Dovers, 2000 p. 96). Progress in this direction, however, is being made in the water management field. The guidance document on public participation for the WFD (Drafting Group, 2002) outlines much of what is expected from participation and provides illustrative case studies as well as lists of some available methods, although no categorisation of methods according to requirements is provided. Categorisations of methods, to different degrees of exhaustiveness, can be found in van Asselt et al. (2001) and Mostert (2003) or, for participatory group model building, Hare et al. (2003). Additionally, for an early and comprehensive review of methods for public involvement in environmental assessment see Sinclair and Diduck (1995). The next two sections of this chapter provide further support for the task of matching methods to participatory water management requirements by describing the use of methods in case studies categorised according to the four participatory management criteria.

8.3 PARTICIPATORY PROCESSES, METHODS AND EVALUATION TECHNIQUES

This section presents a brief description of the variety of participatory processes, participatory methods and evaluation techniques that are illustrated in the case studies. A distinction has been made between participatory methods and participatory processes. Processes are intended as long-term participatory events that may involve the use of a number of different participatory methods to achieve their aims. The subsection on methods describes, in alphabetical order, those used in the case studies. Methods are also listed for evaluating the quality and effectiveness of participation.

8.3.1 Participatory Processes

Group Model Building
Group model building (GMB) (Vennix, 1996) is a methodology for facilitating the 'deep involvement' of a group of individuals in building a model of a particular management system. The goal is to improve group understanding about that system, its problems and possible solutions, which will lead directly or indirectly to better management decisions. In such a methodology, the model itself is not the product of the process. Rather it is the group process, within the framework of model building, involved in identifying system ontology, problems, causes, consequences and solutions, that is responsible for the main outputs of GMB: group consensus, team learning, and improved acceptance of management decisions.

Adaptive Community Learning
Adaptive community learning has been developed over the past five years by Beck et al. (2002b). The prototypical shell of the procedure involves an iterative, cyclical process entailing the following elements, and largely in this sequence:

1. identifying stakeholder concerns for the future;
2. developing mathematical models, as maps of the current science base (with all its uncertainties, knowns, partially knowns, and unknowns), to assist in exploring those concerns;
3. formal, computational assessment of the stakeholder-generated, potential futures;
4. communicating to stakeholders the plausibility or otherwise of their feared/hoped-for futures;
5. identifying the key scientific unknowns (critical model parameters) on which the realisation of potential future outcomes may crucially turn; and

6. designing further experimental/field tests to reduce the uncertainty of the key unknowns, in turn to reduce the uncertainty of any forecast future outcomes.

The cycle of this process is completed in the following way. If, during step 4, stakeholder fears for the future appear to be groundless, or their hopes appear unattainable, then assistance must be provided so that they can begin to reassess and reformulate their concerns. Once this is done, then the procedure returns to the first step, ready for iteration. The scientists participating in the process should then seek to derive a set of priorities based upon these new sets of concerns, so that further scientific effort can be tailored to the concerns of the community (steps 5 and 6), since no environmental problem will ever be sufficiently funded to purchase the scientific effort required for resolving all the unknowns that may be pertinent to the issue at hand. Steps 5 and 6 are therefore essentially about setting priorities for the scientific agenda, as we continually move into the future. Their outcomes should in due course find their way back into step 2, into a revised map of the science base (a revised computational model), with which to explore the evolving landscape of stakeholder hopes and fears.

Social Learning
Social Learning is not a procedure that can be followed, but rather a goal to achieve and a set of principles to be used when selecting and applying specific processes and using specific methods. Whilst the Group Model Building and Adaptive Community Learning principally focus on the development of knowledge and insights into the system, Social Learning also has a strong link to developing the social capital of the management community, a factor that is also considered necessary for improving our management of water resources. As such, social learning is considered a very important concept in participatory methods research (Pahl-Wostl, 2002a, b).

Water management involves many authorities, interest groups, companies, citizens and experts. They all have an interest in the basin, affect the basin or possess relevant information. Together, they need to learn about the basin, how they depend on it and how they may affect it. In the end, they have to arrive at joint action or at least coordinate their actions. They have to learn together to manage together (see http://www.harmonicop.info).

One of the theories on social learning is Bandura's (1977) social learning theory. Social learning, according to Bandura, has two central tenets. First of all, learning is seen as being based upon social imitation of role models ('learning by modelling'), not upon trial and error. Second, learning is a product of reciprocal determinism, in that behaviour and the environment are in a constant feedback loop, adapting each other. However, as noted in the previous chapter, social learning as conceived here is more than a means for improving learning by individuals. It is also about supporting new or established groups to develop effective responses to management issues (Craps, 2003, Mostert, 2004). Social Learning requires that, first, the different stakeholders realise that they are interdependent and that no one is powerful or knowledgeable enough to manage the resource on his or her own satisfactorily. Second, stakeholders have to organise themselves around the main issues at stake and start interacting. To do so, it is paramount that they recognise the differences in the way each frames the issues and in their perceptions and priorities.

The contemporary view of social learning, as reflected in the HarmoniCOP project (Craps, 2003), is that it involves the acquisition of collective skills to collectively thrive in and be able to adapt to a continually changing social, environmental and economic environment. Such skills could enable us to solve the problems of matching the disparate requirements for water supply efficiency, water distribution equity and water quality as described in Chapters 2 and 3. This emphasis, however, on development of the human dimension in management is quite a challenge for water management with its technical and engineering tradition.

8.3.2 Participatory Methods

The methods described here do not form a comprehensive list. Rather they introduce the methods that are used and described in the cases studies in the following section. For a broad range of methods, a recommended book for the interested reader is Wates (2000).

These methods are categorised according to two criteria. The first criterion is whether they are predominantly used for large groups of participants or for medium to small ones. The second criterion is based on the levels of participation (with consultation having been subdivided into consultation and knowledge elicitation), i.e. whether or not the methods can be used to:

- (I) inform stakeholders and the public about management plans;
- (C) consult them on their views about management plans;
- (E) elicit local knowledge about the management system and
- (D) involve them in co-designing management plans.

Methods for large groups

Large Group Response Exercises (I, E, C)
These are facilitated workshops organised to quickly elicit responses to particular questions from large groups of people (up to several hundred

people), normally members of the public (Orth and Sanders, 1998). It involves specifying a few questions and then asking people to write their answers down. The people are then asked to filter their own answers in order to select their most important contribution to the debate and then to come up and display it on the wall. These points are then discussed in a moderated debate.

Mailouts (I)
The public or stakeholders can be kept informed about the planning process through a newsletter that is regularly posted to them.

Questionnaires/Surveys (E, C)
Questionnaires/surveys are structured questions that can be sent to participants to elicit knowledge about the management system or consult them on management plans. Questionnaires have been used extensively by environmental sociology during the last three decades, mainly with the aim to explore people's perceptions of particular problems, measures or policy measures or, more broadly, to analyse the possible change of cultural paradigms towards more ecologically or sustainability ones (Dunlap and Jones, 2002; Olsen et al., 1992; Tàbara, 2001).

Web site provision (I, E, C)
Web sites may be developed to provide a source of information by which the public and stakeholders may regularly be kept up to date with news about the planning process. They can also be used as platforms to run surveys to consult the public and to elicit knowledge from them.

Methods for small- to medium-sized groups or individuals

Capacity building workshops (I)
These are facilitated group training workshops in which participants can be trained in particular techniques useful for the implementation of management plans, e.g. how to maintain and monitor the water bodies created or improved as a result of the management plans.

Card sorting (E)
This is an elicitation method that has roots in experimental cognitive psychology and is practised in the discipline of knowledge engineering. Its strengths are in gathering information about given concepts and how they are categorised in the minds of the subject whose knowledge is being elicited (Gammack, 1987; Maiden and Hare, 1998). These could be used to find out, for example, public and stakeholder perceptions of water issues and the roles and interactions of actors (see, for example, Hare and Pahl-Wostl, 2002).

Focus groups (I, E, C)

Focus groups are small group meetings in which a group of people are brought together to discuss a particular topic with the support of a moderator. Focus groups have been developed and used in sociology for over half a century (Merton and Kendall, 1946; Merton, 1987). Variations on the theme of focus groups are countless and have also been used extensively in environmental planning and Integrated Assessment (IA).

The typical form of focus group gathers participants together who will have never met before and will not form as a group again. Normally, focus groups rely on the interactions between group members to generate qualitative data about the topic of concern (Grabowski et al., 1992). Some designs, however, consult the same participants several times, depending on the complexity of the situation with which to be dealt. IA focus groups (Kasemir, et al. 2003), for example, are facilitated meetings of six–ten people which are repeated half a dozen times with the same group. Such groups contain expert and non-experts on environmental and sustainability issues who discuss possible policy options, supported by computer models which also include socioeconomic factors and variables. IA focus groups are thus a hybrid methodology that can be used to integrate social quantitative and qualitative methodologies, expert and non-expert sources of knowledge, and global and local scales. Variations of these type of focus groups have been used in many diverse environmental policy situations, including water and river basin management, depending on the issues at stake, the available resources, or even time constraints (Tàbara, 2003).

Cognitive mapping (carried out on individuals: E; carried out with a group: E, D)

Cognitive mapping refers to the suite of techniques used to elicit participants' mental models of the world around them and to represent them graphically. Mental models are perceptions of the world and the way it works that allow people to make decisions and operate within it (Doyle and Ford, 1998). Thus these methods can be used to elicit not only ontological knowledge of the management domain (i.e. what are the important things to consider whilst planning), but also the causal and other relational links between these things (why things happen; what may happen). Traditionally, these techniques are used in small groups to construct an agreed group visualisation of how the management system works (usually in the form of a single causal model or a directed graph). This can then be used by the group to discuss and plan management strategy. Good examples of this can be found in methodologies provided by hexagon method (Hodgson, 1992) and causal modelling (Vennix, 1996). Such methods can also be used simply for knowledge elicitation from individuals. A variation of this use of the Hexagon method is described in the Swiss Case Study below.

Interviews (E, C)

Verbal interviews with members of the public or stakeholders can be used to elicit information or their views about a particular management plan. These may take the form of structured interviews in which respondents are asked a set list of questions; unstructured interviews in which the questions asked are not predetermined or semi-structured interviews, in which some broad questions are predetermined whilst the majority of questions depend on the course of the interview.

Joint use of models (I, C, D)

The joint use of models is a way to broaden the field of information available to participants of a collective decision process (Benbasat and Lim, 2000). It does so by providing easy access for a group of people to interact and experiment with a model of the management system, and thus discuss their findings together. Thus the model can act as information provider, can be used to consult people and to help them get more deeply involved in assessing management plans and decision making. The model may be in the form of a computer simulation (Barreteau et al., 2003) or a paper model (Pahl-Wostl and Hare, 2004), used in the same room or distributed across an internet platform.

As Barreteau et al. (2003) point out, joint use of models aims at giving the group more insight into the processes at stake. Providing participants with information about potential consequences of various choices involved in an on-going group decision process reportedly mobilises them more actively in the process (Driessen et al., 2001). It is also a way to alleviate the problem of stakeholders being hesitant to get involved in negotiation. It does so by providing the group, through the model use, with a better understanding of the complexity system and of the heterogeneity of points of view. The model can be then used to simulate dynamic aspects of the actors' relations to specific stakes in the negotiation. The model as such endorses the role of an intermediary object (Vinck, 1999), and mediates the interactions among stakeholders.

Role playing (I, E, D)

A highly specialised form of joint model use is role playing. Social, economic and environmental models of the management system can be converted into role-playing games (RPG) wherein the participants are not simply observing the model from the outside, but actually embedded in the game as actors making decisions about management. The easiest kind of model to convert to role-playing games is an Agent-Based Model (ABM – for a review of ABM in environmental modelling see Hare and Deadman, 2004). In this case, each agent in the model is converted into a role to be played by a participant. The players (as water users and/or managers) play their assigned roles under different environmental and management scenarios. By doing so they can select and test policies to see how their decision making as a group of autonomous and self-interested decision makers affects the policy outcomes. This type of policy analysis, suggesting what is and what may not be an effective policy can then be used directly in the real world decision making process. Other benefits of role playing include helping the participants to learn about the impact of multiple interests on system management, to acclimatise to a particular model and to improve model validation. They can therefore form part of a group model-building exercise or support social learning. As such, RPGs can stimulate learning for players as well as for game organisers, even though the players might only be concerned with how to interact with each other.

RPGs as interactive methods should feature group settings from real life situations. This overlapping of the game with real life is important since they make them different to ordinary games: the RPG becomes no longer disconnected from real life, as stated by Huizinga (1951), and becomes instead useful for simulating real activities. The relation between the world of the game and the world of real life, between RPG and social processes actually appears to be a continuum. In fact, real interactions between a society and its environment are sometimes seen as a form of game in itself (Mermet, 1992) since people act in them as representatives of groups or stakeholders and thus take on specific roles (Innes and Booher, 1999). An RPG can therefore constitute a kind of small-scale model of a society in interaction with its environment and thus can be seen as the 'like societies' upon which scientists and stakeholders may reflect and discuss before working on the world at large (Kohler, 1999) (for further discussion see Barreteau, 2003).

Steering committees (C, D)
These bodies are likely to contain representatives of stakeholder groups whose role is to oversee the planning process and guide it in the correct direction (in a consultative role or in active decision making). The structure and roles of a steering committee and power of its members to direct the selection of methods, design of models or participatory processes, etc. will vary between planning processes.

8.3.3 Evaluation Techniques

Evaluation techniques are used to provide qualitative and/or quantitative assessments of how well the participatory process has developed according to different criteria. Evaluation methods can be distinguished between methods that involve the participants in their own evaluation of the process and methods carried out by external researchers.

Methods for participants' own evaluation

Innovation Assessment

This tool (see UNCHS, 2001) helps to answer the question: Was the participatory process/the project capable of initiating something new? After project termination, community members complete an innovation information sheet, answering the particular questions about the innovation, which include:

- What was the innovation?
- Why was it important?
- Who was involved in its implementation?
- Who will benefit from it? Who will not?

Once the assessment is completed for all proposed innovations they should be ranked in terms of priority for further study. Different measures/innovations can be compared with each other. Such ranking would normally be done during a community workshop.

Sustainability Matrix

Whereas innovation assessment tries to identify the new aspects or ideas that were generated by a project, the goal of the sustainability matrix is to identify the chances that a process once begun can survive under different conditions. The sustainability matrix method (see UNCHS, 2001) can be used during a process to evaluate the sustainability of the participatory project by the participants themselves. Participants are trained in their analytical skills to evaluate their own projects. A matrix is then built up from an evaluation of the participants' sustainability indicators for the project. The participants identify and define those sustainability factors that may hinder or interfere with the continued existence of the process. They also identify and define those factors which support the continued existence of the process and may contribute to their improvement or expansion. They will then develop strategies to offset these threats or take advantage of the opportunities affecting the process.

Participant surveys and interviews

The participants can be asked to evaluate their experience, simply by interviewing them, or through a formalised questionnaire. Varying opinions will provide an understanding of the overall experience from a variety of perspectives. This can be particularly useful for processes that aim at broad representation.

Methods for External Evaluation

Project documentation
Ideally, an evaluation process will be built into the project design. Both in the case of research work and in the case of initiatives that are managed by public authorities, the 'experiment' is more useful if it can be reproduced. For some, this is a criterion to assess the scientific legitimacy of the method. This calls for careful step by step documentation of procedures by the research team to allow others to apply the process with a similar approach. In this connection, a requirements and constraints analysis that is conducted prior to the preparation of group work can be a useful tool. If such rigor is adhered to, then the post-process evaluation has a firm point of reference. Explicit criteria for success become criteria for post-process evaluation, the points at which evaluation take place appear along the project's time line, and the methods are pre-selected and budgeted for.

Cost-benefit monitoring and analysis
Every project has a budget, and many benefit from interested people volunteering their time and resources. At the outset of any project there are implicit assumptions made about how much achieving the stated objectives will cost. By keeping careful track of the actual expenditure of time and money, and by assessing the benefits gained as a result of the process, an evaluation of those assumptions can be attempted.

Experimental observation and comparison of participants' behaviour
The people involved in the process may communicate their enthusiasm and understanding through their body language, their willingness to spend time engaging in activities, and their level of contribution in terms of active discussion. Giving someone the task of recording these observations during and after group work will provide information that can be useful for evaluating the process. This can formalised within a specific experimental setup.

8.4   CASE STUDIES

The following section presents five case studies in applied research on participatory water management taken from across the world. Table 8.2 shows how the studies have been categorised in terms of location, participant types and project goals.

Table 8.2   Classification of the case studies – location, participants and project goals

Case study	Location	Participants	Project goal for organisers
Irrigation management	SENEGAL Senegal River Middle Valley	Farmers Villages SAED	To raise the consciousness of farmers about sharing common problems and the potential benefits of coordinating themselves
Water allocation	AUSTRALIA Gwydir and Namoi river basins	State level policy makers Local government Catchment managers Catchment management boards River management committees Industry groups Irrigators	The development of a DSS for stakeholders to estimate management trade-offs
Urban water management	SWITZERLAND Swiss city	Water utilities Housing associations Manufacturers Consumer forums	To identify the main problems in the management system and identify solutions that will meet the apparently contradictory community norms
Sharing visions for Lake Lanier	USA North Georgia (to the north of metropolitan Atlanta)	Members of the public state, county, and municipality policy makers Environmental and engineering professionals/consultants	The development of shared visions for the future of Lake Lanier, as a first step towards its future stewardship by the community, and the development of the participatory method itself
Transboundary management	PORTUGAL AND SPAIN Tajo, Duero and Guadiana River basins	River basin administrators NGOs Farmers (Aprox. 105)	Improve the stakeholders' knowledge and capacity for the implementation of the WFD in the transboundary context

Table 8.3 shows how they are categorised according to the remaining three participatory management criteria: organisers' participatory goals, the management stages to be supported by the participants and their level of participation. Each study illustrates the implementation of different participatory methods in different water management domains: lake water management, irrigation management, urban and rural water management, and transboundary river basin management (Table 8.4).

Interestingly, as a comparison of these three tables indicates, these case studies represent a contrast in the types of methods applied. This contrast occurs despite, in some cases, the case studies having similar general

Table 8.3   Classification of the case studies – participatory goals, management stage supported and desired level of stakeholder participation

Case study	Participatory goals for organisers							Management stage supported							Level of participation for stakeholders
	Social learning	Increase communication	Elicit local info	Increase democracy	Increase acceptance	Increase value of local info	Conflict reduction	Problem and goal id.	Monitoring	Options assessment	Strategy formulation	Implementation	Evaluation	Model/DSS dev.	
Irrigation management in Senegal	✓	✓	.	.	.	✓	.	✓	.	.	.	.	.	✓	co-thinking
Water allocation in the Gwydir and Namoi Valleys, Australia	.	.	.	.	.	.	✓	✓	.	✓	.	.	.	.	consultation/ co-thinking
Urban water management in Switzerland	✓	✓	✓	.	.	.	.	✓	.	✓	.	.	.	.	co-thinking / co-designing
Sharing visions for Lake Lanier, USA	✓	.	✓	.	.	✓	.	✓	.	.	.	.	.	.	consultation / co-thinking
Transboundary management in Iberian river basins, Portugal and Spain	✓	✓	✓	.	.	.	.	✓	✓	✓	✓	✓	✓	.	consultation

Table 8.4   The application of processes, methods and evaluation techniques across case studies

Process/Method/Evaluation	Senegal	Australia	Switzerland	USA	Portugal and Spain
Group model building	.	✓	✓	.	.
Adaptive community learning	.	.	.	✓	.
Social learning	✓	.	✓	✓	✓
Capacity building	.	✓	.	.	.
Card sorting	.	.	⊕	.	.
Facilitated small group workshops	.	✓	⊕	.	.
Focus groups	.	.	.	.	✓
Cognitive mapping	.	.	✓	.	.
Interviews	.	✓	.	.	.
Joint use of models	✓	✓	⊕	.	.
Large group response exercise	.	.	.	✓	✓
Mailouts	.	✓	.	.	.
Questionnaires	.	✓	.	✓	✓
Role playing	✓	.	⊕	.	.
Steering committees	.	✓	.	.	.
Web sites	.	✓	.	.	✓
Observing participants' behaviour	.	.	.	.	.
Participant surveys and interviews	.	⊕	⊕	.	.
Innovation assessment	.	.	.	.	.
Project documentation	.	⊕	⊕	.	.
Cost benefit analysis	.	.	.	.	.
Sustainability matrix	.	.	.	.	.
Experimental observation	✓	.	.	.	.

Notes: ✓ indicates that the method is described in the text for this case study.
⊕ indicates method was used in case study but not described in the text.

participatory goals, similar management activities and/or having sought to set up similar processes. For example, the Swiss and the Gwydir and Namoi cases both implement a group model building process to aid problem/goal identification and options assessment. Yet the methods they apply are quite different. The methods used represent a bias towards, respectively, building models for use in social learning, and building models used to develop decision support tools. Additionally, social learning does not necessarily mean that group model building is required, as the Senegal case study shows. Instead, this case study focuses on group, or joint, model use and role play. This approach should then be contrasted to the approach to social learning implemented within the Lake Lanier and Iberian river basins case studies. In these cases, learning occurs mainly through facilitated workshops and/or focus groups. The difference between the two approaches can be seen in their intended level of participation. Senegal sought to include participants in co-thinking whilst the Lake Lanier and Iberian case studies focused, in the main, on consultation. This richness in variety of approaches is demonstrated in the remainder of this section.

8.4.1   Irrigation Management in Senegal Middle River Valley

Irrigated systems in the Senegal River Valley[5] are showing cases of abandon, under-use and low yields, in relation to the initial expectations of their designers as well as their funders. Their introduction has modified the coordination habits of farmers in the area, through the construction of physical constraints to using water collectively. The farmers were used to co-operating with each other for the use of space by using social order criteria (notably, the hierarchy of casts and age groups), but now they also have to coordinate the sharing, managing and maintenance of pumping stations and channels (Barreteau and Bousquet, 2000).

Many disciplinary studies within this area have identified important financial and technical issues; however these are just some of the various facets regarding the question of the viability of these irrigated systems. A basic assumption underlying this case study is that coordination patterns among farmers using an irrigated system are also an important influence on its longevity. To assess this assumption, an Agent Based Model (ABM) was developed using a companion modelling approach (Barreteau et al., 2004). The ABM was then translated into a role-playing game to communicate its content to farmers who had been interviewed and to get farmer support in the model's validation (Barreteau and Bousquet, 1999; Barreteau et al., 2001).

Participatory management task
In this case study, three kinds of tasks were to be supported through the use of participatory methods:

1.   social learning about the complexity of the system and how to cooperate to manage it;

2.   validation of the content of an existing model of the irrigation management system;
3.   identification of the irrigation management system.

Participatory methods used
In this case study, two participatory methods were used:

1.   a role playing game; and
2.   the joint use of an Agent Based Model.

   Players (some ten or twelve people, mainly farmers, but also taken from local leaders and extensionists from the state-owned basin management society, SAED) take on the roles of farmers who cultivate plots in an irrigated scheme in the Senegal River Valley. They play out their roles in a room representing the villages (the 'village space') and are divided into two friendship groups. In this room, two tables represent the two groups in the game, which implement collective rules. At the beginning of the game, each player is randomly dealt cards which describe social status, goal for cultivating the plot, and rules for reimbursement of credits. Cards are trilingual: Pulaar, Wolof and French. On the basis of an 'opportunity card' drawn randomly and on the basis of their goal card, players may go to a second room where the map of the irrigation system and plots is illustrated on a chalkboard. In front of this board, in addition to managing their plot, they update their knowledge of the current state of their plot as well as the state of others'. They can also monitor and discuss with others farmer who may also be in front of the board, how the collective rules are really enforced. Back in the village space they share this information with players belonging to their group.
   For the second participatory method, we used a computerised translation of the very same conceptual model as used in the RPG, to which stakeholders had previously agreed, as well as an interface displaying the graphical elements of the game. This new Agent Based Model has been named 'Njoobari ilnoowo'[6] by participants. The modeller managed the computer according to participants' choices, i.e. holding the mouse and clicking on the interface buttons as participants required (see Figure 8.1 for a screen snapshot of the interface). Even though most of the participants had never used a computer before, they were very active in selecting scenarios and discussing the results afterwards, even though they selected only politically correct scenarios. They understood the model and were able to play with it. Groups of ten stakeholders were jointly using this model.

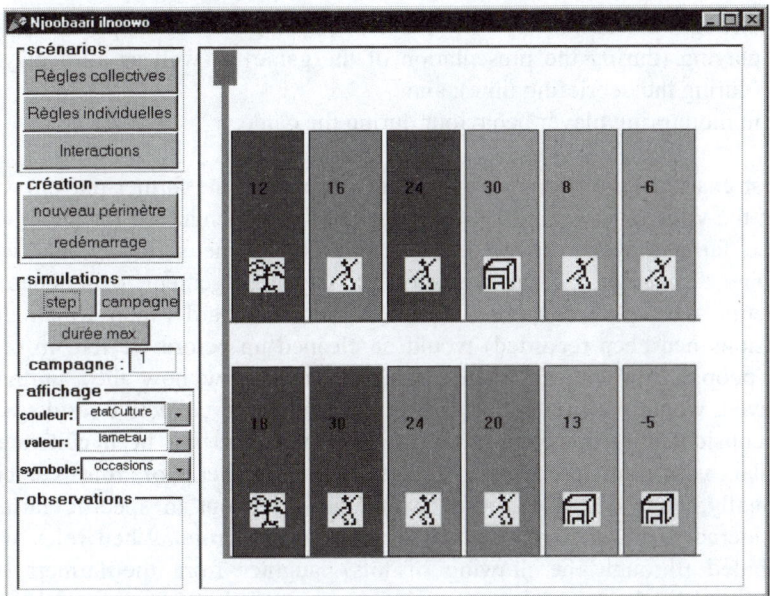

Figure 8.1   Interface of ABM Njoobaari Ilnoowo showing the schematic of the irrigation plots also featured in the role-playing game

Strengths and weaknesses

In terms of social learning, the major strength of both RPG and the joint use of models is their ability to generate discussions about the issues faced daily by farmers. When organising the RPG sessions with stakeholders from the irrigated systems in the Senegal River valley, even in the first batch of short sessions, we received feedback that it was an interesting tool for raising after-session discussions among stakeholders about their collective behaviour in the systems. It was reported to us that such discussions sometimes lasted late into the night in the villages. The most striking effect of all these sessions was the way they stimulated discussions about the participants' own experience of these systems. By sharing their experience with other participants, individuals noticed that theirs was a more common experience than they had first thought. Sharing the same time and space to play the game brought them to better understand their interactions around the virtual irrigated system, and then to understand that the same interactions were occurring in real irrigated systems. In fact the game raised the necessity of having, in reality, a coordination meeting among farmers at the beginning of each cropping season.

In terms of model validation, this occurred through two mechanisms:

1.   through discussion by the players about game assumptions before playing (during the presentation of the game) as well as after playing (during the debriefing time); and
2.   in monitoring player behaviour during the game.

For example, the first time the game was played, the farmer players were from the villages where initial interviews had been conducted for the model. These farmers were observed to consider the game seriously and were convinced enough of the veracity of the management experience to sometimes be quite concerned that our portable board (upon which their decisions had been recorded) would be cleaned up before we left, in order that people from other villages, who did not know how they normally behaved, would not find out. This was especially so if collective results were not considered as being good (i.e. several plots had not been cultivated). Similar validation processes occurred in assessment of role veracity. Normally, once described, roles would be given out to specific farmers considered to be well represented by one specific role. When roles were attributed (through the drawing of lots) laughter from the farmers was interpreted by the research team as questioning the degree to which the role actually did represent farmers' real behavioural patterns. For example, some farmers, who in the real world are not very busy at cultivating, were laughed at if they drew the role of intensive farmers.

Dynamic validation through gaming patterns was less effective. The participants' preference to test scenarios using officially recommended behavioural patterns did not allow for the testing of a large spectrum of alternative behavioural patterns. They also tended to use some of their real attributes, notably their social position, even when they were denying the relevance of these attributes to describe their real behavioural patterns.

In terms of system identification, the participants discussed a lot about assumptions and came to an agreement on a representation of the irrigation management systems. In addition to validation, the RPG induces a model representative of the farmers' shared view, which is a type of system identification. A first experience of interviews and modelling through the companion methodology provides an initial actors' model of their own system, which provides the basis for discussion and progress towards a common representation. However, the impact of this basis on the final result is still to be researched.

The participants also validated the use of the tools in this participatory context since:

1.   they kept on discussing issues long after the game session was finished;
2.   they asked to keep the game to use it by themselves;

3. farmers asked the team to organise a game session at a time when a specific negotiation was required (Daré and Barreteau, 2003).

While the goal of the case study was to reach the third level of participation (co-thinking), the request from farmers for support in their ongoing decision making created the opportunity to use these methods at a higher level of participation.[7] The use of role-playing games at high levels of participation (3+) has been implemented, notably by Hare et al. (2002) and D'Aquino et al. (2003), but this case study highlights the fact that stakeholders themselves recognise this kind of tool, as a legitimate support for participation at a high level.

The joint use of an Agent Based Model was successful in the sense that stakeholders, who had played the game first, were fully able to play with the model, choose scenarios and discuss those scenarios. However, the choice of scenarios was restricted by social constraints, i.e. they preferred to simulate good farmers, even if they recognised that there are other practices to be met in the fields. This tendency was stronger when players did not know each other before the game. It is assumed that they want to impress not only other players but also game session facilitators, organisers and, indirectly, the (European) funding agencies.

This leads to one of the limitations of these methods, about which one must be aware when implementing them: however strict the roles are, the players come with their personal history which completes the palette of their role with either their own behavioural pattern or the patterns they want to test and to show off (Daré and Barreteau, 2003). The game can become a forum for power struggles in which players try to manipulate the game organisers. This mechanism led us as a group of researchers to design a charter describing the approach and its ethical considerations (see http://cormas.cirad.fr for further information).

The difficulties encountered in the joint use of the model occurred mainly when participants did not know each other before the joint use session. Because of the national political situation, in front of the group, individuals could not accept any model representation which did not fit official party lines, such as the inclusion of social status in a country where everybody was supposed to be equal. This problem also occurred in the RPG, but to a lesser degree, since they were also accepting (or rejecting) representations through their play. When participants were familiar with each other, they nevertheless felt as if they were in a public arena, where foreigners (the research team) were observing them, and thus felt compelled to look for 'good farmer' behavioural patterns. Therefore they were all hoping to be allocated with roles of intensive farmers and good payers.

The long-term effects of this approach are difficult to assess. Concerning the specific case study of Senegal, the last experiments were carried out relatively recently (as at the time of publication of this book), so that it would be difficult to speak about long-term successes. Also the conditions necessary for an assessment are not in place. It would require, for example, a specific monitoring process which is difficult to undertake for two reasons:

1. it has not been planned for earlier in the process, therefore relevant indicators might be missing;
2. such an ex-post monitoring does not fall in the organisational scope of a usual research project, which is usually shorter than long term.

This specific problem to assess long-term impact in the Senegalese case study is related to more fundamental problems of long-term evaluation assessment for participatory processes in general. Not only is it practicably difficult to undertake, but even if it is done, the separation of causes is problematic in the extreme. For a given supposed impact, how can one calculate the impact of the approach in comparison to any number of other events which are continuously occurring in the systems being managed?

8.4.2   Sharing Visions for Lake Lanier and the Upper Chattahoochee Watershed

Lake Lanier, located to the north of Atlanta and lying between the development corridors of interstate highways I–75 and I–85, is the single-most important impoundment in Georgia. It is also the subject of intense public and policy scrutiny. Created in 1958 on the Upper Chattahoochee River, the lake occupies 15 400 hectares. Today, Lanier receives more visitors per year than any other Army Corps lake project in the country. Its watershed is some 2704 km^2 in extent, encompassing the foothills of the Appalachian Mountains to the north, and covering a variety of land uses, including significant poultry and pig production, silviculture, and – increasingly from the south – suburbanisation. In 1989 land cover in Lanier's watershed was categorised as: open water 6 per cent, forest 77 per cent, urban 3 per cent, pasture 9 per cent, crops 4 per cent, others 1 per cent. By 1997 the urban category had increased to 10 per cent, largely at the expense of pasture and crops, which had fallen to 5 per cent and 1 per cent, respectively.

Lanier itself is a multi-purpose impoundment, providing hydro-electric power generation, flood protection, drinking water supply and recreational resources. The growing pressure of these land and water uses on Lake Lanier and its watershed are palpable in a variety of ways: Lanier's water resources are the focus of protracted negotiations among Georgia, Alabama, and Florida over access to stream flows in the Chattahoochee River network (including the Apalachicola and Flint basins); throughout our entire project Georgia suffered from a prolonged drought (which extended over four years); 80 per cent of metropolitan Atlanta's water supply is from the surface waters of the Upper Chattahoochee watershed; and the state of Georgia is implementing its Total Maximum Daily Load (TMDL) programme – for comprehensive watershed management – under an especially tight Consent Decree Order from the US Federal District Court (Sierra Club et al. vs EPA). Taken together, the consequences of all these pressures are now manifesting themselves in the costs of providing appropriate wastewater infrastructure. A recently completed wastewater treatment plant for one of the counties (Gwinnett) in Lanier's watershed took $260m to build, where its price might ordinarily have been some $60m. The county not only draws its water supply from Lanier but is faced with the prospect of returning its reclaimed water back to Lanier. This ballooning of costs has come in part from the insistence of local stakeholders on a 'failure-free' infrastructure. Yet in spite of the integral involvement of stakeholders from the outset of the county's plans for the facility, the permitting process for its discharge to the lake has still become the subject of major litigation and, at times, acrimonious debate.

Simply put, Lanier and its watershed are under stress from the pressures of suburban development, hydrologic/climatological variability and change, and the accumulation of nutrients within the lake. Hatcher (1994), for example, has estimated that 80–90 per cent of the phosphorus (P) load entering Lanier is not observed to leave it and is probably sequestered by sediments. Dissolved oxygen (DO) patterns suggest a tendency over the long term towards the occurrence of more extensive volumes of the lake with depressed levels for longer periods of the year. Looking to the future, a crucial question is this: will the capacity of the sediments to retain nutrients remain as great as currently seems the case, in particular, in the face of changing relative rates of loading of sediment, nutrient and organic matter from the watershed? And if it does not, what might be the implications for the lake's ecosystem?

In short, it is fair to conclude that the quality and resources of Lake Lanier are one of the most hotly debated environmental issues in the entire state of Georgia, with stakes that are indeed quite high enough.

Participatory management task

As a research project, our goals were to:

1. develop a concept of environmental decision making in which science-based models are responsive to identified community values, as they evolve in both the short and long term, i.e, the goal was to develop the procedure of adaptive community learning, as it is now being called (Beck et al, 2002b);

2. develop and apply a computational procedure for identifying those scientific unknowns crucial to the 'reachability' of the community's desired/feared environmental futures;
3. improve understanding of basic aspects of lake ecosystem behaviour, with special reference to the roles of the microbial foodweb, sediment-nutrient interactions, and geochemistry.

While lowering the temperature of the debate surrounding Lanier and the Chattahoochee watershed would have been desirable, it was not a goal of the project per se. Conversely, exploration of participatory methods of environmental management was not the only subject of enquiry, although we shall herein restrict our review of the case study to this particular component of it.

Participatory methods used
At the interface between the project team and the stakeholders, two instruments were employed for elucidating the stakeholders' visions of the future: a survey/questionnaire; and a type of large group response exercise (a Foresight Workshop called 'Foresight for Lanier'). In respect of the former, we designed the survey instrument with members of the board of a local home-owners and business-owners association, so that the members of the association at large were to be engaged as the primary group of stakeholders whose concerns for the future were to be elicited (Fath and Beck, 2005). The workshop which was designed and implemented in response to the partial failure of the survey instrument, involved a more varied group of participants (Table 8.2).

Strengths and weaknesses
From the social history of the lake, it is clear in retrospect that our research was entering a highly sensitive arena, albeit not without foreknowledge. In the event, receiving permission to issue our questionnaire to all the members of the homeowners association was the outcome of a finely balanced democratic process (at the board level). In the approach to this permission being granted it became evident that any follow-up survey – essential to the original, motivating hypotheses of the research – would be unwelcome. Subsequent issue of the questionnaire to some small groups of decision makers and professional scientists, i.e, stakeholders distinctly 'other' than the members of the home-owners association, was also found highly unwelcome; so too was our procedure for selecting and inviting participants in the Foresight Workshop, as well as the stakeholders invited to participate therein. Amongst some participants in the Workshop the intervention of the project team in the Lanier problem was viewed as immaterial, even resented.

We have found then that whether or not a team of project scientists strives to be neutral or maximally value free in a case study such as ours, this struggle can easily be perceived by other stakeholders as vain, presumptuous and arrogant. Unconsciously, we may have conveyed the impression of being more interested in the behaviour of members of the community, vis-à-vis their philosophical positions on the man-environment relationship, than in assisting preservation of the cherished piece of the environment. Our procedure of adaptive community learning, nevertheless, has begun to be adapted in the light of this experience, not least in reporting, as we are, on our own behaviour and in dealing with ourselves as a part of the problem.

In formulating the project it had been our intention to use merely the survey instrument, which was accordingly designed expressly with the accompanying computational analysis of stakeholder-generated futures in mind (Beck, 2002; Beck et al, 2002a; Osidele and Beck, 2003). Its goal was to elicit the bounds for a set of numerical 'behaviour definitions', to be assessed with a computational model. The specification of these bounds would ideally be maximally untainted by any prejudices of those assembling the map of the science base to be incorporated into the model of equations (the methodological importance of this is discussed elsewhere; Beck, 2002). In spite of the substantial effort invested in its design, the survey proved to be flawed: on the first account, it turned out that the numerical bounds of the behaviour definitions would ultimately have had to be specified by the project's scientific personnel (the authors of the model); and second, less fatally, the indicators of the future vulnerability of Lanier's water quality were found to be of more or less equal concern to respondents – or at least not radically different. Answering the question of whether the same unknowns in the science base (the model) would have been found to be key to the 'reachability' of a variety of stakeholder visions of the future, for example, is quite important. For it suggests an economy in purchasing more science – of carrying out further scientific work, given a limited budget for such – to clarify the crucial uncertainties attaching to heterogeneous stakeholder perspectives on future hopes and fears for the lake. And in a healthy democracy of stakeholders, just one consensus aspiration for the future would be an unlikely occurrence. Further manipulation of the survey data, in particular, a search for empirical evidence of three of the five social solidarities embraced in Thompson's (1997) interpretation of Cultural Theory, reveals a greater variety of relative priorities amongst the given concerns for a large sub-sample of respondents (Fath and Beck, 2005).

To summarise, we learned from the survey that we – the scientists – had a priori unintentionally constrained what was to be found of concern to the community. An alternative route to stakeholder-derived bounds for the numerical behaviour definitions (of hopes and fears for the longer-term future) had, therefore, to be opened up. The Foresight Workshop, which had not been a part of the project plan, addressed four issues with the 33 members of the community who participated: elicitation of the trends in factors affecting Lake Lanier over the next quarter of a century; expression of stakeholders' personal indicators of the lake's future state; speculation about the patterns of behaviour of the lake in 2030, in as unbridled a manner as possible; and quantification, by way of a sticky dot exercise, of these imagined futures in the terms they themselves had collectively chosen, from both optimistic and pessimistic stances (Figure 8.2).

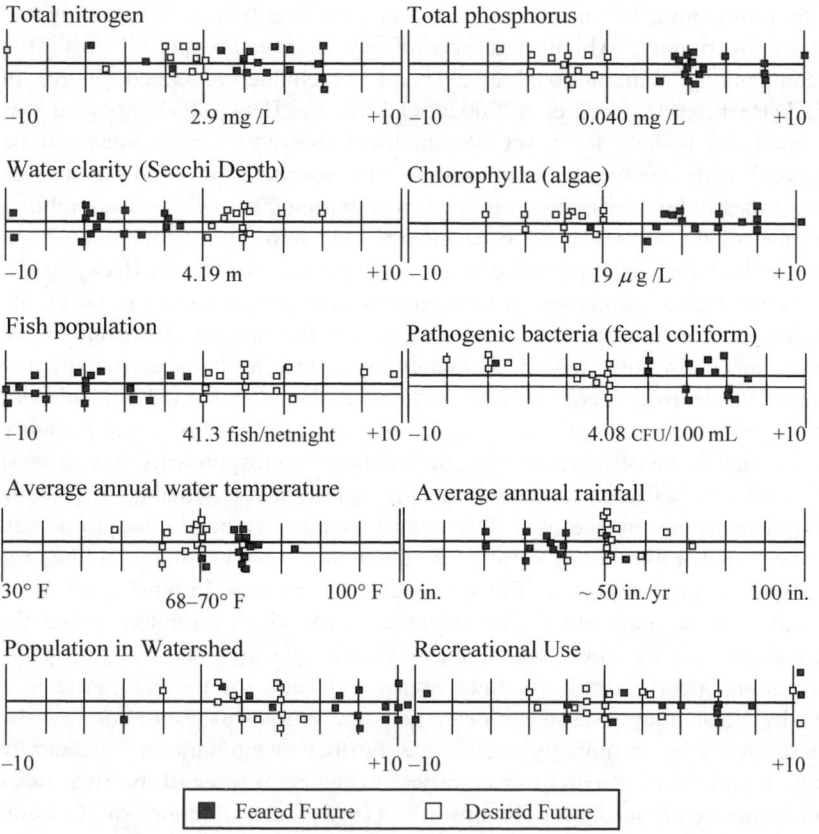

Notes: Speculated changes refer to ten water quality indicators for the lake relative to current values/perceptions; –10 and +10 indicate one-tenth and ten times the current status (from Osidele, 2001).

Figure 8.2   *Transcription of a 'sticky-dot' exercise undertaken by stakeholders during a Foresight for Lanier workshop*

Overall, our project was about the search for a means of managing community-environment interactions in a manner lying somewhere between 'the relatively undisciplined discourse of ordinary language' and 'the algorithmic (but incomplete) models of technical policy analysts such as risk assessors or microeconomists' (Norton and Steinemann, 2001). In these terms the workshop proved the more effective device for translating from the 'language' in which scientifically lay persons perceive their environment to the state variables of a mathematical model. Nevertheless, one can proceed (in detail) from the phrasing of this language to the numerical quantities required for the model and computational analysis in a number of ways and we have thus far adopted but one of the options, as discussed more fully in Osidele and Beck (2003). In procedural terms, we have yet to return to the stakeholders in order to resume the dialogue, informed this time by the outcomes of the computational analyses, themselves enabled, in the first place, by the relative success of the workshop. Unquestionably, our experience of the politics and social unrest surrounding our participation in the Lanier problem has been a factor giving us very significant pause for thought, regarding exactly how to complete one full turn of the cycle of adaptive community learning. The reason is obvious: doing so hinges on our appreciating better how we – the researchers – deal with ourselves in the context of participatory environmental problem-solving. These technical and reflexive, sociological challenges notwithstanding, however, the notion and procedure of adaptive community learning seem not, in general, to be ill founded: indeed we argue elsewhere that they enfold within them the now widely accepted principles of adaptive management (Beck et al., 2002b) –although one can hardly extrapolate to the general from this single, specific case study. We fully expect the procedure itself to be adapted, when it is applied a second time.

8.4.3   Urban Water Management in Switzerland

The dominant infrastructure planning policy of the water supply utility in one of Switzerland's[8] principal cities over the 20th century has been characterised as risk-averse 'worst-case planning' (Tillman, 2001). That means that past patterns of increasing demand have been expected to continue into the future and that supply capacity has therefore been regularly built up to meet ever higher 'worst case' levels of expected demand. This policy worked well until the 1970s in that it met city requirements for high water supply security and high water quality. The policy also appeared to be financially secure and efficient, since infrastructure costs seemed to be proportionate to the demand for water and the water utility was financially supported by the city. However, after another water shortage scare in 1976, as supply was once more increased, demand began to fall and pumping capacity has become unsustainably higher than daily peak demand.

This level of security is very expensive due to the high level of fixed costs involved in developing and maintaining infrastructure. The nature of the costs, such as the need to service interest payments, means that the financial burden will endure for many years to come, even if the infrastructure were to be reduced. Meanwhile, a change in funding arrangements with the city authorities plus a risk to demand-driven income has lead to uncertainty in future financial stability, exacerbated by the fact that the public can reject water price changes by plebiscite. It appears that the continuing oversupply cannot continue indefinitely, but conflict between four norms – not shared by all stakeholders within the community – causes problems when planning the best course of action.

These four norms can be characterised as:

1. that water security must be high;
2. that water saving is good, water-saving technology should be promoted;
3. that water supply utility must be financially secure;
4. that water prices should be fair.

New ideas were needed to bring water demand and supply more into balance whilst meeting the four norms.

Participatory management task
The participatory management task was to bring together the city's water management stakeholders in a group model building process to facilitate (among other things):

- the identification of the city's actual water management problems;
- the exploration of alternative supply and demand management strategies that satisfy the different city norms; and
- an increase in social learning and communication among the stakeholders.

Primarily, however, this was a research project in which new methods for participatory water management were to be developed and tested. As such, there was no specific management decision to be made by the participants. The result of the participation was to move from problem identification to co-thinking and co-designing a palate of possible solutions to these problems.

Participatory methods used
Between autumn 2000 and spring 2003, up to ten participants were included in a series of participatory sessions referred to as the actors' platform. This

platform represented stakeholders from the water utility, the wastewater utility, a manufacturer of water-using technologies, an architects' association, a plumbers' association, a consumers' association, an association for water and gas utilities, and the city council. The project team consisted, at various times, of two facilitators/modellers, an analyst and a psychologist, providing the equivalent of 3.5 person years' of work, generating seven mental models, one conceptual model, four implementations of that model, three questionnaires, two workbooks, and over 45 hours of individual and group discussion time.

The team used many different methods as can be seen in Table 8.4 and in Pahl-Wostl and Hare (2004). Facilitated workshops were organised to elicit knowledge, develop and test models and to discuss findings and possible solutions. Card sorting was used to carry out stakeholder analysis based upon the stakeholders' own viewpoints (Hare and Pahl-Wostl, 2002). Role-playing games were used for social learning about the management system. There was joint use of models, to explore the effects of policy on the system. The focus of this section will however be on the encouragement of social learning through group model building. The technique used was an adaptation/ simplification of Hodgson's method to carry out cognitive mapping to elicit and represent multiple stakeholder perspectives of the management system.

Since the participants each had different levels of experience and authority, there was a fear that some participants might feel that they could not express themselves fully as part of the group. Hence, the cognitive mapping method was combined with principles from the nominal group technique (Delbecq et al., 1975). In concrete terms this meant that the stakeholders were interviewed individually to elicit their cognitive maps and then later asked to present them to the group.

The method used was the following. The stakeholders were initially primed to consider key questions about the water management system in their city, such as: 'What will be the impact of water saving and water supply efficiency measures on the sustainability of the management system?'. This question was sent to them a week before the interview. At the interview itself, the participant was reminded of the question and given 15 blank hexagons. They were then asked to consider key concepts and issues related to answering the question and to fill out each hexagon with one of those concepts or issues. Once all hexagons had been completed, the participant was asked to cluster the hexagons under named categories and then link clusters or hexagons between which the participant thought there was a relationship. The completed cognitive map of one of the participants is shown in Figure 8.3.

In the cognitive map entitled *Unser Weg zum Wassersparen* ('Our road to water saving'), the cluster of concepts categorised as 'Costs' – i.e. key

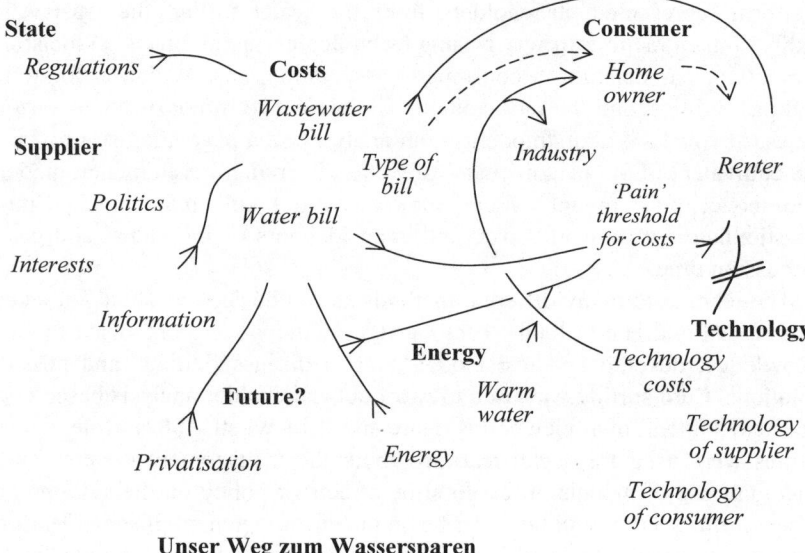

Unser Weg zum Wassersparen

Source: Adapted from Hare and Pahl-Wostl, 2002.

Figure 8.3   A cognitive map developed by a stakeholder

concepts related to consumers' water costs – include 'water bill', 'type of water bill' and 'wastewater bill'. These are part of the interviewed participant's perspective of the system, now grouped and categorised. With the addition of the arrows, comes the relational knowledge. In this example, it can be seen that the stakeholder believes that 'privatisation' will influence the 'water bills' in some way. Note that this is not a full causal model. There is no indication of the way in which charges may be influenced. This was not possible, in the time provided to build the model (45 minutes). Instead, this information was captured, where possible, in an audio-recorded protocol of the meeting with the stakeholder being asked at the beginning of the interview to try and speak out loud about what he was doing and why.

Participants were then asked to present their models back to the group in a follow-up group session, allowing each participant to express their views fully. Once all the models had been presented, they were then discussed by the group which in turn added to the understanding (of both the participants and the research team) about the management system.

The information in these models then was integrated into a single group model of the system (system identification and problem identification). This was done by extracting the commonalities and differences between the models and creating a base model. This base model took many forms over the years, as a structure model, a role-playing game and an influence model. All these formats were used to generate discussions about the key problems affecting the city, to learn about the four norms and, importantly, to explore visually, what the possible consequences (positive and negative) of particular management strategies might be in terms of these four norms (options assessment).

Strengths and weaknesses

The strengths of using the cognitive mapping technique as part of a group model building process was that we managed to elicit the viewpoints of each participant in a representation that could be shared and discussed by all (part of the social learning process discussed in the section on 'Participatory Processes' above). It was also rather a quick method as far as the elicitation side was concerned, taking just over an hour per model. When used adeptly, it can quickly provide the researcher with a view of the diversity and commonality of opinion on a subject. It also has the benefit of being a contrived elicitation method (McGeorge and Rugg, 1992) and thus can overcome the problems of 'knowledge acquisition bottleneck' (Evans, 1988), allowing the elicitation of knowledge that might be suppressed during direct interviews. For the purpose of building models it is also very appropriate in that the method provides the researcher with information that automatically comes structured in terms of ontology and relationship meta-knowledge, providing the foundations of a model.

The weaknesses of our adaptation of the Hodgson's approach for cognitive mapping approach were that the choice of priming questions had to be well thought out in advance. We committed the mistake of priming the participants too much in terms of water saving, a theme that turned out to be not the most pressing problem for the participants as we had earlier thought. However it has to be said that at least the development of the water-saving theme allowed us, the research team, to learn this fact from the participants and thus reappraise some previous research.

The use of this approach has additional specific weaknesses. For instance, one has to make sure that good protocols are taken to ensure that, at a later date, the terse descriptions written on the hexagons can be understood by both the researchers and other participants. This becomes increasingly difficult when participants may use the same words to mean different concepts. As a result, combining and properly explaining models also becomes difficult without good protocols detailing the meaning of hexagons. The researchers were also concerned about the philosophical and practical implications of combining the mental models of seven stakeholders into one base model. We managed to combine the models, but it is still unclear as to what the base model signifies: the views of all the stakeholders or none of them? Naturally this type of problem can, in part, be overcome by getting the stakeholders to validate the base model, as we attempted to do, but it may be better to keep the models separate and integrate only when they are genuinely very similar. In this way, the plurality of views can remain in sight during the subsequent discussion groups. However, this strategy will be expensive if more than one influence model or role-playing game has to be developed to represent each separate model.

Regarding the participatory process as a whole, a final warning relates to the fact that research was the prime motivation for the organisers of the participatory process, rather than a management strategy. Invariably this affects the quality of the participative experience for the participants. For example, the fact that methods are being developed during the process means that the participants cannot be totally informed about what they will be expected to do during the process. New methods can also fail to work, leaving the participants with no gain from their activities. Attention may also stray from achieving real management objectives. For example, because the project was not stakeholder inspired and focused on research, there was no strong impetus at the start of the project to match the process to a particular management decision that had to be made. This meant that it was always unclear what would happen to the results of the participatory management that occurred.

8.4.4 Water Allocation in the Gwydir and Namoi River Basins

The Gwydir and Namoi valleys are both large basins in New South Wales, Australia and both feed into the Murray-Darling Basin. These catchments contain substantial irrigation industries, principally lucerne industries in areas of the upper catchment (mainly for dairy production) and large irrigated cotton industries in the lower catchment. There are also numerous small- to medium-sized towns in these catchments, many of which are economically dependent on these irrigation industries. Past management of water resources in these valleys has focused on the development of the resource, leading to over-allocation and over-extraction of both groundwater and surface water supplies. The last decade has seen substantial reforms at both the Federal and State Government level to the management of water resources. These reforms have included separation of water access from land title, reductions in surface and groundwater allocations, introduction of an extraction cap, changes to access rules in order to protect particular flow levels (especially low flows) and acknowledgement of the environment as a legitimate user of water. Changes to water access are likely to have substantial environmental benefits as well as economic costs in these catchments. The magnitude of these impacts and their distribution is not well understood. In addition there is substantial conflict surrounding the mechanisms by which the environment is protected – many irrigators feel that the ecological benefits of access changes are not certain and have not been tested in a scientific investigation.

Participatory management task
In this section, we report on the participatory tasks involved in a project (Letcher and Aluwihare, 2003; Letcher and Jakeman, 2003; Letcher et al., 2004) focused on the development of decision support systems to assist in future development of water allocation policies in these catchments. These systems are being developed in concert with participatory decision-making processes (which recently produced a water-sharing plan) already in place in these catchments. It is hoped that this process will overcome at least some of the difficulties that arose in both catchments, as a result, through the lack of time and a lack of appropriate communication about the actual levels of stakeholder power through the water-sharing plan development process. Many stakeholders felt they were being offered significantly greater decision-making power through the catchment management boards and other community processes than was eventually the case. In addition there was a feeling that models being used in these processes to justify decisions were not adequately understood or that many of their underlying assumptions were incorrect (or at least untested). This has caused many of these groups to be significantly embittered towards both agency staff and the models they used to analyse these water-sharing plan options. This project aims to get a basic level of agreement on model assumptions and uses before the resulting models are used for decision making in these catchments. It is also hoped that there will be better understanding of the appropriate uses of these models and their associated levels of uncertainty before they are incorporated in a community consultation or participatory decision process.

A particular focus for the case study is the recently released water-sharing plans. These plans include provision for a review of operations and policies after five years of plan operation, and the development of new plans after ten years. The project aims to develop tools and collaborative links that will facilitate improved decision making at these two key decision points (as well as other as yet unforeseen decision points aligning with this timeframe), thereby potentially reducing the problems of mistrust which occurred during the development of the water-sharing plans.

Participatory methods used
Due to the long-term and very large-scale nature of the project and problem focus, a wide variety of participatory methods are being used. The aims of using these methods have been to:

1. encourage better understanding of the models and tools developed as part of the project in order to reduce both mistrust and misuse of models and of model results; and
2. elicit better understanding of the system and processes operating in the catchment through direct incorporation of stakeholder knowledge throughout the project.

The main participatory methods used are as follows:

- Semi-structured and structured interviews. These have been undertaken with various irrigators in both catchments in order to collect information and improve model assumptions, and give a broader range of stakeholders a chance to provide feedback on the models being developed. Interviewees are briefed on the project and its aims and provided with information on the project, the aims of the interview and contact details of project participants. They are invited to contact researchers at any time to provide any kind of feedback on the project, its assumptions and goals or to ask questions about any aspect of the project. A semi-structured conversation then takes place between researchers and the interviewee. Simple quantitative data relating to several key model assumptions (such as on-farm storage sizes, irrigation water practices, and crop rotation practices) are elicited. Detailed questions relating to farm decisions with regard to planting and water use are then asked. Qualitative responses to these are recorded. A short list of questions is used to focus this part of the interview, but additional questions are also raised where necessary depending on the response of interview participants. Most interviews also include an unstructured component in which interviewees are invited to raise other issues that they feel are important to the development of better modelling tools and to policy making in the catchment. This unstructured conversation is also documented. Responses to this part of the interview have focused largely on difficulties that irrigators believe exist in the water-sharing plans for the catchments. Usually, an interview would run for approximately two hours and often concludes with a tour of the property.
- Project steering committee meetings. A core group of stakeholders, including irrigator representatives, State Government agency staff and local government representatives forms a Steering Committee for the project. This committee meets formally twice annually to be briefed on progress and to provide feedback and direction to researchers on model development and assumptions. Membership of this group has been developed through consultation with different agency and community members.

- Facilitated workshops and meetings. Broader community meetings have been held that provide a briefing on the project and model assumptions and request feedback and suggestions on possible changes to these. These meetings included a mix of extension staff, policy makers and technical support staff, as well as irrigators, local government representatives and other interested community members. Feedback has been enabled through both the completion of questionnaires at the end of these sessions and documentation of verbal comments provided throughout these sessions. The additional model developments currently being undertaken were based entirely on the results of a series of these general feedback sessions. Small group meetings are also frequently held throughout the project. Project researchers meet with various stakeholder groups as opportunities arise. For example, presentations and information sessions have been held during irrigator council meetings. Researchers have also visited local councils and government agencies to facilitate collaboration.
- Capacity building in the form of software workshops. Two types of software workshops have been held during the project. The first type of workshop focused on model building and teaching model building skills in the software platform used in the project. This was aimed largely at technical staff at State Government agencies and relevant research institutions to enable these groups to make future modifications to the models and to keep them up to date. It should be noted that a key research agency involved was the Cooperative Research Centre for Cotton, which is closely linked to the irrigation industry in the catchment. The second type was a user workshop where the participants interact with the models through a relatively user-friendly interface (see Figure 8.4). This workshop type was targeted at a much broader audience and is focused not only on training in the use of the DSS (Decision Support System – see Chapter 4) but also is used to elicit feedback on interface design, input values and model assumptions. It was seen as a valuable learning experience for both researchers and participants.
- Mailouts introducing the project, providing contact details and including an open invitation to provide feedback or become involved in the project were also sent out to a large number of individuals and groups in these catchments.

Stakeholders' opinions and perspectives have been used in issue focusing and problem definition, system conceptualisation, the identification of model inputs and development of other assumptions. Scenarios considered by the

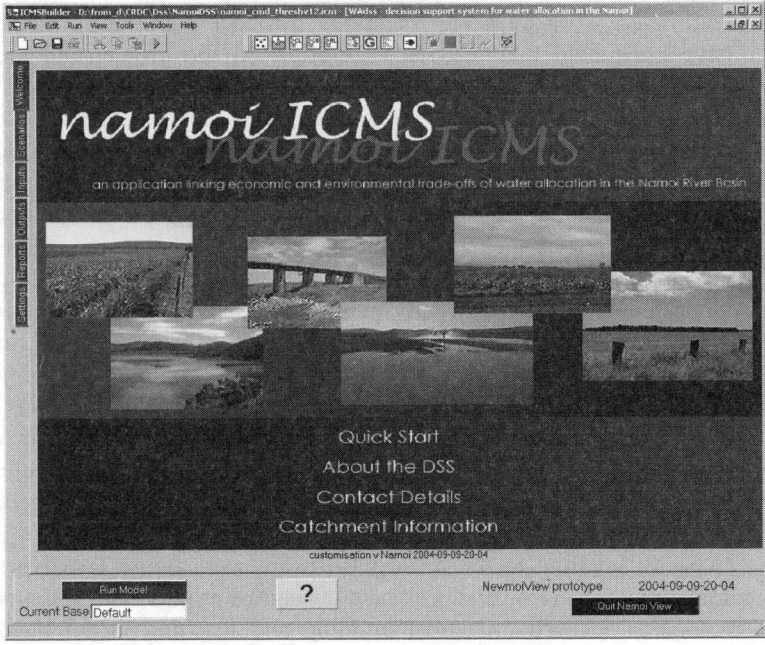

Figure 8.4   The user-friendly interface of the Namoi-ICM

DSS have evolved from options constructed as part of the development of the Water Sharing Plans. These scenarios come from the separate participatory process that involved the Catchment Management Boards.

The different participatory methods used in this project reflect the varying goals of participation. The methods have been chosen to enable a broad range of stakeholders to interact with the project, but also to ensure that key stakeholders, including community representatives and not just State Government agency staff, are given a significant level of authority over the project outcomes (for example through the project Steering Committee). Open discussion and information sessions and mailouts provide an opportunity for individuals, not only representatives, to provide different perspectives on catchment processes and water management. The large number of stakeholders involved in the project means that a variety of methods are required. Community representatives, such as the chairs of irrigator councils in the catchment, tend to hold various representative positions in the catchment, including irrigator representative positions on regional resource management bodies (Catchment Management Boards and River Management Committees). This provides a tight link between the community representation on the project Steering Committee and the key management and decision-making bodies in the catchments. In this way participatory modelling is helping to enable participatory management.

Strengths and weaknesses
The variety of participatory approaches used in the project has facilitated interpretation of the perspectives from a broad range of stakeholders. It has initiated a learning experience for both researchers and stakeholders at a fairly broad level. The long timeframes and personal nature of interaction used (e.g. farm visits and semi-structured interviews, model discussion sessions) have allowed a greater level of trust to be developed between researchers and stakeholders. In most cases it has been found that more complete and useful feedback is provided only after this trust has developed.

The approach being used is very time consuming and requires significant goodwill and effort on the part of both researchers and stakeholders. It would not be appropriate for a relatively simple or small-scale issue, or where the project was expected to be completed very quickly. In addition the representativeness of stakeholders is not guaranteed – for example, urban user concerns were represented by the inclusion of local government representatives rather than through the inclusion of general citizens. These citizens were not excluded from the process (e.g. they were free to attend public meetings) but neither were they actively engaged. This reflects in many ways the bias of the participatory processes underlying the State Government's decision-making frameworks in which urban and industrial concerns are represented through a similar type of participation.

8.4.5   Transboundary Management in Iberian River Basins

The IBERAQUA project (Developing a cooperative regime for the management of shared water basins in the Iberian Peninsula, January–December 2002 – Iberaqua, 2002a, 2002b) is focused on providing knowledge and support for the implementation of the Water Framework Directive (WFD) and the Luso-Spanish Convention (LSC). In particular, the LSC, signed in Albufeira, Portugal on the 30 November 1998 and entered into force on the 17 January 2000, defines a framework of cooperation for the protection of transboundary Iberian surface – and ground – waters, as well as the protection of the ecosystems directly depending on such waters. Therefore, the LSC and the WFD both aim at achieving a good state of shared waters. However, the LSC focuses on issues of institutional cooperation between the two countries, e.g. in sharing information and in the tasks of management, and does not specifically aim at developing public participation or to recover the costs of the improvement of the ecological status of the rivers. In an attempt to support both the LSC and the WFD, IBERAQUA thus focused both on the issues of cooperation between Spanish and Portuguese institutions and on the participation of local stakeholders in the three shared river basins of the Duero, Guadiana and Tajo Rivers (Figure 8.5).

Participatory management task
Specifically, IBERAQUA sought to achieve three main objectives:

1. to carry out new research, from an environmental, administrative, legal and economic perspective, investigating the complementarity between the two legal instruments (WFD and LSC) and identifying the social and institutional mechanisms needed to enhance the effectiveness of their implementation;
2. to provide information to relevant institutions, stakeholders, and water managers about the WFD and the LSC as well as the results of the IBERAQUA research;
3. to facilitate a process of social learning in order to promote debate about institutional change and a better understanding of the functioning, or possibilities for improvement, of the three selected water management regimes.

Participatory methods used
Three participatory full-day workshops were carried out in towns close to the Duero, Tajo and Guadiana rivers. These workshops involved around 35–50 people at a time, divided into focus groups of about 5–10 people with

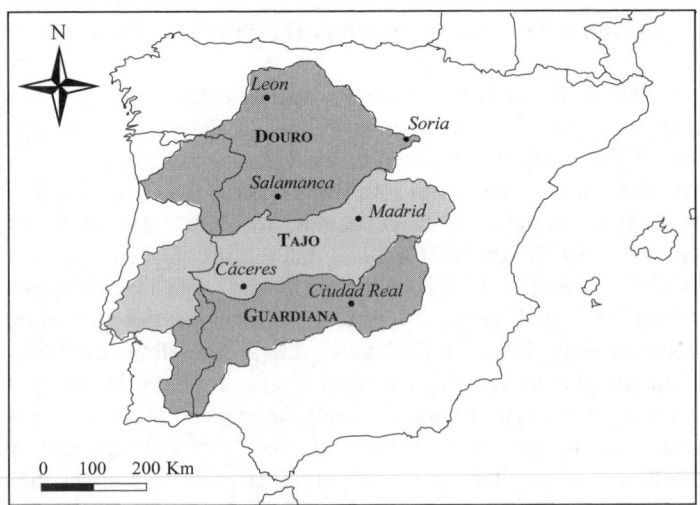

Figure 8.5   The region under transboundary management

support from simultaneous translation, a moderator and a note taker. Such meetings adapted the methodology of IA-Focus groups, but due to time and resource constraints, it was not possible to extend the meetings more than a day. Also IA models were not used, instead only legal and contextual information on the river basins was provided during the focus groups.

Focus groups were complemented with two plenary meetings in which participants were first given a large dossier with some relevant information on the two legal instruments (WFD, LSC) and, at the end of the day, conclusions on the following issues were gathered:

- participants' general reactions to the main contents of the WFD and LSC and their implications for the improvement of the water quality within the selected shared river basins;
- the current state and the possibilities to enhance the institutional cooperation between the two countries on the management of shared river basins;
- institutional gaps and resource needs with regard to the improvement of public information and participation within the selected shared international Iberian river basins.

In total, just over a hundred people were consulted. Previous to the workshops, a questionnaire was delivered to possible participants as well as to other relevant stakeholders in order to better frame the discussions of the focus groups and to obtain secondary information from actors unable to attend to the meetings. The questionnaire had a total of 35 questions and was answered by 55 people, 30 from Portugal and 20 from Spain. A web site was also set up in the early stages of the project in order to give easy access to the participants to the relevant documents and to descriptions of the current situation in the three river basins.

Strengths and weaknesses
IBERAQUA contributed to a greater awareness and understanding of the EC's Water Framework Directive (WFD) and the Luso-Spanish Convention (LSC) in the Iberian Peninsula by fostering cooperation and joint participation of water users and managers involved in the river basins shared between Portugal and Spain. IBERAQUA also helped at providing a platform for discussion about the sustainable management of transboundary river basins to be promoted by inter-institutional cooperation in each of the Iberian states alongside the participation of civil society. However, despite the huge efforts devoted to contacting and establishing the network of relevant actors, the limitations given by the timeframe of the project – only one year in which to investigate three river basins – were evident. The lack of time has limited the

possibilities for integrating the results – mainly of a procedural nature – into the broader institutional and social context of the peninsula.

With regard to the potential of IA-focus groups, it is worth mentioning that such approaches can be used for many purposes at the same time. Indeed, they can contribute to providing in-depth policy-relevant knowledge on complex issues to participants by providing a human interface (via the person of the focus group moderator) to complex information, thus helping to transform otherwise vague or distant information into meaningful knowledge. Furthermore, IA focus groups can enhance the transparency and democratisation of experts' environmental assessments through open dialogue and the framing of problems, causes and solutions in terms more understandable to the community. It is even possible that interpersonal contact with usually difficult-to-contact stakeholders can begin to challenge specific power relationships, introducing equity aspects through direct dialogic participation.

Although in the case of the IBERAQUA project, some very elementary forms of the original IA focus groups methodology were used (mainly shortened and much less elaborate), it was clear that such a methodology faces a series of shortcomings which can be summarised as follows:

- there are critical difficulties in assuring the representativeness and validity of the results which occur through the dialogues. This is very much dependent on the criteria used to select the participants and to the extent the participants have subsequently been able to attend to the meetings. However, in this regard it is important to remember that the aim of IA-focus groups is not to provide representative results in a strict, statistical sense, but to learn new insights, identify new problems and ways of framing the issues at stake and to widen the scope of points of view to be taken into account;
- IA-focus groups must be adapted to their social context, according to each situation. No standard procedure can therefore be universally applied and, as such, they are difficult to institutionalise;
- IA-Focus groups are a relatively new approach which is based on the idea that the integration of knowledge and values is needed, in order to improve the sustainability of policy decisions. There is still considerable resistance by some experts, policy makers and scientists to allow others to participate in what they perceive as their own work and to accept the reformulation of power relations that this entails.

8.5 CONCLUSIONS: LESSONS TO BE LEARNT FROM THE STUDIES

This chapter has illustrated the diversity of participatory methods currently being used in applied research into water management through the examination of five case studies from around the world. It has also provided a categorisation of the case studies to aid the reader in understanding the participatory management context in which these methods have been applied, so that they can better decide what methods might be useful for application to their own management problems. The rest of this section will now try and draw together some general lessons from the individual critiques of the case studies. Whilst contemplating the criticisms of the methods, it is important to bear in mind that the successes and problems associated with particular methods are inextricably linked to the participatory management context of the case study, therefore a method applied in a different context may well perform in a different way. Also as Mostert (Chapter 7) points out, culture also plays a role in determining the success of a process and methods applied. In another culture, problems, such as that of players wanting to always act as the 'good farmer' in the Senegal role-playing game, might not occur.

The case studies presented above share particular themes. The methods employed tend to be quite successful in increasing communication amongst stakeholders and they bring a diversity of knowledge and information into the management process that is enriching. Each method helps to achieve this in different ways. Some methods, such as cognitive mapping, provide quick access to the mental models of participants which represent alternative perspectives. Role-playing games facilitate imaginative and constructive discussion among the public about otherwise unmentioned management issues. Workshops and focus groups carried out with the community have been found to provide good opportunities for 'unbridled' communication that has allowed the practitioners to elicit public knowledge and views about future events, that surveys had not been able to previously provide. The participative building of DSS and other models can help to overcome people's distrust and increase their acceptance of models.

However, there are also common themes that emerge from the case studies in terms of difficulties faced by practitioners. To carry out participatory processes is time consuming and resource intensive. Time, money and stakeholder patience can run out before learning cycles are completed or decisions made. Methods can be difficult to implement when there exists strong resentment or distrust towards outside involvement, or where previous participatory experiences have promised much, but failed to deliver.

Other problems or difficulties faced by participatory methods relate to the issues of recruitment and representativeness of the participants, the role played by the facilitators or 'integrators' in leading the whole process and the problem of translating complex information into a discussable language for the attendant constituencies and policy makers. For instance, in the case of the transboundary management of the Iberian river basins, it was acknowledged from the very beginning that language was a crucial issue, so great effort was made to provide simultaneous translation during the meeting and to translate all the relevant documents in both languages to allow fluid communication among the stakeholders. However, finding the right language for communication is more than a question of translation. Even with the same mother tongue, stakeholders and the public can mis-communicate with one another due to different fields of expertise, or different perspectives. When it comes to constructing common models, as the Swiss case study illustrated, this can be very difficult especially when the same words may have different meanings and vice versa. Gaming environments such as those used in Senegal, may help develop an agreed one-to-one matching of symbol to semantic as people learn in a controlled environment what each other means.

The benefits of being able to elicit multiple and diverse perspectives from stakeholders comes at a high price: the need for rigorous knowledge management and processing. Without thorough cataloguing of knowledge elicited in terms of sources and meaning, the knowledge quickly becomes useless. A wealth of different perspectives also raises the question of what is to be done with all these perspectives. How are they best made use of? As the Swiss case study points out, merely combining them all into a common model may be neither practicable nor meaningful. Simply letting them remain unanalysed whilst trying to make use of all the perspectives brings us back to the problem of resources: who is going to do the work necessary to maintain a perspective on all these views? Yet, if the different perspectives are not used, there is no point in eliciting them in the first place.

As suggested in the Swiss case study and the previous chapter, there is often confusion among researchers between organising participatory management processes, organising participatory research to support management and doing research into participatory management. This confusion can lead to processes being created that by the end of which participants have lost trust, feel exploited or become disappointed. The researcher should therefore always be aware about which type of process he/she is carrying out and communicate this to the participants. Participatory management implies that the participants are going to be involved in an actual decision-making process, unfettered by the requirements of a research agenda. Participatory research implies that participants are going to be helping to collect data and information, etc. for a decision-making process they might not be involved in. Research into participatory management implies that the participants may not be taking part directly in an active decision-making process at all, rather they are there to test participatory methods within a real, yet not 'live', management context. Naturally there are close links between all three categories. Participatory management for example requires some form of participation in the research supporting decision making (e.g. the collection and assessment of data). However, Pahl-Wostl and Ridder (2003) point out that many, especially academic, research projects have no direct link with actual decision making – even when the research is meant to be policy relevant. The case studies, for example, in this chapter predominantly belong to the latter two categories. The Swiss case study in particular is an example of the third category in which no actual final decision making is due to take place. Instead, as a result of the research carried out into participatory methods, a series of ideas were generated by the participants as a by-product which they may or may not make use of in future decision-making processes.

Involving members of the public or stakeholders, as a matter of principle, should provide concrete benefits for them. In all cases, potential participants should know beforehand what benefits they can expect. Realistically, the need to be able to deliver some tangible reward for participation and avoid participant disappointment and mistrust suggests that ideally, participatory processes should principally be stakeholder driven, rather than research driven. This means that participants should ideally be a part of an actual participatory management process rather than research into participation. If research into improving methods is required, a predominantly participatory management process can be combined, if done carefully, with some research on participatory processes to improve methods. Less risky from a participatory management point of view, however, is to carry out research on completed participatory management processes.

Further common themes abound. In both Lake Lanier and the Swiss case study, practitioners reported that a priori assumptions they carried into the process adversely affected the participatory process that they facilitated. There is a need to be always aware of how easy it is, even unconsciously, to influence a participatory meeting when the practitioner is in control of the methods and the reporting. In the case of processes which are research driven rather than purely management driven, the possibility of moving the process away from meaningful management themes is even greater (see also Pahl-Wostl and Ridder, 2003). The type of continuous practitioner self-reflectivity promoted by the Lake Lanier case study is a step in the right direction.

Such self-reflection must lead to the development and meticulous application of evaluation procedures for assessing the effectiveness of participatory processes against the claimed management and participatory goals of the project. Unfortunately, the application of such procedures is not a given. As Table 8.4 indicates, the case studies are not uniform in terms of their rigour in carrying out evaluation. Furthermore, it is also clear that many of the outcomes of participatory processes have to do with the building of new framings and networks of action, which go beyond the specific duration of the project time-spans and the funding body's financial capability. This adds another difficulty in the evaluation of such processes, which cannot be assessed only in terms of 'success' or 'failure' based on a few indicators obtained during or immediately after the end of the project. This theme is also taken up in the Senegal case study: without building in long-term evaluation systems into both the funding application and the setting up of a monitoring process for the project, long-term evaluation is impossible.

Long-term issues are generally problematic in other ways too. The involvement of stakeholders is also a difficult challenge for participatory water management. Adaptive management of any kind takes a long time. Planning and implementing river basin management plans takes a long time. How to keep stakeholders interested in participating over such periods of time is not a trivial concern and is not yet satisfactorily solved by the research community.

As practitioners, we need to employ methods that allow us to think critically about how we ourselves participate and the discipline and maturity to select and abide by behaviours that correspond to our project objectives (Cleaver, 2001, p. 54). If not, things can easily go wrong and our assumptions about participation will remain unchecked. For example, in Cooke and Kothari's book (2001), the collection of essays entitled *Participation: The New Tyranny?*, strong concerns are expressed about differences in private and public accounts of participatory development. Are perceived discontinuities between what is reported by practitioners and what 'really' happened the result of the special challenges posed by personal self-evaluation and trying to be objective about a process in which you yourself play a part? If so, special attention must be paid to evaluation procedures to address this phenomenon. If not, and this idea is explored more extensively through a number of the essays in their book, then there are concerns that participatory processes can become forums for the misappropriation of power, and lead to dishonest or misleading representation.

Obviously, biases do not solely come from researchers and practitioners. It is important to remember that participants also come into such meetings with their own agendas and work-related or cultural biases. The work in Senegal provides a case in point, whereby the irrigators tended to try and role play as a 'good' irrigator rather than as a 'bad' one. This reflects some of the concerns about participation outlined by Cooke and Kothari (2001), particularly when it comes to assuming that increased participation (and the input of local knowledge) is necessarily something that is going to improve management. Good participatory processes may help management to a greater or lesser extent but bad processes will hinder management. The trouble is that neither comes cheap.

NOTES

1. Goals may change during the process of participation, as a result of bottom-up decision making, hence methods may have to be flexible. At the outset it is important that the process designer is aware of his or her top-down goals and that the initial methods are chosen accordingly.
2. As defined in Chapter 7.
3. As defined by the Social Learning Group (2001).
4. As defined by the Drafting Group (2002).
5. Adapted from Barreteau et al. (2001).
6. Translated by authors as 'survival kit of irrigating farmer' (from Pulaar language).
7. Refers to the levels of participation presented in Chapter 7.
8. Based in part on Hare and Pahl-Wostl (2002) and Pahl-Wostl and Hare (2004).

REFERENCES

Asselt, M.B.A. van, J. Mellors, N. Rijkens-Klomp, S.C.H. Greeuw, K.G.P. Molendijk, P.J. Beers and P. van Notten (2001), 'Building blocks for participation in Integrated Assessment: a review of participatory methods', *ICIS Working Paper*, **I01–E003**, Maastricht, The Netherlands: ICIS.

Bandura, A. (1977), *Social Learning Theory*, London: Prentice-Hall.

Barreteau, O. (2003), 'The joint use of role-playing games and models regarding negotiation processes: characterization of associations', *Journal of Artificial Societies and Social Simulation*, **6**(2), downloadable at: http://jasss.soc.surrey.ac.uk/6/2/3.html (last access: May 2005).

Barreteau, O. and F. Bousquet (1999), 'Jeux de rôles et validation de systèmes multi-agents', in M.P. Gleizes and P. Marcenac (eds), *7èmes Journées Francophones d'Intelligence Artificielle Distribuée et Systèmes Multi-Agents*, St Gilles: Hermès, pp. 67–80.

Barreteau, O. and F. Bousquet (2000), 'SHADOC: a Multi-Agent Model to tackle viability of irrigated systems', *Annals of Operation Research*, **94**(1–4), 139–162.

Barreteau, O., F. Bousquet and J.-M. Attonaty (2001), 'Role-playing games for opening the black box of multi-agent systems: method and lessons of its application to Senegal River Valley irrigated systems', *Journal of Artificial Societies and Social Simulation*, **4**(2), downloadable at: http://jasss.soc.surrey.ac.uk/4/2/5.html (last access: May 2005).

Barreteau O., P. Garin, A. Dumontier, G. Abrami and F. Cernesson (2003), 'Agent based facilitation of water allocation : case study in Drome river valley', *Group Decision Negotiation*, **12**(5), 441–461.

Barreteau, O., F. Bousquet, C. Millier and J. Weber (2004), 'Suitability of multi-agent simulations to study irrigated system viability: application to case studies in the Senegal River Valley', *Agricultural Systems*, **80**, 255–275

Beck, M.B. (2002), 'The Manifesto', in M.B. Beck (ed.), *Environmental Foresight and Models: A Manifesto*, Oxford: Elsevier, pp. 61–93.

Beck, M.B., J. Chen and O.O. Osidele (2002a), 'Random search and the reachability of target futures', in M.B. Beck (ed.), *Environmental Foresight and Models: A Manifesto*, Oxford, Elsevier, pp. 207–226.

Beck, M.B., B.D. Fath, A.K. Parker, O.O. Osidele, G.M. Cowie, T.C. Rasmussen, B.C. Patten, B.G. Norton, A. Steinemann, S.R. Borrett, D. Cox, M.C. Mayhew, X.Q. Zeng and W. Zeng (2002b), 'Developing a concept of adaptive community learning: case study of a rapidly urbanizing watershed', *Integrated Assessment*, **3**(4), 299–307.

Benbasat, I. and J. Lim (2000), 'Information technology support for debiasing group judgments: an empirical evaluation', *Organizational Behavior and Human Decision Processes*, **83**(1), 167–183.

Cleaver, F. (2001), 'Agency, and the limitations of participatory processes to development', in B. Cooke and U. Kothari (eds), *Participation: The New Tyranny?*, London: Zed Books.

Cooke, B. and U. Kothari (eds) (2001), *Participation: The New Tyranny?*, London: Zed Books.

Craps, M. (2003), 'Social Learning in River Basin Management', HarmoniCOP WP2, Reference document, Leuven: KU Leuven.

D'Aquino, P., C. Le Page, F. Bousquet and A. Bah (2003), 'Using self-designed role-playing games and a multi-agent system to empower a local decision-making process for land use management: the SelfCormas experiment in Senegal', *Journal of Artificial Societies and Social Simulation*, **6**(3), downloadable at: http://jasss.soc.surrey.ac.uk/ 6/3/5.html (last access: May 2005).

Daré, W. and O. Barreteau (2003), 'A role-playing game in irrigated system negotiation: between play and reality', *Journal of Artificial Societies and Social Simulation*, **6**(3), downloadable at: http://jasss.soc.surrey.ac.uk/6/3/6.html (last access: May 2005).

Delbecq, A.L., A.H.V.d. Ven and D. Gustafson (1975), *Group Techniques for Program Planning: A Guide to Nominal Group and Delphi Processes*, Brighton: Scott, Foresman and Co.

Dovers, S. (2000), 'Beyond EverythingCare and EverythingWatch: public participation, public policy and participating publics', Proceedings of the International LandCare 2000, Conference, Melbourne Australia.

Doyle, J.K. and D.N. Ford (1998), 'Mental models concepts for system dynamics research', *System Dynamics Review*, **14**, 3–29.

Drafting Group (2002), 'Guidance on Public Participation in relation to the Water Framework Directive; Active involvement, consultation, and public access to information', prepared in the Framework of the Common Implementation Strategy of the European Commission and the EU Member States.

Driessen, P.P.J., P. Glasbergen and C. Verdaas (2001), 'Interactive policy making – a model of management for public works', *European Journal of Operational Research*, **128**, 322–337.

Dunlap, R.E. and R.E. Jones (2002), 'Environmental concern: conceptual and measurement issues', in R.E. Dunlap and W. Michelson (eds), *Handbook of Environmental Sociology*, Westport CT: Greenwood Press, pp. 482–524.

Evans, J.S.B.T. (1988), 'The knowledge elicitation problem: a psychological perspective', *Behaviour and Information Technology*, **7**, 111–130.

Fath, B.D. and M.B. Beck (2005), 'Short- and long-term environmental perceptions: a case study of Lake Lanier', *Environmental Modelling and Software*, **20**, 485–498.

Gammack, J.G. (1987), 'Different techniques and different aspects on declarative knowledge', in A.L. Kidd (ed.), *Knowledge Acquisition for Expert Systems: a practical handbook*, New York: Plenum Press.

Glicken, J. (2000), 'Getting stakeholder participation "right": a discussion of participatory processes and possible pitfalls', *Environmental Science and Policy*, **3**, 305–310.

Grabowski, M., A.P. Massey and W.A. Wallace (1992), 'Focus groups as a group knowledge acquisition technique', *Knowledge Acquisition*, **4**, 407–425.

Hare, M.P. and C. Pahl-Wostl (2002), 'Stakeholder categorisation in participatory integrated assessment processes', *Integrated Assessment*, **3**(1), 50–62.

Hare, M.P. and P. Deadman (2004), 'Further towards a taxonomy of agent-based simulation models in environmental management', *Mathematics and Computers in Simulation Journal*, **64**, 25–40.

Hare, M.P., D. Medugno, J. Heeb and C. Pahl-Wostl (2002), 'An applied methodology for participatory model building of agent-based models for urban water management', in C. Urban (ed.), *3rd Workshop on Agent-Based Simulation*, Ghent: SCS– Europe BVBA.

Hare, M.P., R.A. Letcher and A.J. Jakeman (2003), 'Participatory modelling in natural resource management: a comparison of four case studies', *Integrated Assessment*, **2**(4), 62–72.

Hatcher, K.J. (1994), *Diagnostic/Feasibility Study of Lake Sidney Lanier, Georgia, Report Submitted to the Environmental Protection Division*, Atlanta, Georgia: Georgia Department of Natural Resources.

Hodgson, A.M. (1992), 'Hexagons for systems thinking', *European Journal of Operational Research*, **59**, 220–230.

Huizinga, J. (1951), *HomoLudens*, Paris: Gallimard.

Iberaqua (2002a), 'Aplicación de la Directiva Marco del Agua y Convenio Hispano Luso de 1998 en las cuencas hidrográficas compartidas', downloadable at: http://iberaqua.com.sapo.pt/informes.htm (last access: May 2005).

Iberaqua (2002b), 'La participación pública en la gestión de los recursos hídricos de la Península Ibérica', downloadable at: http://iberaqua.com.sapo.pt/informes.htm (last access: May 2005).

Innes, J.E. and D.E. Booher (1999), 'Consensus building as role playing and bricolage: toward a theory of collaborative planning', *Journal of the American Planning Association*, **65**(1), 9–26.

Kasemir, B., J. Jäger, C. Jaeger and M.T. Gardner (eds) (2003), *Public Participation in Sustainability Science. A Manual*, Cambridge: Cambridge University Press.

Kohler, T.A. (1999), 'Putting social sciences together again: an introduction to the volume', in T.A. Kohler and G.J. Gumerman (eds), *Dynamics in Human and Primate Societies*, Sante Fe: Santa Fe Institute, pp. 1–18.

Letcher, R.A. and P. Aluwihare (2003), 'Development of a Decision Support System for the Namoi and Gwydir Valleys', in Proceedings of the International Congress on Modelling and Simulation (MODSIM03), Townsville, QLD.

Letcher, R.A. and A.J. Jakeman, (2003), 'Application of an adaptive method for integrated assessment of water allocation issues in the Namoi River catchment, Australia', *Integrated Assessment*, **4**(2), 73–89.

Letcher, R.A., A.J. Jakeman and B.F.W. Croke, (2004), 'Model development for integrated assessment of water allocation options', *Water Resources Research*, **40**, W05502.

Maiden, N.A.M. and M.P. Hare (1998), 'Problem domain categories in requirements engineering', *International Journal of Human-Computer Studies*, **49**, 281–304.

McGeorge, P. and G. Rugg (1992), 'The uses of 'contrived' knowledge elicitation techniques', *Expert Systems*, **9**, 149–154.

Mermet, L. (1992), *Stratégies pour la Gestion de l'Environnement, la Nature comme Jeu de Société ?*, Paris: L'Harmattan.

Merton, R.K. (1987). 'The focussed interview and focus groups: continuities and discontinuities', *Public-Opinion-Quarterly*, **51**(4), 550–566.

Merton, R.K. and P.L. Kendall (1946), 'The focused interview', *American Journal of Sociology*, **51**, 541–557.

Mostert, E. (2003), 'The challenge of public participation', *Water Policy*, **5**, 179–197.

Mostert, E. (2004), 'Public participation and social learning for river basin management', in Proceedings of Monitoring Tailor-Made IV, Sint Michielsgestel (The Netherlands), 15–18 September 2003, RIZA: Lelystad.

Norton, B. and A. Steinemann (2001), 'Environmental values and adaptive management', *Environmental Values*, **10**(4), 473–506.

Olsen, M.E., G.L. Dora and R.E. Dunlap (1992), *Viewing the World Ecologically*, Boulder, CO: Westview Press.

Orth, K.D. and C.A. Sanders (1998), 'Handbook for the large group response exercise', *Institute for Water Resources report*, 98–R–4.

Osidele, O.O. (2001), 'Reachable futures, structural change, and the practical credibility of environmental simulation models', Ph.D. Dissertation, University of Georgia, Athens, Georgia.

Osidele, O.O. and M.B. Beck (2003), 'An inverse approach to the analysis of uncertainty in models of environmental systems', *Integrated Assessment*, **4**(4), 265–282.

Pahl-Wostl, C. (2002a), 'Participative and stakeholder-based policy design and modeling processes', *Integrated Assessment*, **3**(1), 3–14.

Pahl-Wostl, C. (2002b), 'Towards sustainability in the water sector – The importance of human actors and processes of social learning', *Aquatic Sciences*, **64**(4), 394–411.

Pahl-Wostl, C. and Ridder, D. (2003), 'Participation in Local Level Planning versus Participation in Integrated Assessment', in Proceedings of Monitoring Tailor Made IV, Sint Michielsgestel (The Netherlands), 15–18 September 2003, RIZA: Lelystad.

Pahl-Wostl, C. and M.P. Hare (2004), 'Processes of social learning in integrated resources management', *Journal of Community and Applied Social Psychology*, **14**, 193–206.

Pretty, J.N. (1995), 'Participatory learning for sustainable agriculture', *World Development*, **23**, 1247–1263.

Renn, O., T. Webler and P. Wiedemann (eds) (1995), *Fairness and Competence in Citizen Participation. Evaluating Models for Environmental Discourse*, London: Kluwer Academic Publishers.

Rotmans, J. (1998), 'Methods for IA: challenges and opportunities ahead', *Environmental Modelling and Assessment*, **3**, 155–179.

Sinclair, J. and Diduck, A. (1995), 'Public education: an undervalued component of the environmental assessment public involvement process', *Environmental Impact Assessment Review*, **15**, 241–274.

Sluijs, J. van der and P. Kloprogge (2001), 'The inclusion of stakeholder perspectives in Integrated Assessment of Climate Change', in M. Decker (ed.), *Interdisciplinarity in Technology Assessment. Implementations and their Chances and Limits*, Series: 'Wissenschaftsethik und Technikfolgenbeurteilung', Volume 11, Berlin, Springer, pp. 199–214.

Social Learning Group (2001), *Learning to Manage Global Environmental Risks*, Cambridge, MA: MIT Press, 2 vols.

Tàbara, D. (2001), 'La Medida de la Percepción Social del Medio Ambiente. Una revisión de las aportaciones realizadas por la sociología', (The measure of social environmental perception, a review article of the sociological contributions), *Revista Internacional de Sociología*, **28**, 125–168.

Tàbara, D. (2003), 'Participación cualitativa y evaluación integrada del medio ambiente. Aspectos metodológicos en cuatro estudios de caso' (Qualitative Participation and Integrated Environmental Assessment. Methodological issues in four case studies)', *Documents d'Anàlisi Geogràfica*, **42**, 183–213.

Thompson, M. (1997), 'Cultural theory and integrated assessment', *Environmental Modelling and Assessment*, **2**, 139–150.

Tillman, D. (2001), 'Stakeholder analysis in water supply systems', PhD, ETH-Zürich.

UNCHS (2001), 'The guide for community based environmental information systems (CEMIS)', *Spring Research Series*, **26**, Dortmund.

Vennix, J.A.M. (1996), *Group Model Building*, Chichester: Wiley.

Vinck, D. (1999), 'Les objets intermédiaires dans les réseaux de coopération scientifique', *Revue Française de Sociologie*, **40**(2), 385–414.

Wates, N. (2000), *The Community Planning Handbook*, London: Earthscan.

APPENDIX

Handbooks on participation

This appendix provides the reader with a brief guide to the wide range of handbooks on public participation that is currently available (Table 8.5). A common way to disseminate knowledge and information on participation and water management is by publishing handbooks, manuals and user guides. It is not difficult to find guidance on public participation, participatory tools, community planning, mediation or conflict resolution. The spectrum of already existing guides and manuals is stunning. Some guides are written exclusively on participation and water management in general (*Local Agenda 21 Planning Guide. An Introduction to Sustainable Development Planning*). Others even focus on a specific target group, a special technology or a particular stage within the process of public participation and water management, or a specific area such as the EU. Topics covered are irrigation management in agriculture, coastal zone water management, participation in small-scale rural water supply, wetland management, water quality management (*Public Participation in Making Local Environmental Decisions; The Aarhus Convention – Newcastle Workshop; Good Practise Handbook*) and participation in storm water management.

Despite the popularity of producing handbooks and manuals on participation, their impact remains limited. This is due to the fact that end-user requirements are often neglected. The problem starts with the language barrier. In many cases handbooks on participation are written by social scientists and end-users may be engineers, natural scientists or technicians. Here, not only terminology must be adapted but many of the skills that are necessary to apply tools of participation and facilitation do not necessarily exist within the end-user community. Additionally, the skills needed may vary throughout the participatory process. Another factor that complicates the definition of a target group is that a person who decides about the process of participation in general (i.e. water authority) may differ from the person that carries it out and facilitates participation (i.e. consultant). This must be recognised by the handbook design.

As handbooks have different target groups and different objectives their structures will also vary. Two major groups of handbooks can be distinguished: handbooks that offer selective reference-style reading (A) and handbooks that don't (B).

For handbooks that offer selective reading for quick referencing, the most common structural features are:

A1. a focus on presentation of several tools, methods and techniques;
A2. a process-oriented approach clearly distinguishing different phases of participation; and

A3.   the presentation of case studies as practical experiences or best practice additionally categorised according to locality or used methods.

Handbooks that do not offer their readers different entry points for selective reading mainly focus on:

B1.   the presentation of one tool or method in detail; or
B2.   the explanation of one complex issue in participation such as communication.

Table 8.5 tries to attribute the following categories (Cat.) to a selection of freely available handbooks on participation in water management. Some of the handbooks fit clearly into one given category whilst others fit into several – the dominating categories are indicated.

As can be seen, many handbooks follow a process-oriented approach. That means the different phases of participation are distinguished and tools and methods are presented in that context. It has the advantage that methods, tools and techniques as presented in Section 8.3 ('Participatory processes, methods and evaluation techniques') can be attributed to the most suitable phase. One major disadvantage is the difficulty for readers to quickly access detailed technical information about a tool.

Handbooks also commonly make use of positive case studies and publish them as 'best practice'. The disadvantage is the tendency of human beings to use the positive experiences as a blueprint even if it is stated clearly that this should not be done. Once something is declared best practice, people tend to copy it and as every method, tool and technique as a single application or in its various combinations requires special adaptation to local circumstances, the idea of best practices should be abandoned. Often, as done in this chapter, it is better to present case studies and illustrate that what did not work well and give the reasoning – if possible – why something did not work out as expected. It is also less frustrating to avoid as many mistakes as possible instead of trying to achieve the same good results as pointed out in a so-called best practise.

Table 8.5 A comparison of different handbooks on participation

Title	Author/Publisher	Content in brief
1. EEB Handbook on EU Water Policy under the Water Framework Directive. 60 pages [a]	International Water Affairs and EEB January 2001	The handbook targets the general public and environmental NGOs in particular. It explains the complex WFD and tries to make its content transparent and understandable for interested parties throughout Europe. Besides a general and historical introduction of the legal background it discusses several issues in connection with WFD: integrated river basin management, ecological objectives for surface waters, chemicals policy, groundwater protection and water pricing.
2. Water Management: Guidance on public participation and compliance with agreements. 61 pages [b]	Convention on Protection and Use of Trans-boundary Water Courses and International Lakes. ECE/UNEP, Geneva, March 2000 ECE/UNEP Network of Expert on Public Participation and Compliance	This guideline goes along with the Convention on Protection and Use of Transboundary Water Courses and International Lakes and explains its main issues. Its purpose is to facilitate and achieve compliance with the (legally binding) agreements of the convention. Although not specifically mentioned, the target group of this handbook can be found in water-related governmental agencies and NGOs working on national to international scale.
3. Handbook on Public Participation in Environmental Impact Assessment Procedures in Poland. 65 pages [c]	Ministry of Environment of Poland – Danish Cooperation for Environment in Eastern Europe (DANCEE), January 2002	The book is designed to assist Poland with the implementation of the EU EIA Directive. It covers crucial topics on public participation in environmental decision-making process during EIA. Target group is the public administration involved in implementing participatory processes but also NGOs, (foreign) investors and academia.
4. Supporting Community Management: A manual for training in community management in the water and sanitation sector. 122 pages [d]	IRC/Fmd consultants; Occasional Paper Series 34, Delft 2002	Divided into 2 parts: the 1st part gives an introduction into the theory of concepts and approaches that are useful in the context of community water management and the 2nd part provides tools that help to internalise and use the theory. This book can be distinguished from the others especially because it is a trainer's manual The manual has a clearly defined target group: practitioners that further disseminate and apply the contents of the book.

Notes: a http://www.rivernet.org/general/handbook.pdf (last access: May 2005).
c http://www.mos.gov.pl/aahus/dokumenty/PUBLIC_PARTICIP_in_EIA_Procedu res_in_Poland_handbook.pdf (last access: May 2005).

Strengths	Weaknesses	Cat.
It is very complete in regard to the content of the WFD. It clearly indicates the inconsistencies or issues that were left too vague in the WFD. It is easy to read. The style is adequate.	The term 'handbook' is misleading. The EEB handbook represents a very good critical review and interpretation of the WFD but it is not a handbook in its original sense or guidance for implementing the WFD.	B2
Eight extracts of examples are presented of international co-operation in water management and even how they have learnt from each other. It is well described how water management and compliance to the convention can be achieved in a participatory manner under different legal circumstances. The cases go from Armenia to England to the Russian Federation.	Conclusions that and how participation must take place often remain banal. If it is not possible to provide some further details how 'states should provide for effective public participation rights in their national legal systems', at least some further reading could be given to fill this gap. Also the target group for this book can be assumed but is not defined. The missing table of contents is more than inconvenient.	A3, B2
Comprehensively written. Giving valuable environmental addresses in Poland, web resources. The book gives systematically advantages and disadvantages of techniques of participatory processes. The formal steps of participatory processes in EIA are well described.	Some examples for further reading, especially for the techniques, would have been useful. Style and format is a bit dry. As the targeted reader group is quite large, the content and recommendations are rather designed for public administration than for the other interest groups mentioned.	A1, B2
Good size and structure of the book; well-defined target group; large number of tools presented. Some practical cases and examples given but could be more. Figures, tables and boxes structure the book and make it easier to browse through.	Conditions or circumstances under which tools could be applied are not explained; necessary knowledge and skills of the moderator/ facilitator are not specifically given; book is not very attractive looking. Some hints for further reading would be good.	A1, B2

b   http://www.unece.org/env/water/publications/documents/guidance.pdf
     (last access: May 2005).
d   http://www.irc.nl/page/1919.

Table 8.5 A comparison of different handbooks on participation (Continued)

Title	Author/Publisher	Content in brief
5. Local Agenda 21 Planning Guide. An Introduction to Sustainable Development Planning. · 17 pages [e]	ICLEI 1996 (This free download version provides only the Chapter 4 'Action Planning'. The complete guide comprises 200 pages.)	The intention was to present action planning as one possible tool in community management. Very short. Guides stakeholders in planning processes to develop their own framework (planning) documents and eventually implementation plans.
6. Handbook for the Large Group Response Exercise. 114 pages [f]	Institute for Water Resources; Water Resources Support Centre US, Dec. 1998	Describes the methods of public involvement in ecosystem restoration. Gives a good toolbox for motivation.
7. Public Participation in Making Local Environmental Decisions; The Aarhus Convention – Newcastle Workshop; Good Practise Handbook. 69 pages [g]	DETR, London (UK), 2000	The book explains participation in the context of the Aarhus convention. Accordingly a focus is on information issues. Although following a process-oriented approach this handbook tries to provide detailed information about the different steps of participatory processes in their legal context. A geographical focus is on Europe and the contents relate to environmental issues in general.
8. EU Guidance on Public Participation and the WFD. 199 pages incl. annexes [h]	European Commission 2002 ; Drafting group on public participation for the Common Implementation Strategy for the WFD	This Guidance is the most comprehensive information on the WFD and participation in Europe. The logical structure follows the needs of implementing the directive. By providing a large annex including participatory methods and tools it also serves as a reference book.
9. Water Quality Control Commission; Public Participation Handbook. 17 pages [i]	State of Colorado (USA) 2001	The handbook puts emphasis on informing the public about the formal requirements for public participation in water quality control. It gives detailed information about the agency in charge and the existing regulations in regard to water quality control.

Notes: e http://www.unhabitat.org/cdrom/governance/html/yellop28.htm (Last access: May 2005).

   g http://www.unece.org/env/pp/ecases/handbook.pdf (Last access: May 2005).

   i http://www.cdphe.state.co.us/op/wqcc/GeneralInfo/PublicParticipation/pubpart.pdf (Last access: May 2005).

Strengths	Weaknesses	Cat.
Despite this short version good explanations of strategic planning are provided. Steps of action planning are distinguished. An introduction to detailed steps and the linkage to plans and programmes is provided.	Because of the small size, practical examples are missing. Once the importance of signed agreements among stakeholders is underlined, why not show one of these agreements? Context of the tool/handbook is naturally missing because only one selected chapter of a book is presented. A short introduction could overcome this problem.	B1, the complete guide is: A1, A3
It is based on case studies and real life experiences. That makes it practical. The organisation of the book follows the process approach.	Unfortunately, a critical reflection and examples of what went wrong are missing. Some results could have been presented instead of purely describing the method. Lots of information is found in the annex. This should have been better prepared.	A2, B1
A book like this is helpful since it explains the legal support for participation as provided by the Aarhus convention.	Useful links and ideas for further reading are not provided. This would have completed the more general description of steps in participation. Although named 'good practice' it is not a good practice handbook according to the categorisation.	A2, B2
The amount of given information and different issues raised is surprising. The guidance is mostly complete and underlines the importance of adaptation to new circumstances.	The sometimes moralistic writing style with a raised index finger is disturbing. The use of models in participation is only weakly covered.	A1, B2
Good overview of the legal background to participation and water quality control. All steps for rather formal participation are mentioned from public hearings to petitions.	Although it addresses the public the writing style and format of the handbook are not inviting at all. The handbook rather gives the impression that one should inform the public what they are allowed and not allowed to do rather than looking for constructive collaboration.	B2

f   http://www.iwr.usace.army.mil/iwr/products/reports/reports.htm (Last access: May 2005).
h   http://forum.europa.eu.int/Public/irc/env/wfd/library?l=/framework_directive/
guidance_documents/participation_guidance&vm=detailed&sb=Title
(Last access: May 2005).

PART V

Integrated Modelling for IWRM

9. Software Tools for Hydrological Modelling

Derek Karssenberg, Karin Pfeffer and Marc Vissers

9.1 INTRODUCTION

Models are useful tools for Integrated Water Resource Management due to their combined dependency and independency of the 'real world'. Their dependency consists of the necessity of representing the real world, thereby allowing researchers to use models for making predictions, with associated uncertainty bands, of the future behaviour of the system. This could be referred to as the predictive power of models. At the same time, however, models can be considered as 'laboratory-scale systems' which are partly independent of the system they represent because they can easily be changed or modified for exploring system behaviour under different scenarios. Some researchers consider this exploratory power of models to be more relevant than their predictive power, as the predictive power of models is associated with high degrees of uncertainty, while for exploratory use this uncertainty becomes less of a problem (Bankes, 1993; Oreskes et al., 1994).

Although physical models, which are miniature versions of the world created in the laboratory, have a wide application in water management (such as flumes used for studying river channel evolution), we focus here on mathematical models. In most cases, the mathematical equations need to be solved using numerical algorithms running on a computer, since the size and spatio-temporal variation of their inputs does not allow for manual calculations or analytical solutions.

The application of numerical environmental models in Integrated Water Resource Management is complicated by the wide range of software functionality required and the number of experts required to perform a modelling project. A standard modelling study involves many steps, often commencing with the collection of large amounts of field data, and then processing it to provide input for an existing model or for a model built from scratch. Additional steps include model calibration, evaluation of the model results, and presentation or aggregation of model inputs and outputs for decision making. For each of these steps, different software functionality is needed, and an important issue we are addressing here is how these different tasks can be integrated using existing software. These tasks are undertaken by a variety of experts covering many disciplines. For the necessary scientific knowledge required for the modelling study, application domain specialists play the main part, which in this case are specialists in hydrology or related fields. In most cases, these specialists know a lot about hydrological processes and associated aspects, but their knowledge of information technology is mostly limited, and certainly not at a professional level. Software engineers are therefore employed for the software related tasks in a project, either the development of new software, or the maintenance of existing software. The third group of people involved are the decision makers, who may not be that familiar with either the application domain or the software domain. The challenge is to make these three groups of experts cooperate in a modelling study, and moreover, find software that facilitates this cooperation.

In this chapter, we focus on software and integration of different software components that can be used in hydrological modelling studies for Integrated Water Resource Management. Generally, two types of software are essential: Geographical Information Systems (GIS) and environmental models. In most cases, the role of the GIS is limited to importing spatial data needed for modelling, management of these data in a database, processing these data, and visualisation of model inputs and outputs. With respect to the construction and application of environmental models, we distinguish two approaches. In the first approach, the model is constructed and run with software outside the GIS, since, in many cases, the equations needed for modelling cannot be represented using the build-in functions of the GIS. In the second, more recent approach, the GIS and modelling functionality are merged into one software system, using an environmental modelling language embedded in the GIS. The purpose of this chapter is to describe both approaches in more detail, illustrated with examples, and to evaluate the suitability of both approaches for different types of modelling studies, taking into account the different experts involved in a modelling study.

Although the above-mentioned software, i.e. GIS and environmental models, does provide the tools to handle large amounts of data needed in modelling, to run simple or very complex models, and to evaluate their outputs using standard visualisation routines, additional techniques are needed to provide the models with appropriate inputs and parameter values. In most cases, field or literature data that can be used as model inputs and parameters will be available, but they might not have the correct properties to be directly used in the modelling study. Therefore, advanced techniques are needed to process these data before using them in a modelling study. These techniques include methods to deal with a discrepancy between the scale of measurements and the scale used in the model, methods to interpolate point samples to continuous fields and methods to calibrate model parameters. This chapter will provide a short introduction to these techniques, with references to standard software that can do the job.

Sections 9.2 and 9.3 of this chapter are devoted to a description of the various types of environmental models that might be used. Section 9.4 describes the potential of GIS for database construction and management for modelling. Section 9.5 explains when off-the-shelf models should be used and how these can be linked to a GIS. The next two sections discuss tools to construct new models from scratch or to modify existing models, Section 9.6 dealing with tools running outside the GIS, while Section 9.7 covers environmental modelling languages running inside the GIS. The issue of model input and parameter estimation is dealt with in Section 9.8, followed by the final section that draws some conclusions of the current approaches and discusses issues for future research and development.

9.2   DYNAMIC SPATIAL MODELS

Mathematical environmental models are considered here as a representation of a part of the landscape, including properties and processes above, at or below the land or water surface. The entities represented may be objects or continuous spatial fields as studied by hydrology or associated natural sciences such as biology, ecology, physical geography, geology or meteorology. Besides other types of mathematical models, such as statistical models, dynamic models are widely used in the environmental sciences. The property of a model that makes it dynamic is that it is run forward in time, using rules of cause and effect to simulate temporal changes in the landscape. For this reason, some people refer to dynamic models as forward models. Although dynamic environmental models are often spatial models, in the sense that they represent spatial entities in a landscape, for instance a soil layer and its water content, firstly we introduce the non-spatial approach, or the point model. For this case, the concept of dynamic modelling can be represented by the following equation, which is also illustrated on the left side of Figure 9.1:

$$z(t+1) = f(z(t), i(t), t) \quad \text{for each } t \tag{9.1}$$

In this equation, a certain property, or attribute, of the landscape is represented by the non-spatial state variable z, which can be a continuous variable, for instance groundwater level, or a classified variable, such as a

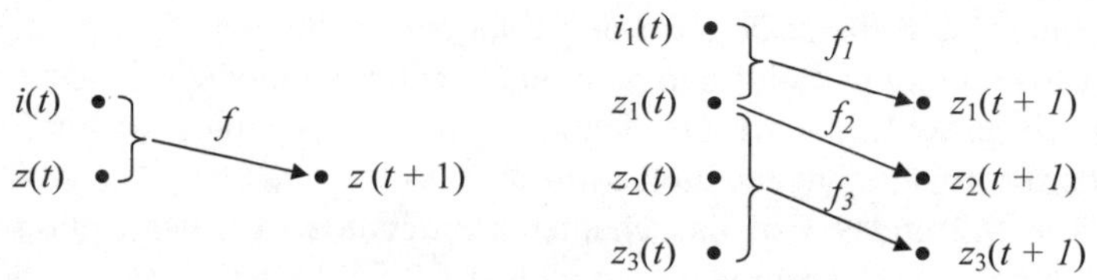

Notes: $i_j(t)$, inputs; $z_k(t)$, state variables; f or f_k, functionals.
Left, one input and one state variable; right, multiple inputs (only one shown) and state variables (three shown).

Figure 9.1   Dynamic non-spatial model

vegetation class. It could also represent an attribute of an object, for instance a lake. The variable z has a value at each moment in time t, and is written as $z(t)$, while $z(t + 1)$ means the value of z at a certain moment later in time. Although z changes in a continuous way through time, which can be represented by a set of differential equations, a discrete representation of time is used here. The letter f represents a functional with associated parameters, operating on the variables inside the brackets. It can be either an update rule, explicitly specifying the change of the state variable over the time slice $(t, t + 1)$, for instance a rule-based function such as cellular automata that uses local neighbourhood interactions to simulate larger scale processes (e.g., Toffoli, 1987), a probabilistic function, or alternatively a derivative of a differential equation describing the change of the state variables as a continuous function (c.f. Gurney and Nisbet, 1998). Equation 9.1 shows that for each moment in time, the value of the attribute at that moment, $z(t)$, is used to calculate that value of the attribute at a later moment in time. This change in z over the period $(t, t + 1)$ is represented by the functional f. The second term $i(t)$ can be zero for all time steps, representing a dynamic model which is not affected from outside, and hence is a closed system. But in many cases, the system represented by a dynamic model has external inputs, also called disturbances or boundary conditions. Examples are rain falling on the ground surface in a model simulating infiltration of water into the soil, or addition of nutrients from agriculture in a model simulating a lake ecosystem. Such inputs are represented in equation 9.1 by $i(t)$, which is, just like z, defined for each moment in time t. The functional f operates on this input and the state variable, as shown in Figure 9.1 on the left. Similar descriptions can be found in Beck et al. (1993), Gurney and Nisbet (1998) and van Deursen (1995).

Note that some models derive $z(t + 1)$ from an input only, which means that equation 9.1 reduces to $z(t + 1) = f(i(t))$. These models are also regarded as dynamic models. Finally, the functional f uses the time t to calculate

$z(t+1)$, which is needed when the processes in the landscape change with time, for instance as a result of climate change.

Equation 9.1 represents the simple case where one state variable z is used; ignoring interaction between different components or processes in an environment, such as deposition of sediment controlled by water level, flow speed or sediment type. Models that simulate interaction between different components of an environment need to include a set of state variables, as illustrated on the right side of Figure 9.1, and can be represented by:

$$z_k(t+1) = f_k\left(z_k(t), k = 1...m\ ;\ i_j(t), j = 1...n\ ;\ t\right) \quad \text{for each } t \quad (9.2)$$

For each state variable z_k, where k represents one of the 1 to m state variables involved, its value at $t+1$ results from a functional f_k on all (or a part of) the state variables $z_k(t)$, $k = 1, ..., m$. In addition, each variable z_k can be determined by a set of $j = 1, ..., n$ inputs i_j. While f in equation 9.1 was a relatively simple functional, f_k in equation 9.2 can be rather complex, representing a complex set of interactions between state variables and inputs, which is called the model structure.

Although the components of some environmental systems can be described by a non-spatial, or one-dimensional dynamic model, many environmental processes include important spatial interactions. For representing these processes, the dynamic model becomes a spatial model, and needs to consider the environment as a two or three-dimensional system, and the variables need to be represented in a two or three dimensional domain. In these cases, the variables and inputs in equation 9.2 become spatial entities, and the functions in that equation become spatial too. Accordingly, spatial relations such as lateral flow of water can be represented. Note that in the spatial case, many parameters used in the functionals will have values changing in the spatial dimension.

Besides the classification of dynamic models into non-spatial and spatial models, they can also be classified as either deterministic or stochastic. A deterministic model has state variables that have a single value for each location in space and moment in time. A stochastic model deals with state variables that in the non-spatial case are random variables, having a certain probability distribution, or in the spatial case, random fields. A dynamic model becomes a stochastic model when its inputs i_j or parameters are stochastic (c.f. Heuvelink, 1998), or when the functional f_k involves a probabilistic rule.

So far, we have mainly looked at how an environmental system or parts of that system can be represented by a model. In applied research, studying this system is not the main aim of modelling; the model is merely an instrument to predict a specified set of properties of the system. In this context, a model is regarded as a system producing a certain number of outputs in which the interest lies. This is shown in Figure 9.2, which can be regarded as a summary of the aspects of this section: a model has external inputs $i_{1...n}$, internal state variables $z_{1...m}$, functionals $f_{1...m}$ with associated parameters $\boldsymbol{p}$, while it generates outputs $\boldsymbol{o}$, which can be regarded as a selection of the state variables in the model.

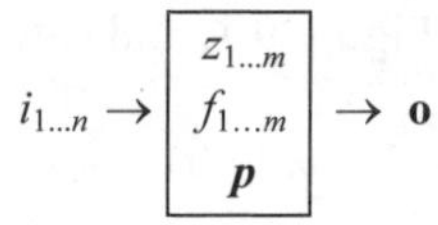

$$i_{1...n} \rightarrow \boxed{\begin{array}{c} z_{1...m} \\ f_{1...m} \\ \boldsymbol{p} \end{array}} \rightarrow \boldsymbol{o}$$

Notes: $i_{1...n}$ inputs; $z_{1...m}$ state variables, $f_{1...m}$ functionals, $\boldsymbol{p}$ parameters and $\boldsymbol{o}$ output variables.

Figure 9.2   Dynamic spatial model as an open system

9.3   THE MODEL DEVELOPMENT CYCLE

A comprehensive modelling study needs to incorporate all steps of the model development cycle (Figure 9.3). The first step of this cycle is the identification of a model structure that is appropriate for the modelling problem under consideration. This is not a straightforward task, since the choice of the model structure depends on several factors, in particular the model outputs required, study site characteristics, practical issues and the modelling aim.

- Model outputs required. The kind of information that is needed for managing a water system, and the required spatial or temporal resolution of this information, help to define the type of model that is most appropriate. For instance, when the height and frequency of peak flows in a river have to be predicted, a rather complex model is needed, including all processes affecting water flow in all system components at a high temporal resolution. The opposite is true when predictions of monthly average discharge are needed. This can be done more appropriately with a simpler model, using larger time steps.
- Study site and field data. To simulate environmental processes at a specific study site, the model needs to embody processes that are important at that site. The set of processes that is dominant will vary across different study sites, and for that reason the same model cannot be applied across all study sites without some adjustments to the model structure (Beven, 2000). In addition, the model structure depends on the properties of the field data available, where properties refers to the

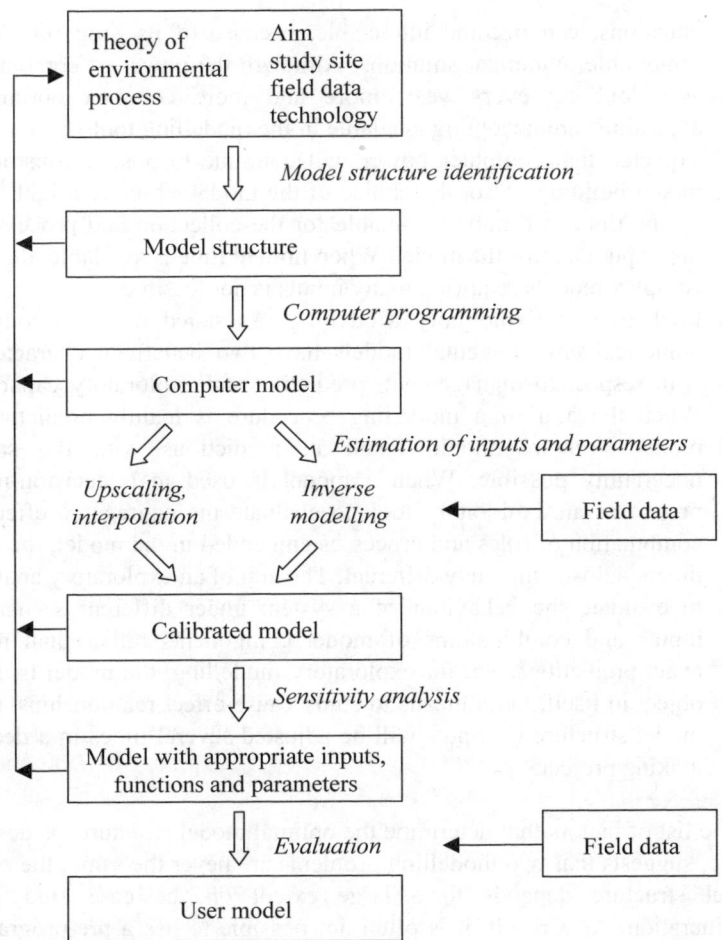

Figure 9.3   The model development cycle

amount, spatial and temporal resolution and precision of the field data. A balance needs to be found between the properties of the field data and the complexity of the model structure, see for instance Beven (2000), de Wit and Pebesma (2001), Donnelly-Makowecki and Moore (1999), Jørgensen and Bendoricchio (1986), van der Perk (1997).

- Practical restrictions. A proposed model structure should be feasible from the technical point of view (Casti, 1997). Whether a model is feasible or not, depends on the model representation, the tool used to program it and the hardware. A complex model, with many variables defined in multiple dimensions, and using a large number of model equations, can become intractable, because of its long run time or impossible numerical solutions. Although the power of computers is still doubling every year, more and more complex optimisation algorithms are becoming available in the modelling tools, and it can be expected that computer power will continue to pose a constraint on model building. Also, the choice of the model structure might depend on the time and money available for the collection and processing of the input data for the model. When limited time is available, the use of complex models requiring many inputs is not feasible.

- Predictive or Exploratory Modelling. As stated in the introduction, numerical environmental models have two beneficial characteristics with respect to management: predictive and exploratory capabilities. When the aim of a modelling procedure is mainly prediction, the model structure should result in predictions with the smallest uncertainty possible. When a model is used in a decision-making project as an exploratory tool, to evaluate the aggregated effect of a combination of rules and processes embedded in the model, the role of the model is completely different. The aim of an exploratory analysis is to evaluate the behaviour of a system under different scenarios of inputs and combinations of model components rather than making exact predictions. So, for exploratory modelling, the model is a study object in itself, i.e. a means to study cause-effect relationships, and its model structure or inputs will be adjusted several times in a decision-making project.

The list of factors that determine the optimal model structure, as described above, suggests that two modelling problems are never the same: the optimal model structure depends to a large extent on the case study under consideration. As a result, it is often not possible to use a pre-programmed off-the-shelf model since none of the existing models will fit the requirements of the model structure identified in the first step of the model development cycle. In these cases, it is far better to program a model from scratch or to modify an existing model until it matches the equations defined in the model structure.

The conversion of the model structure to a working computer program is the second step in the model development cycle, followed by the estimation of model inputs and parameters. Finally, a sensitivity analysis and a model validation have to be performed, resulting in a tool that can be used by decision makers.

Each step of the model development cycle is associated with a specific type of software. Software is needed to:

1. manage large amounts of (field) data associated with a modelling study;
2. to program the model or to modify existing models;
3. to estimate inputs and parameters of a model, to perform a sensitivity analysis and to evaluate model results.

The following sections describe the possible software packages that might be used for each of these steps, their approaches to the modelling problem and their advantages and disadvantages.

9.4   SOFTWARE TOOLS TO MANAGE LARGE AMOUNTS OF (FIELD) DATA

As a result of improved techniques for data collection in the field, such as improved remote sensing techniques and automatic data loggers, an increasing amount of environmental data becomes available. These data have a high potential to improve the quality of environmental models, since empirical data are essential in the steps of the model development cycle involving the estimation of model inputs and parameters, and also in the model evaluation, sometimes referred to as validation. However, a successful application of empirical data in a modelling study is only possible when appropriate tools are used, which are capable of handling high volumes of spatio-temporal data. Most proprietary GIS provide such tools.

GIS come with standard techniques for importing empirical data from different sources to the GIS database. Manually collected field data, such as drainage network or soil type maps can be digitised in a GIS laboratory, while digital mapping tablets are available for storing data in digital form in the field, when linked to a GPS. These data can be uploaded to standard GIS systems. In addition, (real-time) data from automatic data loggers can be imported to the GIS database, without any manual processing. An increasing amount of data from remote sensing images is becoming available, which can be imported to GIS after extraction of the necessary information using image processing software. This software runs mostly outside the GIS, although some GIS packages such as ILWIS (2005) or IDRISI (2005) include image processing software, too. For most areas, digital elevation maps can be retrieved from commercial companies or can be derived from air photography and imported to GIS.

Data imported to a GIS can be managed using spatial database systems included in the GIS. This allows the combining of data from different sources, updating data when new data become available and conversion of data between vector or raster formats. In addition, some GIS include advanced geostatistical interpolation routines for interpolating point data to continuous maps. This is often an important procedure for estimating model inputs or parameters. A GIS also plays an important role in maintaining the quality of the data in the database. Exploratory data analysis (EDA) techniques based on interactive graphics allows users to detect outliers in data sets, caused by measurement errors or errors during manual data import. Since standard GIS do not always provide sufficient interactive graphics for exploring data, digital links have been developed between standard GIS and statistical software providing more advanced exploratory data analysis techniques.

9.5   PROGRAMMING THE MODEL: THE USE OF EXISTING MODELS

As stated above, the first step in the model development cycle is the identification of the model structure, which is a description of the variables and inputs of the model, the model equations used to represent environmental processes and the spatial and temporal resolution of the model. The next step is to convert this to a computer program. In many cases the model must be programmed from scratch. In some cases an existing model can be used, under the condition that such a pre-programmed model fits the model structure envisioned. Since the developers of most existing models focused predominantly on the modelling equations and efficient numerical algorithms to represent these, the capability of these models for database construction and management is limited. As a result, these models need to be coupled to a GIS, since a GIS provides efficient routines related to spatial databases, as mentioned in the previous section. This coupling mechanism needs to include routines to convert data stored in the GIS to the modelling software and vice versa. The first way to do so is the approach referred to as loose coupling (Burrough, 1996), involving manual exchange of data between the model and the GIS. The second approach, referred to as tight coupling, uses additional software that serves as an interface between the GIS and the model, resulting in a seamless link between the GIS and the model. Examples of state-of-the-art hydrological models that are widely used in combination with GIS are MODFLOW (Harbaugh et al., 2000), MIKE-SHE (MIKE-SHE, 2005), DelftWLS (Hesselink et al., 2003). In the following sections an example of applying MODFLOW and associated issues are described. Chapter 12, Section 3.1 provides additional discussion of this approach.

Even though many mathematical models have been developed to simulate the processes that determine groundwater quality, few mathematical models are actually used in groundwater protection programs. This is due to difficulties in data collection, model selection and model implementation (Wang, 1997). In many cases, the difficulties in data collection hinder the use of 3D hydrological transport models, as the input for these models, the ambient groundwater quality, is unknown. Therefore, in most cases other approaches are used to assess groundwater quality. The most commonly applied technique is the DRASTIC (Aller et al., 1987) approach, a GIS overlay technique whereby different maps (such as Recharge, Topography, Conductivity) are added using different weights for each map.

However, knowledge of groundwater flow (e.g. to delineate capture zones or pollution pathways) can be very useful for groundwater protection, sanitation and risk assessment. It could therefore play a major role in spatial planning. Also, the ever-increasing computational power of new computers is making fine-scale regional groundwater modelling possible. This approach was chosen in a study 'groundwater quality mapping of the city of Hengelo, the Netherlands' (Schipper and Vissers, 2003), whereby groundwater flow was modelled using MODFLOW (Harbaugh et al., 2000). The software program (GMS, 2001) was used as the graphical user interface, which has most of the GIS and database functionality required to set up the MODFLOW model.

Figure 9.4 shows an example of an important input to MODFLOW, the geological layers. As the MODFLOW model does not understand zero-thickness layers, GMS could not directly implement the discontinuous clay layers in MODFLOW. Implementation was achieved by exporting the layer data to a database where 'zero-thickness' layers could be assigned to the beneath-laying layers and then brought back to GMS. In a recent update of the program, GMS was extended with a similar technique (Jones et al., 2002), so no additional programming is involved when facing this problem in further studies.

The common output from this type of hydrological model consists of hydraulic heads, represented by isohypses, and the vertical flow component (infiltration or seepage). Since it was not possible to generate more detailed output within GMS, MODPATH (Pollock, 1994) was used. Particles were released in the flow pattern just below the water table in a 50m grid. The tabular output was imported into a database, where transit times and distances were calculated and then exported to a GIS. The distinction of hydrological systems (Engelen and Kloosterman 1996) at a very detailed level, as generated by MODPATH, is shown in Figure 9.5. This map, in combination with other maps such as transit time and transit distance at different depths, is very informative for groundwater quality mapping and estimation. Capture zones of wells and discharge areas can be easily read from the maps, as well as pollution pathways, depths and residence times of polluted groundwater.

In this example we have seen limitations in using off-the-shelf models, when the model input data does not fit the model, and when the model output does not give the desired information. Another problem that is sometimes encountered

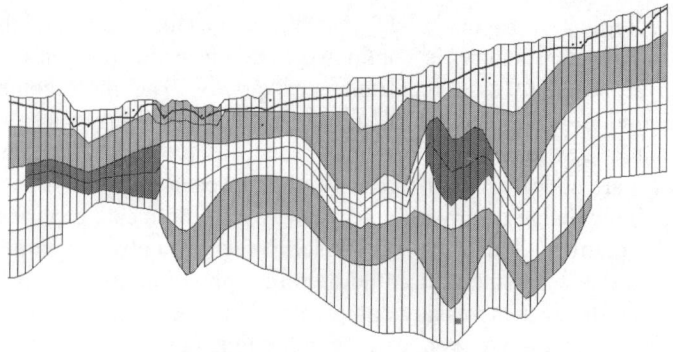

Notes: Cross section of the geological schematisation for the model area at y = 475 (in km, see also Figure 9.5). The grey tones represent clay layers and white indicates presence of sand.

Figure 9.4   Input to MODFLOW

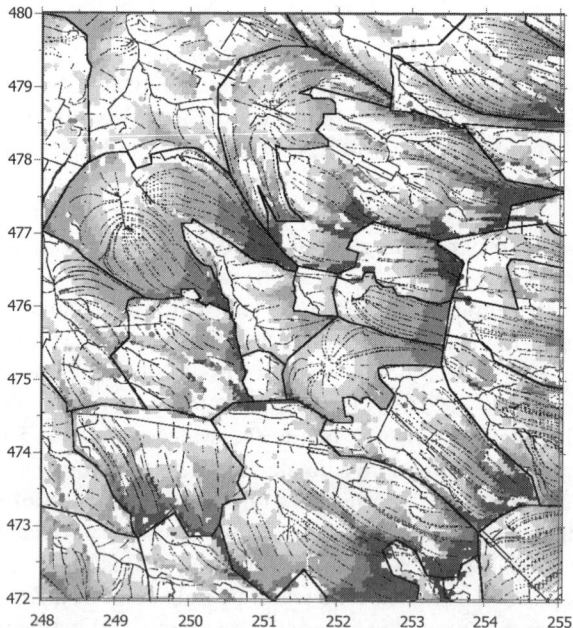

Notes: Transit distance from each location, visualised in GIS, and the resulting subdivision in hydrological systems. The dotted lines represent one fourth of the flow tracks, and the dark lines show the streams in the seepage areas. Coordinates are in kilometres.

Figure 9.5   Output of MODPATH

when using pre-programmed models is the difficulty, or impossibility, to include additional model components. For instance, adding a model component simulating unsaturated zone hydrology or evapotranspiration to the existing MODFLOW software is not an easy task, which can only be done when specialist programmers are available. Also, the coupling mechanism between the GIS and the model is associated with some problems. In the case study described above, manual exchange of data was done following the loose coupling approach. Since human inputs for the data conversion are needed each time that the model is run, it is time consuming to run the model several times with different inputs, and errors are easily made. For the same reason, it is often impossible or difficult to run the model several times in a batch procedure, for instance in the framework of a sensitivity analysis. When the tight coupling approach is followed these problems are not encountered, although it can be time consuming to program the software that interfaces between the GIS and the model.

In spite of these problems, off-the-shelf models are widely used for other good reasons. They have the major advantage that a standard modelling study can be done without much programming. As a result, a specialist programmer is not needed. In addition, these models have been tested and optimised in other research projects, and in many cases a good graphical user interface is provided for running the model, which is not the case when a new model needs to be programmed from scratch.

9.6 PROGRAMMING THE MODEL: MODEL CONSTRUCTION OUTSIDE THE GIS

In Section 9.3, it was shown that the choice of the appropriate model structure depends on many factors, such as the model outputs required and the field data available. As a result, in many cases the optimal model structure is highly specific for a certain case study. In those cases, a pre-programmed model is often not available. Accordingly an existing model needs to be modified, or a new model needs to be constructed. Moreover, when exploratory modelling is done, the development of a new model or the modification of an existing model is a first requirement, since this approach needs to involve a comparison of different model structures.

The choice of an appropriate tool for programming a new model is crucial, since the tool used sets the possibilities and impossibilities regarding certain functionality, and hence determines the types of models that can be developed in the project. Table 9.1 lists the different groups of programming languages that can be used for programming a model. All languages, except the environmental modelling languages discussed in the following section, result in models that are run outside the GIS system. As a result, models built with these languages need to be linked to a GIS using the loose or tight coupling approaches, as described in the previous section.

Generally, all of the languages listed in Table 9.1 can be used for model construction. They differ, however, regarding their concepts, and so the way they are used is very different. A comparison between languages can be made by looking at the entities that are changed by the operators of the language and the type of functionality that is provided by the operators. Both the kind of entities and the functionality of the operators should at least:

1. be compliant with the kind of objects that will be changed by the language and what changes need to be made to them; and
2. represent the thinking level of the user of the language.

Below, we will describe and compare the groups of programming languages running outside the GIS (the first three groups listed in Table 9.1) on the basis of these requirements and some additional items that are also important.

In the first years of the 1980s, when computer modelling was still in its infancy, several research groups started to develop their own hydrological models. These models were built from scratch, using a system programming language such as Fortran or C++. Compared to other languages used for programming a model, system programming languages can be considered low-level languages, which means that many technical details related to how

Table 9.1   Entities and functionality of operators of some programming languages

Language	Entity	Functionality of operators
System programming languages (e.g. Fortran, C++), scripting languages (e.g. Tcl/Tk, Python)	integers, floating points, arrays	adding, summing, looping
Technical computing languages (e.g. Splus, Matlab)	matrices, floating points	matrix inversion, adding matrices, calculating statistics
Graphical modelling systems (e.g. ModelMaker, Stella)	non-spatials states, fluxes	fluxes between states
Environmental modelling languages (e.g., PCRaster, Idrisi)	maps, time series, blocks	summing maps, iterating through time, topological links, transport of water, visualisation

Notes: Top: lower level languages; bottom: higher level languages.

a computer deals with data and computations need to be defined in a program. This is also expressed by the entities and operators of a system programming language (Table 9.1): instead of representing hydrological concepts, these represent concepts used in computer science. Most of the problems of using system programming languages are related to this low level property of these languages. Since efficient use of a system programming language requires much knowledge and experience in computer science, programming the model cannot efficiently be done by an application domain specialist, such as a hydrologist. So, in addition, a software engineer is needed, or the hydrologist needs to be trained in programming. Another problem often encountered is that the modification of the programming code can be a difficult and time-consuming procedure. This can be a serious problem when exploratory modelling is done, or when existing models need to be modified. One of the main problems is the complete absence of a generic approach (apart from the mathematical basis) to dynamic spatial modelling because each program is written by a different team under different circumstances. This lack of standardisation makes it difficult to modify (or even understand) programs developed by others. This last problem is partly solved by the development of standard algorithms that are available to everybody, and are known as numerical recipes (Press et al., 1986).

One of the main reasons why system programming languages are still widely used for programming a model is their generic application: any model can be built with these languages. In addition, when developed in a skilful way, programs written in system programming languages will have shorter run times than any other type of model. A relatively new development is the increasing application of generic purpose scripting languages for programming a model. Although the entities and operators of these languages are comparable to those of system programming languages, scripting languages result in programs that are easier to read or modify because of their simplified syntax. A problem with these languages is that they result in programs that are somewhat slower compared to software written in a system programming language.

Although the description of standard algorithms for numerical modelling has made it easier to develop models using system programming languages, the disadvantages described above that come with using a low level language have remained. One of the methods used to solve this problem was the development of graphical modelling systems (e.g. MODELMAKER, 2005; STELLA, 2005) with built-in functions for dynamic modelling which can be invoked using a graphical user interface. While building a model, the researcher connects these entities on the screen, resulting in a flow diagram similar to graphical representations of models used in scientific publications (Forrester, 1968). Although the graphical representation of a model is not always unambiguous, this approach provides a very easy-to-use environment for inexperienced users, and application domain specialists, without the need for skilled programmers. The main problem of this approach is that these languages are restricted to the development of point models and it is impossible to construct fully spatial models. Although it is possible to construct a model that runs for each separate point location on a map, this approach also has technical difficulties since complicated interface software needs to be written in order to run the model for each location. Moreover, it is not possible to include spatial interaction such as lateral flow of water, since these languages do not include spatial functions. Consequently, the application of graphical modelling systems is in practice restricted to non-spatial (lumped) dynamic modelling.

Another approach for model construction is the use of a technical computing language such as MATLAB, 2005. Just like system programming languages, these languages use a written definition (program) of a model, but the functions used for model building are at a higher level. And just like with graphical modelling systems, pre-programmed functions are available with a lot of built-in functionality. Models are built by combining these functions in a script. The advantage of these languages is the wide range of models that can be built, including both point models and spatial models. The main problems encountered are their restricted functionality to represent a domain consisting of discrete spatial and temporal points. For this domain, built-in functions are not available, and the user needs to give an explicit definition of time steps and spatial discretisation. This shortcoming makes the development of spatial dynamic models still rather difficult.

9.7 PROGRAMMING THE MODEL: MODEL CONSTRUCTION INSIDE THE GIS

In the previous section, all tools described for model programming have two shortcomings. First, there is a mismatch between the entities and functions provided by the language and those needed for efficient model construction in space and time. Either the entities and functions are at a level too close to the computer language, which is the case with system programming languages, or they do not represent concepts needed for both spatial and dynamic modelling, which is the case for graphical or technical modelling languages. The second problem is their need to be linked to a GIS, which may involve difficulties with data exchange. An approach that overcomes these shortcomings is to develop models with an environmental modelling language especially developed for dynamic spatial modelling, embedded in the GIS. Environmental modelling languages running inside GIS have been developed using one of the following three design concepts.

The first design concept is to provide the modeller with building blocks of the language that refer to features and processes existing in the real-world rather than to properties of computers. For modelling processes in two dimensions, such as point processes at several locations on the surface, or surface runoff, maps are used as the building blocks of the model. Each variable z_i in a model is represented by a map with a value for z_i at each location in space. For three dimensional processes, such as groundwater flow, three dimensional entities (blocks) can be used to construct a model (Karssenberg and de Jong, 2005a). The time dimension is explicitly represented using series of those maps or blocks, where each time step is represented by a map or block containing the values for that time step. In addition, the language provides pre-programmed spatial and temporal functions containing algorithms needed for environmental model building, such as different methods for simulating downhill transport of water.

For representing the set of processes that need to be included in the model (f in equation 9.2), these pre-programmed spatial and temporal functions could be combined together if an easy-to-use programming environment was available. Providing such a programming environment that allows a modeller to construct models using his or her understanding of environmental processes rather than computer expertise can be considered the second design concept of environmental modelling languages.

The third design concept is to embed such a language in a GIS providing generic tools for database management and visualisation of the data read and written by the model. It is important that these tools can deal with data which have a spatial and temporal component, since most inputs and outputs of dynamic environmental models will be spatial (such as maps of groundwater level), and temporal (such as the change in water level through time).

So far, many standard GIS (e.g. ESRI, 2005; IDRISI, 2005) have failed to fulfil all the above mentioned design concepts, mainly because of their limited set of spatial functions and a lack of built-in functionality to deal with temporal data, both regarding model construction and data visualisation. This limitation has driven specialist research groups to develop new modelling languages with sufficient functionality embedded in GIS, for example GRASS (2005) and PCRaster (PCRaster, 2005; van Deursen, 1995; Wesseling et al., 1996), and the latter is used here to illustrate the concepts. PCRaster includes 120 spatial and non-spatial functions on map grids that can be glued together in a dynamic modelling script. Table 9.2 shows an example script taken from a study aimed at finding a site for establishing a new ski piste (ski run) in an Alpine area resulting in the least impact on the environment. The example script is a highly simplified script taken from this study assessing the impact of one alternative ski piste location on erosion triggered by runoff

(Pfeffer, 2002). The aim of the script is to:

1. generate a scenario of the location and geometry of the piste, and decrease the infiltration capacity of the soil in the area covered by the piste;
2. simulate the variation of run-off in time and space as a function of a spatially and temporally variable input of water to the soil surface, which is assumed to be a measure of the amount of erosion; and
3. to aggregate the spatially and temporally variable run-off on the piste to a non-spatial value which can be used in a multi-criteria analysis.

The script is structured in the *binding, areamap, timer, initial* and *dynamic* section, each having a specific meaning in the model. The *binding* section links names of variables used in the script with file names. For instance, the digital elevation map of the area (filename: dem.map) is linked to the

Table 9.2   PCRaster script

```
binding
 Dem=dem.map;       # elevation map (m)
 Clone=clone.map;   # mask of the area
 TopPiste=toppiste.map;
 PisteL=800;        # length of piste (m)
 PisteW=200;        # width of piste (m)

areamap
 Clone;

timer
 1 28 1;

initial
 # generation of scenario
 Ldd=lddcreate(Dem,1e9,1e9,1e9,1e9);
 Dist=spreadldd(Ldd,TopPiste,0,1);
 Centre=cover(Dist lt PisteL,0);
 Piste=spread(Centre,0,1) lt PisteW/2;
 ICap=if(Piste then 10 else 40);

 TotRO=0;

dynamic
 # modelling
 Input=timeinput(RainMelt);
 RO=accuthresholdflux(Ldd,Input,ICap);

 # aggregation
 TotRO=TotRO+RO;
 report PRO=areaaverage(TotRO,Piste);
 report runoff.tss=timeoutput(Piste,Runoff);
```

variable name Dem, a synonym used in the script to refer to that map. The *areamap* section defines the modelling area with a 'clone' map of the study area. The spatial functions in the *initial* section are run only once, at the start, from top to bottom. This section can be used to define static spatial models (not shown here) using a sequence of operations, or to generate an input scenario, defined in space. The latter is shown in the example script giving a sequence of operations generating an input scenario of the location and geometry of a ski piste. The *lddcreate* function requires the digital elevation model (Dem) to generate a local drain direction map (Ldd, Figure 9.6) with a flow direction in each cell to one of its neighbouring cells, using the 8 point pour algorithm (Burrough and McDonnel, 1998). The toppiste.map (Figure 9.6) represents the location of the top of the piste that needs to be generated. Here, it is an input map, although it could also be created in the script, by just entering spatial coordinates of the location of the top of the piste that has to be generated. Since the piste needs to be oriented downhill of this location, the local drain direction map can be used to define the centre line of the piste. This is done with the spread *lddfunction* creating the map Dist (Figure 9.6) with a distance path downstream of TopPiste over the local drain direction map. The centre line (Centre) of the piste is the section of this path with distances from the top location less than the length (PisteL) of the piste. The piste (Piste, Figure 9.6) is defined by the area that is closer to this centre line than half the width (PisteW) of the piste.

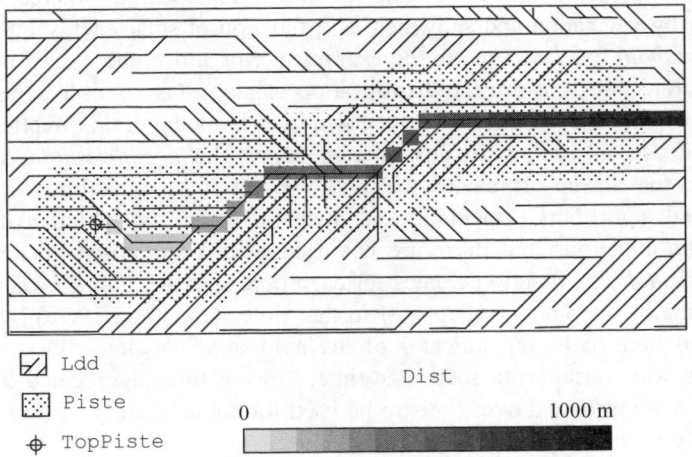

Ldd

Piste

TopPiste

Dist

0   1000 m

Notes: The figure shows a zoomed area containing the ski piste of the whole modelling area shown in Figure 9.7a. The general flow direction is from left to right.

Figure 9.6   Map variables used in the model to create the ski piste

Although a piste affects the soil's susceptibility to erosion in many different ways, it is assumed to cause an impact on the infiltration capacity only. This is represented by the last line in the *initial* section generating the map ICap, which contains for each cell the infiltration capacity (mm/h). The *if...then...else* function assigns an infiltration capacity of 10 mm/h to the area containing the piste, while other cells are assigned a higher infiltration capacity of 40 mm/h. The infiltration capacity is used in the *dynamic* section to simulate run-off through time.

Dynamic modelling can be undertaken using a sequence of operations by means of functions in the dynamic section. This sequence is executed for each time step, while the number of time steps is given in the timer section. Although a wide range of run-off models implementing processes in all components of the hydrological cycle have been built with the embedded modelling language of PCRaster (Karssenberg 2002a; PCRaster 2005; van Deursen 1995), Table 9.2 shows a highly simplified model to explain the concepts. In the example script, the number of time steps is 28, where each time step represents three hours. The *timeinput* function in the script reads, for each time step, a map with the amount of net rain + snowmelt, resulting in an input of water to the surface for each grid cell, given in the map Input. Note that this map Input is different for each time step, representing the temporal (and spatial) change in snowmelt and rainfall. In the more extended source script of the same model, both net rain and snowmelt are simulated in the same model script by adding functions representing interception of rainfall by vegetation and snowmelt as a function of solar energy input. The *accuthreshold* function used in the example script allows the Input of water to infiltrate until the threshold infiltration capacity (ICap) is reached. The excess of water is assumed to flow down over the local drain direction map, allowing for infiltration in downstream cells. The *accuthreshold* function assumes that all run-off reaches the outflow point in the same time step. More advanced algorithms (kinematic and dynamic wave) are included in other PCRaster functions, but these are not used in this simplified version. The *accuthresholdflux* function creates for each time step the map RO where each cell contains the amount of run-off in that time step (Figure 9.7a), which is assumed here to be an indicator of the amount of erosion. Since RO is a variable with variation in space and time, it needs to be aggregated over the area of a ski piste and over time, to be used for compensatory aggregation in a multi-criteria analysis.

The last three lines in the example script (Table 9.2) aggregate the results over time and space. The line resulting in TotRO accumulates the runoff over time, for each cell. This is done by adding for each time step, the amount of run-off for that time step (RO) to the map TotRO. TotRO is set for each cell to zero at the start of the model run, which is defined by the last line in the

(a) one time step (time step 10) of the temporal map variable RO, surface run-off

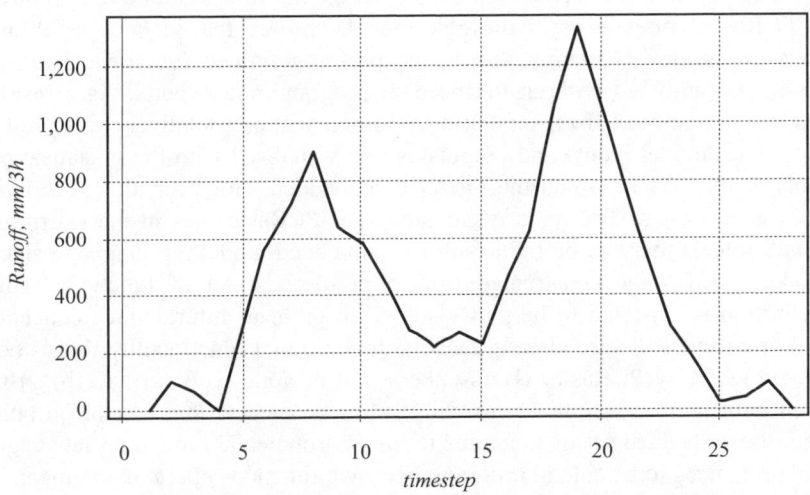

(b) average runoff on ski piste, time series variable runoff.tss

Figure 9.7   Output of the PCRaster model

initial section. At the last time step, TotRO contains for each cell the cumulative runoff that occurred during the model run. The last line calculates the average value for total runoff on the ski piste. This is done with the *areaaverage* function, which calculates the average of TotRO over the piste area on Piste. The result of this statement is saved on hard disk by means of the *report* keyword. For the case that the change in the amount of run-off through time on the piste is required for additional analysis, it can be stored in a time series file according to the last line of the script: the *timeoutput* function stores for each time step the average run-off on the piste in a time series file (Figure 9.7b).

PCRaster provides standard routines for visualising spatio-temporal inputs or outputs of a script, which were, for example, used to create Figures 9.6 and 9.7. These routines can be used ad hoc during the model building and testing. After a model is finished, standard software can be invoked that generates a graphical user interface (GUI) on top of the model script, which makes it much easier for decision makers to use the model. Creating the GUI involves a minimal amount of work, since it is automatically generated from information contained in the model script, while the standard visualisation routines of PCRaster are used by the GUI to display model inputs and outputs.

It should be noted that the example given above is highly simplified. Examples of models built with PCRaster simulating all processes involved in rainfall-run-off modelling can be found in de Roo et al. (2000), Karssenberg (2002a), Kwadijk (1993) and PCRaster (2005). An evaluation of the usefulness of PCRaster for building hydrologic models showed that its successful and wide application is mainly due to the pre-programmed functions that can easily be combined without the need of programming experts. As a result, models can be built from scratch or modified within a relatively short time. Moreover, model inputs and outputs can be visualised with the visualisation tools of the GIS in which the model is embedded. However, there are also some weaknesses. The main disadvantage of PCRaster lies in the restricted set of models that can be built with the embedded modelling language since models need to be constructed from a pre-defined set of functions. This restriction is expected to be partly solved in the near future, since concepts and prototype software already exist with additional functionality that is not yet provided by PCRaster (Karssenberg and de Jong, 2005(a) and (b)). But even with these additions, there will always be models that cannot be built with the embedded set of functions of an environmental modelling language, and users need to be able to program their own functions operating on maps in a system programming language. This is possible in most environmental modelling languages such as PCRaster.

9.8 SOFTWARE FOR ESTIMATION OF INPUTS AND PARAMETERS

The estimation of the model inputs and parameters is another step in the model development cycle and requires considerable attention, since the model outputs are strongly dependent on the value of the inputs and parameters. In this step, the model inputs $i_{1...n}$ and the parameters $\mathbf{p}$ are required for each location in the spatial domain of the model, at a resolution corresponding to the spatial and temporal resolution used in the model. In some cases, field data are available that directly fulfil these requirements and no additional calculations have to be performed. However, in most cases, field data are only available for a limited number of locations and for a restricted number of moments in time. In these cases, considerable pre-processing is needed before the data can be used in the model. There are two common approaches for preparing the model input: (1) interpolation and up-scaling (Figure 9.8, left) and (2) inverse modelling (Figure 9.8, right).

The inverse modelling procedure uses the model itself for estimating inputs or parameters. Conversely, the approach of up-scaling and interpolation involves techniques that are run independently from the model, i.e. outside the model as shown in Figure 9.8 (left). Interpolation techniques are used to convert sparse data that are available at a limited number of locations or moments in time, to a map with inputs or parameter values for all locations in the modelling area and for all time steps. A large set of these techniques is available, ranging from simple techniques, such as nearest neighbourhood interpolation, to more complicated (geo-)statistical techniques, such as kriging. The choice of the appropriate technique depends on many factors, in particular the number of field data available, the availability of additional (soft) information and the precision required (c.f. Burrough and McDonnel, 1998; Cressie, 1993). Most standard GIS packages include simple interpolation routines, while an increasing number of packages also include standard geostatistical techniques, for instance ESRI (2005), IDRISI (2005), PCRaster (2005). When more advanced techniques are needed, interpolation needs to be done using geostatistical software running outside a GIS, such as GSLIB (2005) or Gstat (2005).

While interpolation involves estimation of inputs and parameters for each location in the modelling domain, up-scaling involves a transformation of the field data to the resolution of the model being used. In many cases the resolution of the field data and the resolution applied in the model differ. In order to use the field data in the model, an up-scaling or down-scaling procedure needs to be performed. Up-scaling and down-scaling theory is built around a key concept called support (Bierkens et al., 2000; Blöschl, 1996; Blöschl and Sivapalan, 1995). The spatial domain of a dynamic spatial

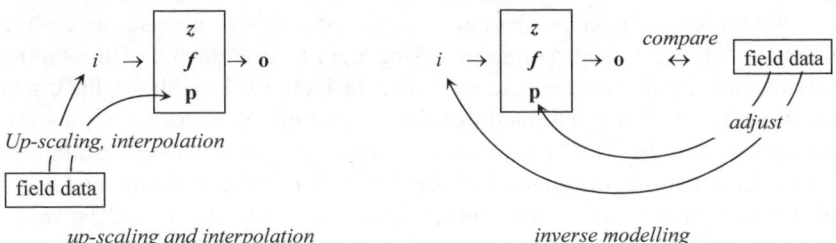

Figure 9.8   Estimation of inputs and parameters

model, is subdivided (i.e., discretised) into a finite number of sub-areas, while the temporal domain is subdivided into sub-intervals. The area of these sub-areas and the length of these sub-intervals are called the support of a model. It is the largest area (or volume) and time interval for which the properties represented by a model are considered homogeneous. These sub-areas or sub-intervals are called support units. The values of the model inputs, variables and parameters are representative for the support used in the model, while the functions need to be representative of the change in model variables occurring over a time step, at the support of the model. The term support can also be used for field measurements, representing the area (or volume) and time interval for which the measured properties are considered homogeneous, and for which only the average value is measured and not the variation between them. The term scale refers to the same concept as support, where a large scale refers to a large support. The term scale transfer means changing the support, while up-scaling and down-scaling refer to increasing and decreasing the support, respectively. An up-scaling or down-scaling method refers to the procedure describing how to calculate changes in input values, parameters, or a function in a model when the support is changed.

Up-scaling and down-scaling methods are important for environmental modelling, since the values and the spatial pattern of most environmental attributes, when measured in the field, depend on the support of measurement. Many examples illustrating the problem of scale in a wide range of environmental studies, and the up-scaling and down-scaling methods to solve this problem, are given in Bierkens et al. (2000), Blöschl and Sivapalan (1995) and Burrough and McDonnel (1998). Standard software for up-scaling and down-scaling hardly exists, since the procedure that needs to be followed is very specific for the kind of data and the kind of model under consideration (Karssenberg, 2002b). For this reason, application domain specialists are frequently needed to define good up-scaling methods that can be used in a modelling study.

When field measurements of inputs and parameters, or appropriate up-scaling procedures to estimate inputs and parameters of a dynamic model are not available, inverse modelling is the only method for estimating inputs and parameters of a dynamic model. Unlike up-scaling, inverse modelling estimates the inputs and parameters using field measurements of the output variables of the dynamic model as shown in Figure 9.8 on the right. Using inverse modelling, it is assumed that the best set of values for the inputs and parameters of a dynamic model corresponds to the set of values resulting in the smallest possible difference between the output of the dynamic model and field measurements of the same output variable(s) (McLaughlin and Townley, 1996). The difference between the output and field measurements is reflected by an objective function (sometimes called goal function) which is a mathematical procedure to calculate the aggregated difference between a vector of model outputs and field data, where the lowest outcome of the objective function mostly represents the smallest difference between outputs of the dynamic model and field data.

The procedure of inverse modelling comprises an iteration of three steps:

1. select a set of inputs and parameters for the dynamic model;
2. run the dynamic model with this set of inputs and parameters; and
3. calculate the value of the objective function.

The iteration is stopped when the set of inputs and parameters with the lowest value of the objective function is found. The number of iterations that is needed can be reduced by using results of previous iterations in a better selection of inputs and parameters in step 1, where the selection is expected to result in a lower value of the objective function. If inverse modelling is only used for finding parameter values, it is also called calibration. Moreover, if the aim of inverse modelling is to obtain model outputs that exactly fit field data, the term conditioning or data-assimilation is commonly used.

A wide range of inverse modelling techniques exist (Beasley et al., 1993; Falkenauer, 1998). While GIS do not provide software tools that include standard inverse modelling techniques, some pre-programmed models come with these techniques. In most cases, however, a separate software package needs to be used, such as MATLAB or PEST (MATLAB, 2005; PEST, 2005). Coupling the environmental model to such an inverse modelling software package is not an easy task; it always involves additional programming. Other relatively complicated algorithms have been described in literature (e.g. Duan et al., 1992; Gupta et al., 1998) for which pre-programmed software is not always available.

9.9 SUMMARY AND CONCLUSIONS

Modelling in Integrated Water Resource Management involves a large number of diverse tasks that need to be executed, as represented by the procedural steps of the model development cycle. A complete integration of all of these steps in one software environment or tool will not be available within the coming ten years, and researchers will have to deal with coupling several packages. In some cases, integration is already possible, as shown by the approach of model construction inside the GIS, where GIS operations and model construction is done with the same tool. The technical aspects of software integration are further discussed in Chapter 12.

If we look at the different steps in the model development cycle, it can be concluded that the researcher is provided with many good tools for importing and managing model data and for model construction, while the set of tools for estimating inputs and parameters is somewhat limited, or more difficult to use for technical reasons. The wide range of GIS systems provides modules needed for data import, management of large data sets and visualisation. In most cases these modules provide sufficient routines for a standard modelling project, although more tools are needed for temporal data in GIS. We discussed in this chapter several approaches for model construction from scratch and the approach of using existing models. It was shown that the choice of the appropriate software depends on many factors, and there is certainly not an optimal tool that can be applied in all cases.

Although science provides many techniques for the estimation of inputs and parameters in a modelling study, the development of easy-to-use tools that embed these techniques, linked to GIS or modelling software, is somewhat in its infancy. Nowadays, many GIS include standard interpolation routines, but more advanced interpolation, up-scaling techniques and inverse modelling techniques are not yet integrated into GIS, models or model construction tools. As a result, the step of estimating inputs and parameters can be considered one of the most difficult steps in a modelling study, from the viewpoint of software technology available today.

REFERENCES

Aller, L., T. Bennett, J.H. Lehr and R.J. Petty (1987), *DRASTIC: a Standard System for Evaluating Groundwater Potential Using Hydrogeological Settings*, Report 600/2-85/01, Ada, OK: US Environmental Protection Agency.

Bankes, S. (1993), 'Exploratory modeling for policy analysis', *Operations Research*, **41**(3), 435–449.

Beasley, D., D.R. Bull and R.R. Martin (1993), 'An Overview of Genetic Algorithms: Part 1, Fundamentals', *University Computing*, **15**, 58–69.

Beck, M.B., A.J. Jakeman and M.J. McAleer (1993), 'Construction and evaluation of models of environmental systems', in M.B. Beck, A.J. Jakeman and M.J. McAleer (eds), *Modelling Change in Environmental Systems*, New York: John Wiley and Sons Ltd.

Beven, K.J. (2000), 'Uniqueness of place and the representation of hydrological processes', *Hydrology and Earth System Sciences*, **4**, 203–213.

Bierkens, M.F.P., P.A. Finke and P. de Willigen (2000), *Upscaling and Downscaling Methods for Environmental Research*, Dordrecht, the Netherlands: Kluwer.

Blöschl, G. and M. Sivapalan (1995), 'Scale issues in hydrological modelling: a review', *Hydrological Processes*, **9**, 251–290.

Blöschl, G. (1996), *Scale and Scaling in Hydrology*, Vienna, Austria: Technische Universität Wien, Institut für Hydraulik, Gewässerkunde und Wasserwirtschaft.

Burrough, P.A. (1996), 'Opportunities and limitations of GIS-based modeling of solute transport at the regional scale', in D.L. Corwin and K. Loague (eds), *Special SSSA Publication Application of GIS to the Modeling of Non-Point Source*

Pollutants in the Vadose Zone, Madison, US: Soil Science Society of America.

Burrough, P.A. and R.A. McDonnel (1998), *Principles of Geographical Information Systems*, Oxford, UK: Oxford University Press.

Casti, J.L. (1997), *Would-be Worlds: How Simulation is Changing the Frontiers of Science*, New York, US: J. Wiley.

Cressie, N. (1993), *Statistics for Spatial Data*, New York, US: Wiley.

de Roo, A.P.J., C.G. Wesseling and W.P.A. van Deursen (2000), 'Physically based river basin modelling within a GIS: the LISFLOOD model', *Hydrological Processes*, **14**, 1981–1992.

de Wit, M.J.M. and E.J. Pebesma (2001), 'Nutrient fluxes at the river basin scale. II: the balance between data availability and model complexity', *Hydrological Processes*, **15**(5), 761–775.

Donnelly-Makowecki, L.M. and R.D. Moore (1999), 'Hierarchical testing of three rainfall-runoff models in small forested catchments', *Journal of Hydrology*, **219**, 136–152.

Duan, Q., S. Sorooshian and V. Gupta (1992), 'Effective and efficient global optimization for conceptual rainfall-runoff models', *Water Resources Research*, **28**(4), 1015–1031.

Engelen, G.B. and F.H. Kloosterman (1996), *Hydrological Systems Analysis, Methods and Applications*, Dordrecht, the Netherlands: Kluwer.

ESRI – Environmental Systems Research Institute, http://www.esri.com, (Last access: May 2005).

Falkenauer, J. (1998), Genetic algorithms and grouping problems, New York, US: Wiley.

Forrester, J.W. (1968), *Principles of Systems. Text and Workbook*, Cambridge, MA, US: Wrigh-Allen Press, Inc., Chapters 1–10.

GMS (2001), *GMS Groundwater Modeling System Version 3.1 Reference Manual*, Provo, US: Brigham Young University.

GRASS, http://www.geog.uni-hannover.de/grass/ (last access: May 2005).

GSLIB, http://www.gslib.com (last access: May 2005).

Gstat, http://www.gstat.org (last access: May 2005).

Gupta, H.V., S. Sorooshian and P.O. Yapo (1998), 'Toward improved calibration of hydrologic models: Multiple and noncommensurable measures of information', *Water Resources Research*, **34**(4), 751–763.

Gurney, W.S.C. and R.M. Nisbet (1998), *Ecological Dynamics*, New York, US: Oxford University Press.

Harbaugh, A.W., E.E. Banta, M.C. Hill and M.G. McDonald (2000), *MODFLOW-2000, the US Geological Survey modular ground-water model – user guide to modularization concepts and the ground-water flow process*, Reston, Virginia: US Geological Survey.

Hesselink, A.W., G.S. Stelling, J.C.J. Kwadijk and H. Middelkoop (2003), 'Inundation of a Dutch river polder, sensitivity analysis of a physically based inundation model using historic data', *Water Resources Research*, **39**(9), 1234, DOI: 10.1029/2002WR001334.

Heuvelink, G.B.M. (1998), *Error Propagation in Environmental Modelling with GIS*, London, UK: Taylor and Francis.

IDRISI, http://www.clarklabs.org (last access: May 2005).

ILWIS, http://www.itc.nl/ilwis (last access: May 2005).

Jones, N.L., T.J. Budge, A.M. Lemon and A.K. Zundel (2002), 'Generating MODFLOW grids from boundary represtentation solid models', *Groundwater*, **40**(2), 194–200.

Jørgensen, S.E. and G. Bendoricchio (1986), *Fundamentals of Ecological Modelling,*

Amsterdam, the Netherlands: Elsevier.

Karssenberg, D. (2002a), 'The value of environmental modelling languages for building distributed hydrological models', *Hydrological Processes*, **16**(14), 2751–2766.

Karssenberg, D. (2002b), *Building Dynamic Spatial Environmental Models*, Utrecht, The Netherlands: Knag/Faculteit Ruimtelijke Wetenschappen Universiteit Utrecht.

Karssenberg, D. and K. de Jong (2005a), 'Dynamic environmental modelling in GIS: 1. Modelling in three spatial dimensions', *International Journal of Geographical Information Science*, **19** (5), 559–579.

Karssenberg, D. and K. de Jong (2005b), 'Dynamic environmental modelling in GIS: 2. Error propagation modelling', *International Journal of Geographical Information Science*, **19** (6), 623–637.

Kwadijk, J.C.J. (1993), *The impact of climate change on the discharge of the River Rhine*, Utrecht, the Netherlands: Koninklijk Nederlands Aarderijkskundig Genootschap / Faculty of Geographical Sciences.

MATLAB, http://www.mathworks.com (last access: May 2005).

McLaughlin, D. and L.R. Townley (1996), 'A reassessment of the groundwater inverse problem', *Water Resources Research*, **32**, 1131–1161.

MIKE-SHE, http://www.dhisoftware.com/mikeshe (last access: May 2005).

MODELMAKER, http://www.modelkinetix.com/modelmaker (last access: May 2005).

Oreskes, N., K. Schraderfrechette and K. Belitz (1994), 'Verification, validation, and confirmation of numerical-models in the earth-Sciences', *Science*, **263**(5147), 641–646.

PCRaster, http://www.geog.uu.nl/pcraster (last access: May 2005).

PEST, http://www.sspa.com/pest (last access: May 2005).

Pfeffer, K. (2002), *Integrating spatio-temporal environmnetal models for planning ski-runs*, Utrecht, The Netherlands: Knag/Faculteit Ruimtelijke Wetenschappen Universiteit Utrecht.

Pollock, D. W. (1994), *User's Guide for MODPATH/MODPATH-PLOT, Version 3: A particle tracking post-processing package for MODFLOW, the U. S. Geological Survey finite-difference ground-water flow model*, US Geological Survey Open-File Report 94-464, p. 249.

Press, W.H., S.A. Teukolsky, W.T. Vetterling and B.P. Flannery (1986), *Numerical Recipes in Fortran 77, The Art of Scientific Computing (First Edition)*, Cambridge, UK: Cambridge University Press.

Schipper, P.N.M. and M.J.M. Vissers (eds) (2003), *Groundwater Quality Maps Hengelo* (in Dutch), Vol. SV-60, Gouda, The Netherlands: SKB.

STELLA, http://www.hps-inc.com/softwares/Education/StellaSoftware.aspx (last access: May 2005).

Toffoli, F. (1987), *Cellular Automata Machines*, Cambridge, MA: MIT Press.

van der Perk, M. (1997), 'Effect of model structure on the accuracy and uncertainty of results from water quality models', *Hydrological Processes*, **11**, 227–239.

van Deursen, W.P.A. (1995), 'Geographical Information Systems and Dynamic Models, Utrecht, The Netherlands', Koninklijk Nederlands Aardrijkskundig Genootschap/Faculteit Ruimtelijke Wetenschappen, Universiteit Utrecht.

Wang, X. (1997), 'Conceptual design of a system for selecting appropriate groundwater models in groundwater protection programs', *Environmental Management*, **21**(4), 607–615.

Wesseling, C.G., D. Karssenberg, W.P.A. van Deursen and P.A. Burrough (1996), 'Integrating dynamic environmental models in GIS: the development of a Dynamic Modelling language', *Transactions in GIS*, 1, 40–48.

10. Integrated Modelling: Construction, Selection, Uncertainty

Anthony J. Jakeman, John P. Norton, Rebecca A. Letcher and Holger R. Maier

10.1 INTRODUCTION

Integrated water resource management (IWRM) is basically a tool to achieve more sustainable outcomes in catchments or watersheds. Uncertainty, subjectivity and compartmentalisation are three notions that characterise the problem of achieving sustainability in catchment systems. There is uncertainty and subjectivity about what sustainability is, how to reach it and about the representation of system processes affecting it. In addition, there is compartmentalisation of natural resource management and policies, so much so that one policy may conflict with another in its environmental or socio-economic objectives. IWRM embraces these problems and emphasises ideas of community choice, precaution, risk, learning and adaptive management. Precaution is often recommended where there is doubt about the sustainability of a system. The level of precaution and the risk of a dire outcome need to be addressed in the participatory process. Active adaptive management uses policy implementation to achieve two closely linked objectives: robustly sustainable outcomes and accelerated learning about the system. Robustness of desired outcomes requires monitoring of the system and revision of management actions to deal with unforeseen changes, such as new disturbances, unpredicted consequences of earlier actions and additional demands on the system. It clearly requires continued acquisition of new knowledge about the system, which will partly come as a result of monitoring but may also pose a need to perturb the system. For this reason accelerated learning may involve a compromise between perturbing the system enough to cause clearly interpretable responses and leaving undisturbed aspects of the system which seem to be in a satisfactory state.

A key ingredient to facilitate such a way forward for IWRM is Integrated Modelling and, in particular, Integrated Scenario Modelling (ISM). In ISM we refine our knowledge about system processes and linkages iteratively through modelling and by a comparison of model outputs with observed behaviour. This knowledge is then used to simulate the effects of uncontrollable (e.g. climate) and controllable (e.g. human activities) catchment drivers on selected outcomes that serve as indicators of sustainability. Transparent use of ISM can promote system thinking, learning and understanding, formulation of realistic management objectives and design of adaptive management strategies. The setting of ISM within an Integrated Assessment (IA) framework is discussed in this chapter, bringing out the roles that the different sciences can play in achieving better sustainability outcomes. Lessons are drawn from some of our previous IA studies. The utility of ISM, and hence IA, for integrated water resource management can be strengthened by further development of methods to assess the confidence that policy changes will have on predicted outcomes, and to show where more system knowledge and data collection are most needed.

This chapter concentrates on integrated modelling from the point of view of integrating models into the decision-making process, arguing the benefits and issues that arise, and especially pointing to some of the lessons that have been learnt and gaps that need addressing.

10.2   FINDING A PRACTICAL APPROACH TO IDENTIFYING SUSTAINABILITY

Concepts of sustainability are developed in Chapter 2. Broadly, sustainability can be interpreted as a state or state trajectory that satisfies the so-called triple bottom line of socially, economically and ecologically acceptable behaviour for present and future generations. While it is difficult, if not impossible, to specify what human activities in a system are sustainable, it is a simpler task to contrast the features of a more sustainable system with an unsustainable system.

It also seems sensible to admit that what precisely should be sustained will always be in the eye of the beholder. One person or interest group will weigh the elements of the triple bottom line differently from another – for instance the degree of pristine function of a landscape versus socioeconomic function. Given this subjectivity and the uncertainty of recognising sustainability and how to reach it, integrated water resource managers tend to put emphasis on certain indicators of sustainability and a target level for them; for example a lower limit for satisfaction of basic human needs (access to safe water, health protection, etc.), an upper limit for erosion, water quality concentration, pollutant load, or a lower limit on restoring native fish populations. The achievement of such targets, however, may conflict with other desirable targets, so compromise is needed. Also, it may make sense to allow some targets to vary spatially and temporally, sacrificing one area or one time period for another. This concept underpins many natural resource management strategies such as the development of reserves or national parks. Understanding the integrated nature of the benefits of these mosaic systems of land use and management is generally at a very early stage.

Subjectivity, uncertainty and potential conflict imply that setting targets for IWRM must involve continuing choice for the community. There will always be trade-offs to be identified across a multi-dimensional spectrum of possible system states. Selection of a particular set of targets may initially be based on a relatively narrow vision, but eventually should be based on a broad perception of benefits and costs. The selection should also be moderated by the quality of the existing knowledge base and the capacity to take actions to achieve those targets.

A key topic discussed in this chapter is how, from a modelling perspective, science and social science can be integrated to assess policy options and other system drivers, and identify trade-offs that offer strong prospects for more sustainable outcomes. We will also offer some thoughts on where the sciences need improvement to enhance the advice available to policy makers and catchment managers.

10.3   INTEGRATED ASSESSMENT AND INTEGRATED SCENARIO MODELLING

10.3.1   Integrated Assessment

Integrated Assessment (IA) is a procedure that is extremely pertinent to IWRM. It has been defined as

> Integration of knowledge from different disciplines with the goal to contribute to understanding and solving complex societal problems, that arise from the interaction between humans and the environment, and to contribute in this way to establishing the foundation for sustainable development. Modelling and participatory processes should include stakeholder groups and the public at large [www.tias.org – last access: May 2005]

The key features of IA summarised by Jakeman and Letcher (2003) are that it is a problem-focused activity using an iterative, adaptive approach that links research to policy; possesses a transparent interactive procedural framework that enhances communication; is a process enriched by stakeholder involvement (see Chapters 7 and 8) and dedicated to adoption; connects complexities between the natural and human environment, recognising spatial dependencies, feedbacks and impediments; and attempts to recognise essential missing knowledge.

Integrated Scenario Modelling (ISM) is a core part of many IA exercises. It involves a model as an approximation of selected aspects of the system under study. The model (Figure 10.1) allows simulation of how input drivers (scenarios) such as climate and human activities yield output variables representing the states of the system (as shown by indicators). In IA, the system is extended to link policy and management to the controllable human activity inputs. Targets or indicators of sustainability are functions of the output variables, usually simple (e.g. an average, maximum or minimum level). Thus ISM can be at the centre of IA, connecting policy and institutional drivers to sustainability indicators. Multi-criteria analysis (MCA), as referred to in Chapter 2, is a technique for informing trade-offs. It can be used formally or informally, in conjunction with ISM outputs, to assess the sensitivity of trade-offs to assumptions or system drivers. Overarching the IA procedure is the conduct of participatory processes. Iteration among the steps, as we learn and model more about the system, is another essential feature of IA.

Figure 10.1 demonstrates the process of Integrated Scenario Modelling. Information flows in two directions, from policy makers and stakeholders into the conceptualisation of the model, and from the model results showing

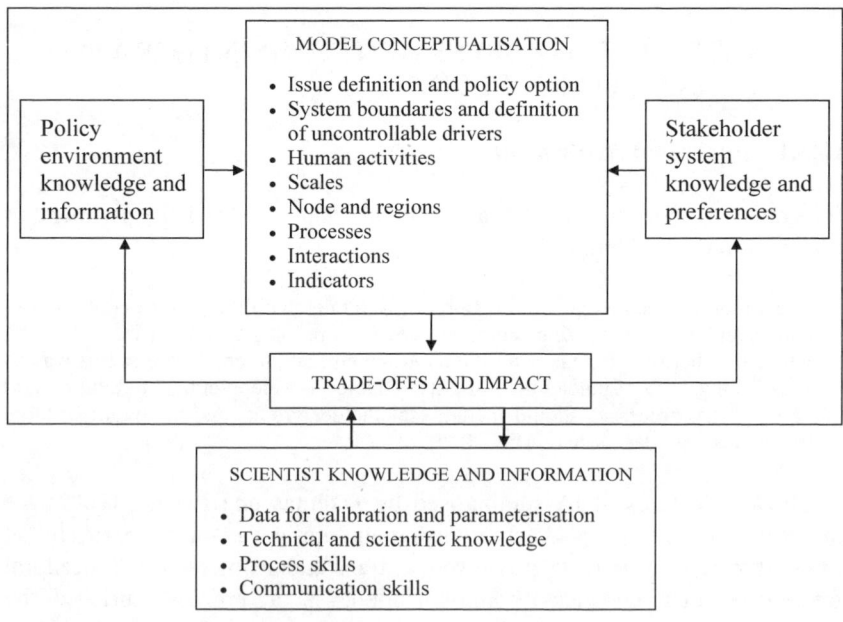

Source: Adapted from Letcher and Jakeman, 2003a.

Figure 10.1   Conceptual framework for Integrated Scenario Modelling

trade-offs and impacts to inform stakeholder and policy preferences and system understanding. Scientific knowledge, including tools and techniques as well as process understanding, informs the model conceptualisation. Scientists also learn through their interaction with stakeholders and policy makers and through the interdisciplinary perspective provided by the Integrated Assessment. The model conceptualisation process includes specifying model equations and also other assumptions such as the location of nodes where indicators are calculated, preferred spatial scales, and the types of policy options to be considered by scenarios. This model conceptualisation process is necessarily trans-disciplinary as issues and policies and their impacts influence both natural and human systems.

Social science has several roles here, including identification of sustainability targets, enhancing the understanding of links and dependencies between people and the natural and modified systems, and analysing policy, institutions, governance and participatory methods. Like other sciences it offers characteristic model types, and non-model-based assessment methods, to the ISM core, particularly for assessment of the social and/or economic impacts of scenario options. Science and engineering offer technology to support model use and development, such as the storage, management and analysis of large databases and the visualisation of results from ISM. They provide the means for interest groups to interact personally with models, test scenarios and observe predicted system changes. They also provide established ways to specify, analyse and communicate uncertainty quantitatively, although not for all the different types of information that arise in environmental management situations.

IA is a valuable procedure for IWRM because it is about assessing options for what to do, where, when, how and with whom. ISM is a key tool for investigating this. Model components can be a mixture of different types, for example quantitative and qualitative, physics-based or empirical (see Chapter 9).

10.3.2 Model Integration

Here we are concerned with model integration, not from the perspective of how different models can be integrated (see Chapter 11 for various frameworks), but about how models can be integrated into decision making. There are two primary distinctions to be made about how models are integrated into management decision making. The first is between the types of model: either process-oriented models containing detailed internal workings, or management-oriented models with no more detail than needed to represent the relations between specific inputs and outputs. An integrated process model consists of a number of interlinked smaller process models, the overall structure being determined by knowledge of the mechanisms. By contrast, models for integration into management are often statistically based, with a relatively simple structure chosen empirically, perhaps because of the difficulties of acquiring and representing detailed process knowledge. They are likely to be constrained by analytical convenience and economy (parsimony in number of parameters), necessary for statistical efficiency.

The second important distinction is between different management decision-making structures into which the model is embedded. In the simplest, and by far the most common structure, the model is used to predict the outcomes of a number of alternative decisions in one or more future situations, and the decision with the preferred predicted outcome is chosen. As this procedure does not involve examining any actual outcome, it amounts to open-loop control, which is susceptible to the effects of modelling error and uncontrolled inputs. In the second structure, decision making is based on rules to derive the decision from observed differences between the desired and actual outcomes: closed-loop control. The role of the predictive model is now to predict the effects of alternative decision-making rules. This alternative is more complicated, because it implies a monitoring system and the ability to revise management action as events unfold. In some instances, this might not be feasible. When it is, it offers the feedback-control advantages of reduced sensitivity of outcomes to variations in the system, and to unforeseen disturbance inputs. It also poses the feedback-control danger of instability or too much variation of the outcomes if the management action is too slow, inappropriate and/or based on excessively delayed or error-prone information about actual outcomes.

Figures 10.2 and 10.3 show the roles of process-based and input-output models in decision making. The difference is the absence of information about internal, unobservable system behaviour when employing an input-output model. In the figures, choice between decisions is represented as iteration to find the 'best' outcomes. In practice the procedure can be either sequential (iterative) or batch (looking simultaneously at all possibilities), depending on how predictable the alternative choices are. Figure 10.4 shows the process of using a predictive model in the design of a set of decision rules for use in a closed-loop arrangement.

The task of integrating individual process models or management models into a whole (as distinct from integration into a decision-making structure) can be done in a determinate or an adaptive, self-organising manner. The former assumes that overall system behaviour is known, whereas the latter supposes that the model components can interact in a way that enables overall system behaviour to emerge.

Potential difficulties associated with integration of process models include:

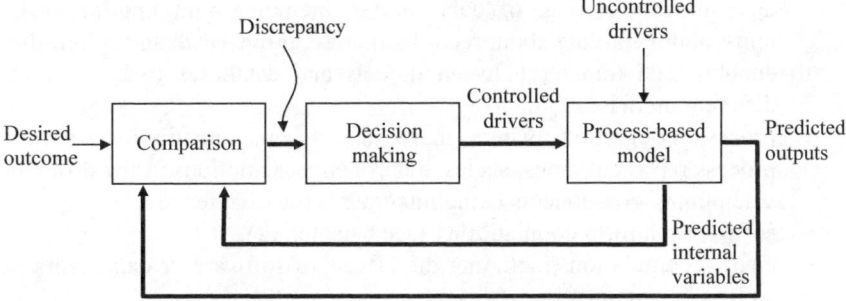

Note: Bold lines show loop involved in iterative decision making.

Figure 10.2   Decision making based on process model

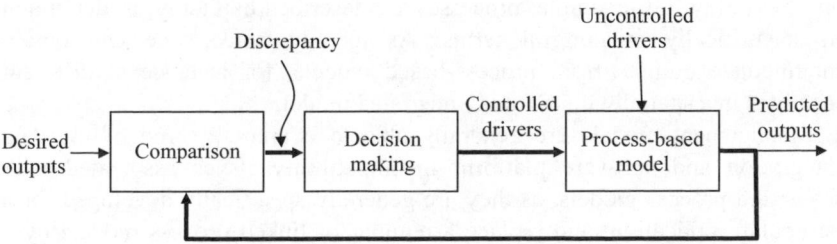

Note: Bold lines show loop involved in iterative decision making.

Figure 10.3   Decision making based on management-oriented input-output model

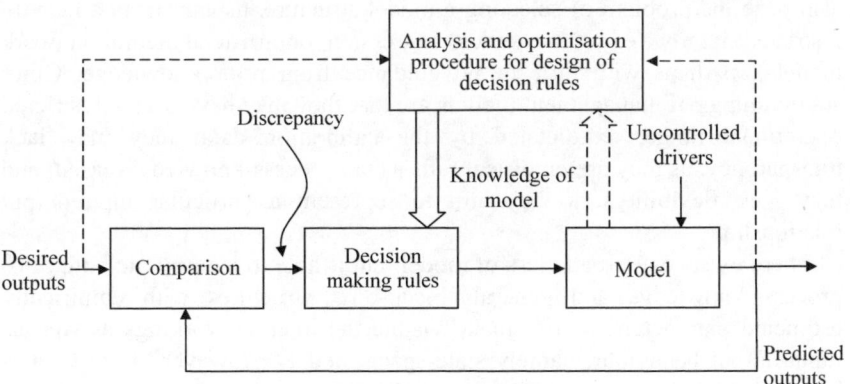

Note: Dashed lines indicate information used by design procedure.

Figure 10.4   Model-based design of decision rules

- data integration (e.g. of data format, including sampling intervals, units, and meta-data about record structure, provenance and so on) that enables data transfer between models and databases to be read by different models;
- process integration, where there may be incompatibility between process representations, scales and system assumptions in the different disciplinary components being integrated (see Chapter 11);
- software platform compatibility (see Chapter 12);
- error accumulation (including the effects of software or data errors as well as uncertainty);
- large data requirements; and
- high model complexity, and high likelihood of over-parameterisation.

The main advantages of integrated process models include transparency and flexibility. For example, processes are described explicitly, in detail and in scientifically meaningful terms. As already noted, one can obtain intermediate outputs from process-based models, for instance at different locations in a spatially distributed, integrated model.

Management models are generally able to overcome some of the data integration and software platform incompatibility issues associated with integrated process models, as they are generally specifically developed for a particular application, and replace a number of linked process models by a single input-output model. This also reduces model complexity and the potential for error accumulation.

However, although management models are generally less data-intensive than process models, they nonetheless demand input and output data that is adequate for model calibration and validation to an acceptable standard. They also pose the problem of selecting a model structure, usually from a heavily restricted family (e.g. time series, regression or artificial neural network models), perhaps with little or no guidance from prior knowledge. Other shortcomings of management models are that they may have a very restricted operational range, as dictated by the calibration data; they may lack transparency, as they are empirical rather than process-knowledge-based; and they lack flexibility, as they aim to represent a particular input/output relationship.

There exists one broad class of model that is able to incorporate both prior process knowledge and general 'black-box' structures with empirically estimated parameters, and to make visible the internal workings as well as input-output behaviour, namely state-space models. However, these models have substantial problems with systematic structure selection, choice of state variables, merging of prior and empirical information and adaptation to changing situations, which have not yet been fully resolved. One notable use of state-space models is in the identification, from input and output records, of models with relatively simple structures but time-varying parameters. Here the parameters are treated as state variables with known yet flexible dynamics, such as random walks (Norton, 1975, 1976; Young et al., 1991), allowing them to be found by standard state-estimation algorithms (Norton, 1986; Young, 1984). Selected groups of parameters can be permitted to vary, then their time variation and effects on model performance examined, and explanations found on the basis of process knowledge. The understanding gained in this way may suggest specific improvements to the model, building up a constant-parameter model with a structure that only incorporates the process knowledge important for the input-output behaviour.

As mentioned earlier, both process and management models can be integrated using determinate or self-organising approaches. In the determinate approach, models are linked in a way that predetermines overall system behaviour. In contrast, self-organising approaches establish linkages between component models by trial and error, enabling overall system behaviour to emerge in response to changes to individual component models. Agent-based modelling (Feuillette et al., 2003; and Chapter 11) is an example of a self-organising approach. Advantages of the self-organising integration framework are that it provides a flexible framework for the integration of environmental, social and economic models; it is stochastic; it can cater for spatial distribution of processes and for simulations over extended periods (subject to the possibility of error accumulation), and it has the potential to be adaptive.

10.4   KEY CONSIDERATIONS FOR ISM

10.4.1   Exploratory Simulation and/or Optimisation

Once models are constructed and parameterised, the next challenge is how to produce the information needed to assist decision making. At one extreme is systematic one-shot optimisation of the system. Here a single answer is determined, relating a specified or preferred set of outcomes, usually with multiple objectives, using a traditional optimisation technique such as hill climbing. The advent of evolutionary optimisation methods has changed the situation drastically, as they produce a number of near-optimal solutions (e.g. the 'top 20') and can be configured to yield, deliberately, a number of diverse solutions, rather than converging on a single optimum. This may be especially valuable when a management decision also has to take account of factors not modelled, and can exploit freedom of choice between diverse alternatives. In any such optimisation, the controllable driving variables in the system are varied within permitted ranges, but there is a danger that the relatively narrow focused modelling needed for this procedure does not reveal important complexities and dependencies in the system.

A less formal alternative is to use simulation to explore more fully the effects of controllable and uncontrollable scenario variables on indicators of system response, before or instead of trying to specify any optimisation goal. This suggests an intermediate, two-stage procedure, such as exploration followed by optimisation, depending on whether it is found possible to express the management objectives as an optimisation goal, and if so, on the size of the search space (i.e. the range of potential options). If optimisation is attempted, it can in principle be risk based, including reliability, robustness, vulnerability and resilience in the criteria, so long as uncertainty is taken explicitly into account in the model. ISM may yield fuller understanding of inter-dependencies and may point to better trade-offs than the outcomes of pre-specified optimisations. Compared to pre-specified optimisation, it is more cumbersome and less predictable in its demands on time and resources, but the range of input variations explored can be reduced as understanding of the modelled behaviour accrues.

Adopting the second alternative, the decision-making process starts by assessing the impacts of each proposed course of action (management scenario and associated catchment drivers), using an integrated model, as sketched in Figure 10.5. The various environmental, social and economic criteria used to discriminate between management scenarios require the model outputs to be integrated, by techniques such as multi-criteria analysis (MCA, Chapter 5), to make a choice of management action possible. A large number of MCA approaches have been proposed, including the weighted sum method, compromise programming, multi-attribute utility theory, ELECTRE and PROMETHEE (Barron and Barrett, 1996; Brans and Mareschal, 1990; Buede, 1992; Roy, 1991). All these approaches utilise stakeholder-defined weightings to rank alternatives in accordance with the adopted performance criteria. A crucial issue is how to elicit weightings from stakeholders; common experience is that individuals, even from apparently homogeneous groups with similar interests, nominate widely differing weights (Mousseau et al., 2003).

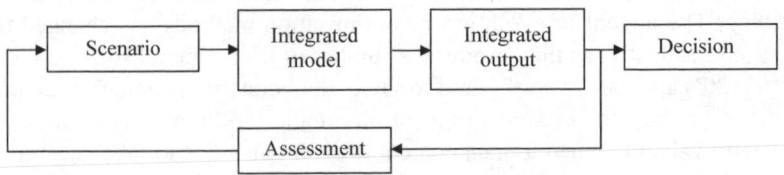

Figure 10.5   Simulation-based decision making

This procedure only covers initial decision making, not adapting the management scenarios or choice as new information arrives or the outcomes evolve. In feedback-control terms, it consists of open-loop optimisation, not design of a closed-loop control scheme, and is thus vulnerable to unexpected changes.

When the number of potential management options is large, formal optimisation methods may be considered, as applied in optimisation-based decision making discussed earlier. By using evolutionary algorithms, such as genetic algorithms (Goldberg, 1989), model outputs can be used to direct the search for an optimal solution (Figure 10.6) while following the overall decision-making process in Figure 10.5.

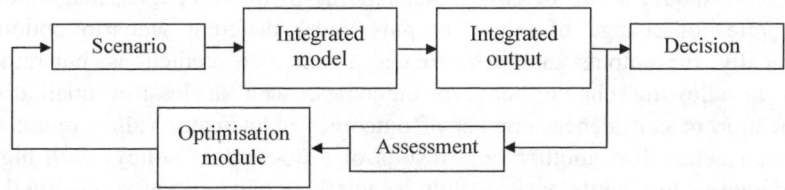

Figure 10.6   Optimisation-based decision making

The decision-making processes of Figures 10.5 and 10.6 depend on comparison of outcomes of alternative scenarios, through one or more model output values. These outputs are highly uncertain: the model inputs are subject to natural variation, the model parameters are estimated from limited data and the model structures are unlikely to represent the processes exactly. Moreover, the integration of model outputs is generally subjective, for instance employing stakeholder-defined weightings for multiple criteria. It is thus essential to consider the sensitivity of the results to uncertainty and to subjectively specified parameters, as discussed in Section 10.6.

10.4.2   Types of Scenarios and Indicators

For modelling, whether mechanised as pure exploratory simulation, pure optimisation or a mixture, scenarios and indicators must be selected. In optimisation, the scenarios are automatically adjusted to meet pre-specified indicator objectives. In exploratory simulation, scenarios are only constrained by computing load, practical constraints on the controlled inputs and the need to keep the effects on indicators within acceptable ranges.

A useful dichotomy in categorising scenarios is between controllable and uncontrollable influencing variables. For the latter, ISM must establish the sensitivity of the model indicators to the characteristics (range, frequency of extreme events, short-term variability, etc.) of uncontrollable variables such as climate. Some boundary conditions also constitute uncontrollable influences. We may not wish, or be able, to model in detail some of these items, e.g. price changes for agricultural inputs or products, labour market variables, trans-border water supply and upstream water quality. Controllable variables are those that can be influenced by instruments such as regulation, education, incentives, subsidies and public or private investment.

10.4.3 Broad Objectives of ISM

The complexities and uncertainties of integrated modelling dictate that its objective should be to increase understanding of the directions, magnitudes and rates of change of model outputs under different scenario options. Typically, the outputs cannot be treated as accurate predictions, but rather aim at allowing choice between outcomes, with at least a qualitative indication of confidence: one set of outcomes or indicator values might be thought better than another (e.g. results of a do-nothing policy) with high, moderate or low confidence. Ideally, predictions have a known quantitative measure of confidence but this is seldom possible at present. The extent to which confidence in the predicted differences between outcomes of alternative policies has to be conveyed to a decision maker depends, of course, on the decision maker's attitude to risks, and also on other information and influences that are not modelled. Even when a model cannot provide high enough confidence to permit a decision, it may still be valuable in clarifying just what improvements in prediction confidence are needed. As discussed later, existing methods for quantifying uncertainties have severe limitations which new research needs to address.

10.4.4 Key Modelling Considerations

What to include, and what not to include, in an ISM activity should be considered explicitly at the outset. The physical, socioeconomic and institutional boundaries of the system being modelled, and the aspects of behaviour to be covered, need clear definition. Boundary conditions can then be incorporated as constraints or part of the input scenarios, and perturbed in line with stipulated assumptions. Modelling for natural resource management commonly faces the following issues:

- Climate variability and extreme episodes: variability can affect the economic returns on investment as well as ecosystem response, while episodes such as floods can have a profound effect on outputs. As will be seen, both raise issues of appropriate time periods and time steps over which to model. They are also intimately linked to risk acceptance.

- Choice of model complexity: once the basic processes are decided upon, there is still much scope for selecting the level of detail, including the spatial and temporal scales. If there is a lack of field data this will limit model complexity, because it limits ability to validate the model. For example, in modelling flow and sediment transport in a river, spatial data on catchment attributes may allow a finely structured model, but this detail is unwarranted if flux measurements for calibration cannot support it.

- Scenarios beyond the business-as-usual: environmental or social change may require substantial changes to the current situation as input controls. Public and private investments, policy incentives and new institutional arrangements may be needed.

- Long lags: the timeframes for investment returns and for ecosystem response to changes constrain the period and temporal resolution of both the model runs and indicator monitoring. Delays in monitoring or consequent action have the potential to destabilise the system, so have to be modelled if continuing active management is contemplated.

- Narrowing modelling objectives: in addition to keeping the types of models, scales, system boundaries, etc. as simple as practical, it is critical to keep the level of integration of issues and disciplines manageable.

- Model uncertainty: it is desirable to reduce and, wherever possible, characterise uncertainty; the latter needs attention by IA/ISM researchers.

- Error accumulation: currently this is mostly ignored and also needs more attention from researchers.

- System representation: the capacity to characterise feedbacks and interactions while keeping model components and linkages effective yet efficient. Nodal network structure for river networks: this is a valuable mechanism for integrating spatial scales and is addressed next, but see also Chapter 11.

10.4.5   Scales and Nodes of Analyses and Outputs

Scale includes the time period and spatial extent over which a model must run (the domain) and the time and space steps (the discretisation). Selection of spatio-temporal scales for the component subsystems is a key item for credible ISM. Scale must be fine enough to avoid loss of significant information in the inputs and system response, but no finer than is warranted by the availability and quality of the data. As well as increasing complexity, discretisation intervals that are too small may well result in over-parameterisation, increasing parameter uncertainty, and may even cause poor numerical conditioning by having adjacent samples so close in value that rounding errors are significant.

In resource management, certain immutable factors guide the selection of scale. One is the level at which decisions require support; another is the location and nature of desired model-output indicators. In catchment management, these locations translate into nodes in the stream network (and their associated, residual sub-catchments) where management and land and water use can be compared with other scenarios and nodes.

The specific breakdown of a system into sub-systems depends on the management questions being asked and the nature of the data and other prior knowledge. The real objectives often turn out to be less broadly based and less demanding than first perceived, allowing simplification of the model or its use.

The possibility of cutting a complex model into sections which can be analysed or experimented upon largely independently, before combining the results, has a strong bearing on the assessment of uncertainty propagation through a complex model, as discussed next.

10.4.6   Uncertainty and Sensitivity Needs

Natural systems present considerable difficulties for modellers, compared, for instance, with engineered systems. One is the sheer complexity of internal behaviour arising from physical, chemical and biological processes, and dynamic, multidimensional interactions. Another factor is that interactions may occur in more than one medium. Moreover, the range of time and space scales characterising the media or subsystems is likely to be wide. To compound these difficulties, inaccessibility of internal system states and outputs for measurement, and of inputs and parameters for perturbation, often reduces the ability to test and learn individual aspects or modes of system behaviour. Consequently ISM entails a high degree of uncertainty which, for integrated assessment and management to be credible, must be described and reduced as far as possible. Credibility requires that model parameters be identifiable (Norton, 1986) as well as plausible and able to match observed output behaviour.

Integrated models for resource management are thus subject to many uncertainties, due to measurement and sampling errors in inputs and calibration data, parameter uncertainty and model-structure assumptions. Errors can accumulate in the course of simulation, especially when integrating over time or aggregating over a spatial domain, or when unstable behaviour occurs. They may also cascade, as sub-model outputs become inputs to successive ones, e.g. progressing down a catchment, and may add through interaction between sub-models, e.g. at confluences. Few useable techniques (but see Heuvelink, 1998) exist for assessing the evolution of uncertainty in integrated models, yet this is essential if reliable conclusions are to be drawn from them.

An additional benefit of assessing the sensitivity of outputs to uncertainty in inputs, parameters and model structure, is that it can point to how the model can be simplified. Conventional sensitivity assessment, based on perturbation and Monte Carlo trials, incurs very heavy computing to discover which combinations of uncertain items are most important and how far they can vary before the model output changes significantly.

A new approach being investigated by the authors is to pose sensitivity analysis as selective exploration of the feasible set of parameters, inputs or model structure indices that give a specified range of output behaviour. This range is expressed as a set, defined by a collection of constraints on realistic, acceptable behaviour leading to a given qualitative outcome. Uncertain inputs or parameters are not characterised by probability distributions, but are allowed to vary within a feasible range. The focus on sets removes any need to assume linearity between cause and effect, continuity of the output or even quantification of the output. As part of this approach, the robustness of the relative merit of a particular alternative with respect to another alternative is defined as the smallest joint change in model inputs/parameters, as given by a certain distance metric (e.g. Euclidean distance, mutual information (Fraser and Swinney, 1986)), that results in equivalence of the two alternatives: the 'limit state'. The new approach will be adaptive, combining searches, Monte Carlo trials and feature extraction by methods suggested by descriptive multivariate analysis. By using optimisation approaches such as evolutionary algorithms, the shortest distance from the current state to the limit state surface can be determined. Alternatively, simulation can be used to explore the features of the feasible sets, guided by an optimisation algorithm which seeks, for example, to find the parameter combination which has maximum or minimum range allowed by the output-acceptability constraints, i.e. the combination to which the outputs are respectively least or most sensitive.

Advantages of this approach include the absence of any need to characterise the probability distributions of uncertain inputs/parameters, and the ability to produce a quantitative robustness measure which relates any two alternatives.

One disadvantage is the difficulty of the optimisation problem of determining the shortest distance from the current state to the limit state, particularly for complex, integrated models. Another is that there is no indication of the likelihood that the changes in inputs or parameters associated with the shortest distance from the current to the limit state will occur.

Control of error accumulation also requires attention. The first task here is to identify where accumulation is problematic, through analysis and exploratory simulation. The problem must then be mitigated by modifying model structure or imposing constraints. Consider, for example, a hydrograph of stream flow at a node which has an increasing trend in error caused by errors upstream. A remedy here is to compute at multiple time steps, longer steps having lower resolution but less bias. The ordinates of the hydrograph computed at shorter time steps can then be constrained by knowledge of the total volume of the hydrograph computed at the longer interval. Further research is required on error control in such contexts.

10.4.7   Other Considerations

There are basic principles (Jakeman and Letcher, 2003) that should guide the capability of models constructed for ISM. Thus ISM may need to allow simulation of climatic variability and episodic events that may have a profound effect on outcomes. So strong may be potential environmental or social decline that ISM may need to incorporate changes in resource activities that go beyond business-as-usual scenarios to consider long-term simulation of a range of public and private investments, policy instruments and institutional arrangements. Modelling of long leads and lags may be necessary, as the timeframes for returns on investments and for ecosystem response affect both the period and the temporal resolution over which models are run. To minimise uncertainty in ISM results, the system representation must characterise essential feedbacks and interactions without excessive complexity in model components and linkages. Good focusing of modelling objectives is crucial in this respect. In addition to simplifying but not oversimplifying the types of models, scales, system boundaries, etc. it is critical to keep the level of integration of issues and disciplines manageable.

We argue that at present most ISM exercises violate one or more of these principles. For example, hydrologists may simplify the economics and/or the ecology and economists or ecologists tend to simplify the hydrology. The causes of such violations are understandable. There is also a tendency to employ a model because one is comfortable with it or simply because it is available, rather than select or build one that suits the objectives and is consistent with the accuracy of the other model components. The timeframe for providing an answer to policy makers is often short. There are other resource constraints, particularly lack of access to other disciplinary expertise in the team and in some cases lack of understanding and/or methods for integrating the knowledge from all the disciplinary components. These are exacerbated by the difficulties in building teams and keeping them vibrant, difficulties which are partly inherent and uncontrollable and partly due to the poor rewards and tenure conditions for researchers who work in multidisciplinary teams. The latter should be addressed institutionally at various levels.

10.5 DIFFERING TREATMENT OF ISM AMONG THREE CASE STUDIES

In three IWRM case studies presented by Jakeman and Letcher (2003), many factors affect the way integrated scenario modelling and assessment is undertaken. They include the nature and scale of the issues, data and information availability, time scale in which an assessment must be produced, and the stakeholders involved. Table 10.1 illustrates that in IWRM, the context shapes the approach. Crucially, the process of assessment should be transparent, with the assumptions and other limitations spelt out as far as possible, to assure stakeholders of its validity.

A key difference among the case studies is the scale of the IA problem. Clearly in the 100 km^2 Mae Chaem sub-catchments, relationships can, and often must, be modelled in more detail than in one of 40 000 km^2 (Namoi). Thus a crop and water-balance model is used in the former but only empirical relationships are applied to predict yields in the latter. Correspondingly, short- to medium-term effects of climate variability have been included in the two smaller-scale studies and could have been in the larger one for a little more effort. However, in the Namoi case the interest is in more complex, long-run effects of capital investment on water allocation decisions. On the other hand the hydrology is modelled daily in all three cases in order to consider river extractions with that time resolution, and because accurate enough modelling with a daily step is feasible even in the Namoi.

The treatment of the economic component in the three case studies differs according to both the modelling scale and the issues being considered. In the Namoi case, regional farmers have relatively few crop rotations to choose from, but a broader range of capital investment decisions. This reflects the long-run, capital-intensive nature of the off-allocation water issue. In the Yass study, a very broad range of farm types and land use is considered but for shorter-run decisions. In this catchment at this scale, water issues are influenced by a broader range of land uses, both through direct extractions and indirectly by forest cover change and farm dam development. Capital investment was not considered crucial for this system and was not modelled. In the Thai case, the focus on household scale meant that factors influencing household decision making, such as uncertainty about outcomes, were taken into account, but decisions to invest in capital were not considered crucial.

Table 10.1   Comparison of three case studies

Catchment	Mae Chaem	Yass	Namoi
Spatial scales			
Area (km²), nodes	100 (x 5), 2	1000, 4	40,000, 16
Activities	Seasonal irrigated and dryland crops	Farm forestry Viticulture Irrigated cropping Grazing	Rotation based irrigated and dryland options
Policies	Erosion control Forest encroachment Upland development Infrastructure investment	Farm Dams Volumetric conversions Daily flow extraction rules Forestry/salinity Environmental flows	Off-allocation and reduction in groundwater allocations Sleeper licence activation Volumetric conversions Daily flow extraction rules Environmental flows
Time scales for hydrology, economics and crop models	Hydrology – daily Economics– seasonal Crop – 10 day	H – daily E – 20 years C – subannual	H – daily E – 20 years C – non-varying
Economic modelling	Short run Linear Programming (LP)	Short run LP	Long run Dynamic Programming, Short run LPs
And Decision basis	Expectations-based	Perfect knowledge	Perfect knowledge
Production/yield model	Crop-water balance, climate influenced	Empirical model Climate influenced	Empirical model, not climate influenced

Source: Jakeman and Letcher (2003).

10.6   BENEFITS AND DIFFICULTIES OF ISM

Integrated Scenario Modelling for IWRM has many benefits. It provides: a way of exploring and explaining tradeoffs; a long-term memory of the project methods; a visible and accessible collection of models, methods, visualisation and other tools; a focus for integration across researchers and stakeholders; a training and education function; a tool for adoption by stakeholders; and a potentially transparent analysis. In the next sub-sections we draw from our personal experiences to illustrate some of these benefits.

10.6.1 Involvement in Modelling

In particular, ISM promotes engagement by stakeholders in systems thinking which can assist people in appreciating one another's perspectives. In our project work in the catchments of northern Thailand over the last few years (e.g. Merritt et al., 2004), the modelling focus has substantially enlarged the number of government organisations involved, from the Land Development Department to include Royal Forestry, Royal Irrigation, Agriculture, and the Office of the National Water Resources Committee. These agencies see themselves contributing to the development of ISM tools in order to understand and assess options to address erosion, water supply, forestry protection, subsistence needs and agricultural development. The departments work together in developing and incorporating the modelling components in a software system for widespread application. The modelling has also provided a focus for capacity building through training and the development of training materials. This focus has had the benefit of exposing managers and researchers from otherwise fairly narrowly focused disciplinary perspectives to other ways of thinking about change in the system. In this way it has enhanced their integrated system understanding.

10.6.2 Stakeholder Involvement

Our work in the Namoi Basin over the last four years has involved integrated assessment of water allocation options (Letcher and Jakeman, 2003). A focus on ISM with stakeholders has been successful in gaining strong industry and government backing for expansion of this work in the Namoi and into the adjacent Gwydir Basin (see also Chapter 8 in this book). Transparency in the assumptions of the model developed for the Namoi has allowed stakeholders to identify which components of the model and which geographical areas are preferred for extension of the work. In addition, the explicit incorporation and acknowledgement of stakeholder views and system understanding in model development has meant that a broad range of stakeholders have been empowered by their understanding of the models used for management decisions in their system.

10.6.3 Insights

In both these projects the ISM tool and exercises have also provided information and insights that would not have otherwise been possible. For example, in Thailand we could calculate the trade-off in allowing agricultural expansion to provide a subsistence level of rice; we could calculate the increase in erosion and short-term income, and the reduction in forest cover, required to meet this subsistence deficit. Scenarios investigating the impact of rapid and large-scale price changes in agricultural markets showed that not only economic and social outcomes are affected by these changes but also the environmental health of the catchment. The influence of climate on the nature of this impact has also been demonstrated. It can be shown that the magnitude of negative impacts from a range of catchment changes, both exogenous economic factors and policy decisions, are greater in times of drought, when people are more vulnerable to these impacts.

In the Namoi, the initial stakeholder focus was on allocation, but through ISM their concern additionally focused on other access rules. It also clarified that the timing of impacts was important, not merely the average impact. The cumulative impact after a series of dry years manifested as a major concern. As with the Thailand case, the estimation of the impacts and the possible trade-offs would not have been possible without models that are predominantly quantitative.

10.6.4   Software as a Means to an End

All of the IA projects in which we have participated have reinforced the rather obvious point that software development must be undertaken with a clear picture of the target audience, the specific issues and the uses. Thus while a sophisticated, object-oriented software platform may be both useful and desirable in some circumstances, in other cases a spreadsheet-based model may be more useful for extending project ideas and science. Having different software products aimed at different audiences can also be a useful outcome for a project. On the other hand, software development should not be the primary objective of the work undertaken. The software is a tool to enhance communication and interaction between different disciplinary teams. It should only be a focus of the project in so far that it encourages communication of ideas and enhanced understanding of the integrated nature of the problem.

10.6.5   Interpersonal Matters

The ultimate success and lessons learnt through an ISM project will depend critically on the personalities and aims of those involved in the project. One key requirement of ISM and IA is that the parties involved are able to respect and acknowledge the contribution from other disciplinary components. During some of our early experiences we found that different disciplinary teams were often too tied to their own software or modelling concepts, and ended up developing their own independent modelling systems which displayed their prior ideas largely without change. In these cases, many of the participants did not want to compromise their prior ideas or exploit the experience of the other teams to develop something unique and interdisciplinary. When these problems can be overcome, the project value can be much greater than the sum of its parts. Integration should not be about simply linking different component models. It should enhance participants' understanding of the interactions between system components, and also provide direction for research to fill critical gaps among the disciplinary components of the project.

The communication required within the research team and between researchers and stakeholders is extremely time- and energy-consuming. A significant component of any IA project is communication between these groups. This means that IA or ISM is not always an appropriate technique for considering management problems. Where a problem is relatively simple or has a very short timeframe, the time necessary to manage this communication properly means that a simpler, less comprehensive approach should be used. In general, if you do not intend to pay due attention to stakeholder views then you should not ask for them in the first place. A project that claims to be participatory, but does not allow appropriate time and resources for building trust between researchers and stakeholders, risks alienating, as well as disenfranchising, stakeholder groups and making future management efforts more difficult.

10.7   ENHANCING THE PROSPECTS FOR IWRM

We see several ways to achieve greater progress in IWRM and future assessment of sustainability outcomes. Some lie predominantly in the hands of politicians and policy advisors, others with the scientists and social scientists. To avoid policy compartmentalisation and instil system learning, the processes of adaptive management (Holling, 1978) and active adaptive management (e.g. Allan and Curtis, 2003) of our 'environment' must be institutionalised and adopted across all relevant sectors. This must include the monitoring and evaluation of active and passive experiments to see what does and does not work and where there are gaps. Systematic representation of our knowledge and how it changes and accrues is vital so that we have a platform on which to build and test. ISM, and modelling in general, has a role here. One of the challenges is not to disenfranchise catchment communities, and perhaps politicians also, by increasing the uncertainty in their eyes through unsystematic representation of accrued knowledge.

Given the complexities and uncertainties of integrated modelling, it should be accepted that its broad objective is to increase understanding of the directions and magnitudes of change under different options. Typically, it cannot be about accepting or treating simulation outputs as accurate predictions. A key advance required is for ISM to allow differentiation between outcomes, at least with qualitative confidence. For example, a particular set of outcomes or indicator values might be categorised as overall better than, worse than or no different from another set (for instance a do-nothing, current situation) with high, reasonable or low confidence. This is enough to facilitate a decision as to the worth of adopting a policy or controllable change. ISM analyses must be able to differentiate between policies and specify what knowledge or data will provide leverage to improve the differentiation. As noted earlier, it is often impractical at present to produce a quantitative confidence level for predictions by integrated models. Currently, methods for quantifying uncertainties have severe limitations; Norton et al. (2003) and Jakeman and Letcher (2003) discuss new research required to address this glaring deficiency.

We know some of the important information that needs to be gathered to progress the integrated management of water resources through IA. The social sciences can offer insight and information into decision making and adoption processes previously ignored in many scenario-based models. In particular, social survey data linking information about decision making and adoption to biophysical and socioeconomic characteristics of farmers, industries or households is a key to developing more sophisticated ISM and other policy analyses (e.g. Curtis et al., 2001). Very little of this type of data exists for most catchment situations. In addition, biophysical scientists are often not in a position to extract and understand the implications of such data. Further use and development of participatory methods (e.g. Haslam et al., 2003; Chapter 8) for ISM building is one way of extracting and using such information. These techniques have the bonus of allowing stakeholders inside the model development phase, to ensure they have a better understanding of, and opportunity to feed into, the assumptions underlying these types of models. Hare et al. (2003) present one of the recent comparisons of different participatory processes.

IA takes time. This needs to be recognised by all parties involved in IWRM. The time scales necessary for IA mean that the nature of the management problem and stakeholders' views will change throughout the life of the project. Problem definition needs to be sharp enough to allow for useful interaction between researchers and stakeholders, but also flexible enough for the tools and understanding being developed still to be useful at the end of the IA project. While success of IA projects will breed interest from decision makers, the latter group needs to allow sufficient time for assessments and policy implementation, thereby reducing the current piecemeal approach to IWRM. Although adaptive management is becoming widely recognised as a desirable aim, it implies a commitment to monitoring and updating of policies and implementation over a period commensurate with proper assessment of their effectiveness: a fair trial. This period will often exceed the life of a government.

While clearer guidance to management is a principal aim of any IA or ISM exercise, it is important to recognise that the most useful outcome may be in the learning experience of researchers and stakeholder groups. In other words it may be overly optimistic to assume that any single research project will, on its own, greatly improve the sustainability of the system. We argue that in many cases the concept of sustainability is not fixed and that improved understanding of the nature of IWRM attained by participants in any project or exercise is an outcome worth achieving.

ACKNOWLEDGMENTS

The authors are grateful to their colleagues who have worked with them on IWRM projects. We are also indebted to the Australian Centre for International Agricultural Research, which supported the funding of our work in Thailand, and to the Cotton Research and Development Corporation for funding the work in the Namoi and Gwydir catchments.

REFERENCES

Alan, C. and A. Curtis (2003), 'Learning to implement adaptive management', *Natural Resource Management*, **6**(1), 25–30.

Barron, F.H. and B.E. Barrett (1996), 'Decision quality using ranked attribute weights', *Management Science*, **42**(11), 1515–1523.

Brans, J.P. and B. Mareschal (1990), 'The PROMETHEE methods for MCDM; the PROMCALC, GAIA and BANKADVISOR software', in C.A. Bana e Costa (ed.), *Readings in Multiple Criteria Decision Aid*, Heidelberg: Springer-Verlag.

Buede, D.M. (1992), 'Overview of the MCDA software market', *Journal of Multi-Criteria Decision Analysis*, **1**, 59–61.

Curtis, A., M. Lockwood and J. MacKay (2001), 'Exploring landholder willingness and capacity to manage dryland salinity in the Goulburn Broken catchment', *Australian Journal of Environmental Management*, **8**(2), 79–90.

Feuillette, S., F. Bousquet and P.L. Goulven (2003), 'SINUSE: a multi-agent model to negotiate water demand management on a free access water table', *Environmental Modelling and Software*, **18**, 413–427.

Fraser, A.M. and H.L. Swinney (1986), 'Independent coordinates for strange attractors from mutual information', *Physics Review A*, **33**(2), 1134–1140.

Goldberg, D.E. (1989), *Genetic Algorithms in Search, Optimization and Machine Learning*, Reading, MA: Addison-Wesley.

Hare, M., R.A. Letcher and A.J. Jakeman (2003), 'Participatory modelling in natural resource management: a comparison of four case studies', *Integrated Assessment*, **4**(2), 62–72.

Haslam, S.A., R.A. Eggins and K.J. Reynolds (2003), 'The ASPIRe model: actualising social and personal identity resources to enhance organisational outcomes', *Journal of Occupational and Organizational Psychology*, **76**, 83–113.

Heuvelink, G.B.M. (1998), *Error propagation in Environmental Modelling with GIS*, London: Taylor and Francis.

Holling, C.S. (1978), Adaptive *Environmental Management and Assessment*, Chichester: Wiley.

Jakeman, A.J. and R.A. Letcher (2003), 'Integrated assessment and modelling: features, principles and examples for catchment management', *Environmental Modelling and Software*, **18**, 491–501.

Letcher, R.A. and A.J. Jakeman (2003), 'Application of an adaptive method for integrated assessment of water allocation issues in the Namoi river catchment, Australia', *Integrated Assessment*, **4**(2), 73–89.

Merritt, W.S., B.F. Croke, A.J. Jakeman, R.A. Letcher and P. Perez (2004), 'A biophysical toolbox for assessment and management of land and water resources in rural catchments in Thailand', *Ecological Modelling*, **17**, 279–300.

Mousseau, V., J. Figueira, L. Dias, C. Gomes da Silva and J. Climaco (2003), 'Resolving inconsistencies among constraints on the parameters of an MCDA model', *European Journal of Operational Research*, **147**(1), 72–93.

Norton, J.P. (1975), 'Optimal smoothing in the identification of linear time-varying systems', *Proceedings Institute Electrical Engineers*, **122**, 663–668.

Norton, J.P. (1976), 'Identification by optimal smoothing using integrated random walks', *Proceedings Institute Electrical Engineers*, **123**, 451–452.

Norton, J.P. (1986), *An Introduction to Identification*, London and New York: Academic Press.

Norton, J.P., R. Nathan, G. Podger and R. Vertessy (2003), 'Sensitivity-assessment needs of complex simulation models for integrated catchment management', in D.A. Post (ed.), *Proceedings of the International Congress on Modelling and Simulation, MODSIM 2003, Townsville, Queensland, July 14–17*, vol. 4, pp. 1667–1672.

Roy, B. (1991), 'The outranking approach and the foundations of Electre methods', *Theory and Decision*, **31**, 49–73.

Young, P.C. (1984), *Recursive Estimation and Time Series Analysis*, Berlin: Springer-Verlag.

Young, P.C., C. Ng, K. Lane and D. Parker (1991), 'Recursive forecasting, smoothing and seasonal adjustment of non-stationary environmental data', *Journal of Forecasting*, **10**, 57–89.

11. Typology of Models and Methods of Integration

Rebecca A. Letcher and John Bromley

11.1 MODELLING ISSUES OF INTEGRATED WATER RESOURCES MANAGEMENT

Issues associated with integrated water resources management (IWRM) are generally characterised as being complex, multi-scale and multi-disciplinary in nature. The complexity of these issues has meant that model-based approaches have been one commonly applied method for considering various system components and their interactions. Model development for sustainable water management has come from a wide range of disciplinary perspectives, including hydrological, economic, agronomic and ecological perspectives. Models have been used to consider; groundwater and surface water management, resource allocation, water pollution (thermal, nutrients, sediments, pesticides, salinity), land degradation and erosion. Current research efforts are focused heavily on better integration of these different disciplinary approaches to sustainable water management.

This chapter provides an overview of modelling techniques used to consider IWRM from three main disciplinary perspectives: hydrological, ecological and socioeconomic. Issues related to the treatment and consideration of spatial and temporal scales in these models are also discussed. Several approaches to model integration and their application to sustainable water management are also reviewed.

11.2 ISSUES RELATING TO MODEL DEVELOPMENT FOR IWRM

Integration of models, disciplines and stakeholders in assessment of natural resource management issues has been strongly supported internationally. Park and Seaton (1996) advocate the linking of scientific research to policy. They stress the need for an integrated approach, particularly with the social sciences, for making this come about. Geurts and Joldersma (2001) state that 'policy analysts that use traditional formal modelling techniques have limited impact on policy makers regarding complex policy problems'. They argue that 'these kinds of problems require the combination of scientific insights with subjective knowledge resources and improved communication between various parties involved in the policy problem'. Villa and Costanza (2000) argue that different modelling approaches need to be integrated into higher level simulation models because of the

> increasing complexity and multidisciplinarity of environmental research and management problems, the spatial and cultural delocalization of research groups, and the increasing recognition of the need for a multiplicity of scales to be considered at the same time.

Integrated modelling however comes with it's own set of difficulties.

One key issue to consider when integrating models is scale, with respect to both the overall scales at which the issue is modelled and the scales at which individual component models are applied. This is especially the case when the models are derived from very different disciplines. Processes at larger scales may often be modelled using simple empirical relationships while other processes may be more appropriately modelled using detailed spatially distributed models. Model objectives will also affect the choice of models and scales. Environmental problems vary in scale from those that are localised, to large-scale issues occurring over basin or even global scales. For integrated modelling of different environmental issues, a compromise between these scales must often be achieved based on the policy or management focus of the research. Ewing et al. (1997) recognise the importance of this issue of conflicting scales in terms of integrated environmental management, stating that 'in the case of catchment management, one of the difficulties often faced arises from the fact that catchment boundaries, often do not coincide, for example, with administrative or social boundaries (Syme et al., 1994), with ecological regions (Omernik and Griffith, 1991), or to what Weatherford (1990) refers to as 'hydrocommons'. Norton (1996) suggests that environmental problems are, in this sense, essentially problems of scale'.

The main issue to consider when developing any model is that of modelling objective or problem focus. In general the type of model which is developed, the way in which spatial and temporal scales are treated, and the level to which the model incorporates components from different disciplines will depend critically on the objectives of the model development exercise. In many cases these will also be limited by data availability and system understanding.

11.3   REASONS FOR MODELLING

When choosing the type of modelling approach to be used, it is important to consider three main issues: what is the purpose of the model; what types of data are available; and, what requirements are there on the scales and formats of model outputs? This section focuses on the purposes of model building. The next section discusses issues of scales and data.

Models are generally built to satisfy one or more of five main purposes:

1.   Prediction;
2.   Forecasting;
3.   Management and decision making;
4.   Social learning;
5.   Development of system understanding or experimentation.

These purposes place different requirements on the model structure, scales and accuracy.

11.3.1   Prediction

Prediction involves estimating the value (quantitative or qualitative) of a system output in a specified time period, using knowledge of the system inputs in the same time period. Models are often developed to predict the effect of a change in system drivers or inputs on the system outputs. For example, a model may predict a change in the probability of an algal bloom occurring in a dam given that there is going to be an increase in the level of nutrients delivered to the dam. Predictive models may be very simple (often empirical) or may be more complex. In many cases increased complexity of a model does not lead to improved predictive performance, so many successful predictive models have relatively simple structures that are well grounded in observations. Predictive models are generally required to have some level of accuracy in reproducing historic observations of system outputs. For integrative models, validating the predictive accuracy of these models is often difficult due to a lack of appropriate data for validation.

11.3.2   Forecasting

Forecasting refers to predicting the value of a system output in future time periods, without knowledge of the values of system inputs in those periods. For example, a model may use observed rainfall today to forecast the chance of rainfall tomorrow. Time series methods are very commonly used for forecasting problems. The accuracy of forecasting models can only be tested by comparing the difference between 'forecast' values and historic observations.

11.3.3   Management and Decision Making

Models are frequently developed for management and decision-making purposes. The term 'decision support system' is often applied to models that have been developed to aid decision making. These models may be simulation based (i.e. developed to answer 'what if' type questions) or optimisation based (developed to provide the 'best' option under a given objective, subject to constraints). Management and decision-making models are usually required to accurately differentiate between the various management options being tested. This usually requires the model to give accurate estimates of the magnitude and direction of changes in system outputs in response to changes in system drivers.

11.3.4   Social Learning

The use of models for social learning is an increasingly important development area. Of particular interest is the recent popularity of agent-based models. In this case, models are developed to allow individuals (not the model builder) to learn and experiment with the way in which the system may work and the way their individual actions may interact with the actions of others to create system outcomes. Models developed for social learning generally have a large emphasis on the importance of social interactions between individuals or groups and may include representations of many less well-known or understood processes. The emphasis of accuracy in models developed for social learning tends to fall more on the plausibility of interactions and outcomes than the predictive accuracy of the model (see also Chapters 7 and 8, in this book).

11.3.5   Developing System Understanding

Models are frequently developed to summarise and integrate available knowledge of system components in order to improve understanding of the entire system and the way it may react to changes in system drivers. Models that are developed to improve system understanding or for experimenting on a system, may include components that are less certain (to test the potential effect of the assumed structure on the system) than those used for prediction, forecasting or decision making. These models tend to be 'research' models, accessible to the model builder and other researchers, as opposed to social learning models that are generally developed with a large non-technical audience in mind. As with social learning models, model accuracy tends to be considered in terms of plausibility and possible implications for the system rather than history matching.

11.4   MODEL CLASSIFICATION

Models from various disciplines can largely be classified according to four criteria: whether they are process or data-based; how they treat space; how they treat time; and whether they are agent-based or developed to simulate averaged system outcomes.

11.4.1   Is the Model Process-based or Data-based?

1. Process-based models generally rely on a priori assumptions about model structure. These assumptions tend to come from theory relating to physical, chemical, biological or socioeconomic processes. These structural assumptions may range from simple to complex.
2. Data-based models include empirical models and systems models where structure and behaviour are inferred from system outputs, inputs and other prior knowledge. These models generally do not rely on a priori assumptions relating to structure, or may rely on only the simplest, non-process-based assumptions.

11.4.2   How Does the Model Treat Space?

There are four basic approaches that models use to handle space:

1. Non-spatial models do not make reference to space. For example, simple predator-prey models used in ecology may not refer to any particular spatial scale.
2. Lumped spatial models provide a single set of outputs (and calculate internal states) for the entire area modelled. For example, the impact of a change in nutrient delivery to a lake may be modelled using a simple function as a total change in biomass for the entire lake system. In this case the lake system is not disaggregated into smaller units and the interactions between parts of the lake system are not considered.
3. 'Region'-based spatial models provide outputs (and calculate internal states) for homogenous sub-areas of the total area modelled. These sub-areas are defined as homogenous in a key characteristic(s) relevant to the model, such as homogenous soil types or similar agricultural production systems. For example, the lake system may be disaggregated into

riparian areas within 1–2m of the shore line, the creek leading into the lake and the deeper lake system. Interactions between these three 'regions' are then considered by the model.

4. Grid or element-based spatial models provide outputs (and calculate internal states) on a uniform or non-uniform grid basis. Neighbouring grid cells may have the same characteristics but are still modelled separately, as opposed to homogenous region-based spatial models where these areas would be lumped together. For example, when considering the impact of land use changes on terrestrial ecosystems, the landscape may be divided into a uniform grid, where the descriptors for each grid cell are based on either a single measurement within that cell (e.g. landcover, species distribution, soils). These cells may then be modelled either independently or as a connected series of cells (i.e. each cell affects the outcomes in neighbouring cells) depending on the way in which the model has been conceptualised.

For integrated models, the entire model may not operate using a single approach. For example, a grid-based lake hydrodynamic model may be used to feed a single spatially averaged output into an economic or ecological model. Different spatial scales can lead to many difficulties in integrated models, as the spatial scales of interest in one component model may be quite different to those of a model from a different discipline.

11.4.3   How Does the Model Treat Time?

There are three basic approaches to dealing with time:

1. Non-temporal models are those that do not make reference to time. For example, key ecological attributes of a landscape may be considered to be patch size and connectivity. These may be modelled for different scenarios from a static land use or management decision using appropriate ecological indicators. This is essentially a simple model of ecological impact of land use change that has no reference to time.
2. Lumped temporal models generally provide outputs over a single time period, such as average annual outputs. For example many nutrient and sediment models output an average annual load, rather than an annual or daily time series. By definition a model that is developed for forecasting purposes cannot be lumped temporally.
3. Dynamic models provide outputs for each time-step over a period. For example a model may calculate the change in the system condition each day, month or year. This approach is usually taken when the response of the system to a time varying input (such as rainfall) is required.

As with their treatment of spatial scales, integrated models do not necessarily have to integrate components working at the same temporal scale. The outputs of one component may be aggregated or disaggregated before being input into another component model. The main consideration here is that the choice of aggregation or disaggregation method is generally subjective and may affect the model outputs. Any such effect needs to be considered when interpreting model results and, if the effect is too great, the model may need to be modified (for example component models may need to be redesigned to work at a more appropriate scale).

11.4.4   Is the Model Agent-based or Developed to Produce the Averaged Characteristics of some Population or Phenomena?

Agent-based models, also commonly referred to as multi-agent systems or individual-based models, consider a system to be made up of a number of individual 'agents' that interact with each other (see for example Hood, 1998; van der Veen and Otter, 2001). These models are based on the theory that detailed knowledge and information are only available on the properties of individuals and that system properties are a potentially non-linear consequence of agent properties (Hood, 1998). Agent-based models are mainly used to understand the consequences of these types of interactions between individuals for the whole system. Thus the concept of investigating 'emergent behaviour' of the system as a result of individual interactions is considered to be a key concern of agent-based modelling. These types of models are more commonly developed for ecological or socioeconomic applications.

The more traditional approach to modelling is to simulate an averaged system outcome (at some scale), by modelling whole of system behaviour using assumptions developed by theory or observation.

11.5   HYDROLOGICAL MODELLING APPROACHES

A wide range of models exists for modelling hydrological processes. For the purposes of this chapter, hydrological processes are considered to be the generation and routing of rainfall-runoff or streamflow, and also of catchment pollutants, such as nutrients, sediments and salinity. Hydrological models can be either process-based or data-based, or a combination of both. Many relevant reviews of hydrological models have been undertaken previously. For example, Merritt et al. (2003) conducted a review of erosion and sediment transport models. Beck (1987) reviewed the sources of uncertainty in water quality modelling, providing a detailed discussion of the problem of parameter identification in models of medium to high complexity. Sui and Maggio (1999) reviewed the integration of GIS with hydrological models. Wheater et al. (1993) provided a classification of rainfall-runoff models. Croke and Jakeman (2001) also provided a good overview of hydrological modelling.

This section provides three very different examples of hydrological models and gives an indication of the types of modelling objectives these models would be used to address.

11.5.1 An Example of a Data-based Model (NRCS Curve Number Approach)

The NRCS (formerly SCS) curve number approach is an empirical (or data-based) model, using tables of curve numbers (CN) for combinations of soil group, vegetation cover type and condition (many categories), hydrologic condition and antecedent runoff condition. The estimates of the curve numbers were obtained from a large number of field measurements taken in the United States, and thus need to be verified/modified for use in other regions. The curve number approach is based on an empirical equation that relates runoff (Q), to rainfall (P), potential maximum retention after runoff begins (S), and an initial abstraction (I_a) that represents all losses that occur before runoff begins.

$$Q = \frac{(P - I_a)^2}{(P - I_a) + S} \tag{11.1}$$

Based on studies of a large number of small agricultural catchments, I_a can be approximated using the empirical relation $I_a = 0.2S$. This gives the runoff equation used in the NRCS curve number approach

$$Q = \frac{(P - 0.2S)^2}{(P + 0.8S)} \tag{11.2}$$

where $S = (1000/CN) - 10$. For combinations of different soils, vegetation and condition within a catchment, an area-weighted average of the CN value is used. A full description can be found in NRCS (1986).

This type of model can be implemented as a lumped temporal and spatial model, and is commonly used in management and decision making or social learning applications where limited data are available, or where coarser outputs may be acceptable.

11.5.2 An Example of a Mixed Process And Data-based, Dynamic, Spatially Lumped Model (IHACRES)

The IHACRES model consists of a non-linear loss module that converts rainfall to effective rainfall, and a linear routing model that converts the effective rainfall to streamflow. This model structure is demonstrated in Figure 11.1. Symbols used in this figure are summarised in Table 11.1.

The non-linear module comprises a storage coefficient c, a time constant for the rate of drying τ_w of the catchment at a fixed temperature (20°C), and a factor f that modulates τ_w for changes in temperature. In the subcatchments used in this example, a configuration of two parallel storages in the linear routing module is implemented; one represents quick flow and the other

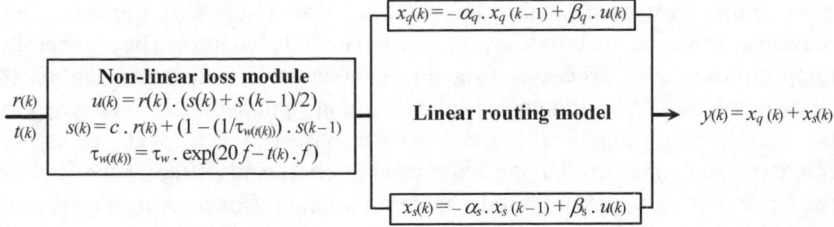

Figure 11.1   IHACRES model showing the configuration of two parallel storages implemented in the routing module.

Table 11.1   Symbols used in Figure 11.1 for variables and parameters in the IHACRES rainfall-runoff model.

Model inputs and outputs at timestep k	
$r(k)$	Rainfall
$t(k)$	Temperature
$s(k)$	Soil moisture index
$u(k)$	Effective rainfall
$y(k)$	Streamflow
$x_q(k)$	Quick flow volume
$x_s(k)$	Slow flow volume

Model parameters	
c	Volumetric storage coefficient of catchment
τ_w	Drying rate of catchment
f	Temperature modulation of drying rate
α_q, α_s	Quick and slow flow recession rates
β_q, β_s	Fractions of $u(k)$ for peak response

represents slow flow (as shown in Figure 11.1). Each storage is characterised by a time constant (or equivalently the rate) of its unit hydrograph recession (α_q and α_s). The proportional volume of the quick flow (v_q) to slow flow (v_s) storage response completes the parameterisation of the linear routing model. A detailed description of this version of the IHACRES model is provided in Jakeman and Hornberger (1993).

This style of model is generally referred to as a conceptual model, mixing data-based and process-based components. It can be used as a lumped spatial model, but could also be applied as part of a region-based spatial model. These types of models are commonly used for all modelling purposes. Conceptual models are typically based on the representation of the catchment as a series of internal storages. They usually incorporate the underlying transfer mechanisms of pollutant and runoff generation within their structure, representing flow paths within the catchment as a series of storages, each requiring some characterisation of its dynamic behaviour. They generally lump representative processes over the scale at which outputs are simulated (Wheater et al., 1993). Parameter values for conceptual models have typically been obtained through calibration against observed data such as stream discharge and concentration measurements (Abbott et al., 1986), usually from the catchment to which the model is being applied. Conceptual models tend to suffer from problems associated with the calibration of parameter values from limited sets of observed data (Jakeman and Hornberger, 1993). Most calibration techniques used for conceptual models of medium complexity (say more than six parameters) are capable of finding only local optima at best. This means that there are many possible 'best' parameter sets available.

11.5.3   An Example of a Grid-based, Dynamic, Process-based Hydrological Model (TOPOG)

TOPOG was initially developed as a catchment scale hydrological model that linked three dimensional terrain attributes with a simple description of water movement (O'Loughlin, 1986). The program has received on-going attention and now is a package that incorporates eight computational programs. The TOPOG program simulates dynamic water, carbon, solute and sediment balances of catchments. The model operates on a continuous basis and considers both point and non-point sources of pollution. The model requires detailed information on topography, soils, climate and vegetation (Grayson et al., 1999).

The approach is based on two assumptions:

1.   Steady state conditions are assumed to prevail in draining hillslopes; and
2.   The potential gradients that determine the direction of lateral subsurface flow are assumed to be dominated by elevation.

The rainfall-runoff module in TOPOG simulates the hydrologic behaviour of the catchment and how this is affected by changes in vegetation. The development of local surface saturation on a hillslope is considered to occur when the accumulated water flux Aq passing across an element of contour length b exceeds the product of the local soil transmissivity T and the local surface gradient M (O'Loughlin, 1986). The accumulated water flux is the product of the upslope partial catchment area A and the areal drainage flux q. Apart from the consideration of appropriate values for T and M, the use of the above equation relies on the ability to estimate A. Surface runoff will be generated where rain falls on a soil that is saturated at the soil surface. TOPOG is capable of simulating rainfall-runoff over daily time-steps or over intervals as small as minutes.

This style of process-based model which is generally used over fairly small spatial scales (less than 10's of km^2), is most often applied to improve system understanding or for experimentation. These models are commonly applied on a grid basis, with detailed description of processes occurring within grid cells and of the links between grid cells. These process descriptions rely on various parameter values that are, in theory, measurable in the cell or catchment. In practice, however, many parameters cannot be measured, either at the appropriate scales, or at all in some cases. This means that many parameter values are either calibrated or merely set to a constant, which leads to additional uncertainty in model outputs (Beck et al., 1995; Wheater et al., 1993). Even in situations where parameters can be 'measured' within the catchment, errors in the measurement of important characteristics, and differences between model grid scales and measurement scales will also create uncertainty in results (Bloschl and Sivapalan, 1995). These difficulties are further exacerbated by problems with simply 'scaling up' small-scale parameters (such as soil properties) to the large scale, where these values may lose meaning (Seyfried and Wilcox, 1995). These problems limit the usefulness of these models to prediction or forecasting applications.

11.6 ECOLOGICAL MODELLING APPROACHES

There have been many definitions of ecology over the years, each one tending to be a product of its time. Ecology was originally defined in the mid-nineteenth century by the German biologist Ernst Haeckel as the relationship of organisms with their environment. However, this simple statement was made at a time when biology was a very different discipline than it is today. Over the years increased understanding of the complex web of processes that determine the abundance and distribution of organisms and the inter-relationships between organisms and the environment, at all scales from the microscopic upward, has led to the development of more comprehensive definitions of the subject. Although many modern definitions exist, that proposed by the Institute of Ecosystem Studies (IES), is representative:

> Ecology is the scientific study of the processes influencing the distribution and abundance of organisms, the interactions among organisms, and the interactions between organisms and the transformation and flux of energy and matter
> [IES, 2003]

Complexity is the recurring theme throughout the field of ecology. The full understanding of real world ecosystems is not possible through the application of purely mathematical or experimental approaches. The only practical way is to simplify and represent systems as numerical models. In fact the application of numerical models in ecology is almost compulsory if we wish to understand the multitude of functions of an ecosystem; it is simply not possible to represent the inter-relations of the many components within an ecosystem without the use of a model as a synthesis tool.

Some general overviews of ecological models can be found in Jørgensen and Bendoricchio (2001), Gillman and Hails (1997), Blasco and Weill (1999) and Hannon and Ruth (1997).

11.6.1 Trophic Networks

Lumped spatial and/or temporal models are often used to construct a trophic (feeding habits/food relationships) web or network representing the complex relationships between organisms or between organisms and the environment. They can also be used to simulate the response of an ecosystem to changes in external factors (e.g. climate change). A good example of a lumped spatial and temporal trophic network is that of Carrer and Opitz (1999), quoted in Jørgensen and Bendoricchio (2001). This model was constructed using the ECOPATH software. ECOPATH is a public domain software released by ICLARM (International Centre for Living Aquatic Resources Management, Manila, Philippines) for balancing steady state ecosystem models, and is described by Christensen and Pauly (1992).

This model describes the set of trophic interactions taking place within the Palude della Rosa, a shallow water area in the northern part of the Venice Lagoon. The objective was to quantify the mass and energy transfers between the system components. Data on hydrobiology, sediments, algae, planktonic and benthic communities were used to produce a model of the energy flows among the various biological components of the region. Calibration of the model was achieved using a mass balance equation to ensure that total input balanced total output. The model was dynamic, in that it produced a monthly time series of outputs, but it only considered a steady state response.

11.6.2   Modelling Population Dynamics

Population models are dynamic models that track the growth or decline in the number of individuals. A population is defined as a collective group of organisms of the same species. Each population has several properties, such as population density, birth rate, death rate, age distribution, dispersal, growth forms and so on. Another important factor is the carrying capacity of an ecosystem for a particular species; populations below the carrying capacity will tend to increase, while those above this capacity will decrease. These models are generally process-based and may be agent-based or top-down.

The first population model, the Lotka and Volterra model, was developed as early as the 1920s (Volterra, 1926). Since this time a huge number of others have been developed and a comprehensive review of all types is not possible. Instead one example, the 'wildebeest model' described in Hannon and Ruth (Hannon and Ruth, 1997), is used as an illustration.

The wildebeest model was developed for a wildlife park on African grasslands. Wildebeest are eaten by lions and shot by rangers attempting to manage the ecosystem. The model was constructed using STELLA, a simple icon-based language that facilitates the construction of models of any dynamic process, such as population changes. It is a lumped spatial model, and the input data are shown in Table 11.2.

Given the above data it is possible to construct a model to calculate an average death rate of this particular group of wildebeest (Figure 11.2). Once constructed and calibrated, it is then possible to use the model to assess the impacts of different culling strategies and lion populations on total wildebeest numbers, or perhaps on the calf population alone. A typical output is shown in Figure 11.3, which shows total wildebeest population for the next 20 years for a particular strategy.

Table 11.2   Input data for the wildebeest model

Variable Data	
Number of lions in the park	500
Lion kill rate	3.8 – 4.5 wildebeest per lion per year
Shooting strategy	Wildebeest shot for first 4 years
Calf survival rate	0.35 – 0.48
Population census for calves, yearlings, 2-year olds and adults	Available for first 6 years

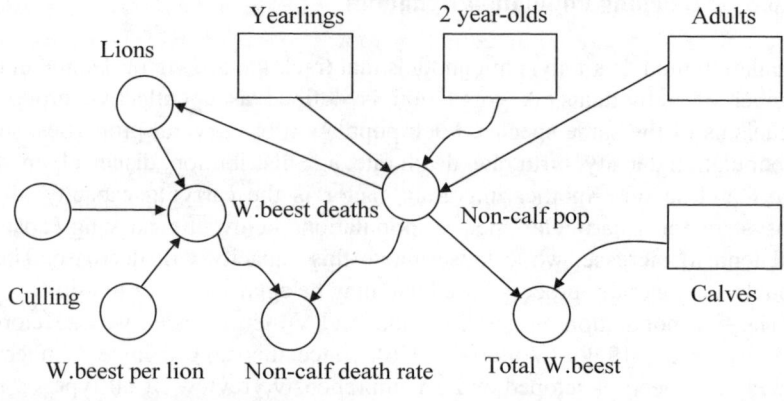

Source: Hannon and Ruth (1997).

Figure 11.2   Wildebeest model

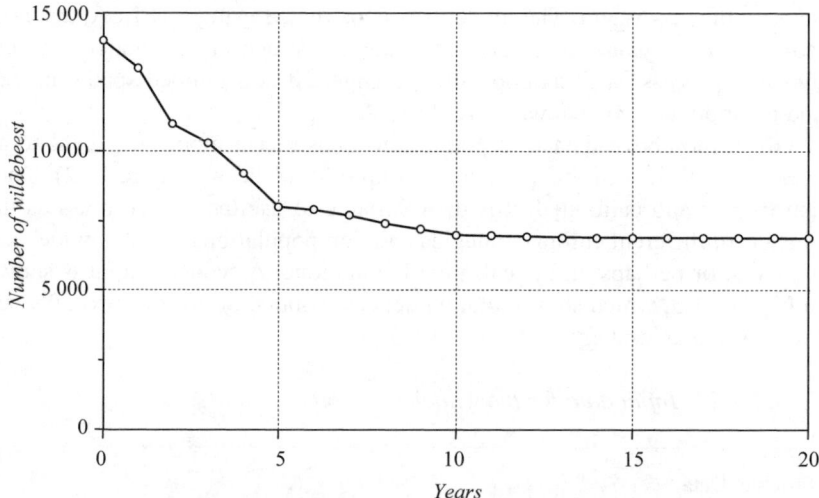

Figure 11.3   Typical output from the wildebeest model

11.6.3   Biogeochemical Models

Biogeochemical models attempt to capture the dynamics and cycling of biochemical and geochemical compounds in an ecosystem. Over the past 25 years there has been increasing demand for dynamic biogeochemical models, which can be used to solve a wide range of pollution-related problems, ranging from groundwater contamination to air pollution issues. When used for pollution control, they are required to account for the fate and distribution of both the pollutants and of naturally occurring compounds. There are many varieties of biogeochemical models but one of the more widely used types are eutrophication models. Eutrophication is the tendency for nutrient levels in lakes to increase, often as a result of artificial inputs through the activity of man. More often than not the results are damaging to the ecosystem. It is the impact of increases in phosphorous and nitrogen levels that cause most of the damage. These types of models are closely related to pollutant models developed in hydrological applications although they are generally more focused on the fate of pollutants than their generation, which is the case with hydrological applications. They generally follow the model types described in Section 5.

11.6.4 Ecotoxicological Models

Ecotoxicological models are increasingly applied to assess the risk of emissions of chemicals to the environment. They can be divided into two groups; fate models which predict concentrations of a chemical in, for instance, a lake or an animal, and effect models which translate the concentration present into an effect on the organism, population, or ecosystem.

Fate models fall into three groups:

1. Models that map the fate and transport of a chemical in a region or country, so-called MacKay type models (Mackay, 1991);
2. Models that simulate a specific case of toxic pollution such as discharge from an industrial source into a lake or river;
3. Models that focus on the fate of a locally used substance. For instance the use of pesticides on agricultural land will pose a potential threat to local surface and groundwater sources. A model can be used to investigate the impact of this practice, often in the form of a worst-case scenario.

Effect models can be divided into five groups, according to the scale:

1. Single organism models: these simulate the effect of toxic substances on single organisms;
2. Population scale models: models that look at the impact on specific populations;
3. Ecosystem models: these models are concerned with the effect of toxic substances on entire ecosystems:
4. Landscape models: models that examine the effects of chemical changes

on a number of inter-related ecosystems.

5.   Global models: a typical example of a global model is one that simulates the decomposition of the ozone layer due to the emission of particular gases such as freon.

Currently over 20 000 chemicals are in use around the world. Of these, 2500 are used in large volumes and pose the greatest threat to the environment. Under EU law, a full ecotoxicological evaluation of 140 of these chemicals is required. Reliable ecotoxicological models are required for this purpose, and an extensive list is presented in Jørgensen and Bedoricchio (2001).

A good example of an ecotoxicological model is that used to simulate the contamination of agricultural products by cadmium and lead (Jørgensen and Bendoricchio, 2001). This is a type 2 fate model (see above). Agricultural products are contaminated with lead and cadmium from air pollution, the application of sludge as a soil conditioner, and from the use of fertilizers. The model was constructed using STELLA. The results provided a good match with observed data, though it proved more difficult to obtain good matches during the second and third years once municipal sludge had been applied as a conditioner (Figure 11.4). The model demonstrated the importance of heavy metals from atmospheric fallout and also those originating from plant residues.

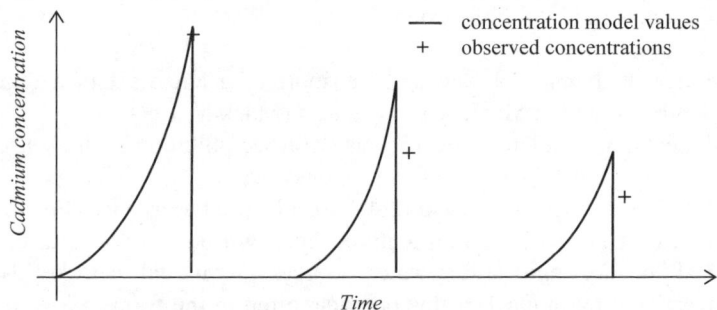

Figure 11.4   Validation of the cadmium concentration model values against observed concentrations

11.7   SOCIOECONOMIC MODELLING APPROACHES

Social scientists and economists rely on a variety of qualitative and quantitative approaches to consider questions related to IWRM. Quantitative techniques consist of both model-based and non-model-based assessment approaches. In many cases a mix of approaches is required to consider the different aspects of IWRM. Due to the focus of this chapter on quantitative, and specifically model-based techniques, this section describes a number of model-based socioeconomic approaches. However, it is important to recognise that all approaches are likely to require some qualitative components to consider the very broad range of IWRM questions.

As with other disciplines, different types of modelling approaches have been developed to address different types of modelling questions. This section outlines several broad groups of socioeconomic models and the types of questions they have been developed to address.

11.7.1   The Spatial Distribution of Impacts of Change on Groups of Producers or Industries

Production models are generally used to consider the regional-scale, spatial distribution of impacts and trade-offs resulting from changes in policy or other factors. These types of models normally divide an area, such as a catchment or basin, into a number of regions (e.g. sub-catchments) on the basis of 'relatively homogenous' production systems and policy scales. Each of these regions is then treated as though it is managed by an individual farmer. This allows 'averaging' or aggregation of decision making to a scale appropriate for the types of impacts being considered. This assumption means that resources, such as land and water, are assumed to be transferable between farmers within a region. These models place emphasis on the differences between farmers from different regions rather than on differences within regions. This enables large-scale water trading and reform issues to be considered. In particular, conflicts between upstream and downstream use can be identified. These models are essentially process-based models, as they rely on a priori assumptions about system behaviour (ie. relating to decision-making processes). They use a region-based spatial disaggregation, and are generally dynamic.

In IWRM, regional-scale production models are used to investigate the spatial distribution of socioeconomic and environmental impacts, such as those resulting from changes in water policy or water trading. These models are also able to indicate if water is likely to be bought into or sold out of a region for alternative production options. They can be applied to consider 'optimal' allocation of water within a basin given an objective. Impacts are generally limited to first-order impacts only (ie. direct impacts on water users in the region). This means that secondary impacts on towns and industries dependant on the activities of water users are not considered. These models may be used to identify whether or not the magnitude of first-order impacts is large enough to warrant further investigation of these types of second-order impacts. Examples of the application of this type of model can be found in Letcher et al. (2004), Evans et al. (2003), Hall et al. (1994), Rosegrant et al.

(2000), Ringler (2001) and McKinney at al. (1999).

The strength of regional-scale production models is their ability to consider spatial trade-offs, both socio-economic and environmental, at reasonably large scales. They do not, however, allow the user to consider impacts on individual farmers. Nor do they consider the second-order impacts on towns, agricultural-dependent industries and employment. Limited information about first-order impacts on employment may be obtained, so long as regional labour supply constraints are included in the model formulation.

11.7.2　The Impact of Changes on the Regional Economy

Input-output models are used to consider the flows of goods and services in the economy (see, for example, Black, 1997). These models assume that the economy can be divided into a number of sectors. Horton (2002) states that:

> the fundamental premise of this technique is that changes in production levels of an economy's basic industries, arising from either changes in output or changes in demand, will, through various and extensive inter-industry linkages, produce an iterative process of spending, income creation, and re-spending, thereby changing the production levels of other, directly and indirectly related industries.

Thus, when undertaking analysis of the impacts of water trading or changes in water allocation policies, these models are often used to consider the second-order impacts on regional industries, employment and regional income. They assume fixed-input coefficients, which are generally derived from data at one point in time, as well as linearity (ie. constant returns to scale and constant ratios of inputs to production for each sector). Multipliers are used to indicate the strength of linkages between a particular sector and the regional economy (see Morison and Zorzetto, 1995). A lack of supply-side constraints is also assumed.

Examples of input-output models can be found in Leistritz et al. (2002) and Fischer and Sun (2001). These models may be lumped temporal or dynamic and are process-based, relying on theory and a priori assumptions about system behaviour for their structure.

17.7.3　Representative Farm (Household) Models

Representative farm models are commonly used to simulate the impact of water reforms and other policy changes on individual farmers or households. This type of model relies on identification of a 'typical' or 'representative' farm (or household) in a given area. Production decisions made by this farm, subject to various resource constraints, are generally considered by the model. This model may take the form of a simple farm budget, or may be a complex simulation or optimisation based procedure. Taylor and Adelman (2003) provide a review of agricultural household models. These models are generally non-spatial, but may be dynamic or lumped temporal models. They are generally process-based in that they rely on a priori assumptions about system behaviour. They are top-down models, that is, impacts on the system are assumed to be represented by the average impacts on the individual, rather than being a complex outcome of self-organising system behaviour. Examples of representative farm models can be found in Berbel and Gómez-Limón (2000), Köbrich et al. (2003) and Schlizzi and Boulier (1997). One common issue with developing representative farm models is deriving 'typical' or representative farms for an area. In some cases, clustering and analysis of statistical data is used.

Representative farm models and regional-scale production models are often classified by economists according to their use of optimisation algorithms. Optimisation algorithms are themselves generally only used where assumptions relating to decision making are based on a 'profit maximising' or 'minimising costs' style of assumption. It is, for example, entirely possible to construct representative farm models that apply linear programming, dynamic programming or simpler 'decision rules' formulations. The decision about which approach should be used will generally depend on whether or not farmers (or households) are assumed to be making long- or short-run decisions and whether or not they are profit maximising. This will in turn depend on the focus required by the modelling question. There are several common choices of assumptions that need to be made when constructing economic models, particularly for production models. These include:

- Decisions are made on a long-run or short-run basis;
- Labour supply is, or is not, a constraint on decision making;
- Decisions are made to maximise profit given any resource constraints, or are based on other motivations;
- Decisions are made subject to perfect knowledge or with uncertainty.

11.7.4   Choice Models

Choice modelling, or a choice experiment, is one of a number of stated preference techniques used to estimate the value that the community places on various environmental outcomes. This method is capable of producing estimates of the values of changes in individual attributes as well as the value of aggregate changes in environmental quality (Morrison et al., 1996). This method uses surveys to identify respondents' preferences for environmental outcomes. Respondents choose their most preferred resource option from a number of alternatives. This allows estimation of the value of multiple resource options. Choice modelling is based on the assumption that consumers seek to maximise utility when they make choices.

Morrison et al. (1996) reviewed a number of stated preference techniques and concluded that choice modelling had considerable potential for providing useful and valid estimates of environmental values. These models are data-based, generally lumped temporal or non-temporal and lumped spatial or non-spatial. Examples of the application of a choice modelling approach can be found in Whitten and Bennett (2001), and Bennett and Morrison (2001). The strength of choice modelling is in its ability to consider the impacts of policy change on non-monetary values, such as recreational or environmental values.

11.7.5   Urban Water Demand Models

These models are generally based on the estimation of demand curves for urban water, assuming a given functional form, using observations of water demand. Empirical relationships between household water demand and price are generally calculated. Factors such as rainfall or evaporation may also be used to explain seasonal fluctuations in demand. These models are generally constructed by water supply authorities for demand forecasting and pricing purposes. They assume that all households in a city, or some subgroup, can be represented using a single demand function.

The most common, and simplest, function for estimating urban water demand is:

$$Q = a\,P^b \tag{11.3}$$

where Q is household water demand, P is price and a and b are parameters derived from analysing observed demand and price data. These may be measured over a variety of temporal scales (e.g. seasonal, annual, monthly). This form of the demand curve is often used as it easily allows a constant price elasticity of demand to be estimated (b). In order to improve the fit of the model to observations, it is often assumed that this function holds only for excess water use, above some minimum necessary threshold (sometimes considered to be equal to indoor water use).

Many other forms of demand model have been used in the past, including more complicated econometric models of demand as a function of both price and climate (see, for example, Renwick et al., 1998). Other functional forms of the demand curve have also been assumed.

Urban demand models allow predictions of demand to be made given changes in price (demand management). Where the model is being used to simulate future water demand, a model of population growth is also required to obtain total demand. Application of an urban demand model can be found in Ringler (2001).

11.7.6 Agent-based Models

An agent-based model considers a system that is made up of a number of individual 'agents' that interact with each other (for examples, see Hood (1998), van der Veen and Otter (2001); see also Bousquet and le Page (2004), Hare and Deadman (2004) for reviews of agent-based modelling applications in ecosystem and environmental management). In particular, the implications of cooperation and collusion between individuals on system outcomes and the stability of such arrangements are a focus of many agent-based modelling studies.

Hood (1998) recommends that agent-based models are used to complement 'top-down' modelling approaches where assumptions of linearity are often made, rather than as prescriptive models. One advantage of agent-based models is the way in which they are not constrained by the system, rather the system properties emerge from agent interactions (Hood, 1998). Also assumptions of linearity and equilibrium, common in economic models, do not need to be made. Van der Veen and Otter (2001) stress the possibility of using these models for considering highly spatially disaggregated land use decisions.

Agent-based models rely on detailed knowledge of individual characteristics and the representation of a large number of individuals. As such, data and computational limitations generally mean that only a relatively small number of individuals (e.g. hundreds) can be considered. This limits the spatial scale at which they can be used, and limits their capacity to consider catchment or basin-scale problems.

Applications of agent-based methods for considering natural resource problems can be found in Barreteau and Bousquet (2001) and Becu et al. (2001).

11.8   METHODS FOR INTEGRATION OF MODELS FOR IWRM

Effective IWRM requires managers to make informed decisions about many social, economic and environmental trade-offs likely to arise from any change in land or water management. The complexity of interactions between social, economic and environmental systems means that these types of trade-offs are difficult to estimate or analyse without the use of integrated models. These models are generally developed to allow decision makers to estimate the magnitude and direction of the outcomes arising from a variety of policy decisions or other interventions.

The term 'integration' or 'integrated model' is used by researchers and modellers in different ways. At least five different uses of the term 'integration' can be identified in the literature. Integration may refer to:

1. Integration of models – requires combining two or more models of different system processes at a variety of scales. These processes may be biological, chemical, physical, economic or social. Models may be combined to describe more than one aspect of the physical or biological features of the catchment, such as the surface water and groundwater systems. However, integration may also involve combining modelling techniques across disciplines such as ecology and economics. Obviously this type of integration may involve not just the integration of models but also the integration of different disciplines, scales and issues.

2. Integration of disciplines – involves the integrated consideration of two or more disciplinary views of a management problem. For example an ecologist may view a pollution problem as impacting on ecosystem viability, whereas an economist may see the same issue as a trade-off between the costs of pollution reduction in the catchment and the benefits accrued by the impacted ecosystem. An integrated approach to such a problem may need to reconcile these two views of the causes and effects of the problem, in order to characterise the interrelationships between components of the system.

3. Integrated treatment of issues – arises because suggested management options for many catchment problems have impacts on other resource and environmental issues within catchments. For example management options for dryland salinity often involve reforestation of a significant proportion of the upper catchment. This may also reduce the amount of erosion in the upper catchment, improving water quality and reducing sediment and nutrient discharge to the lower catchment. However, large scale reforestation may also effect the amount of runoff that is generated, potentially 'drying up' the catchment, and reducing water availability to downstream users, and possibly even increasing salt concentrations in the short to medium term. Considering the effects of management options on a range of resource and environmental issues within the catchment may improve decision making and reduce the impact of negative externalities generated by these decisions. It may also change perceptions of the seriousness of a problem to consider a broader range of the impacts generated by managing the problem.

4. Integration of scales – must be considered since resource and environmental issues occur at a variety of temporal and spatial scales. While catchment boundaries may determine the most appropriate scale

for hydrological issues such as runoff generation or erosion, social and economic boundaries are unlikely to concur with these boundaries. Important processes in the economic system may occur at household or farm scale. Social boundaries may follow electoral boundaries or may be linked to infrastructure such as roads and schools. Even within the physical system of the hydrological cycle, the groundwater and surface water systems operate at very different spatial and temporal scales. The surface water system is likely to respond to a rainfall event within hours or days, while the groundwater system may continue to respond for many years. Treatment of issues at different scales requires some compromise between the scales of component processes, and often a more simplified representation of some parts of the system.

5. Integration with stakeholders – the level and success at which research outcomes are applied and adopted will often depend on how connected stakeholders are to the research output and how relevant research outcomes are made to policy and extension activities. Integration with stakeholders may vary from simple updates of research to community groups, to large-scale inclusion of stakeholder views and knowledge at all stages in a project. Project outputs may be focused by the requirements of stakeholder groups, and local knowledge or views may contribute to the understanding of the system. Various classifications of the types of integration between stakeholders and researchers have been given in the literature. Biggs (1987) defines four types of relationship – contract, consultative, collaborative and collegiate – which differ in terms of who is responsible for decision making at various stages of the research (taken from Martin and Sherington, 1997). Pretty (1995) defines seven types of participation (manipulative, passive, by consultation, for material incentives, functional, interactive, self-mobilization) and argues that the term 'participation' should not be accepted without further clarification.

These types of integration are not totally independent of one another. In many cases the distinction between the types of integration is not clear. For example an integrated treatment of environmental, social or economic issues may require an integration of modelling techniques at a variety of scales. Some level of stakeholder integration is also likely to be a feature of any integrated modelling exercise.

In this chapter the focus of the term 'integrated model' is used for models in which two or more types of disciplinary components are linked. This may mean coupling models from different disciplines, or approaches that allow the development of 'systems' models that naturally cross disciplinary boundaries. Other aspects of integration, such as stakeholder participation in model development are dealt with elsewhere.

The previous sections provide a brief overview of common modelling approaches from three key disciplines of IWRM. This section focuses on methods by which models and other assessment approaches may be used in an integrated modelling approach. Several methods of model integration have been used IWRM. This section focuses on the two main integration approaches that have been applied:

1. Coupled complex models, including:
    -   node-link (semi-distributed) approaches
    -   grid-based approaches; and
2. Bayesian belief networks.

Lee and Howitt (1996) provide a review of integrated approaches to river basin management.

11.8.1   Coupled Complex Models

The approach of coupling complex models involves combining complex models from different disciplines to come up with an integrated outcome. Coupling may be loose, where outputs from models are linked together 'manually' or externally to the original models, or tight where the component models are engineered to share inputs and outputs. The term 'complex' model refers to models of varying levels of complexity but reflects that the functions and representations within these models would be expected to be more complex than is the case with system dynamics approaches, meta-models and Bayesian approaches. The conceptual framework for a coupled complex model generally represents links between system components, so that nodes often represent detailed component models, while links correspond to data passing between models. These models are able to incorporate feedback. Two different 'spatial' approaches are commonly applied in IWRM applications when coupling complex models: node-link approaches and grid-based approaches.

Node-link (semi-distributed) approaches

One common conceptual approach to model integration involves the use of node-link systems, or semi-distributed modelling approaches. This general method of integration treats the catchment system as a series of interacting, homogenous regions. The concept of 'homogenous' is applied in terms of various ecological, physical, social or economic characteristics, usually defined by the model question being considered. Common characteristics underlying the definition of spatial 'lumps' in the model are topography, climate, soils, geology, ecological community and farm production. Spatial lumps are generally considered to be intersections of these key characteristics so that each region or modelling unit considered by the model is 'relatively homogeneous' in terms of these characteristics. Model scales and components may be river reaches or links, nodes (generally individual points along a river) or regions, depending on the type of processes being considered. In many cases a model may have both nodes and links or nodes and regions, with key integration between disciplines often occurring at nodes. These systems allow for some spatial disaggregation of processes, while incorporating the different scales of system processes explicitly in the model conceptualisation.

Node-link approaches to model integration have been widely applied for sustainable water management. This has been particularly the case for water quantity management, such as water allocation modelling, both from an operation and control perspective (usually engineering based) and a more integrated simulation perspective.

The System-Wide Initiative on Water Management (SWIM) is an integrated economic-hydrologic model that has been developed to consider water demand and supply and solute transport. It has been applied in the Maipo River Basin in Chile. While this application is specific to this catchment, the integrative framework has been developed to be sufficiently generic for application to other catchments and issues (McKinney et al., 1999; Rosegrant et al., 2000).

The model is based on a node-link network approach. Nodes are physical entities, representing demand and supply points. Demand nodes in the model include irrigation off-takes, industrial plants and households. Supply nodes include rivers, reservoirs and groundwater aquifers (McKinney et al., 1999; Rosegrant et al., 2000). The model has been developed to account for the interactions between water allocation, farmer input choice, agricultural productivity, non-agricultural water demand, and resource degradation, to estimate the social and economic gains from the allocation and efficiency of water use (McKinney et al., 1999; Rosegrant et al., 2000). It is intended to estimate the economic benefits of water use for different demand management instruments, including markets for tradeable water rights based on production and benefit functions with respect to the agricultural, urban and industrial sectors.

The economic modelling component includes an optimisation model to estimate returns to water use. Both instream and offstream uses are modelled. Instream uses include flows for waste dilution and hydropower. Offstream uses include diversions for agriculture and municipal and industrial uses.

Crop yields are calculated externally using a crop model that accounts for water, salinity and irrigation technology as variables. Hydrologic modelling is undertaken internally. SWIM includes a component model for flow and salt balance and transport (McKinney et al., 1999; Rosegrant et al., 2000).

Other examples of the application of the node-link integration approach to IWRM can be found in Greiner (1998, 1999), Letcher et al. (2004), Merritt et al. (2004), Simons et al. (1996), Belcher et al. (2004), Chowdary et al. (2005) and Lui and Yao (1995).

Grid-based approaches

Grid-based modelling approaches are those where all or most models in the system operate on a cell-based spatial disaggregation. This overcomes some problems with differences in process scales by considering the operation of all processes at a smaller spatial scale than that on which the smallest scale process occurs. Generally fluxes of various system components, such as rainfall runoff, erosion, nutrients or even 'biodiversity' or species populations, are modelled as interactions between neighbouring grid cells. This approach is also widely applied for model integration, particularly where ecological function of the terrestrial system is of primary importance.

The NERC/ESRC Land-use Programme (NELUP) is an integrated model for analysing the impacts of land use and management options on catchment systems. The prototype modelling system was developed on the River Tyne catchment in Northern England (O'Callaghan, 1995). The NELUP model integrates modules describing the hydrology, ecology and economics of the catchment system (O'Callaghan, 1995). The hydrological model used in NELUP is the SHE model, used to simulate flow and water quality in the catchment and to predict the hydrological consequences of changes in land use. A solute transport component was also added to the SHE model for incorporation in NELUP (Adams et al., 1995; Dunn et al., 1996).

The ecological models used in NELUP were developed specifically for this purpose (Rushton et al., 1995). This component predicts the likelihood of occurrence of individual species or species-assemblages per unit area (O'Callaghan, 1995).

The economic component of NELUP is based on a recursive linear programming approach (Moxey et al., 1995). The main economic model of NELUP represents the catchment as a single macro-farm, maximising total returns to agriculture and forestry in the catchment. NELUP has also been extended to enable farm-level economic modelling, with the use of NELUP's sister-program FLEUR (Oglethorpe and O'Callaghan, 1995). Crop yields under alternative fertiliser and grazing management regimes are simulated using the EPIC model (Moxey et al., 1995).

Other applications of a grid-based approach to integration can be found in Vatn et al. (1997), Weber et al. (2001) and Möller and Kulhmann (1999).

11.8.2   Bayesian Belief Networks

Bayesian networks are based on an approach to probability theory developed by Thomas Bayes, an eighteenth century English clergyman. The technique has been successfully applied for many years in fields such as medicine and artificial intelligence (Charniak, 1991; Heckerman et al., 1995). However, it is only relatively recently that the technique has been applied to resolve environmental issues (Kuikka and Varis, 1997; Varis, 1998), and watershed management in particular (Ames and Neilson, 2001; Borsuk et al., 2001).

So far, environmental case studies have not generally involved a wide range of variables, but have been restricted to specific issues. Part of the reason for this limited approach is the restriction imposed by computer speed and memory. Bayesian networks deal with large amounts of inter-linked data and it is only with the advent of high-speed, large memory, desktop personal computers that it has become feasible to set up and operate sufficiently large networks to cope with complex environments.

Bayesian networks are used to simulate systems containing some degree of uncertainty caused by imperfect understanding or incomplete knowledge of the state of the system, randomness in the mechanisms governing the behaviour of the system, or a combination of these (Jensen, 1996). They can be used to assist decision making based on the best information available and are especially useful in situations where a large number of interlinked factors need to be taken into consideration. This makes them ideally suited as a tool to aid decision making in the field of natural resource management, where problems are complex and data often scarce and uncertain.

A Bayesian network consists of a series of nodes, representing variables that interact with each other. These interactions are expressed as links between variables; the links, however, are not permitted to form a closed loop. A node representing variable 'A' will be linked to a number of 'parent' nodes, B_1, B_2, ..., B_n, on which it is dependent. The links or 'edges' are expressed as probabilistic dependencies, which are quantified through a set of conditional probability tables (CPTs). For each variable the tables express the probability of that variable being in a particular state, given the states of its parents. As more data or knowledge becomes available these tables are updated, and the associated uncertainties reduced. For variables without parents, an unconditional distribution is defined.

A simple Bayesian network is shown in Figure 11.5. The boxes are network variables, which represent the most important factors relating to a particular decision or action. They are linked together so that a change in one will result in a chain reaction of impacts on all the linked variables in the direction of the links. The design of the network is based on a

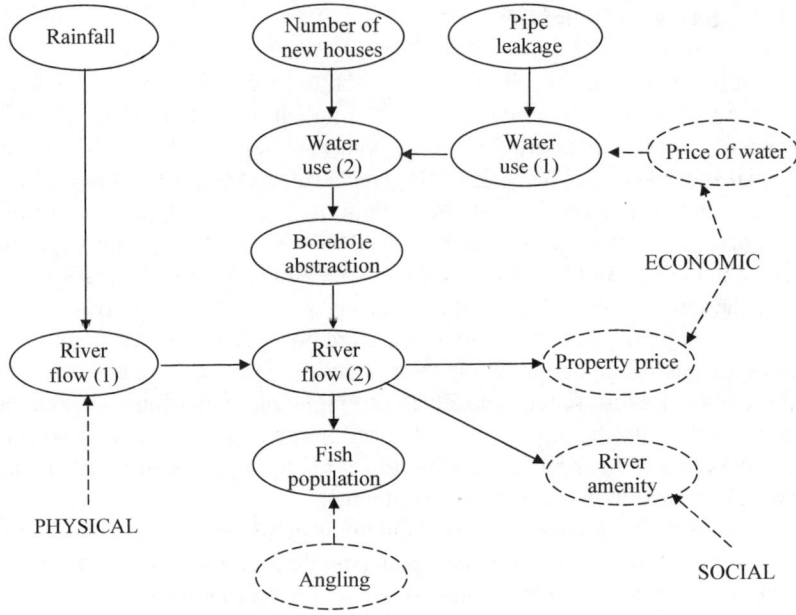

Figure 11.5   Simple Bayesian network

conceptualisation of the problem and the outcome of discussions with stakeholder groups.

In Figure 11.5 the links between 'Number of new houses' → 'Water use (2)' → 'Borehole abstraction' → 'River flow (2)' indicate that the construction of new houses in the region can ultimately have an impact on low river flows. This follows because new houses need to have water, which in the example is provided from groundwater sources contributing base flow to the river; more new houses mean increased groundwater abstraction, leading to a decline in groundwater levels which in turn causes a reduction in base flow to the river. But the impacts go further; a severe reduction in low flows during the summer, for example, could adversely affect the price of property along its banks as well as devaluing the river as a public amenity. It may also reduce fish stocks, with adverse consequences for local angling clubs and for the river ecology in general.

In the example shown, however, it is not only the construction of new houses that can impact on river flow, there are several more: reducing 'pipe leakage', changing the 'price of water' and more obviously 'rainfall' will all, to a greater or lesser extent, have an impact. The example also demonstrates that networks can incorporate variables of any type, economic, social, or physical. The ability to link diverse types of information is a key characteristic of Bayesian networks and one that makes them particularly suited for the problems of integrated water management.

The ability of Bayesian networks to integrate information lies with the nature of the 'links', the behaviour of which is defined by the construction of conditional probability tables (CPTs) for each variable. A CPT simply quantifies the probability of a variable being in any particular state, given the states of the variables linked to it (i.e. the 'parent' variables). An example CPT, based on the network shown in Figure 11.5, is given in Table 11.3. Here the 'child' variable we are dealing with is 'Water use (1)', which is defined to be in one of three states, 'increase', 'no change', and 'decrease'. The 'parent' variables, that have a direct impact on 'Water use (1)', are 'Pipe leakage', for which three states are defined; a reduction of 0 per cent, 5 per cent or 10 per cent, and 'Price of water', which is also given three states; 'up' (+10 per cent), 'no change', or 'down' (−10 per cent). The selection of states is the decision of the user. Whether verbal descriptions are used, or quantitative states (either numbers or intervals), or even a simple true or false statement depends upon the objectives of the network.

The example CPT shown in Table 11.3 tells us that with no reduction in leakage, but a 10 per cent increase in price, there is a 5 per cent probability of water use increasing, a 65 per cent chance it remains unchanged and a 30 per cent chance of a decrease. Selecting different combinations of states for 'Pipe leakage' and 'Price of water' will change the probability of 'Water use (1)' being in any particular state. This is the mechanism by which the links are made between variables.

Table 11.3   Conditional probability table

Pipe leakage	Price of water		Water use (1)		
			Up	No change	Down
0%	Down	(−10%)	0.2	0.75	0.05
5%	Down	(−10%)	0.1	0.3	0.6
10%	Down	(−10%)	0.05	0.25	0.7
0%	No change		0.1	0.9	0.1
5%	No change		0.05	0.1	0.85
10%	No change		0.0	0.05	0.95
0%	Up	(+10%)	0.05	0.65	0.3
5%	Up	(+10%)	0.05	0.5	0.45
10%	Up	(+10%)	0.05	0.15	0.8

Notes: 'Pipe leakage' and 'Price of water' are the parent variables of the child variable, 'Water use (1)'.

The conditional probability tables constructed for each variable, such as that shown in Table 11.3, are based on the best information available. This may be in the form of a set of data. For instance, in our example, the information linking price change to water use may come from historical data relating consumption to price change, or perhaps from the results of studies in other areas.

Tables may also be constructed using the output from models in the place of observed data. Again in our example the data for the CPT linking 'Borehole abstraction' and 'River flow (2)' could come from the output of a groundwater model. A rainfall-runoff model might provide the data for the link between 'Rainfall' and 'River flow (1)'.

In some instances the data available for a particular link will be limited or even non-existent. In these cases it may be necessary to fall back on 'expert opinion'. Reducing low flows in the river for example will tend to affect the price of properties along its banks. This is represented by the link between 'River flow (2)' and 'Property price' in Figure 11.5. But there is likely to be little data available to indicate the extent to which prices are affected. In this case an expert opinion may be introduced, which although not rigorous, still represents the best estimate available.

Bayesian networks thus allow the joint use of objective and subjective information. It should be stressed that networks do not replace existing environmental, economic or social models; instead they are able to take the output from these models and convert it into a format suitable for inclusion within a CPT.

An integral feature of Bayesian networks is that when they are compiled, results are presented in the form of probability distributions rather than single values. An example of output for the network in Figure 11.5 is presented in Figure 11.6. Here the network has been run to assess the impact of building 10 000 new houses in the region. The states of the variable affected by the construction of houses are presented as a probability distribution, rather than a unique figure. In each box the column of figures on the left represents the percentage probability that the variable is in the state defined in the right-hand column. The percentage figure is also given as a bar graph. Thus, given the construction of 10 000 houses 'Water use (2)' is shown to have a 66.7 per cent probability of being between 0.06–0.08 million m^3/day. But because of the uncertainty of the data there is also a chance the variable might be in other states, as shown by the distribution. Likewise property values adjacent to the river are shown to have a 39.1 per cent chance of falling in value by between 8–10 per cent; but the wide distribution reveals considerable uncertainty about the result. The explicit representation of uncertainty provides a transparent means of representing the impact of different management options without concealing the considerable element of uncertainty that invariably exists with water resource planning.

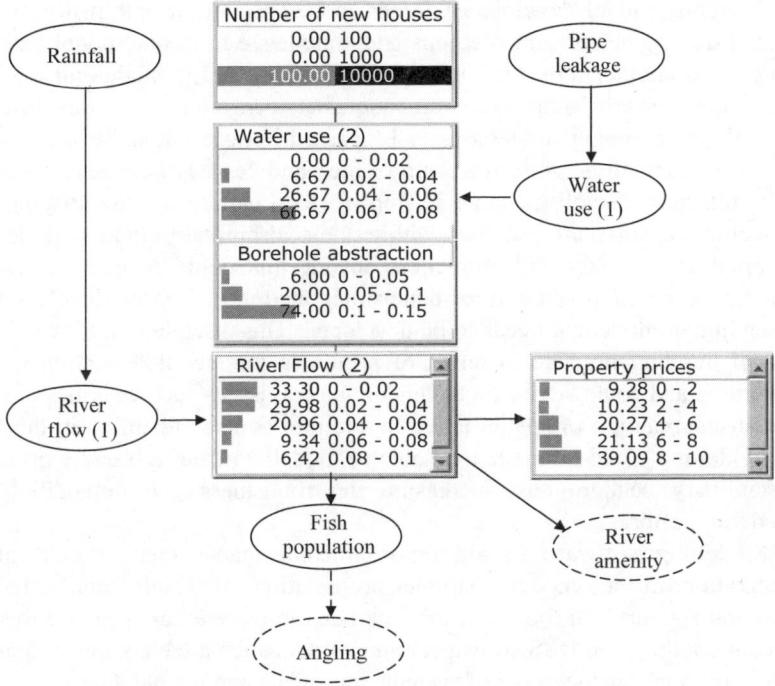

Figure 11.6   Example of output from network shown in Figure 11.5

Applications of Bayesian networks for environmental management problems can be found in Bacon et al. (2002), Borsuk et al. (2004), Bromley et al. (2005) and Rieman et al. (2001).

11.9   CONCLUSIONS AND FUTURE DIRECTIONS

This chapter has demonstrated the very broad range of modelling approaches available for considering issues of Integrated Water Resources Management, from a variety of disciplinary and interdiscplinary perspectives. While a single universal classification system for models across all disciplines is difficult, it is possible to classify most models by several key characteristics: treatment of space, treatment of time, whether the model is process-based or data based, and whether the model is agent-based or averaged. This classification system is useful for generalising many of the issues in model development and for allowing the lessons from model development in one discipline to spread to other disciplines and fields.

Currently model development tends to be specialised within disciplines, often limiting the spread of lessons and knowledge from one model building domain to another. Fortunately the advent of integrated modelling tends to mean there is now more communication between modellers from different disciplines, allowing for lessons to be passed between modellers. However this communication of results, approaches and lessons between modellers from different disciplines could be improved. In particular many disciplinary modelling experts are isolated within their disciplinary field and do not communicate widely with modellers outside this field. In order for model practice to be improved and for better integrated models to be developed the discipline of modelling needs to be developed. This discipline needs to inform model building practice in terms of protocols for model development and reporting, and could advise modellers on general issues such as issues of scale and disaggregation of spatial units. In addition general advances in the field of modelling could be made available to modellers from a broader group of disciplinary backgrounds, increasing the robustness and defendiblity of modelling efforts.

Modelling software to aid environmental management should allow integration of sub-models, simple presentation of results and effective decision support. All too often this has been interpreted as meaning that we need modelling and DSS software frameworks which are elaborate enough to allow for a very wide range of systems, problems and people. Our contention is that the opposite is much nearer the truth: we need software that is no more elaborate than is required by the specific questions being put about a specific system and no more elaborate than justified by the data, and hence quite specific to the application. The more integrated the model, the more likely is it to need rigorous simplification to keep it manageable and testable. If it is to be properly tested, its assumptions and structure will also be heavily conditioned by the methods available to test it. Moreover, its interface with its users should, as far as possible, be designed with their cooperation, and will therefore also vary greatly from case to case. This argument is not to be taken as saying that generality is unachievable; rather we suggest that generality should reside in the methodology (i.e. the rules of good practice) in widely applicable technical tools, and not in a 'one size fits all' software vehicle.

We need to accelerate our development and use of integration methods and applications. The potential for development of new integration methods is enormous. While we need more vision for what these would look like, much of that will come from lessons learnt in practical applications and from sharing experiences through a revitalised league of modellers. There is no substitute for a large base of shared experience; at present, some lessons can be drawn from the small number of integrated assessments undertaken by any one group, but it is arguable that this is not enough to constitute an emerging discipline.

Overall model development should be problem focused and should be tailored to solving real-world problems in an effective manner. Models should be no more complex than necessary to adequately resolve issues, or to identify important trade-offs. We should also focus on testing models more heavily to ensure their components represent meaningful and necessary interactions. Finally we should encourage honest and open reporting of model results, including model failures as well as model successes to ensure past mistakes are not repeated or, even more importantly, that poor model practice is not embedded in our science.

REFERENCES

Abbott, M.B., J.C. Bathurst, J.A. Cunge, P.E. O'Connell and J. Rasmussen (1986), 'An introduction to the European Hydrological System – Système Hydrologique Européen, 'SHE'. 1. History and philosophy of a physically-based, distributed modelling system', *Journal of Hydrology*, **87**, 45–59.

Adams, R., S.M. Dunn, R. Lunn, R. Mackay and J.R. O'Callaghan (1995), 'Assessing the performance of the NELUP hydrological models for river basin planning', *Journal of Environmental Planning and Management*, **38**(1), 53–76.

Ames, D. and B. Neilson (2001), 'A Bayesian decision network engine for internet-based stakeholder decision-making', in G. Shelke, *Bridging the Gap: Meeting the World's Water and Environmental Resources Challenges*, Orlando, FL: American Society of Civil Engineers (ASCE).

Bacon, P.J., J.D. Cain and D.C. Howard (2002), 'Belief network models of land manager decisions and land use change', *Journal of Environmental Management*, **65**, 1–23.

Barreteau, O. and F. Bousquet (2001), 'From a conceptual model to its artefacts: building experiments using the SHADOC model' in Proceedings of the International Congress on Modelling and Simulation (MODSIM2001), Canberra, Australia, 1123–1128.

Beck, M. B. (1987), 'Water quality modelling: a review of uncertainty', *Water Resources Research*, **23**(8), 1393–1442.

Beck, M.B., A.J. Jakeman and M.J. McAleer (1995), 'Constuction and evaluation of models of environmental systems', in M.B. Beck and M.J. McAleer (eds), *Modelling Change in Environmental Systems*, England: John Wiley and Sons, pp. 3–35.

Becu, N., P. Perez, A. Walker and O. Barreteau (2001), 'Catchscape: An integrated multi-agent model for simulating water management at the catchment scale, a Northern Thailand case study', in *Proceedings of the International Congress on Modelling and Simulation (MODSIM2001), Canberra, Australia*, 1141–1146.

Belcher, K.W., M.M. Boehm and M.E. Fulton (2004), 'Agroecosystem sustainability: a system simulation model approach', *Agricultural Systems*, **79**(2), 225–241.

Bennett, J.W. and M.D. Morrison (2001), 'Estimating the environmental values of new South Wales rivers', Report No. 2, Asia-Pacific School of Economics and Governance, Canberra: The Australian National University, downloadable at: http://ncdsnet.anu.edu.au/pdf/jbennett/envnsw01.pdf (last access: May 2005).

Berbel, J. and J.A. Gómez-Limón (2000), 'The impact of water-pricing policy in Spain: an analysis of three irrigated areas', *Agricultural Water Management*, **43**, 219–238.

Biggs, S. (1987), *Proposed methodology for analysing farmer participation in the ISNAR OFCOR study*, London: Overseas Development Institute.

Black, J. (1997), 'A dictionary of economics', *Oxford Reference Online*, Oxford: Oxford University Press.

Blasco, F. and A. Weill (eds) (1999), *Advances in Environmental and Ecological Modelling*, Amsterdam, London, New York, Oxford, Paris, Shannon, Tokyo: Elsevier Health Sciences, 230 pp.

Bloschl, G. and M. Sivapalan (1995), 'Scale issues in hydrological modelling', in J.D. Kalma and M. Sivapalan (eds), *Scale Issues in Hydrological Modelling*, England: John Wiley and Sons, pp. 9–48.

Borsuk, M., R. Clemen, L. Maguire and K. Reckhow (2001), 'Stakeholder values and scientific modelling in the Neuse river watershed', *Group Decision and Negotiation*, **10**, 355–373.

Borsuk, M.E., C.A. Stow and K.H. Reckhow (2004), 'A Bayesian network of eutrophication models for synthesis, prediction and uncertainty analysis', *Ecological Modelling*, **173**, 219–239.

Bousquet, F. and C. Le Page (2004), 'Multi-agent simulations and ecosystem management: a review', *Ecological Modelling*, **176**(3–4), 313–332.

Bromley, J., N.A. Jackson, O.J. Clymer, A.M. Giacomello and F.V. Jensen (2005), 'The use of Hugin to develop Bayesian networks as an aid to integrated water resource planning', *Environmental Modelling and Software*, **20**(2), 231–242.

Carrer, S. and S. Opitz (1999), 'Trophic network model of a shallow water area in the northern part of the Lagoon of Venice', *Ecological Modelling*, **124**, 193–219.

Charniak, E. (1991), 'Bayesian networks without tears', *Artificial Intelligence Magazine*, **12**(4), 50–63.

Chowdary, V.M., N.H. Rao and P.B.S. Sarma (2005), 'GIS-based decision support system for groundwater assessment in large irrigation project areas', *Agricultural Water Management*, **75**(3), 194–225.

Christensen, V. and D. Pauly (1992), 'ECOPATH II – a software system for balancing steady state ecosystem models and calculating network characteristics', *Ecological Modelling*, **61**, 169–186.

Croke, B.F. and A.J. Jakeman (2001), 'Predictions in catchment hydrology: an Australian perspective', *Marine Freshwater Research*, **52**, 65–79.

Dunn, S.M., R. Mackay, R. Adams and D.R. Oglethorpe (1996), 'The hydrological component of the NELUP decision-support system: An appraisal', *Journal of Hydrology*, **177**(3–4), 213–235.

Evans, E.M., D.R. Lee, R.N. Boisvert, B. Arce, T. A. Steenhuis, M. Prano and S.V. Poats (2003), 'Achieving efficiency and equity in irrigation management: an optimization model of the El Angel watershed, Carchi, Ecuador', *Agricultural Systems*, **77**, 1–22.

Ewing, S.A., R.B. Grayson and R.M. Argent (1997), 'Research Integration in ICM: Review and Discussion Document', 1/97.

Fischer, G. and L. Sun (2001), 'Model based analysis of future land-use development in China', *Agriculture, Ecosystems and Environment*, **85**, 163–176.

Geurts, J.L.A. and C. Joldersma (2001), 'Methodology for participatory policy analysis', *European Journal of Operational Research*, **128**, 300–310.

Gillman, M. and R. Hails (1997), *An Introduction to Ecological Modelling: Putting Practice into Theory. Methods in Ecology*, Oxford, Malden: Blackwell Science Inc, pp. 216.

Grayson, R., R. Argent and A. Western, (1999), 'Scoping Study for the Implementation of Water Quality Management Frameworks', *Final Report*, CEAH Report 2/99, May 1999, University of Melbourne.

Greiner, R. (1998), 'Catchment management for dryland salinity control: model analysis for the Liverpool Plains in New South Wales', *Agricultural Systems*, **56**(2), 225–251.

Greiner, R. (1999), 'An integrated modelling system for investigating the benefits of catchment management', *Environment International*, **25**(6/7), 725–734.

Hall, N., D. Poulter and R. Curtotti (1994), 'ABARE model of irrigation farming in the Southern Murray Darling Basin', 94.4, Canberra: ABARE.

Hannon, B. and M. Ruth (1997), *Modelling Dynamic Biological Systems,* New York, Berlin, Heidelberg: Springer-Verlag, pp. 399.

Hare, M.P. and P. Deadman (2004), 'Further towards a taxonomy of agent-based simulation models in environmental management', *Mathematics and Computers in Simulation Journal*, **64**, 25–40.

Heckerman, D., Mamdani, A. and M.P. Wellman (1995), 'Real world applications of Bayesian networks', *Communications of the ACM* (Association for Computing Machinery), **38**(3), 24–26.

Hood, L. (1998), 'Agent Based Modelling', Greenhouse Beyond Kyoto – Conference Day 2: Tools for an Uncertain World, 31 March–1 April 1998, Bureau of Rural Sciences, Canberra Australia, downloadable at: http://affashop.gov.au/product.asp?prodid=13231 (last access: May 2005).

IES (2003), 'The Institute of Ecosystem Studies (IES) defintion of Ecology', downloadable at http://www.ecostudies.org/definition_ecology.html (last access: May 2005).

Jakeman, A.J. and G.M. Hornberger (1993), 'How much complexity is warranted in a rainfall-runoff model?', *Water Resources Research*, **29**(8), 2637–2649.

Jensen, F.V. (1996), *An Introduction to Bayesian Networks*, London: UCL Press, pp. 178.

Jørgensen, S.E. and G. Bendoricchio (2001), *Fundamentals of Ecological Modelling*, Amsterdam, London, New York, Oxford, Paris, Shannon, Tokyo: Elsevier, 530 pp.

Köbrich, C., T. Rehman and M.Khan (2003), 'Typification of farming systems for constructing presentative farm models: two illustrattions of the application of multi-variate analyses in Chile and Pakistan', *Agricultural Systems*, **76**, 141–157.

Kuikka, S. and O. Varis (1997), 'Uncertainties of climatic change impacts in Finnish watersheds: a Bayesian network analysis of expert knowledge', *Boreal Environment Research*, **2**, 109–128.

Lee, D.J. and R.E. Howitt (1996), 'Modeling regional agricultural production and salinity control alternatives for water quality policy analysis', *American Journal of Agricultural Economics*, **78**, 41–53.

Leistritz, F.L., J.A. Leitch and D.A. Bangsund (2002), 'Regional economic impacts of water management alternatives: the case of Devils Lake, North Dakota, USA', *Journal of Environmental Management*, **66**, 465–473.

Letcher, R.A., A.J. Jakeman and B.F.W. Croke (2004), 'Model development for integrated assessment of water allocation options', *Water Resources Research*, **40**, W05502.

Lui, G. and L. Yao (1995), 'A study of an intelligent operation decision support system for a large-scale water resources system for inter-basin water transfer', *IAHS Publication*, **231** (Modelling and Management of Sustainable Bain-scale Water Resource Systems), 417–426.

Mackay, D. (1991), *Multimedia Environmental Models. The Fugacity Approach*, Boca raton, Ann Arbor, London and Tokyo: Lewis Publishers, pp. 257.

Martin, A. and J. Sherington (1997), 'Participatory research methods – implementation, effectiveness and institutional context', *Agricultural Systems*, **55**(2), 195–216.

McKinney, D.C., X. Cai, M.W. Rosegrant, C. Ringler and C.A. Scott (1999), *Modeling water resources management at the basin level: Review and future directions*, Colombo, Sri Lanka: International Water Management Institute.

Merritt, W.S., R.A. Letcher and A.J. Jakeman (2003), 'A review of erosion and sediment transport models', *Environmental Modelling and Software*, **18**, 761–799.

Merritt, W.S., B.F. Croke, A.J. Jakeman, R.A. Letcher and P. Perez (2004), 'A biophysical toolbox for assessment and management of land and water resources in rural catchments in Northern Thailand', *Ecological Modelling*, **171**, 279–300.

Möller, D. and F. Kuhlmann (1999), 'ProLand: A new approach to generate and evaluate land use options', in *Proceedings of IX European Congress of Agricultural Economists*, Warsaw, Poland.

Morison, J. and Zorzetto, A. (1995). 'The economic impact of irrigated agriculture in the Namoi Valley region', Department of Land and Water Conservation, Water Resources, September 1995.

Morrison, M.D., R.K. Blamey, J.W. Bennett and J.J. Louviere (1996), 'A comparison of stated preference techniques for estimating environmental values', *Research Report*, **1**, Canberra: The University of New South Wales.

Moxey, A., B. White and J. O'Callaghan (1995), 'The economic component of NELUP', *Journal of Environmental Planning and Management*, **38**(1), 21–33.

Norton, B.G. (1996), 'Integration or reduction: two approaches to environmental values', in A. Light and E. Katz (eds), *Environmental Pragmatism*, London: Routledge, pp. 105–138.

NRCS (1986), 'TR-55: Urban hydrology for small watersheds', *Technical Release*, **55**, June 1986, US: Natural Resources Conservation Service, Conservation Engineering Division.

Oglethorpe, D. and J. O'Callaghan (1995), 'Farm-level Economic Modelling within a River Catchment Decision Support System', *Journal of Environmental Planning and Management*, **38**(1), 93–106.

O'Callaghan, J. (1995), 'NELUP: An Introduction', *Journal of Environmental Planning and Management*, **38**(1), 5–20.

O'Loughlin, E.M. (1986), 'Prediction of surface saturation zones in natural catchments by topographic analysis', *Water Resources Research*, **22**(5), 794–804.

Omernik, J.M. and G.E. Griffith (1991), 'Ecological regions versus hydrological units: frameworks for managing water quality', *Journal of Soil and Water Conservation*, **46**, 334–340.

Park, J. and R.A.F. Seaton (1996), 'Integrative research and sustainable agriculture', *Agricultural Systems*, **50**, 81–100.

Pretty, J.N. (1995), 'Participatory learning for sustainable agriculture', *World Development*, **23**(8), 1247–1263.

Renwick, M., R. Green and C. McCorkie (1998), 'Measuring the price responsiveness of residential water demand in California's urban areas', Report prepared for California Department of Water Resources.

Ringler, C. (2001), 'Optimal water allocation in the Mekong River Basin', **38**, Bon: Centre for Development Research, University of Bonn.

Rosegrant, M.W., C. Ringler, D.C. McKinney, X. Cai, A. Keller and G. Donoso (2000), 'Integrated economic-hydrologic water modeling at the basin scale: the Maipo river basin', *Agricultural Economics*, **24**, 33–46.

Rushton, S.P., A.J. Cherill, K. Tucker and J.R. O'Callaghan (1995), 'The ecological modelling system of NELUP', *Journal of Environmental Planning and Management*, **38**(1), 107–116.

Schlizzi, S.G.M. and F. Boulier (1997), '"Why do farmers do it?" Validating whole-farm models', *Agricultural Systems*, **54**(4), 477–499.

Seyfried, M.S. and B.P. Wilcox (1995), 'Scale and the nature of spatial variability: field examples having implications for hydrologic modeling', *Water Resources Research*, **31**(1), 173–184.

Simons, M., G. Podger and R. Cooke (1996), 'IQQM – A hydrologic model for water resource and salinity management', *Environmental Software*, **11**(1–3), 185–192.

Sui, D.Z. and R.C. Maggio (1999), 'Integrating GIS with hydrological modeling: practices, problems, prospects', *Computers, Environment, Urban Systems*, **23**, 33–51.

Syme, G.J., J.E. Butterworth and B.E. Nancarrow (1994), 'National Whole Catchment Management: A Review and Analysis of Processes', 1/94, LWRRDC, Canberra.

Taylor, J.E., and I. Adelman (2003), 'Agricultural household models: genesis, evolution, and extensions', *Review of Economics of the Household*, **1**, 33–58.

van der Veen, A. and H.S. Otter (2001), 'Land use changes in regional economic theory', *Environmental Modelling and Assessment*, **6**, 145–150.

Varis, O. (1998), 'A belief network approach to optimisation and parameter estimation: Application to resource and environmental management', *Artificial Intelligence Magazine*, **101**(1–2), 135–163.

Vatn, A., L.R. Bakken, H. Lundeby, E. Romstad, P.K. Rorstad, A. Vold and P. Botteweg (1997), 'Regulating nonpoint-source pollution from agriculture: An integrated modelling analysis', *European Review of Agricultural Economics*, **24**(2), 207–229.

Villa, F. and R. Costanza (2000), 'Design of multi-paradigm integrating modelling tools for ecological research', *Environmental Modelling and Software*, **15**, 169–177.

Volterra, V. (1926), 'Fluctuations in the abundance of a species considered mathematically', *Nature*, **188**, 558–560.

Weatherford, G.D. (1990), 'From Basin to "Hydrocommons": Integrated Water Management Without Regional Governance', *Natural Resources Law Centre Western Water Policy Project Discussion Series*, Boulder: University of Colorado.

Weber, A., N. Fohrer and D. Moller (2001), 'Long-term land use changes in a mesoscale watershed due to socioeconomic factors – effects on landscape structure and functions', *Ecological Modelling*, **140**, 125–140.

Wheater, H., A.J. Jakeman and K. Beven (1993), 'Progress and Directions in Rainfall-Runoff Modelling', in A.J. Jakeman, M. Beck and M. McAleer (eds), *Modelling Change in Environmental Systems*, England: John Wiley and Sons, pp. 101–132.

Whitten, S.M. and J.W. Bennett (2001), 'Non-market values of wetlands: A choice modelling study of wetlands in the Upper South East of South Australia and the Murrumbidgee River floodplain in New South Wales', *Research Report*, **8**, Canberra: The University of New South Wales.

12. Software and Software Systems: Platforms and Issues for IWRM Problems

Andrea E. Rizzoli and Robert M. Argent

12.1 INTRODUCTION

Traditional water resource management has often required the support of software systems for various activities. In these, mathematical models were used to analyse physical processes such as stream-flow routing, rainfall-runoff processes, and crop production simulations. The results of these studies were fed to the decision makers, e.g. the catchment management authority, which decreed and ruled how water should be allocated among users. Analysis of the social and economical impacts of these management decisions was rare, generally only occurring for large-scale projects, such as the building of a new dam, rather than for operational management.

Previous chapters have shown how Integrated Water Resource Management (IWRM) calls for new approaches in modelling: an approach that encompasses integration of models with GIS (Chapter 9), integration between modelling and management through scenarios (Chapter 10), and integration of different forms of knowledge in the modelling process (Chapter 11). The practice of IWRM means that the interrelationships and the interdependencies of the different systems (economic, hydrologic, ecological, social, agricultural) increase and this makes modelling considerably harder than before. Cutting away the unnecessary parts of the model is a well-assessed and useful practice, which helps in managing the complexity of a model. For instance, to compute the runoff flow response in a river section, land use classes can be aggregated to approximate the percentage surface runoff directly contributing to the result. This is possible since the modelling objective is clear, the model is largely mechanistic and it is possible to neglect unnecessary details, thanks to reasonable approximations. Integrative modellers (a new breed of modellers created by the needs of IWRM) often cannot do this. They are faced with problems requiring the multi-objective analysis approaches of Chapter 5, involving different modelling domains and complex interrelations, often with positive and negative feedbacks. An integrated model never returns the 'right' answer, being more generally used in scenario-based approaches to management (Chapter 10).

Software systems play a fundamental role in all of this, since they must provide the medium to support the modelling of IWRM processes. A software system is not simply the implementation of a mathematical model; it must also support decision making and collaborative workflow management. Software systems must then evolve along with the modellers' needs and they must increase in flexibility, ability to integrate across disciplines, and possibility to reconfigure and reuse existing code and knowledge.

This chapter explores the roles of software systems in providing support to IWRM, particularly in the integration of software components. It starts with a discussion of the roles of software systems in IWRM, and then introduces the concept of software components as smaller and more flexible software units that are needed to fulfil those roles. Finally, a few application development systems for integrated water management are reviewed.

12.2   THE ROLE OF SOFTWARE AND SOFTWARE SYSTEMS

In IWRM there is a spectrum of activity that can take place, including planning, design, monitoring, data warehousing, operation, policy development and decision support. Many of these aspects have been discussed in previous chapters, and in almost all cases the use of software has been identified as an integral part of the process. In this, software refers to computerised tools such as spreadsheets, databases, systems for developing models, and the models themselves. Essentially, software is pervasive in IWRM, and fulfils a number of roles. The primary role of interest to many researchers, managers and policy makers, is in the form of models – algorithmic representations of system behaviour. Models are used in all of the design, assessment and operation aspects of IWRM, and Chapter 11 has provided detail of the types of models that are applied in areas of IWRM.

To explore the broader roles of software in IWRM, and to identify the issues related to the use of software systems, it is useful to consider an example, such as restoration of a section of river, or establishment of a new housing development on the edge of a large city. This type of activity encompasses planning, design, construction, monitoring, data management, operational policy and implementation.

In planning, software is used for both conceptual and concrete processes. On the conceptual side, software provides the capability to explore alternative options for design, layout and installation, such as comparing alternative water use strategies in a new housing development, and supporting decision making on these alternatives. In this kind of work, as noted previously, different approaches and mathematical tools are available, but to ensure that the decision process is consistent, transparent and repeatable, a methodology must be rigorously adopted.

In design, software fulfils roles that include costing and sizing of components, such as water supply, roads and drains, as well as, again, supporting comparison of alternative technologies and implementation options.

In construction, where it is part of the IWRM activity, software is used for planning and operation, but can also extend to day-to-day processes of industry, such as project management, timing, scheduling, supply and logistics.

Before, during and after any focussed IWRM activity, such as a river restoration or housing development, there is a role for software in monitoring the system. Monitoring of environmental variables is used for emergency warning (e.g. real-time flood forecasting), baseline setting, compliance reporting, assessment of effects and impacts, and to record values of variables of interest to system managers. A range of software activities are also currently used in IWRM to gather, store and make readily available the host of environmental data that are gathered. An example of this is the recent increase in environmental data warehouses accessible via the Internet and, as part of this, the provision of environmental information metadata. In using these warehouses and metadata, researchers, planners and managers can readily obtain either the data relevant to their problem situation, or a greater knowledge of what data are available, and where they can be obtained. This is useful in many IWRM situations where relevant data may not be available from traditional sources, such as government institutions, but has to be gathered from various academic and one-off monitoring studies.

A key process in system monitoring is that of the measurement and assessment of indicators. In IWRM, the strategic goals and the concerns of stakeholders are translated into operational criteria, and these are in turn transformed into physical and socioeconomic indicators. For example, the indicators may evaluate the performance of water supply to civil, agricultural and industrial users (including hydro-power production), compliance to river water quality standards and flood control. The indicators are of considerable use in modelling, as they are often used to simplify the link between modelling and management. Indicators, such as habitat area for a given species, tend to be more robust and more readily calculated than individual outputs of system components, such as the population of a given species in a river reach.

Operational aspects of IWRM that use software include realtime forecasting, supply and demand monitoring and control, operation of infrastructure, system evaluation and policy development. In evaluation of system performance, the system behaviour is first simulated to estimate values of relevant system indicators under alternative management policies. System monitoring is then used to assess the performance of the system and to allow managers the opportunity to adjust operation, and, sometimes, to also adjust the models of system behaviour.

Thus there exists a range of roles for software in IWRM. For much of this range, there is a reasonably standard set of tools and software applications. However, the modelling portion of IWRM software has been, and continues to be, rapidly developing. The use of new software development theories and operational paradigms is steadily growing, and many tools are now available for construction of models. These range from programming tools to application development systems. Programming tools support coding and compilation of models. Application development systems, while supporting coding and compilation, provide the broader range of features required to build models of complex system behaviour, such as sub-model construction, linking of sub-models, simulation support, optimisation and multi-criteria analysis tools and GIS routines. Application development systems can also support the integration of these functions into models of IWRM system behaviour, and provide features for design, construction, testing, calibration and validation of different system models, in line with the model development process given in Chapter 9. The following sections provide an overview of the software engineering approaches that have recently come to the fore in the area of model development, management and use in IWRM.

12.3 SOFTWARE FOR INTEGRATED WATER RESOURCE MANAGEMENT

Previous sections have shown how software for IWRM must cover many roles, including planning, design, monitoring, operation, policy development and decision support. Traditionally, each role has been fulfilled by a dedicated piece of software. Such software tends to be monolithic – with one single tool for one job, although they do sometimes support water management at an integrated level, accounting for the multiple factors that affect water management.

In the near future, it will be less common to see software performing all the tasks required to fulfil one of these roles, since this is a bad design choice in terms of software reusability. Software components – small and flexible modules of software – can often be generic enough to provide functions that are common and shared among many tasks and roles. Despite the modularity and flexibility of software components, monolithic software systems are still common. They are the side-effect of the integration of legacy systems in modern applications.

12.3.1 Monolithic Software

To better understand why monolithic software is still very popular, it is beneficial to consider MODFLOW (McDonald and Harbaugh, 1988), a well-known groundwater flow model. In the original MODFLOW implementation, the authors wanted to provide users with a model to solve a contaminant transport problem. MODFLOW can be used for scenario evaluation and to assess the impact of different remediation strategies.

MODFLOW has been seen as a key component for use in water management studies, but it was not designed with integration in mind, and the use of MODFLOW as a software component within an IWRM problem is not a straightforward activity. Haagsma and Johannes (1994) presented this problem in general terms, while an example is found in Havnø et al. (2002), where data exchange with MODFLOW within an IWRM problem is made via text data files. The example of MODFLOW in Chapter 9 shows integration through manual exchange of data files. A similar experience is described by Nalbantis et al. (2002), who exploit the high modelling quality of MODFLOW to test water management policies that have been obtained using a simpler model approximation of the groundwater system.

In wishing to apply MODFLOW to IWRM problems the software designers are confronted with a hard choice; either spend a considerable effort in adapting MODFLOW to make its resources available, or re-implement its functions in a truly modular and component-based software form. For small applications, the first choice is often the less expensive, and it also allows access to pre-packaged science that has been validated by hundreds (if not thousands) of users. On the other hand, when planning an investment over a longer period, reusable components are generally preferred for environmental applications.

The reader should also not think that all monolithic software is inherently badly designed. First of all they have been designed with the aim of producing software applications, not components, and secondly their internal software architecture sometimes reflects modern advances in fields such as software engineering and decision support systems. They include internal components such as database management systems (often enhanced by geographic data management features); a set of models and related tools such as calibration routines and numerical integration schemes; visualisation, user interaction and reporting modules. Their primary limitation is the inability to export their internal components to the increasingly connected and integrated outside world.

12.3.2   The Decomposition of Software into Components

To design for the future, attention must turn to software components. Recent developments open the way to a more modular and flexible approach to software coding. Two examples are Sun Microsystems J2EE and Microsoft .NET software technologies. They aim to provide the developer with a technology enabling the creation of applications that are secure, robust and inter-operable and they are centred on the concept of software components.

Szyperski et al. (2002) define a software component to be a unit of composition with contextually specified interfaces and explicit context dependencies only. A software component can be deployed independently and is subject to third-party composition. In other words, it is a piece of software, which allows the user to implement a set of functions to achieve one or more tasks. The functions are published via an application programming interface (API), which is machine readable. Software components can be embedded into larger components, which use the functions provided by the sub-components. Software components can be encapsulated in graphical user interfaces (GUI) to make their functions more available to the user.

Software for IWRM can therefore be decomposed into components and objects, where components operate and transform objects. Objects are software structures packaging data and functionality together, but they differentiate from components since their state is made accessible. Decomposition is based on the functions required to perform the software roles discussed previously.

It is noted that execution of a given role can be mapped to a sequence of steps. As an example, in the case of policy assessment and development for IWRM they are (Soncini-Sessa et al., 2002; Chapter 4):

1. Expression of stakeholder preferences and goals;
2. Identification of the indicators used to assess movement towards goals;
3. Development of a conceptual framework, encompassing:
   - objective functions
   - decision problems
   - conceptual model formulation;
4. Analysis, including formulation of detailed models and management policies;
5. Assessment of system performance under a range of scenarios.

In Figure 12.1, the policy-making process in IWRM is represented. Stakeholder preferences and goals (e.g. better water quality) are transformed into indicators (e.g. tonnes of nitrogen) by means of an 'assembly' operation. In some cases, this operation can be assisted by a software component, which facilitates the process of indicator definition. Such a component should provide data management functions and also knowledge management functions, to model the process of indicator construction from informal stakeholder preferences and goals.

In establishing a conceptual framework for the problem, indicators are transformed into objective functions, which, in turn, are combined, with a (conceptual) model of the system, into a decision problem. This approach has been developed in the field of Systems Analysis, as shown by ReVelle et al. (1997), where a decision problem is composed of a set of objectives and a set

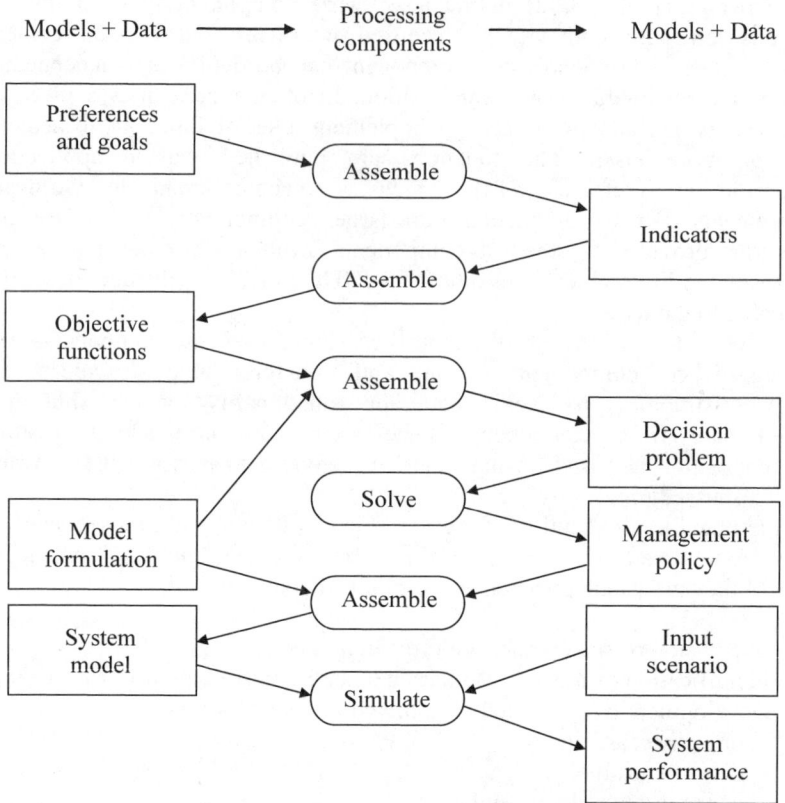

*Figure 12.1   A sequence of transformations generates catchment
           management policies and evaluates their performances*

of constraints. Note that the model of the real world system under study is
one of the problem constraints. Formulation of a system model encompasses
the steps outlined in Chapter 9, including consideration of structure, inputs,
sensitivity assessment and validation. The specification of a decision problem
can be performed using various software components, since different
functions are required: data management, model management, and statistical
processes for model calibration and validation. The union of these
components can constitute an application development system. The solution
of a decision problem returns a management policy. Software components
providing optimisation functions are required to compute the solution.
Finally, the management policy is applied to a formulated model to provide a
tailored model of system behaviour. This system model is used to assess
system performance under a range of alternative input scenarios. A
component providing simulation functions is required during this phase.

12.4 CLASSIFICATION OF MODERN SOFTWARE COMPONENTS

The example of policy development in IWRM served the purpose of introducing different software components in action. Now, the different types of components that may be required are classified into categories:

- Data storage and manipulation components;
- Knowledge representation components;
- Modelling components;
- Operational components;
- User interface components.

Data, knowledge and models are created using the components in the first three classes, which are objects, while operational components, such as simulators, inference engines and optimisation algorithms, transform the objects into new or modified objects, according to the scheme of Figure 12.2.

The following describes the main features of these classes and introduces some examples.

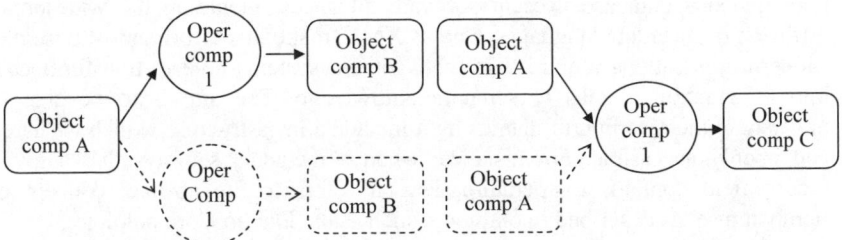

Figure 12.2   Alternative operational components can be applied to the same object (A); alternative versions of an object are transformed by the same operational component (B)

12.4.1   Data Storage and Manipulation Components

At the lowest level in an imaginary hierarchy of software components for IWRM are the data storage components. Yet, they play a fundamental role, since they provide the software developer with all the tools required to retrieve, edit, process and analyse environmental data. These components are readily available as commercial packages. For instance, a useful set of components is provided by the consortium promoting HDF, the Hierarchical Data Format. HDF is a physical file format for storing scientific data. HDF also provides a high-level API to access a collection of utilities and applications for manipulating, viewing and analysing data in the HDF format.

Other software components, such as ESRI MapObjects, are specialised for geographical information processing.

Not all data storage and management problems have yet been solved, and it is worthwhile to mention data harmonisation and data interoperability as one of the most pressing problems faced by both model developers and model users. The wide variety of available data formats results in developers tightly connecting database components, where the potential for reuse is somewhat limited. It is therefore noteworthy to mention two initiatives, INSPIRE and MURMUR. The former, the Infrastructure for Spatial Information in Europe, is a recent initiative launched by the European Commission, which aims at making quality geographic information readily available. The latter, the MurMur project, is aimed at defining a new approach for database description and manipulation that would fully support storage and definition of multiple perspectives of the same information, in multi-scale databases.

12.4.2   Knowledge Representation Components

It was noted earlier that IWRM software often relies on carefully designed datasets, obtained by rigorous fusing of different data sources into a homogeneous database. Recent software advances, including the widespread diffusion of metadata languages such as XML, make this effort almost obsolete. Modern applications require data management systems able to transform data into information, thanks to semantic knowledge. The aim is to be able to understand the meaning of data using a metadata infrastructure, which is shared and openly accessible. For instance, when a metadata set says that a given record field contains temperature data, it refers to the abstract concept of 'temperature' as described in ontology, such as the Dublin Core ontology.

In the future there should eventually be a convergence of data and knowledge, since data items will acquire a meaning, becoming 'facts', and making inferences on these facts will allow extension of the knowledge base. Research efforts in this direction are ongoing, as testified by the Ontoknowledge, the Ontoweb and the Protégé research projects.

12.4.3   Modelling Components

A key class is represented by software components for modelling IWRM systems. In this context, modelling is defined as the set of operations that creates and edits models, and that stores and retrieves models from permanent storage.

Model definition
Model creation can be supported at various levels, from concept definition to implementation. Chapter 11 reported a number of possible modelling types

that can be employed in IWRM, and detailed high-level approaches to model integration. Here, the focus is on supporting the implementation of models in machine executable format, using a range of possible modelling formalisms. The current modelling languages available on the market reflect this situation. Each modelling language is versed in a limited number of formalisms, often not more than two. Examples include Matlab and ACSL for continuous systems, and Simscript for discrete event systems.

A problem of incompatibility arises when seeking to integrate models across platforms, across languages and across formalisms. For example, given model A, designed with tool X, and model B, designed with tool Y, how can the output of model A be linked with the input of model B? Even assuming that the same operating environment (such as .NET or J2EE) is being used, model drivers still need to be created to route communications. Model reusability would be limited. Similar problems are to be faced when trying to apply an optimisation tool to a model: there is an interface specification problem. This problem is commonly solved by avoidance – model developers avoid the problem by either creating or repackaging models in ways that ensure cross-model compatibility, or develop wrappers or interfaces that provide the required interpretation or exchange features. Chapter 11 has described the model integration methods that can be employed under these conditions.

A declarative approach to modelling offers a solution to the incompatibilities that arise when working across platforms, languages and formalisms. Declarative modelling uses a powerful model representation language, which is independent of the model implementation and of the programming language used to implement the executable code. This approach has been initiated by Geoffrion's 'structured modelling' (Geoffrion, 1987) and has been developed in the field of management science, from Muhanna's model description language (1994) to successful commercial applications such as the General Algebraic Modelling System (GAMS, Brooke et al., 1998), through component-based model management (Kottemann and Dolk, 1992; Dolk and Kottemann, 1993). In environmental modelling the work of Muetzelfeldt and Massheder (2003), which originates from the Prolog model of an ecological system, as described by Muetzelfeldt et al. (1989), is acknowledged.

In the conventional procedural approach, a model is implemented as a series of assignments and instructions to be executed by the computer. Flow-control structures (e.g. if, then, while) and the model equations, expressed as assignment instructions, are listed in the same file. This is not surprising, but consider a simple program to compute the average of a series of numbers. In this it would be surprising to find the data (i.e. the numbers being averaged) listed as constants in the source program file rather than being sourced externally. This example, originally presented by Muetzelfeldt (2004), suggests the desirability of applying a numerical integration routine on another set of equations in the same way that an averaging routine would be applied to another set of data.

Thus, in the declarative approach, a model is represented as a series of facts. Imperative statements and flow control instructions are stripped away from the declarations and it is then up to the model compiler to translate the model specification into machine executable code.

The advantage is that the declarative model specification is truly portable and can be automatically parsed by a machine. Interfacing two models can be automatically done. With the advent of the Semantic Web (Berners-Lee et al., 2001) it will be possible to declare model interfaces referring to shared ontologies, thus facilitating input data preparation and output data interpretation. Finally, processing components can be clearly separated from model specification, enabling different simulation algorithms to be applied to the same model.

Archiving and documenting models

A key element of a software system for IWRM is a model base. This is the place where models can be stored. An early example is provided by EcoBas (Hoch et al., 1998), a system for the documentation of mathematical descriptions of ecological processes. EcoBas provides a language that is an extension of XML, designed to represent models in a clear and communicable manner, according to declarative modelling principles.

Another example of a system for accessing archived models is the Ecosystem Services Database (Villa et al., 2002). It is a web-accessible knowledge base for quantifying the value of ecosystem services. It links a relational database for temporally and spatially explicit data, with dynamic simulation models and analysis algorithms.

Finally, the model base must be complemented by a documentation system, which can assist the modeller in managing all the aspects of documentation, from code comments through to recommendations on appropriate use of a component or multi-component model. Such a system, which is essential to good integrated modelling, must ensure that information is never repeated but rather drawn together from different sources to form appropriate documentation.

12.4.4   Operational Components

Data, knowledge and models are objects, which need to be put into action to produce new data, new knowledge and new models. In Figure 12.1, they appear in the first and last column. The operational components are the processes that apply to those objects. They are the engines of application development systems.

For example, a statistical analysis component can process a data set and extract new data, which are statistical indicators. A simulation algorithm can take some time series, feed them into a model, simulate their behaviour and return a new set of time series. An inference engine can examine facts stored in a knowledge base to infer new facts. Finally, an optimisation algorithm can use data and a model to generate new data that can guide operational or policy decisions in IWRM.

Traditionally models, data, simulations and optimisations were all packaged together and it was very difficult, if not impossible, to evaluate the results of simulation after having changed the model. The greatest freedom was to change some parameters, but not the structural definition of the model itself. Alternatively, the modeller could be interested in evaluating the impact of using different algorithms in the model. Figure 12.2 shows these two alternative situations. It is clear that the aim is to make operational components independent of object components.

There are different architectural solutions to enable the independence of operational components from objects. The three case studies reported in this chapter present the reader with various alternatives, but in all of these systems the interface between the object component and the operational component plays a key role. It is via the interface that component separability is achieved and for this reason it must be carefully designed. Where the interface of an object is specified by means of a metadata language, as described in the previous sections, operational components can automatically combine with objects. Providing operational components with a semantically rich description of their teleology (i.e. their usage and application) assists users in the decision-making process, and can guide and direct the workflow.

This approach, with some limitations, has been successfully applied in commercial products such as GAMS (Brooke et al., 1998) and AMPL (Fourer et al., 2002). In both these software packages, designed to solve various mathematical programming problems, solvers are independent of model formulations. This allows testing of various solution strategies and provision of a model library, as with GAMS.

12.4.5   User Interface Components

Operational components and objects interact in a workflow to provide different software roles, but the user also needs to interact with these components. User interface components could be seen as a subclass of operational components, since they process data to make it more available and understandable to the enduser.

There are many user interface components on the market, since their application is not limited to a particular domain. These components are past the research stage and well into maturity. As usual, the major players tend to get the biggest share of the market and Visual Basic and Java Beans are two of the best-known components to be used in the coding of a graphical user interface.

With these programmable graphical components, the programmer can design complex applications that provide an interface to all the phases where the user must interact with the application, such as data visualisation and model design. The Object Modelling System (Kralisch et al., 2004) is an example of how existing components can be reused to create the graphical user interface of a model design application.

12.5   DEVELOPING INTEGRATED WATER RESOURCE MANAGEMENT APPLICATIONS

Data, knowledge, model, operational and user components are often assembled in a tailored way for particular IWRM problems. In some cases, the model base and the database are large enough to give the user the impression of being able to model practically anything, see for instance the Lakemaker architecture (Del Furia et al., 1995). Such systems are often sufficient for decision makers since they bring the required computing power to their desktops, but other categories of users, who are good modellers but not software developers, are often frustrated in their efforts to access the power and resources provided by these tools.

To provide the capability to access and use the components that are available or required for IWRM, there is a clear need for application development systems. These systems not only support creation of the component parts for integrated models of system behaviour, but also allow system analysts to create their own workflow implementing a decision support system. The basic building blocks are the components discussed previously. Software component integration here plays a fundamental role as is shown when using tools such as Java 2 Enterprise Edition and Microsoft .NET.

Notable instances of application development systems, albeit with different ranges of functions, are TIME (Rahman et al., 2004), OpenMI (Gijsbers et al., 2002), the Object Modelling System (Kralisch et al., 2004), the Integrated Modelling Toolkit (Villa, 2001), ModCom (Hillyer et al., 2003), and TwoLe (Soncini-Sessa et al., 1999).

The remainder of this chapter focuses on three of these environments: TIME, OpenMI and TwoLe. The first two are relevant for their generic approach to modelling, the latter for being an environment for policy making and decision support, which displays several of the features described in the previous sections.

12.6   CASE STUDY: THE TIME MODELLING ENVIRONMENT

One initiative, which is producing an application development system for IWRM, is currently underway in Australia. The system is known as TIME

(The Invisible Modelling Environment), and is being constructed by the Cooperative Research Centre for Catchment Hydrology (CRCCH), a national multi-party research centre that spans research and industry in the areas of catchment hydrology and management. The CRCCH, established in 1994, is working to deliver to resource managers the capability to predict the impacts of land use and water management decisions at the whole-of-catchment scale. The method used for this delivery is a catchment modelling toolkit, within which the bulk of the outcomes of the Centre's research are delivered as software components that fit into an integrated toolkit. To achieve this aim, an application development system was required that supported construction of components arising from individual research projects, and also the combination of these components into larger models of system behaviour for use by catchment managers.

The experience of the CRCCH partners with application development systems started in the mid 1990s with construction of two systems, the Interactive Component Modelling System (ICMS – formerly Integrated Catchment Modelling System) and Tarsier.

The ICMS was originally constructed using the concepts of the Open Modelling Engine (OME) (Reed et al., 1999; Rizzoli et al., 1998), wherein a strong class-based structure supports linking and information transfer between different data, knowledge and model components in the form of domain objects. Active construction of the framework continued until the early 2000s. In the resulting application development system, a GUI provides relatively straightforward access to all stages of component construction, and for deploying models of system behaviour an extra GUI layer, termed the 'public user interface', is used to provide user-friendly access to the underlying objects.

The Tarsier application development system (Watson and Rahman, 2004; Watson et al., 1998) is constructed using the 'observer pattern' of software engineering design (Gamma et al., 1995), thereby providing strong support for data sharing and message transfer. Operationally, Tarsier works as a system that uses data, knowledge and model components, in the form of DLLs, to support rapid construction of models of system behaviour. These DLLs play the role of operational components referred to previously. Tarsier has an extensive library of components, which continues to expand in parallel with ongoing environmental applications using the system.

Together, experience with ICMS and Tarsier provided the background, and much of the core design strategy, for development of TIME. The concept in TIME is to provide a lightweight (almost 'invisible') model kernel upon which a broad range of data and model components can be layered. These components can range from hydrological components, such as rainfall-runoff tools, to support components that provide analysis, manipulation and visualisation functionality.

The basic high-level architecture of TIME is shown in Figure 12.3, where

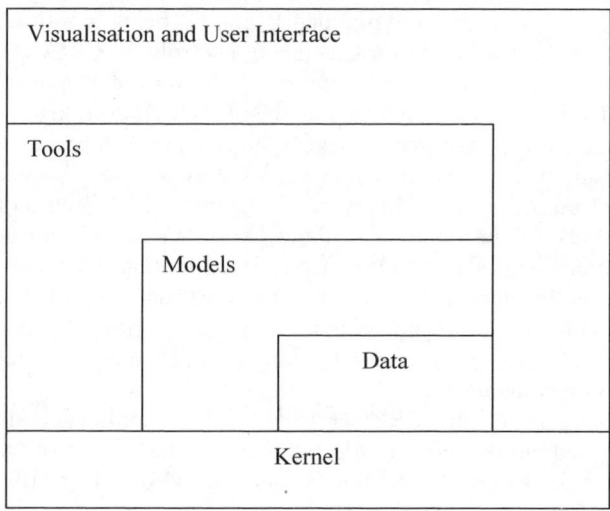

Figure 12.3   High-level architecture of TIME

the definitions for generic concepts, such as 'data' and 'model', are included in the Kernel. Definitions for common data types, such as 'time series' and 'raster' are positioned in the Data layer, while component hydrological models reside in the Models layer. The Tools layer contains the bulk of the operational components of TIME, such as model linking and auto-generation of model GUIs. The highest layer, Visualisation and User Interface, is to some degree a meta-layer, as it contains user interface components that use the functions provided by the lower layers (Rahman et al., 2004).

One of the key functional aspects of TIME is the pervasive use of metadata. TIME is built using the .NET environment, which in addition to providing a multi-language capability for component construction, also provides support for metadata-based model operation. In TIME this allows for the definition of a set of core metadata tags, at the kernel level, that are used by the TIME system to aid or control model operation. TIME uses metadata tags in variable classification (e.g. input or output), setting of numeric constraints on parameters (e.g. between 0 and 5) and in identifying variable aliases (e.g. ET, also known as evapotranspiration). Provision of the tags within software components allows the TIME system to use introspection to automatically utilise protocols for data type information and handling, such as data bounding and type matching between components supplying and receiving data. Automatic GUI generation for models is provided by TIME through analysis of model inputs, outputs, parameters and bounds, and generation of relevant visual controls.

Development of TIME, mainly through expansion of available components, is continuing through the period 2003–2006. The basic TIME Kernel has existed largely unchanged since 2001, with recent additions of extra metadata tags. The advantages of a stable Kernel are considerable, allowing developers within different organisations to work largely independently when developing models and tools.

12.7 CASE STUDY: THE OPEN MODELLING INTERFACE AND ENVIRONMENT (OPENMI)

Another example of an application development system is the Open Modelling Interface and Environment (OpenMI). This is being developed as part of a European Commission 5th Framework Programme research project HarmonIT, over the period 2002 to 2005. The HarmonIT consortium consists of partners from some eight European countries and involves design, development and implementation of a system for improved linking of hydrological models, including component-based models of system behaviour built from data, knowledge, model, operational and user interface components. The impetus for this work lies with the European Water Framework Directive, and the outcomes are intended to support catchment management and integrated planning activities across and, potentially beyond, Europe (Gijsbers et al., 2002).

Development of the OpenMI draws on the experience of the main commercial and research partners based in the Netherlands, Denmark and the United Kingdom, who between them have been involved in development and deployment of many of the hydraulic and hydrology system models currently used across Europe. These include pipe flow, 1D and 2D hydraulics, 3D hydrodynamics, river, floodplain, rainfall-runoff and groundwater models. Although the processes simulated by these system models are often linked, and need to be modelled interactively, the capacity to undertake the required linked modelling has been limited. By developing communication standards for modelling and model linking, the OpenMI will provide the methods whereby the necessary communication and linking can take place. The OpenMI also draws upon the generic application development system of Blind et al. (2001), where concepts of system architecture for model linking were explored.

Beyond model linking, it is intended that the OpenMI will facilitate migration of existing models to a new standard that increases model inter-operability, improves accessibility and reusability, and which will, in time, become a standard for development of new models.

The initial concept of the OpenMI architecture was to provide a platform independent model that allowed mapping to a range of languages and environments with relative ease. The architecture was the first aspect of the

OpenMI to be developed.

The OpenMI architecture consists of a small set of interfaces that focus on the problem of linking components and models. A pull-based pipe and filter architecture is used, within which 'linkable' data, knowledge or model components exchange data of pre-defined formats in a specified manner. Data are exchanged between provider components and acceptor components, with roles defined according to component data requirements. In data exchange, linkable components handle data requests individually and in sequence, reflecting a single-threaded system. Data requests are defined simply by a 'GetValues' call which generally returns the specified values, although in cases where manipulation, such as aggregation or interpolation, are required, additional data operations are specified.

In operation, the exchange of data is initiated by a single data, knowledge or model component, and thereafter automatically, and autonomously, as each component receives and requests relevant data (Gijsbers et al., 2003). In the approach of OpenMI, the role of models as objects is downplayed, with respect to the functionalities provided by operational components, which embed models.

Implementation of the OpenMI software has been initiated using the .NET environment, and Java implementation has also been considered. Implementation of the OpenMI includes development of a range of Use Cases that include linking river (1D) and river (1D) models, river (1D) and floodplain (2D) models, and river (1D) and groundwater (3D) models. The models used in such implementations are those of the commercial research partners, and so will provide immediate benefits in terms of on-ground application. Development of the OpenMI also has associated with it the construction of a range of test models, as well as tools for creating and monitoring model links, so together these offer researchers and developers an environmental modelling approach that supports legacy model linking and the capacity to create new, readily linkable models.

12.8   CASE STUDY: TWOLE, A TOOL FOR INTEGRATED RESERVOIR MANAGEMENT

TwoLe, a two-level decision support system, provides a final example of an application development system for IWRM. The top-level – planning – concerns the design and synthesis of optimised reservoir management policies, while the bottom-level – management – enables simulation of the optimised policy under different scenarios. TwoLe therefore provides an environment for the system analyst at the planning level, and it also provides a traditional decision support tool for scenario comparison and analysis at the management level.

The software architecture of TwoLe revolves around the concept of domain objects. Domain objects provide an object-oriented view of data. A single domain object can be associated with multiple models, that is, multiple model representations are allowed for the same entity. This feature is relevant for model integration and model composition. An example is provided by considering alternative mathematical models for a catchment. Essential catchment data (e.g. surface, digital elevation model, average rainfall, rainfall measured in gauging stations), are members of the 'catchment' domain object. This object can be modelled by a parsimonious model, a physical-based model, or a black box model. All these models are legitimate representations of the same entity and they can be interchanged in the compound model of the water system.

Domain objects are the keystones of TwoLe architecture, and models and tools complete the picture. Models are classified as either compound or basic, with compound models being made up of basic models. The tools perform transformation on models, as described earlier, and therefore correspond to operational components. The main operational components available in TwoLe are calibrators, optimisers and simulators. A calibrator applies data series to a model returning a calibrated model. Such a model can be simulated to perform validation tests, using a simulator. A simulator can also be used to evaluate the impact of a reservoir management policy applied to a water system. Finally, optimisers can be applied to decision models to produce management policies. A decision model is a model of a water system with an objective function, while a management policy is a prescriptive model which can be plugged onto a water system to create a new model of system behaviour: the regulated water system. Figure 12.4 shows a diagram representing a system model that is applied to a regulated water system to produce simulation results. The system model feeds historical precipitation scenarios on the catchment, which in turn returns a catchment outflow used by the management policy, together with the current reservoir level and the water demand of the users, to compute how much water should be released from the reservoir network.

TwoLe is designed and implemented according to object-oriented technology. Technically, the interface of a model in TwoLe is composed of interface variable objects. Following a systems analysis approach to modelling, interface variables are classified into input, state and output variables. In the current TwoLe implementation, models are described by difference equations. A model is a class with a 'run' method which transforms the input and the state interface variables, evaluated at time t, into the output interface variables at time t and the state interface variables at time $t + 1$.

TwoLe software components are written in C++, mostly for performance issues, since high computational efficiency is demanded by the core of the dynamic programming optimisation algorithms of TwoLe. The components have been encapsulated in a graphical user interface written in Java, which enables the systems analyst to exploit all the functions in an easy and intuitive way.

TwoLe has been successfully applied to the problem of integrated management of Lake Maggiore, also known as Verbano, a natural lake with an area of 210 km^2 managed by trans-national Italian and Swiss accounts for the different interests: flood protection, navigability and ecosystem preservation for the Swiss users; hydropower generation, irrigation, environmental flows and flood protection on the Ticino river for the Italian users. Since some objectives are conflicting and there are many decision makers, the problem is therefore multi-objective with multiple commission. The regulation policy, designed with the help of TwoLe, accounts for the different interests: flood protection, navigability and ecosystem preservation for the Swiss users; hydropower generation, irrigation, environmental flows and flood protection on the Ticino river for the Italian users. Since some objectives are conflicting and there are many decision makers, the problem is therefore multi-objective with multiple decision makers (Soncini-Sessa et al.,

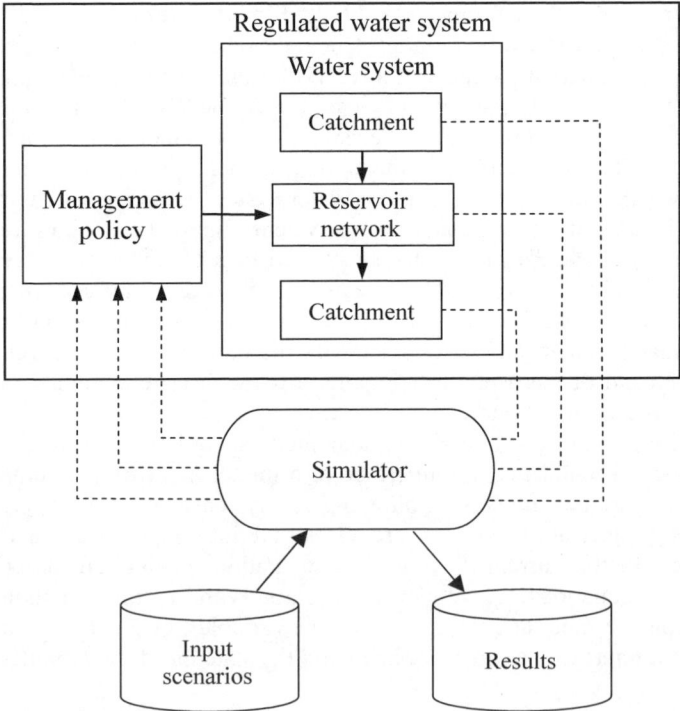

*Figure 12.4	Simulation of a regulated water system in TwoLe*

2000). The problem can only be solved by looking for a solution that integrates over domains and disciplines and is a classic example of an integrated water resource management problem.

12.9   CURRENT AND FUTURE RESEARCH

The case studies presented in this chapter are examples of the current research efforts that are focusing on the development of component-based application development systems, and the associated problems of compatibility, interoperability, interfacing and semantics. Almost every month it seems that another environmental research group announces development of a system that embraces this approach. Each system has a different combination of language, platform and modelling method support, and an associated component specification. This naturally raises problems of interoperability, if developers wish to extend the practice of component re-use from their own to other frameworks. Of course, many research groups are aware of these problems and are working to address them. One example, using two of the systems mentioned previously, is the development of an OpenMI interface component within the TIME environment, aimed at allowing models built using TIME to access the methods of models conforming to the OpenMI specification.

The answers to interoperability problems lie partly with good use of component metadata systems, partly with good semantics, and partly with the use of sound interface specifications. Component metadata provides the information needed to determine if the component can perform a desired task, semantics are used to ensure that what passes to and from the component is expressed in a correct and expected manner, and interface specifications are used to ensure proper component operation by, for example, making clear the process to correctly call a required method. The solutions to these problems sit not only in the technical domain, but require good communication between researchers, developers and users to achieve outcomes that are shared and workable.

Beyond the development of application development systems and improved interoperability lies the research area of mixed model concept support. At present many modelling solutions use constrained model concepts, such as stochastic modelling with discrete time. Expanding environmental modelling to include a range of research groups and disciplines will require development of more tools that support multi-method modelling, such as discrete and continuous time, lumped and distributed processes, or deterministic and stochastic operation.

Other areas of current and future development include distributed resource access, web services and distributed computing. These technologies can work well with component-based approaches, allowing components to be accessed from, or run on, remote sites that act as hosts for both components and component processing. In the processing area, development of the Grid also promises opportunities for faster distributed processing of the complex, dynamic, spatially-distributed, multi-component modelling often used for environmental problem exploration. Successfully using these kinds of resources will again take much work in the interoperability areas described previously, and it is likely that the key areas of interfacing, metadata and semantics will be the focus of development activity for much of the near future.

12.10   CONCLUSIONS

The discussion and examples presented in this chapter have highlighted some general trends in development of software systems for environmental problem solving. These systems of software have, in many circumstances, advantages over more traditional collections of applications for problem solving, in terms of reduced duplication, simpler reusability, improved interoperability and more flexibility. These systems are well supported by modern software engineering theory and practice, built around the concept of components that perform specific tasks, and the provision of development systems that support selection, connection and execution of components in applications tailored to specific problem situations. This method of software construction is of particular use in IWRM, where problem situations often differ from place to place, and even from time to time in a given place. Additionally, the requirements of participatory processes for open model development and software usage are met through transparent component selection and operation.

Three examples of application development systems were presented, but the list could have been much longer, since the needs of IWRM bring scientists and software engineers together in the development of new software systems in most environmental-related research areas, from ecology to agriculture, from hydrology to air quality modelling.

While looking at future applications which promise even deeper integration and interoperability due to advances in distributed and grid computing, the current challenge is to make these software systems available to a wider group of users, to fully support the needs of the new paradigm of integrated water resource management.

REFERENCES

Berners-Lee, T., J. Hendler and O. Lassila (2001), 'The semantic web', *Scientific American*, (May), 28–37.
Blind, M.W., L. Wentholt, B. van Andrichem and P. Groenendijk (2001), 'The

Generic Framework – An open framework for model linkage and rapid decision support system development', in F. Ghassemi, D. White, S. Cuddy and T. Nakanishi (eds), *MODSIM 2001 International Congress on Modelling and Simulation*, 4, (December), Modelling and Simulation Society of Australia and New Zealand, pp. 1601–1606.

Brooke, A., D. Kendrick, A. Meerhaus and R. Raman (1998), 'GAMS, a User's Guide', Washington, DC: GAMS Development Corporation.

Del Furia, L., A. Rizzoli and R. Arditi (1995), 'Lakemaker: a general object–oriented software tool for modeling the eutrophication process in lakes', *Environmental Software*, 10(1), 43–64.

Dolk, D.R. and J.E. Kottemann (1993), 'Model integration and a theory of models', *Decision Support Systems*, 9, 51–63.

Fourer R., D.M. Gay and B.W. Kernighan (2002), *AMPL: A Modeling Language for Mathematical Programming*, Duxbury Press Brooks Cole Publishing Company.

Gamma, E., R. Helm, R. Johnson and J. Vlissides (1995), *Design Patterns: Elements of Reusable Object-Oriented Software*, Reading, MA: Addison-Wesley.

Geoffrion, A.M. (1987), 'An introduction to structured modeling', *Management Science*, 33, 547–588.

Gijsbers, P.J.A., R.V. Moore and C.I. Tindall (2002), 'HarmonIT: Towards OMI, an Open Modelling Interface and Environment to harmonise European developments in water related simulation software', *Hydroinformatics 2002, Fifth International Conference on Hydroinformatics*, Cardiff, UK: International Association of Hydraulic Engineering and Research.

Gijsbers, P.J.A., E. Brakkee, J.B. Gregersen, L.E.P. Hanssen, S. Hummel, R. Brinkman, S. Vanacek and S. Westen (2003), *OpenMI Architecture – Report B System Specification*, HarmonIT Project.

Haagsma, I.G. and R.D. Johanns (1994), 'The interaction of ground water and surface water studied by loosely coupled models', *Water Down Under 94, 25th Congress of The International Association of Hydrogeologists / International Hydrology & Water Resources Symposium of The Institution of Engineers*, Australia, 2 (A) 93–98.

Havnø, K., H. Refstrup, J. Sørensen and B. Gregersen (2002), 'Integrated water resources modeling and object-oriented code architecture', *Proceedings of the 1st Asia-Pacific DHI Software Conference, DHI Software*, downloadable at: http://www.dhisoftware.com/Bangkok2002/Proceedings/Proceedings.htm (last access: May 2005).

Hillyer, C., J. Bolte, F. van Evert and A. Lamaker (2003), 'The ModCom modular simulation system', *European Journal of Agronomy*, 18 (3–4), 333–343.

Hoch, R., T. Gabele and J. Benz (1998), 'Towards a standard for documentation of mathematical models in ecology', *Ecological Modelling*, 113, 3–12.

Kottemann, J.E. and D.R. Dolk (1992), 'Model integration and modeling languages: A process perspective', *Information Systems Research*, 3, 1–16.

Kralisch, S., P. Krause and O. David (2004), 'Using the Object Modeling System for hydrological model development and application', in C. Pahl, S. Schmidt and T. Jakeman (eds), *iEMSs 2004 International Congress: Complexity and Integrated Resources Management*, Osnabrueck, Germany: International Environmental Modelling and Software Society.

McDonald, M.G., and A.W. Harbaugh (1988), *A modular three-dimensional finite-difference ground-water flow model*, U.S. Geological Survey Techniques of Water-Resources Investigations 6 (A1), US Geological Survey.

Muhanna, W.A. (1994), 'SYMMS: A model management system that supports model reuse, sharing and integration', *European Journal of Operational Research*, 72,

214–243.

Muetzelfeldt, R. (2004), *Declarative modelling in ecological and environmental research*, EUR 20918, European Commission, downloadable at: http://www.decmod.org/documents/dmeer.pdf (Last access: May 2005)

Muetzelfeldt, R. and J. Massheder (2003), 'The Simile visual modeling environment', *European Journal of Agronomy*, **18**, 345–358.

Muetzelfeldt, R., D.S. Robertson, M. Uschold and A. Bundy (1989), 'The use of Prolog for improving the rigour and accessibility of ecological modelling', *Ecological Modelling*, **46**(1), 9–34.

Nalbantis, I., E. Rozos, G. Tentes, A. Efstratiadis and D. Koutsoyiannis (2002), 'Integrating groundwater models within a Decision Support System', in *Proceedings of the 5th International Conference Water Resources Management in the Era of Transition, Athens, 4–8 September 2002*, European Water Resources Association.

Rahman, J. M., S.P. Seaton and S.M. Cuddy (2004), 'Making frameworks more useable: using model introspection and metadata to develop model processing tools', *Environmental Modelling and Software*, (19)**3**, 275–284.

Reed, M., S. M. Cuddy, and A.E. Rizzoli (1999), 'A framework for modelling multiple resource management issues – An open modelling approach', *Environmental Modelling and Software*, **14** (6), 503–509.

ReVelle C.S., E.E. Withlatch and J.R. Wright (1997), *Civil and Environmental Systems Engineering*, Upper Saddle River, NJ: Prentice Hall.

Rizzoli, A.E., J.R. Davis and D.J. Abel (1998), 'Model and data integration and re-use in environmental decision support systems', *Decision Support Systems*, **24**, 127–144.

Soncini-Sessa, R., A. Castelletti and E. Weber (2002), 'Participatory decision making in reservoir planning', in A.E. Rizzoli and A.J. Jakeman (eds), *Integrated Assessment and Decision Support, Proceedings of the First Biennial Meeting of the International Environmental Modelling and Software Society, June 2002*, 1, International Environmental Modelling and Software Society, 334– 339.

Soncini-Sessa, R., A.E. Rizzoli, L. Villa and E. Weber (1999), 'TwoLe: a software tool for planning and management of water reservoir networks', *Hydrological Sciences Journal*, **44** (4 August), 619–631.

Soncini-Sessa, R., D. Canuti, A. Colorni, E. Laniado, F.B. Losa, A.E. Rizzoli, L. Villa, B. Vitali and E. Weber (2000), 'Use of multi-criteria analysis to resolve conflicts in the operation of a transnational multipurpose water system, the case of Lake Verbano (Italy-Switzerland)', *Water International*, **250**(3), 334–346.

Szyperski, C., D. Gruntz and S. Murer (2002), *Component Software – Beyond Object-Oriented Programming*, Boston, MA: Addison Wesley.

Villa, F. (2001), 'Integrating modelling architecture: a declarative framework for multi-paradigm, multi-scale ecological modelling', *Ecological Modelling*, **137**, 23–42.

Villa, F., M. Wilson, R. de Groot, S. Farber, R. Costanza and R.M.J Boumans (2002), 'Designing an integrated knowledge base to support ecosystem services valuation', *Ecological Economics*, **41**, 445–456.

Watson, F.G.R. and J.M. Rahman (2004), 'Tarsier: A practical software framework for model development, testing and deployment', *Environmental Modelling and Software*, **19**(3), 245–260.

Watson, F.G.R., R.A. Vertessy, R.B. Grayson and L.L. Pierce (1998), 'Towards parsimony in large scale hydrological modelling – Australian and Californian experience with the Macaque model', *EOS, Transactions*, **79**(45), F260–F261.

Index